ON RECORD

"Jim Vieira and Hugh Newman have thoughtfully assembled a truly worthwhile collection of accounts herein. Take it for your library, and you'll return to it again and again over the years."

Ross Hamilton, author of
The Mystery of the Serpent Mound, A Tradition of Giants,
and *Star Mounds: Legacy of a Native American Mystery*

"Essential book on the existence of giant skeletons and giant races in the Americas. It catalogues, chronicles and records original accounts and assesses their authenticity and reality, with a great summary of all the evidence to date. A perfect addition to the ancient mysteries bookshelf."

Andrew Collins, author of
Göbekli Tepe: Genesis of the Gods,
From the Ashes of Angels, and *The Cygnus Mystery*

"I, like most people, thought that stories of giants associated with the building of mounds and other ancient sites were the result of the mythology that surrounds the sites, including stories of the Devil being involved, and people turned to stone for dancing on the Sabbath. However, having read the tour-de-force *Giants on Record*, by Hugh Newman and Jim Vieira, I have now changed my mind. The avalanche of evidence unearthed by the authors leaves the reader with no option but to agree with them. Illustrations include photo-copies of many original news headlines and stories that repeatedly say the massive bones from many ancient graves were taken away for study by the Smithsonian, who now deny all knowledge of many of these bones, even though their own records confirm they once had them. The reasons why this conspiracy of silence has occurred are even more controversial! This is essential reading for anyone interested in history, archaeology, or ancient sites."

Geoff Stray, author of
Beyond 2012: Catastrophe or Awakening,
The Mayan and Other Ancient Calendars,
and *Glastonbury Underground: Searching for the Lost Treasure of Avalon*

"Jim and Hugh have put together what is by far the best compilation of everything that is known about the reports of "giant" skeletons recovered in America from the 1700s to the late 1900s. They included a thoughtful summary of the influence of hoaxed reports and exaggerations that have clouded our modern view of these anomalous finds and what is left is a mystery. You won't find any wild or utterly fantastic claims in it. The unvarnished truth is that many huge human skeletons were genuinely found in mounds, stone chambers, and what are thought to be Native American grave sites. These cluster around a range of 7 to 8 feet in eight, but there are credible reports of far larger ones. The book is well illustrated and contains excellent sections from Ross Hamilton. Unlike Dewhurst's awful hodgepodge of newspaper clippings (many of which were repeated), *Giants on Record* is a well organized, logical, and thoroughly researched book."

Dr. Greg Little, author of
Path of Souls: The Native American Death Journey,
The Illustrated Encyclopedia of Native American Mounds & Earthworks,
and *Mound Builders: Edgar Cayce's Forgotten Record of Ancient America*

GIANTS
ON RECORD

America's Hidden History,
Secrets in the Mounds and
the Smithsonian Files

JIM VIEIRA

HUGH NEWMAN

AVALON RISING
PUBLICATIONS

Glastonbury, Somerset, UK
books@avalonrising.co.uk

First published 2015 AD
This edition © Jim Vieira & Hugh Newman 2015 AD

Published by Avalon Rising Publications.

British Library Cataloguing in Publication Data
Vieira, J and Newman, H.
Giants On Record

Avalon Rising Publications
Dragon Clan Offices
31-33 Benedict Street
Glastonbury, Somerset, BA6 9NB
United Kingdom

ISBN: 978-0-9567865-1-7
Also available in hardback and ebook formats.

AVALON RISING
PUBLICATIONS
Glastonbury, Somerset, UK
books@avalonrising.co.uk

Front cover and jacket design by Jake Ewen.
www.jakeewen.com

Contact the authors directly at: info@megalithomania.co.uk

ABOUT THE AUTHORS

Jim Vieira is a stonemason, researcher and writer. As well as exploring and writing about the stone sites of New England, he has collated over 1,500 newspapers and scholarly accounts of giant skeletons being found in North America and around the world. He has written for *Ancient American* magazine, *The Heretic* (UK) and local Massachusetts newspapers. In 2012 he created the online blog *The Daily Giant* that showcased a giant report every day for nearly two years. He controversially had his TEDx talk removed from the Internet (much like Graham Hancock and Rupert Sheldrake). He is the star of the History Channel TV shows *Search for the Lost Giants* (2014) and *Roanoke: Search for the Lost Colony* (2015) with his brother Bill. He lives in Ashfield, Massachusetts.

Hugh Newman is an explorer, antiquarian and author of *Earth Grids: The Secret Patterns of Gaia's Sacred Sites* (Wooden Books, 2008). He has been a regular guest on History Channel's *Ancient Aliens* in the last five seasons and featured in *Search for the Lost Giants* with Jim and Bill Vieira. Since 2006 he has been organising the *Megalithomania Conference* (UK, US and South Africa) and since 2013 the *Origins Conference* in London with Andrew Collins. He runs regular tours and expeditions worldwide. He also writes for numerous magazines and has a Bachelor of Arts Honours Degree (BA Hons) in Film and Journalism from London Guildhall University. His worldwide adventures and lectures can be seen at www.youtube.com/megalithomaniaUK. His main websites are www.megalithomania.co.uk and www.hughnewman.co.uk. He lives in England.

TOP TEN GIANT DISCOVERIES IN NORTH AMERICA

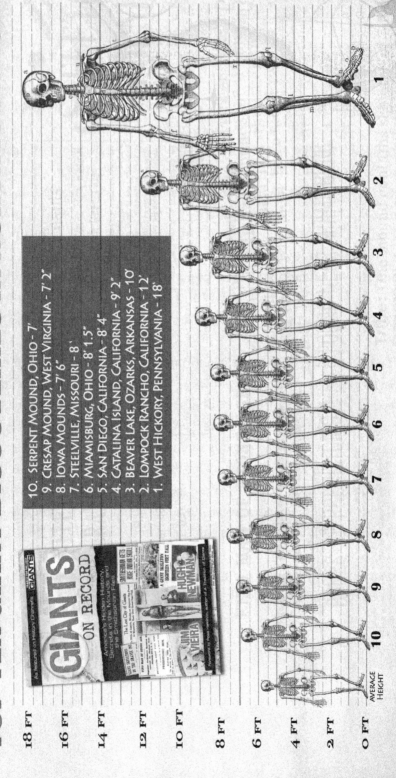

10. SERPENT MOUND, OHIO - 7'
9. CRESAP MOUND, WEST VIRGINIA - 7'2"
8. IOWA MOUNDS - 7'6"
7. STEELVILLE, MISSOURI - 8'
6. MIAMISBURG, OHIO - 8'1.5"
5. SAN DIEGO, CALIFORNIA - 8'4"
4. CATALINA ISLAND, CALIFORNIA - 9'2"
3. BEAVER LAKE, OZARKS, ARKANSAS - 10'
2. LOMPOCK RANCHO, CALIFORNIA - 12'
1. WEST HICKORY, PENNSYLVANIA - 18'

18 FT
16 FT
14 FT
12 FT
10 FT
8 FT
6 FT
4 FT
2 FT
0 FT

AVERAGE HEIGHT

1   2   3   4   5   6   7   8   9   10

TABLE OF CONTENTS

Acknowledgements

Hugh Newman would like to thank all his family for their support and encouragement, Ross Hamilton—"godfather of giantology" for his insight, guidance and editing of the book, Geoff Stray, Cee Hall, Micah Ewers, Bill Vieira, Gretchen Gerstner, Kyle, Seth, Josh and all the Ashfield crew, and Linus of course. Thanks to JJ Ainsworth, Andrew Collins, Greg Little, Jeffrey Wilson, Barbara DeLong, Micah Hanks, Renée Fleury, Greg Maestro, Ted and John and all at Left/Right Productions for making a great TV show, David Hatcher Childress, Michael Tellinger, Emmanuel Martin, David Hatfield, Susan Malleson, Shaun Kirwan, Kristan T. Harris, James Swagger, Bill Busha, Marcia K. Moore, Terje Dahl, Larry Bohlen, Bruce Cunningham, Andrew Gough, Stuart Mason, Wayne May, Gil Zamora, Graham Hancock, Giorgio Tsoukalos, and Jake Ewen for the cover and graphic design skills. Finally, to our departed friends John Michell, Patrick Cooke, Anthony Roberts, John Agnew, Philip Coppens, Sunbird and the wonderful Leslie LaBoda.

Jim Vieira would like to thank the entire Vieira and Gerstner clan but most importantly brother Bill for his support throughout this project. Also thanks to producers John Marks, Ted Bourne and Carmen Garcia of Left/Right studios and History Channel executive Matt Ginsberg for helping to bring this story to the History Channel. Thanks to Ross Hamilton, Micah Ewers, Greg Little and Graham Hancock for inspiring my research and for being examples to try and emulate. I would like to thank my father Edward for instilling in me a love of a good mystery and my mother Margaret for a lifetime of selfless service to others. Finally, thanks to Linus the cat for being a faithful friend through thousands of hours of research.

There were till then left the race of giants, who had bodies so large, and countenances so entirely different from other men, that they were surprising to the sight, and terrible to the hearing. The bones of these men are still shown to this very day, unlike to any credible relations of other men.

- Flavius Josephus, 93 AD

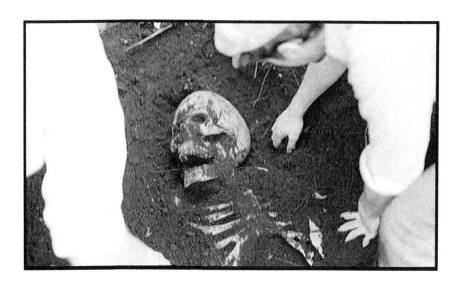

For all Indigenous Americans
ancient and modern.

Foreword

The Tall Ones
by Ross Hamilton

Giants on Record is an outgrowth of the internet age coupled with solid research endeavors the old-fashioned way of hands-on detective work. So many libraries, museums, private residences, and cemeteries have been visited in our efforts that if you added-on all the interviewing of knowledgeable people, the list would go on for pages and pages.

Jim and Bill Vieira, Hugh Newman, and prolific researcher Micah Ewers are like lions that have championed the cause of the continuing retrieval of information dealing with an overly fantasized, intellectually marginalized, and professionally ostracized sector of humanity. These four men and others who share their vision are doing something that literally requires courage to dare present publicly in this age of academically controlled archaeologies.

In a fairer world, our researches would without doubt have benefitted from the keyed-in professors of anthropology who would already have thoroughly documented the extensive tenure of the tall people in the ancient Americas, Europe, and places of the East. However by some strange twisting-about of luck probably reflecting the mediocre development of social justice and intellectual honesty, it has become the responsibility of our researches to bear the burden substantiating a populace who often stood upwards from seven feet in height with proportionate figures. More to the point, the professional ethnologists of the world should perhaps be explaining the *missing skeletons* along with loss of context supporting the tall people's existence, not us.

And missing they are. For a number of sound reasons, the bones are hardly accessible for the court of research science. These reasons include the fanatical leveling of scores-of-thousands of Indian graves beginning in earliest colonial times seeking artifacts to sell as well as clear the land for farming and towns. The chemically delicate condition of the older skeletons is noted in some of the accounts as the blackening processes of oxygen disintegrated the bones before the eyes of the exhuming parties. But there was also the silly practice of disarticulation to isolate the skulls and long bones of large size for turnover to collectors curating evidence of anomalies. Add to these points the dark aspects of racial prejudice and the understanding that Native people were without rights alive or dead, and you have a *mojo cocktail* of white sectarianism that would disorient even the most sober and reliable jurist.

And this is no joking matter, for so repressed has this information been that it belies the public knowledge—something that should be unconscionable today. These forgotten folk, many of whom would be as giants if they walked among us now, lived not only in America's past, but as other evidence points, many parts of the ancient world. As Hugh explains ahead, some of their stories are so very old they have reverted to legend, folk tradition, classical myth, and even fable.

Our work here is a straightforward attempt at restoring to the light of common acceptance the evident existence of these people. As becomes obvious in much of Hugh and Jim's chronicles, peerage social systems featuring men and women of large stature in pre-contact America proliferate among our best sources. That coupled with an astute exposé of a concerted effort within an early twentieth century National Museum to apparently do away with the bones and falsely declare these people never existed, has placed our efforts more in the frame of a service worthy for the sake of an historical narrative.

There was a sort of cottage industry mania in the later nineteenth century—a craze that so alarmed the National Museum and related concerns that they took it upon themselves to upturn, loot, and leave to the elements the great majority of remaining Indian cemeteries throughout the east and central United States. The only criteria was that they showed some promise of significant artifactual caches.

In perspective of the time, the universities had not yet developed any archaeological programs, so all was undertaken by interested men, including fortunately some trained physicians and others of background in the sciences of the time. Although their activities weren't inclusive enough (by means of disciplines involved) to stem the tide of bigotry and loss of compassion for Native folk, it has helped us a modicum to get a reasonable grasp on the enormity of the problem. Yes, Native people were often considered to be somewhat sub-human, a dark projection that is even today in the process of complete eradication. Now we appeal to the reader to take a moment to reflect on the ease with which the undercurrents of early American racial discrimination influenced the public imagination to the point of permitting settled efforts at writing history with extreme prejudice.

ORIGINS OF THE TALL ONES

According to the Native accounts, e.g. the early French and Spanish—as well as not a few of the sources documenting the physical condition of the native leadership's remains, these people were, by-and-large, comely and attractive to the eye. Some of their ancient folk traditions held that they were, (as claim also some traditional Japanese), descended from a race of divinely endowed beings, but had through disgrace lost the mastery of earth-and-sky, devolving rapidly to plain mortals. At a time not as long ago as one might believe, a wiser humanity stewarded the earth to the condition of a true paradise. The people, fauna, and flora lived far longer than now, and as they became older, they continued to grow incrementally. The period of a person's youth took a very long time to fade.

> *"....They stated that the bones belonged to one of the big buffaloes, which roamed over the plains during the times of their fathers. At that period, the Happy Hunting Ground was on earth, but was afterward removed beyond the clouds by the Great Spirit, to punish his children for bad conduct."*[1]

There was a hallowing element stirred by the wind and waters in those days that is all but absent today. It is remembered across the globe as mana or manna, by means of which Nature achieved true balance. With the agricultural arts of a spiritually enhanced landscape millennia ago, the mana rose as the source of vital sustenance impregnating the vegetation, revealing all vestigial aspects—allowing very tall and well-endowed people to appear for a time and thrive. All this has been taken from our comprehension as we struggle with restoring the subconscious memory of our humanity.

Now this also may be an important point to grasp: without the mana in the water, soil, and air vitalizing and perfecting the living plants and trees, the people in time saw their orènda degrade in potency and dissipate. Likened to the East Indian ojás, orènda was in part definable as the most spirited essence born of nourishment enabling the performance of otherwise formidable tasks intellectually and physically.

The progressively retreating power of the divine orènda in short order restricted the vision of the internal world, and in a remarkably brief period the general populations descended from possession of supernal wisdom to simple human traits. It is said as well that this spiritual power's loss was hastened through sexual sporting with both sexes responsible for the laxity. They found themselves diminishing in stature, diminishing in years; but perhaps with all tallied, the greatest loss of all was memory—a senility that seems to have affected the entire human race.

> *"They suppose their ancestors to have been more perfect, both in intellectual & bodily formation, than the present race. They were of very large stature, both men and women, attributed in part to their abstinence from sexual intercourse during the early years of life. In those days the men at a hundred years were equal to those of the present race at seventy. A gradual degeneration has at last brought them to their present state and is now working imperceptibly among all the Indian tribes."* [2]

Vine Deloria (in *Red Earth, White Lies*) notes that even within the memory of some Indian people, the age of 200 years was attained—and perhaps not uncommonly. After the disengagement of the mánitou systems' gathering arms of linear earthen and stone walls punctuated with artificial mounds and terminus caves to polarize and convert the land's magnetic flows in maintenance of the mana, the people knew great difficulty wanting for the reestablishment of a reliably potent orènda. A similar story seems to have happened throughout prehistoric Britain and around the world where standing stones, dolmens, and temple structures were operated by people who yet grasped the workings of a very subtle yet understated magnetic field.

A Tradition of Tall People

In America the bones that we have found evidence for—the ones the anthropologists and museum curators say never existed—were in feasible theory those of the generations that had instituted the protocols of selective marriage to stay the will of nature. In this way it is believed they may have at least outwardly retained some resemblance to their revered forebears of preceding millennia. But it was also held, it would seem, that their children's orènda was hopefully kept preserved by this means (the creation of lineages), and so the offspring of the noble class were carefully protected against worldly influences until a certain age. Nonetheless, and although it seems to have worked to keep strength and tallness in families, selective mating in hindsight crafted an artificial suspension—an effort that postponed what nature odds-on would otherwise have dictated as fated. Yet it is fortunate for us to have been left these important clues as artifacts that, suitably discerned, leave us with working answers pertinent to the origins of the Tall Ones as a once worldwide social phenomenon.

> *"Measurements taken of the skeleton while still in the grave indicated an individual approximately 7.2 feet tall. He would have been a splendid figure in any society and the darling of a primitive basketball team."* [3]

The bones we have uncovered seem large to us: seven-footers can be imposing even on a professional basketball court. It seems quite apparent the indigenous people had been practicing deliberate and selective intermarriage among families that had tall members—a social phenomenon in some respects akin to some European royal families in centuries passed. Unlike in Europe however, instead of seeking out wealth and power as a first cause, the native folk of the Eastern Woodlands sought robust physicality as a motive for establishing their leaders—this being an indication of descent from a venerable stock of elite status known to exhibit administrative talents. It was from these people that their public figures were developed—wealth and power coming along in due course.

An additional important factor of the tall people having survived seems to be that the woodlands of North America were abundant with food and open spaces to the degree that wars were not fought as often as they were upon other territories around the ancient globe. Such conditions coupled with their believed hierarchically structured village systems giving leeway to an overall egalitarian vision, may have stayed the grand stature resulting in so many such skeletal remains being witnessed by the European settlers in the Eastern U.S. Since the rest of the world's larger and stronger men were often enough placed on the front lines of battle throughout Asia and Europe, that version of DNA was not as available for procreation, and the populations of larger men knew steady depletion; while in America, conditions may have favored the survival of the very tall, allowing their numbers to remain considerable as evinced through their oral traditions.

Sadly, though consistently birthing some commanding and muscular individuals, uncounted generations practicing selective breeding may in theory have exacerbated an already impaired immune response to the European smallpox. Here is conceivably a measure of irony, for if not for the poxes the Europeans brought, who knows how things may have turned out for the Native populations?

IGNORANCE, RACIAL INTOLERANCE, AND CONSPIRACY

Bear in mind that 'giant' is used herein more in the spirit of, though not as, a homonym, i.e. having more than one aspect, which Hugh and Jim explain ahead in better perspective. I've never been completely comfortable with the use of the term 'giant' to describe these people because the term was once and has again become a tool of academics agreeable to further berating the last vestiges of information concerning the reality of the people of whom this book treats. Without much critical thought, these men are willingly extending the misanthropies of their predecessors through certain fields of education and communication, further abetting the abject racial bias already too long leveled against our indigenous people. Overwhelmed by the mass-marketed science of today, the fact of our Native ancestry's physicality being superior in many respects to the populations of today is treated as nonsense.

Left unchallenged, notorious characters like the twentieth century's Aleš Hrdlička of the National Museum (see chapter 8) will appear from time to time employing presentist philosophy in declaring the belief in exceptional stature in ancient times insulting to anyone of intelligence. Even now a correct view over the past is blocked by men who, though long dead, influence academia through partialities that support some current models. Advancements in technology may help in some respects to be rid of these shadows—but not always—in that interpretation can be imperceptibly tainted with old concepts. Any time hypotheses of ancient Native folk are put up by non-Indians, there too often we still see adherence to well established party lines that through preference have survived from the nineteenth century. Good examples of this kind of Jim Crow mentality are not hard to find because even just a century ago, such an attitude flourished in virtually every university.

So could there have been a conspiracy headed by a ranking anthropologist seated in Washington, D.C. to gather and remove, on a permanent basis, evidence of an admirably robust and otherwise remarkable race or (sub-race) of people? The following chapters as thoughtfully arranged by Hugh and Jim may provide a clear and obvious answer to that question. Bearing in mind that such remains were already long missing from other regions of the world, we can see how it may have been a relatively easy affair to control and censure the anomalies of our Native American burial sanctuaries.

In sum, basically any way we look at it, the real problem may ultimately lie in the inability for men to leave courteously alone the established libraries, repositories, and cemeteries of the world's past. It has been out of our regular severing of connections with past histories that we have found ourselves no better off than orphans having no knowledge of our parents. This book is an effort toward amending that problem.

Bless us all with the wisdom of our ancestors
Ross Hamilton, September 2015

PREFACE

Recently an article from a satirical website claimed that a Supreme Court ruling forced the Smithsonian Institution to admit to the historic destruction of giant skeletons. It was published not long after the *Search for the Lost Giants* TV show had aired with a headline that read: "*Smithsonian Admits to Destruction of Thousands of Giant Human Skeletons in Early 1900s.*"[1] The article was convincing, and this apparent exposé of the National Museum hit a chord with people. Straight away, we were inundated with emails from people believing the story was real.

If such a story were true it would be front-page worldwide news. However, when an Internet post is mentioning a startling find and not verifying any of the professionals involved, real organizations or institutions they belong to, you can quickly conclude that it is a misrepresentation of facts. Maybe someday, the Smithsonian will admit to the irony of this story.

The over willingness to believe seems to be the culprit for such stories gaining life. This is the reality we have had to deal with in writing this book, as hoaxes and exaggerations were often reported as the truth. This is also a challenging subject to research because of the lack of physical evidence and the moral and ethical implications of investigating human remains. When the Native American Graves Protection and Repatriation Act (NAGPRA) was passed in 1990, any remaining giant skeletons and bones were removed from public display and buried according to the traditions of individual tribes. We often get asked: "where are the bones?" and we reply: "ask the Smithsonian and the Native Americans."

Even with these obstacles, we have done our best to chase down every account to the end and to be as impartial as possible. This book is not trying to be a long scientific paper but rather an assemblage of data and documents that have been hidden in libraries and local historical societies, and quietly shunned by academia for the last two centuries. Unfortunately several hoaxes clouded serious research into the existence of giants so it is perhaps pertinent to look at some of these deceptions, as they have become the bane of researchers seeking the truth of the North American giants.

THE CARDIFF GIANT

The Cardiff Giant was one of the most famous hoaxes in United States history. Purportedly, it was a 10-foot-long "petrified man," uncovered on October 16, 1869 by workers digging a well behind the barn of William C. 'Stub' Newell in Cardiff, New York. Both it and an unauthorized copy made by P. T. Barnum are still on display. The giant was the creation of

a New York tobacconist, atheist George Hull, who decided to create the giant after an argument at a Methodist revival meeting about *Genesis 6:4* stating that there were giants who once lived on Earth. Hull hired men to carve out a 10 feet, 4.5 inch long block of gypsum in Fort Dodge, Iowa, telling them that it was intended for a monument to Abraham Lincoln in New York. He shipped the block to Chicago, where he hired Edward Burghardt, a German stonecutter, to carve it into the likeness of a man and swore him to secrecy. It was later exposed as an elaborate fraud.

THE MARTINDALE MUMMIES
Yosemite Valley, California

The controversial Martindale Mummies were said to have been discovered 1n 1885, in California's Yosemite Valley. A team of miners led by G.F. Martindale reported finding the remains of a woman nearly seven feet tall, who was holding a mummified child. The mummies were claimed to have been found in a cave behind a wall of rock.

The Mummies were acquired by *Ripley's* in February 1998 from Dr. Larry Cartmell (*Ripley's Believe It or Not!* is a franchise founded by Robert Ripley in 1918 that collects strange artifacts). The mother and child mummies were first displayed in Scranton, Kansas in 1899. The origin and authenticity of the Martindale Mummies remained a mystery for a long time but in 1996 simple x-rays and CT scans of the mummy quickly revealed it was a sideshow fake that had done the rounds for half a century.

9-FOOT MUMMY
The Anderson Intelligencer, December 4, 1895
Cartersville, Georgia

This is a report of a 9-foot-tall mummy being housed at the court of Judge Edgar Orr of Atlanta. The mummy was at a museum on Decatur Street after a financial dispute closed down the museum. We have read dozens of newspaper articles and book entries that described Judge Orr as a respected and prominent judge in the Atlanta area, which made the case initially more interesting. Many people stopped in to view the mummy and the article tells us that it had "long coarse hair" and the "huge frame is well proportioned, considering that it is so large." We are informed that:

> *"The advertisement has attracted the attention of the*

Smithsonian Institution doctors and professors and that institution has sent several osteologists at different times to make expert examination of the mummy. Dr. Priorleau, Professor Stelle and Professor Lucas all examined the mummy, determined its authenticity and concluded it was between 500 and 1000 years old. The examinations were made with the intention of purchasing the mummy to put in the National Museum in Washington D.C. Copies of the advertisement of the sale were taken by the professors of the National Museum and it is expected that representatives of the Institution at Washington will be present at the sale of the museum next Monday. All the experts who have examined the giant mummy, which is nearly nine feet in length, think it is a curiosity fit to be placed in the National Museum."

This mummy also turned out to be a fake after further analysis.

Finally, all over the Internet we have the unfortunate remains of a 2002 Photoshop contest of giant skeleton creations. The *Worth 1000* website hosts numerous design competitions and in 2002 they featured one focusing on giant skeletons.[2] Many of these examples of graphic design have been reported to be genuine by some researchers for over 10 years. They have featured in various books and on the *National Geographic* website.[3]

In the course of researching this subject, the authors have uncovered hoaxes, exaggerations, mismeasurements, use of faulty regression formulas, other honest mistakes and even downright deceptions. However, those only comprise a small amount of the reports that we are dealing with. We do not claim that all the accounts presented in this book are true, but rather present them so the readers can examine, research and make their own conclusions. We have investigated many of the accounts to their source, with some coming to a dead-end, so there is no way to verify them. Other (often famous) accounts we found to be hoaxes, while others were accurately measured and reported by the Smithsonian and other well-known authorities.

The story of the North American giants may be consumed by

controversy, intrigue, hoaxes, and disinformation, but please take a look for yourself and make up your own mind, as there are simply too many accounts to ignore.

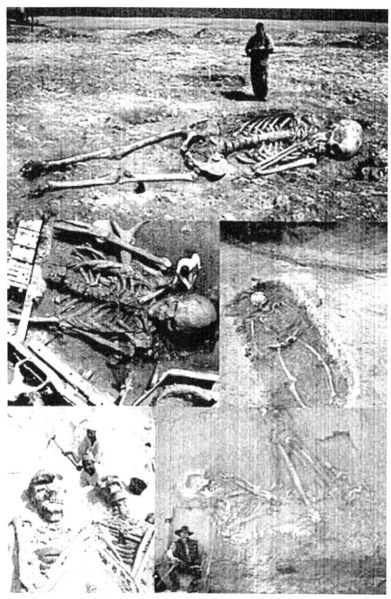

Various giant skeleton hoax photos courtesy of www.worth1000.com

Beyond the realms of Gaul, beneath the sunset
Lieth an island, girt about by ocean,
Guarded by ocean - erst the haunt of giants.

Geoffrey of Monmouth, *History of the Kings of Britain,* **1150 AD**

INTRODUCTION
FE-FI-FO-FUM
BY HUGH NEWMAN
"I SMELL THE BLOOD OF AN ENGLISHMAN"

Giants have always been part of British culture. Hundreds of legends, stories, folk-tales, and even the chronicles of King Arthur have these ancient gods involved, and have been part of a tradition for thousands of years. There are well-known stories such as *Jack-the-Giant-Killer* (that later became the fairy-tale *Jack and the Beanstalk*), Brutus battling with the giant Gogmagog, and the construction of hundreds of megalithic sites attributed to these beings.

In Europe there are the Ice Giants of Nordic tradition, the Tuatha Dé Danann and Formorians of old Ireland, Hu Gadarn of Celtic tradition, Cronus and the Titans of Greece and the one-eyed Cyclops of Homer's tales. Further afield there are the Thunderous Rakshasas of the Indian Ramayana, the Gigantes of the Middle East, and even in the Bible there are matter-of-fact accounts of mighty warriors, and tribes such as the Nephilim, Rephaim, Anakim and the Canaanites. Some examples, like King Og of Bashan and Goliath—who was defeated by David—even had their heights described in detail, and were attributed as the builders of megalithic temples in the Bible lands.

These traditions have become part of our psyche, and are now the stuff of legend. Most people believe they are just tales, poems and

1

bedtime stories read to children, startling them with the mighty roar of "Fe-Fi-Fo-Fum." As they are no longer part of our historical timeline, the giants have been sidelined and absorbed into the imaginary world. But what if these giant humans really did exist? What if mighty races of titans really did rule parts of the ancient world?

In the past giants were seen as gods, elementals, and aspects of the sacred landscape, that would bring fertility to the crops, affect weather, and remind us of a greater power beyond our scope of reason. The more one looks into these tales of old, the more one realises they exist in almost every country on every continent.

> *"Everyone is fascinated by the question of whether races of mighty beings once roamed the earth, shaping the landscape and building huge enclaves of earth and stone which are still associated with their name. Such legends are universal; often they point to magical and meteorological phenomena crediting the giants with a definite, if dangerous, supernatural ability."* [1]

When I was nine years old my family moved to a quaint village on the outskirts of Cambridge. Cherry Hinton was known for its cherry orchards and private airport, but not much else. Upon the local Gog Magog Hills, however, legends of giants were part of the school playground chatter. There were rumours that a giant was still buried at the sacred spring that was called 'Giant's Grave' or 'Magog's Grave,' which has a 20 ft island in the middle of it said to be the resting place of a local titan. It is directly across the street from the Robin Hood and Little John Pub. Little John was a legendary giant who accompanied the medieval hero of Nottingham on his escapades through Sherwood Forest. His influence obviously reached this part of East Anglia too. In the pub's car park a chunky monolith sits with a mysterious footprint carved in it that to this day no one knows how it got there or who carved it out.

When I reached the tender age of twelve I joined Netherhall secondary school that was at the base of Lime Kiln Hill, part of the Gog Magog Downs. Chalk clunch was excavated from this hill and was used for building several of the university buildings on the other side of town.

The 3 ft wide footprint stone in Cherry Hinton, in the *Robin Hood and Little John* Pub.

Twice a week our class had to scale the side of the hill as part of physical education, not realising that in the distant past it was once the abode of mysterious and extremely tall inhabitants.

As the years rolled by, with daily school runs past the Giant's Grave and the Gog Magog Hills, I discovered Wandlebury Hill Fort that lies a few miles southeast of Cherry Hinton. Now a country park, its history is shrouded in mystery, and I became obsessed with the place and started looking deeply into the mysteries of the area around the Gog Magogs. Immediately a number of references of giants emerged. One local tradition, relative to the origin of the hills said there,

> "...was a very large cave, which was inhabited by a giant and his wife (a giantess) of extraordinary stature, whose names were Gog and Magog." [2]

On 27th May 1854, a short item appeared in the *Cambridge Chronicle* that described a find by workmen who were preparing the land for the first reservoir for Cherry Hinton upon Lime Kiln Hill. Nine skeletons were found:

> "Several of them were of large size, and were evidently the remains of men who reached to a greater height than ordinary men in the present day." [3]

According to local researcher and archaeologist Michelle Bullivant, "*this*

3

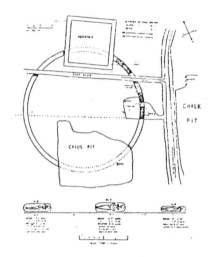

War Ditches, Cherry Hinton: Plan showing
three of the nine giant burials

*sparked local interest as to a possible race of giants having once lived upon
the hills.*"[4] Unfortunately this is the only record of that particular discovery
and many more could have been discovered but it gave some clout to the
giant legends that persist around the Gog Magog Hills.

These hills are named after Gog and Magog, who, in British
mythology were the giant sons of some of Roman emperor Diocletian's
wicked daughters who were banished to the island of Albion (an ancient
name for England) where they mated with demons.

Like in North America, giants are often linked to mounds,
earthworks and hill-forts. Bartlow Mounds are a group of seven mounds
remarkably similar to many in America (most notably Grave Creek
Mound in West Virginia and Miamisburg in Ohio). Heydon Ditch,
also in Cambridgeshire, has eerie stories of giant warriors, but when it
was excavated in the 1950s several taller-than-average skeletons were
unearthed. A similar, although much grander ditch is the Devils Dyke. In
Legends of the Fenland People (1926), Christopher Marlowe describes an
old story associated with the dyke saying it was constructed by "*...a race
of giants, renowned alike for cunning, strength and ferocity*".[5] Is that what
the ancient British giants were really like?

"*The ancient Britons were remarkable for the large stature of their bodies; their eyes were generally blue, which was esteemed a great beauty; and their hair red or yellow, though in many various gradations. They were remarkably swift of foot, and excelled in running, swimming, wrestling, climbing, and all kinds of exercises in which either strength or agility were required. Accustomed to hardships and despising cold and hunger, in retreating they plunged into the morasses up to the neck, where they remained several days. They painted their bodies with a blue dye extracted from woad, and at an early age they were tattooed in a manner the most ingenious and hideous; and in order to exhibit these frightful ornaments in the eyes of their enemies, they threw off their clothes in the day of battle. When advancing to the combat their looks were fierce and appalling, and their shouts loud, horrid, and frightful."* [6]

If we survey other parts of Britain, legends of giants emerge again and again. Hundreds of ancient megalithic sites have 'Giant' in their name. The first known name of Stonehenge was 'The Giants' Dance.' Stonehenge is a later Saxon name. 'Giant's Grave,' 'Giant's Hill,' 'Giant's Causeway,' 'the Sleeping Giant,' 'Giant's Well,' and 'Giant's Bed' are some further examples.

The discovery of giant skeletons is clearly more than just an American phenomenon, so let's take a look at some examples of accounts

Bartlow Mounds in Cambridgeshire, UK are similar to those in America.

from the British Isles, before we head across the Atlantic Ocean.

'The Giants' Dance,' now called Stonehenge, is without doubt the most famous archaeological site in Britain. It is unique in style, as no other stone circles have lintels and precision-carved stones like this one. The earliest known depiction of Stonehenge shows a giant helping Merlin the wizard building the great stone circle. It comes from a manuscript called *Le Roman de Brut* by poet Wace dated to around 1150 AD[7] (based on *History of the Kings of Britain* by Geoffrey of Monmouth), but was not published until the early-to-mid 1300s. In the illustration it shows Merlin directing a giant human to move a stone lintel into place. In the text it explains that Merlin is constructing a burial place for Aurelius Ambrosius, an ancient King. However, *History of the Kings of Britain* also states that the monoliths originally came from Africa.

> *"Giants of old did carry them from the farthest ends of Africa,*
> *and did set them up in Ireland when they lived there."* [8]

The original 'Giants' Dance' stone circle was said to have been constructed by giants at Mount Killarus in Ireland, then Merlin magically transported them over to Salisbury Plain. How this might have been done remains a mystery.

There are hundreds of mounds, earthworks, woodhenges and other megaliths spread out around Salisbury Plain that are part of the greater Stonehenge complex. These are ignored by most visitors to Stonehenge, but some early antiquarians soon found that something quite remarkable was often hidden within them.

In *Journey into South Wales* (1802) George Lipscomb describes not only a suit of armour belonging to a giant warrior at Warwick Castle, but he also states:

> "...it should be remembered, that Leland, in his "Collectanea", quotes the respectable authority of his friend, Sir Thomas Eliot, as recording, that himself had seen, at some place, near Salisbury, a skeleton which measured fourteen feet ten inches in length." [9]

In the *British Critic*, Volume 42, pg 544, 1813, the following is reported,

> "Such were the arms found with a skeleton of large dimensions, in a remarkable barrow, on the verge of Wiltshire, by the road leading from Salisbury to Blanford."

In *A Theological, Biblical, and Ecclesiastical Dictionary* (1830), it describes a 9 ft 4 in skeleton unearthed near Salisbury in 1719. It also recounts a mound named 'Giant's Grave' next to St Edmunds Church. This church was part of the original college founded by the Bishop of Salisbury, Walter de la Wyle in 1269, and is located a few miles from Stonehenge.

I now live in the town of Glastonbury in Somerset, less than 80 miles west of Stonehenge. The legendary *Isle of Avalon* has a few giants hidden within its records too, more often than not linked with the stories of King Arthur. At the current location of Glastonbury Abbey in the 1190s AD, a great oak coffin was discovered by the monks sixteen feet below the surface between two small pyramids. A controversial object was also found, at only eight feet below the surface. The infamous lead cross had this carved on it in Latin *"Here lies interred the famous King Arthur on the Isle of Avalon."* This became a sensation, and some say a hoax. However, the skeleton that was excavated was said to be close to 9 feet tall.[9]

"It was absolutely gigantic. It appeared to be much taller than an average man, and the space between the eye sockets was as wide as the palm of a man's hand." [10]

Giraldus Cambrensis, a respected historian personally examined the bones and the grave about four years after the discovery and pronounced it a genuine find. In 1278 in the presence of King Edward 1 and Queen Eleanor, the remains were transferred to inside the Abbey. Then, in 1962-63, after doing some additional excavations at the grave site, Dr. Ralegh Radford, an archaeologist, *"confirmed that a prominent personage had indeed been buried there at the period in question."* [11]

Now I could go on and on and add more accounts from Britain, but that is beyond the scope of this book.

My intense interest in megaliths and prehistoric earthworks led me to America in the autumn (fall) of 2008. After exploring the incredible stone sites of New England (that Jim writes about in his introduction and chapter 5), the next stop on my trip was Arizona, where I was housesitting for fellow author David Hatcher Childress. In his home library one book grabbed my attention and within two days I had read the whole manuscript. It was *A Tradition of Giants* by Ross Hamilton.

This masterful analysis of the giants in the Ohio Valley inspired me to look around Arizona and California for more examples, so after visiting many of the petroglyph sites of the Southwest, I headed to Hollywood to stay with a friend and her delightful dog called Earl, and decided to investigate the Lompock Rancho giant account from 1819, that was only a few miles from her house. The Lompock giant, said to be over 12 feet tall was said to have had double rows of teeth. I hired a car and drove to the area of the so-called ranch, but after asking some locals for the whereabouts of its location they had no information. I eventually found the exact place where it should be, but it was no longer a ranch. It was Vandenburg Airforce Base, and they did not want any giant hunters going through their barbed wire gate. We go into much further detail about this particular account in the *Double Rows of Teeth* chapter.

I undertook various investigations of reports of giant skeletons, and became enthralled by the prehistoric Mound Builders, and the mighty landscape artifacts they left behind. In October 2011 we organised a Megalithomania Conference in Glastonbury, Connecticut. We had Ross Hamilton and his colleague Jeffrey Wilson speaking at the event. This is also where I met Jim Vieira. Many discussions took place and research was shared. Jim's work on the giants of New England piqued my interest and we stayed in touch thereafter.

In late 2012, I went on a road trip with my partner at the time, starting in New England, heading to Pennsylvania, West Virginia, Ohio, Indiana, Illinois, Kentucky, Michigan and Wisconsin. I read hundreds of giant accounts and Jim provided me with many more to research, as we traveled through the landscape of the "Tall Ones." We visited numerous mound sites that giant skeletons were excavated from and learning from Ross and Jeffrey was an eye-opening experience. It integrated me with the incredible sacred landscape of the tribes of old, the earth temples they constructed, and a wisdom tradition that has faded drastically since the arrival of the white man.

We visited Grave Creek Mound, the Marietta Earthworks, Portsmouth Earthworks, Serpent Mound, Miamisburg, Seip Mound, Newark Earthworks, Chillicothe, Story Mound, Norwood Mound, Aztalan, Mound City, Fort Ancient, numerous other Adena, Hopewell and Fort Ancient culture sites, historical societies and museums, and our last mound stop was McKee's Mound in Pennsylvania. However we had set an intention to see a giant skeleton with our own eyes, and on the last day of our trip we visited the bizarre Mütter Museum in Philadelphia. Numerous scary carcasses, heads and other organs, as well as elongated skulls from Peru and extreme skeletal deformities were on display, but in the center of the darkened room a magnificent 7 ft 6 inch tall skeleton towered above us.

We had met our giant.

We looked through the records at the museum and discovered that it had been sold to Mütter Museum in 1921, and that the seller from

"Northern Kentucky" in the signed agreement stated that the buyer must never reveal its origins. Could a mysterious 7 ft 6 in skeleton found in the giant-occupied region of America really be one of the great giants of old?

The story of ancient America is not what I had originally thought. Its deep prehistory, high culture, architectural mastery, sacred teachings, and ultimately what it has to teach us about our origins is what is now at stake.

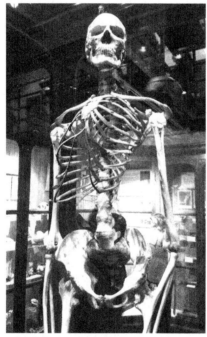

7 ft 6 inch skeleton at Mütter Museum with
rare signs of acromegaly or gigantism.

Today we see giants in various ways: as intellectual giants, philosophical giants, or great leaders and sportsmen; but do these compare to the characters in the story that is about to unfold?

Take a look for yourself, as these giants were *really* here, living where *you* live now, and they were as commanding and powerful, and had just as many supernatural abilities as the folk tales about them. We hope this book opens a door into this mysterious lost world once ruled by an elite tribal network of once great human beings.

Map of reported Giant Discoveries featured in this book over 7ft tall across the United States. Courtesy of Cee Hall and Google Earth.

11

INTRODUCTION

NEW ENGLAND MYSTERIES
BY JIM VIEIRA

FIRST DISCOVERY

Everyone loves a mystery, but why is that? Is it because a mystery is more fun to dive into than hard science? Or is it that people love a mystery because they know intuitively that something is wrong with present theories?

It is now time to explore one of the greatest mysteries in human history—a mystery that just happened to find me several years ago as I accidently fell down the *rabbit hole*. I was never able to think the same about the past. This strange story has had many twists and turns and unexpected discoveries for me, but it started over twenty years ago as I strolled through the forest with my brother and our friends.

As stonemasons, my brother and I have always been intrigued by stone constructions all around the planet, especially some of the more enigmatic megalithic sites. Even in our local part of New England, we

Hawley serpent wall. Left: Effigy of serpent's head. Right: Turtle effigy.

12

would marvel at the amazing accomplishments of colonists who laid down over 250,000 miles of stone walls crisscrossing the landscape. To put it in perspective, this is roughly the distance to the moon.

One day as we walked through the forest in Hawley, Massachusetts a few miles from my house, a strange-looking wall caught our attention. This was no ordinary wall—it climbed up a twenty-foot ledge and ended in seven huge multi-ton blocks possessing a serpent's head as the last stone. My brother and I were puzzled at the effort to create such a thing and asked why a colonist would be memorializing the form of a serpent. I ruminated on this for quite a while and then, serendipitously, a wonderful book called *Manitou* by James Mavor and Byron Dix (1989) came my way.

Byron Dix and Dr. Bary Fell at Calendar II. Coutersy of James A. Garfall.

Jim Mavor was a naval architect and professor who designed the submersible sub *Alvin*, featured in National Geographic deep sea documentaries. Byron Dix was an optical designer and archaeoastronomer. Their book describes a multi-year investigative effort that attempts to make the case that Native Americans in the Northeastern United States built with stone for ceremonial and astronomical purposes. In fact the oldest currently

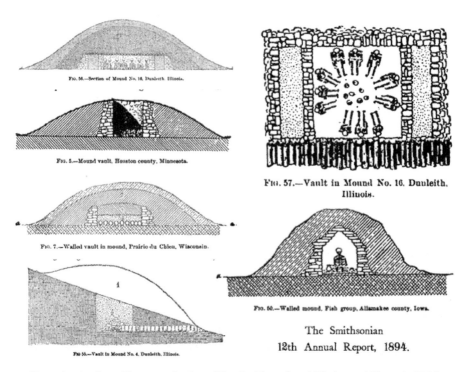

Fig. 56.—Section of Mound No. 16, Dunleith, Illinois.

Fig. 5.—Mound vault, Houston county, Minnesota.

Fig. 7.—Walled vault in mound, Prairie du Chien, Wisconsin.

Fig. 55.—Vault in Mound No. 4, Dunleith, Illinois.

Fig. 57.—Vault in Mound No. 16, Dunleith, Illinois.

Fig. 50.—Walled mound, Fish group, Allamakee county, Iowa.

The Smithsonian
12th Annual Report, 1894.

Stone tombs found in mounds, from The Smithsonian 12th Annual Report, 1894.

Ancient Stone Vault within the Kurtz Mound, Missouri
Antiquities of Missouri, Gerrard Fowke, 1910.

recorded stone structure in the country was built by the Maritime Archaic people in Labrador, which is in the far Northeast. This was a child's burial mound with a stone cist at L'anse Amour, Newfoundland dated to 7,500 years. The Maritime Archaic people built stone mounds, stone cairns and are most likely responsible for the mysterious standing stones on unpopulated Coffin Island in the far reaches of frigid Labrador.

Looking around our country you find native peoples engaging in stonework construction from coast-to-coast in ancient times. A little known fact is how extensive some of this construction was. Native American civilizations such as the Adena (1000-200 BC), Hopewell (200 BC-500 AD) and the so-called Fort Ancient (1000-1750 AD) peoples built stone mounds, massive stone wall complexes, stone hilltop forts, stone chambers, and stone tombs all over the eastern half of the country. Structures like the 55 feet high stone mound with a 182 feet base that once existed in Licking County, Ohio, littered the landscape of ancient America. Most of these were dismantled for colonial use. When this man-made stone mountain was taken down to build a dam, multiple burials were found beneath the structure. Stone kivas and cliff dwellings found in the Southwest are also ancient reminders of Native American proficiency in stonework.

NORTH WALL, SHOWING ABUTTING STONES, IN MOUND NO. 2

FEATURES OF BRENNER MOUNDS NOS. 1 AND 2

Dry stone walling in Brenner Mound, Missouri.

ANCIENT NEW ENGLAND STONEWORK
IN THE HISTORICAL RECORD

As I continued to explore the woods and fields of New England in an attempt to find evidence of pre-colonial stonework, I decided to turn my attention to historical documents to see if the early colonists made any mention of pre-existing stonework when they arrived. Some notable finds were as follows: John Pynchon, in a letter to John Winthrop Jr. dated Nov. 30, 1654:

> *"Sir I heare a report of a stonewall and strong fort in it, made all of Stone, which is newly discovered at or neere [sic] Pequot, I should be glad to know the truth of it from your selfe [sic], here being many strange reports about it."*

Henry Baker, *History of Montville*, Connecticut, 1896; pg.31:

> *"Owaneco . . . . afterwards gave them each [two Englishmen who had rescued him from drowning] one hundred acres of land, which transaction was afterwards confirmed by the General Court, and ordered to be surveyed and laid out about a mile or two west northerly of the ancient Indian fence, provided Oweneco hath good right to said land, and is not prejudicial to any former grant."*

Notes to Wawekas Hill, or Mohegan's Watchtower and Tombstone, c. 1769:

> *"Aged people whose fathers remembered the days of Uncas... uniformly called (Wawekas) Hill by the name of the Indian Watch Tower....The Fort upon this Hill was a large square building erected in the Indian manner of unpolished stone, without mortar, embanked with earth. The remains of this structure have been visible until within a few years. It probably stood in good repair in the days of Uncas; and though more than one hundred thirty years have passed since that time, but for the depredations of those who wished to enclose their farms with stone fences, it might have stood firmly at the present day."*

Equinox Stone Chamber, Gungywamp, Connecticut.
Believed to be the chamber described by John Pynchon in 1654

Dry-laid stone chambers litter the woods of the Northeast and there is much controversy about who built them. Theories range root cellars from colonial construction to ancient Celts and Native Americans having built them. Whoever built them—and when—has had people debating for over 50 years. Historical documents such as those above would seem to indicate that some of these structures may indeed be pre-colonial and most likely Native American.

FIG. 289.—Stone heap with two cavities, Fayette county, West Virginia.

FIG. 290.—Section of stone heap with triangular cavity, Fayette county, West Virginia.

Strange stone heap mounds in West Virginia, with entrances and chambers.

A Giant problem in New England

What I then found transformed my thinking about ancient America and sent me on a quest to uncover the truth of it. The quest continues to this day. In George Sheldon's 1895 *Town History of Deerfield, Massachusetts,* I found a most curious passage on page 78:

> "At the foot of Bars Long Hill, just where the meadow fence crossed the road, and the bars were placed that gave the village its name, many skeletons were exposed while plowing down a bank, and weapons and implements were found in abundance. One of these skeletons was described to me by Henry Mather who saw it, as being of monstrous size—'the head as big as a peck basket, with double teeth all round.' The skeleton was examined by Dr. Stephen W. Williams who said the owner must have been nearly eight feet high."

I was astonished and told my brother about the account, and he was dumbfounded. Sheldon was a noted historian, a former state Senator of Massachusetts and one of the first preservationists in the country as well as an amateur archaeologist. Dr. Stephen West Williams was a well-respected physician in Deerfield who taught anatomy at Berkshire College. I couldn't wrap my head around what this account meant—double rows of teeth were something I had never heard of. Spurred on by this discovery, I then visited local libraries and read through thousands of pages of town and county histories of New England. What I uncovered both amazed and shocked me. Accounts of seven-foot-plus skeletons unearthed with double rows of teeth were reported in Martha's Vineyard, Middleboro, Hadley, Newton, and Wellfleet (all in Massachusetts), as well as Concord and Portsmouth, New Hampshire, and Rockingham, Vermont:

The Story of Martha's Vineyard, Charles Gilbert Hine, 1908, pg.136:

> "Some 15 years ago the skeleton of an Indian Giant in almost perfect preservation was dug up in the same locality (Cedar Tree Neck), the bones indicated a man easily six feet and a half possibly seven feet high. An unusual feature was a complete

double row of teeth on both the upper and lower jaws."

History of the Town of Rockingham, Vermont. 1907, Lyman Simpson Hayes pg. 338:

> "When the earth was removed from the top of the ledges east of the falls, a remarkable human skeleton, unmistakably that of an Indian, was found. Those who saw it tell the writer the jaw bone was of such size that a large man could easily slip it over his face and the teeth, which were all double, were perfect."

History of the Town of Middleboro, Mass. Thomas Weston, 1906, pg. 400:

> "A few years ago when the highway was straightened and repaired, remains were found. When his skeleton was measured by Dr. Morrill Robinson and others, it was found that the thigh bone was four inches longer than that bone in an ordinary man, and that he had a double row of teeth in each jaw. His height must have been at least seven feet and eight inches."

I also found over 100 accounts of seven-foot-plus skeletons reported unearthed in towns across the region, often mentioning strange anatomic anomalies such as jawbones being so large they fit over the face of the finder. After finding the account of an 8-foot skeleton from Deerfield with double rows of teeth and a skull *"as big as a peck basket,"* I decided to visit the library that George Sheldon founded—the Pocumtuck Valley Memorial Association Library and Museum. Sheldon was one of the most respected historians in the country at the time. He was the museum's first president, and maintains legendary status at the prestigious Deerfield Academy to this day. I found correspondence from Admiral Byrd and other luminaries in his personal letters. At the museum's library, I showed one of the employees the giant skeleton account from the Deerfield town history, and asked if he could lead me in any direction towards unraveling this mystery.

He put in front of me Sheldon's *Archaeological Scrapbook*. Sheldon

George Sheldon's
Archaeological Scrapbook.

had pasted together newspaper accounts about the Mound Builders, the Zuni Indians, and giant skeletal finds. Accounts of 7- and 8-foot skeletons in Ohio, a nine-foot skeleton unearthed in Randolph County, New York, and a 7-foot skeleton with double rows of teeth in Hadley, Massachusetts were pasted into his scrapbook. I then found the 1883 book of *Curiosities and Relics* from the library and museum in Deerfield that had a listing of a thigh bone of an "at least" 8-foot skeleton that was on display until recently. I spoke with a physical anthropologist who fairly recently reinterred the remains as part of the *Native American Graves Protection and Repatriation Act* (NAGPRA), who verified the information.

We investigated the giant skeleton account with double rows of teeth and found what is believed to be the exact location of the burial site as we filmed *Search for the Lost Giants* (History Channel, 2014). A series of meetings with the local farmers (who have owned the Bars Hill Farm area for generations) helped us locate the site. Although we understandably could not dig at the area because it is a protected Native American burial site, a survey was carried out using ground penetrating radar. The GPR technician scanned a 12 x 4 feet stone slab of some sort as well as two large cylindrical artifacts.

It is noteworthy that there is very little stone to be found in the Deerfield area. The GPR technician also verified that something had been removed from the depression pit we surveyed. You can see this in episode 1 of the series. This graphic shows what the tomb may look like.

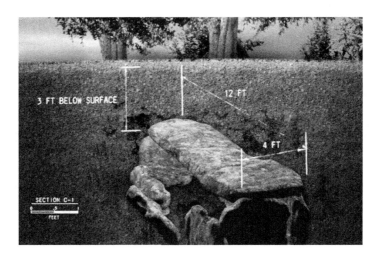

Armed with these strange accounts and a desire to figure out the implications of what I had found, I decided to go to a conference in Connecticut run by now co-author Hugh Newman who invited researchers to speak on the mysteries of ancient America. Hugh is an earth mysteries writer and explorer who has traveled the world studying enigmatic megalithic sites. He had become interested in the stone structures of New England in recent years and had been investigating the same mystery as I had. What I found was that nearly all the speakers talked about encountering similar giant accounts in their research. Ross Hamilton in particular grabbed my attention as he spoke of working with Native Americans investigating this topic. I quickly became friends with Hugh and reached out to Ross who ended up being a mentor to me on the subject.

I quickly read Ross Hamilton's book *A Tradition of Giants*, which he compiled with the help of his friend Vine Deloria Jr., a Lakota elder and scholar. Ross's book is an extremely well researched and very balanced look at this controversial subject. Ross also uncovered multiple accounts of over seven-foot skeletons with double rows of teeth throughout the Ohio Valley. What I decided was that I would use Google Books to see how far this story went. With digitization of a large body of historical documents and the ability to use key words, I saved thousands of hours accumulating more reports. I teamed up with west coast researcher

Micah Ewers and together we amassed over 1000 individual accounts of giant skeletons being unearthed in the past in the United States and over 500 more worldwide.

So this is where I stand now, working with Hugh, Ross and Micah trying to figure out this mystery. I have sought the opinion of numerous anthropologists and archaeologists on this matter. The official position is that these reports constitute a collection of hoaxes, misidentified animal remains, disarticulation, measuring (anthropometry) errors, inaccurate regression formulas, and rare cases of acromegaly and pituitary gigantism. I certainly do not think every report is valid or that all anthropologists and archaeologists are involved in some wide-sweeping cover-up, but I do believe there is a mystery here and a form of obfuscation that keeps the truth hidden. As the reader will find, our research has revealed that a fair number of these accounts represent very reputable people, real places, and real events. There are reliable measurements such as 26, 28 and 29-inch femurs and skulls with circumferences of 26, 28, 30, 32, 36 and 40 inches that are well out of the normal range.

Many of these reports are from well-known historians noting the actions of respected physicians. Anatomic anomalies such as double rows of teeth and jawbones that could be placed over the face are reported from Martha's Vineyard, Massachusetts to Catalina Island, California and

all around the country. These reports are often buried obscurely in voluminous town and county histories in an era of inefficient communication. How is it possible that all these respected people through decades of time can be reporting such things without it being public knowledge?

I leave it to the reader to decide what to think of all this but predict that most rational and logical people will agree with the authors that there is a mystery here that requires further investigation.

Deerfield historian and early
giantologist George Sheldon.

1

EARLY EXPLORERS

A common theme in the early historical record is settlers encountering giant Native Americans in many parts of the country. As far back as the 1500s when the Spanish navigators were exploring the coast of the Americas, sightings of live giants were being recorded. Not only does this put the whole phenomenon into an historical perspective, it also points to the fact that it was only in the last few hundred years that they died off. Three captains of Spanish ships reported these taller-than-average native people on their expeditions to America, as well as Sir Francis Drake, Captain John Smith, a Smithsonian professor, and several other notable eyewitnesses.

GIANTS ALONG THE MISSISSIPPI RIVER, 1519

In 1519, a year before Ferdinand Magellan witnessed the Patagonian giants in Southern Argentina, Spanish explorer Alonzo Álvarez de Pineda was mapping the coastline of the Gulf Coast, marking the various rivers, bays, landmarks, and potential ports, declaring that they belonged to the king of Spain. After navigating his way between Florida and Mexico, he sailed back to the mouth of the Mississippi River. Pineda was the first Spanish explorer to sail up the Mississippi, and reported on large settlements of villages inhabited by local giants, not far from where the river empties into the Gulf of Mexico. There he *"found a large town, and on both sides of its banks, for a distance of six leagues up its course, some forty native villages."* [1]

He quickly discovered that these giants were not dangerous, so

Pineda and his crew settled among them to recuperate and carry out repairs to their four ships. Pineda detailed the abundance of gold found in the river, and how the Indians wore plenty of gold-engraved ornaments. He also noted that other than giants, the tribes also had a race of tiny pygmies. Pineda described the tribes that settled near the Mississippi river as: "*A race of giants, from ten to eleven palms in height and a race of pigmies only five or six palms high.*"[2] (Webster's Dictionary defines a palm used as a unit of measurement to range from seven to ten inches, so the giants were at least 6 feet 7 inches to 8 feet tall).

On his return from Tampico to the Mississippi, Pineda unknowingly sailed right past a tribe of equally huge Texas Indians.[3] (Matagorda Bay is located about one hundred miles below modern-day Galveston). Historian Woodbury Lowery, along with several others, placed "*the giant Karankawas*" nation around Matagorda Bay at that time. Furthermore in a report on the Karankawas, John R. Swanton, of the Bureau of American Ethnology, describes the men as being:

Alonso Alvarez de Pineda.

> "*...very tall and well formed.... Their hair was unusually coarse, and worn so long by many of the men that it reached to the waist. Agriculture was not practised by these Indians, their food supply being obtained from the waters, the chase, and wild plants, and, to a limited extent, human flesh; for, like most of the tribes of the Texas coast, they were cannibals.... Head-flattening and tattooing were practised to a considerable extent.*"[4]

However it was also recorded that they:

> "*...do not eat men, but roast them only, on account of the cruelties first enacted against their ancestors by the Spanish.*"[5]

So that's OK then! Anyway, when Pineda returned, he presented Francisco

Pineda's map of the Gulf Coast, 1519.

de Garay, the Spanish governor of Jamaica, with the first maps and sketches of the entire Gulf Coast. These maps also included Pineda's writings about the race of giants living there. These sketches and writings were archived by the famous Spanish chronicler Martín Fernández de Navarrete. They can be found today by visiting the *Archivo General de Indias* in Seville, Spain.

A few years later in 1523, as the Spanish fleet discovered, dominated, and overran the Caribbean Islands, a strange report came forth via historian Peter Martyr who assisted at the Council of the Indies. The account was originally shared by a native who was Christianized and taken to Spain:

> *"The report ran that the natives were white and their king and queen giants, whose bones, while babies, had been softened with an ointment of strange herbs, then kneaded and stretched like wax by masters of the art, leaving the poor objects of their magic half dead, until after repeated manipulations they finally attained their great size."* [6]

THE PATAGONIAN GIANTS, 1520

Meanwhile, on the most southern tip of South America, giant rumblings were afoot. Although this account is not one from North America, its place in the historical timeline makes this short summary worthy of inclusion. During his busy schedule of sailing around the area now known as Patagonia, Ferdinand Magellan, much to his surprise, found a naked giant dancing and singing on the shore. Magellan sent one of his men to go on land to make contact and ordered him to dance and sing to the giant, to show friendship. The look on the chosen man's face was not recorded, but must have been one of surprise and fear!

The frolicking worked and they were able to be alone with the giant. Antonio Pigafetta, who kept a diary of the journey, later turned it into a book called *Magellan's Voyage: A Narrative Account of the First Circumnavigation*. He wrote:

> *"When he was before us, he began to marvel and to be afraid, and he raised one finger upward, believing that we came from heaven. And he was so tall that the tallest of us only came up to his waist."* [7]

They spent some time on the island, hunting with the huge natives, building a storehouse for their supplies, and devising a cunning plot to kidnap two of them and take them back to Europe. The first part of the treacherous plan worked, and they managed to get them on the ship, but they both died before Magellan could show off his prized possessions. Why he didn't keep the bones to prove his claim is unknown, but the decaying bodies, and terrible smell may have been a good enough reason.

Britain soon got involved and in 1578 Sir Francis Drake made contact with the same Patagonians of the *Tehuelche* tribe but placed them at 7 feet 6 inches tall, as outlined by his nephew in *The World Encompassed* (1628):

> *"Magellan was not altogether deceived in naming these giants, for they generally differ from the common sort of man both in stature, bigness and strength of body, as also in the hideousness of their voices: but they are nothing so monstrous and giant-*

*like as they were represented, there being some English men as
tall as the highest we could see, but peradventure the Spaniards
did not think that ever any English man would come hither to
reprove them, and therefore might presume the more boldly to
lie."* [8]

GIGANTVM
REGIO

In 1580 a Spanish captain, Pedro Sarmiento, was said to have seen
giants in the same area according to an historian on his voyage. Another
narrator, Anthonie Knivet, who accompanied the circumnavigator
Thomas Cavendish in 1592, wrote of two Patagonians twelve feet tall,
and a boy whose height was over nine feet.[9] Willem Schouten and Jacob
Le Maire, two Dutch circumnavigators, touched down in Patagonia in
1615 and found some graves made of heaped stones, one of which they
opened and saw within it *the bones of human beings ten and eleven feet in
stature."* According to Robert Silverberg there were other similar reports
like this.[10]

John Wood, of John Narborough's 1670 expedition made no
reference to their great stature, only that: *"none of the seven Patagonians he
met were not much above six feet".*[11] However, other eyewitness accounts
suggest otherwise. Harrington and Carmen returned there in 1704,
with reports that corroborated the Spanish version. Horace Walpole,
the English historian and gothic novelist, published *An Account of the
Giants Lately Discovered: In a Letter to a Friend in the Country* following
the return in 1766 of Captain John Byron, who had circumnavigated the
world in the HMS Dolphin. Word leaked out that the crew had seen nine-

foot-tall giants in South America.[12] Then in 1741 survivors of a shipwreck, John Cummins and John Bulkeley, made note that they were "*of a middle stature.*" Whoever they were, some of them were very tall, as they wrote the following:

> "*I never was more astonish'd than to see such a set of people, the stoutest of Our Grenadiers would appear nothing to them... Nothing in Nature could appear more terribly frightful that these people did both Men and Women...their Horses appear'd so small in Comparison to their Riders, tho' when I was near them I observ'd that their Horses were of the Common Size, and Our People on Board, who were looking at us thro' their Glasses, said we look's like meer Dwarfs to the people we were gone amongst...these People who in size come the nearest to Giants of any people I believe in the World'.* [13]

There is still debate about the authenticity of some of these reports, even though there are quite a few of them. Can the chroniclers really be that confused that they cannot determine the approximate height of someone standing before their very eyes?

Detail from *A Representation of the Interview between Commodore Byron and the Patagonians*. 1773.[14]

The White Indians of Duhare, 1521-1526

In early 1521, a secret voyage from Spain was undertaken by Francisco Gordillo and Pedro de Quejo. They sailed over to America and along the Carolina coast to capture Native American slaves and scout out potential locations for new Spanish colonies. They managed to capture seventy members of the Chicora tribe to bring back to their homeland.

> *"The chiefs of the province of Chicora, a portion of what is now South Carolina, were famous for their height, which was supposed to prove their royal blood."* [15]

While Gordillo and Quejo treated the enigmatic Chicora Indians with treachery, their relationship with the Duhare peoples were much more gentlemanly. This was probably because the inhabitants of Duhare were described as looking European, with red or brown hair, tan skin and gray eyes. Strangely, for this part of the world, the men had full beards and towered over the Spanish. They did not appear to be Native American.

One of the kidnapped Chicora Natives was taken back to Spain and christianized. He was named Francisco de Chicora. He learned their language and started working for Spanish explorer Lucas Vazquez de Ayllón. They met with the court chronicler, Peter Martyr, and he talked with him at length about his people, homeland and about neighboring provinces. Ayllón was a member of the *Real Audiencia in Santo Domingo* (the first court of the Spanish crown in America). De Ayllón had received from Charles V in 1523, a grant for the land explored in 1521 by Francisco Gordillo and slave trader Captain Pedro de Quejo

Soon after this, he set sail to create a colony in America and eventually landed in this area of the Santee River. He visited with many of the Native American tribes in the area and recorded their customs, rituals and ways of living. The report on the Duhare stated:

> *"Ayllon says the natives are white men, and his testimony is confirmed by Francisco Chicorana. Their hair is brown and hangs to their heels. They are governed by a king of gigantic size, called Datha, whose wife is as large as himself. They have five children. In place of horses, the king is carried on*

*the shoulders of strong young men, who run with him to the
different places he wishes to visit."* [16]

Datha was described by the Spanish as being a giant, the largest man they
had ever seen. He had a wife as tall as him. He wore brightly colored
paint or tattoos on his skin that distinguished him from the commoners.
Duhare can either be translated as "di-hAicher - place of the Clan Hare"
or, as researcher Richard Thornton points out, if the Duhare came from
west of the Shannon River in Ireland, it meant, "du'hEir – place of the
Irish." Datha was a Medieval Irish Gaelic word that meant "painted," that
could be linked with the pigments or tattoos that Datha's skin was covered
with (that is a similar style to ancient Irish body art).[17] These unusually
European characteristics have been noted all across ancient America,
particularly when giants have been reported.

One of the things that stood out with this culture was that they
bred many types of livestock including ducks, chickens, geese and even
deer. According to the Spanish chroniclers, the Duhare worked large
herds of domesticated deer and made cheese from their milk. Although
this might sound odd, this technique has been recorded in the annals
of Irish monks before dairy cows became the norm.[18] The Santee River
Natives also grew large amounts of corn and an unrecognized grain, as
well as potatoes and other vegetables. However it does raise questions of
how they developed these advanced farming practices. Were there earlier
connections between America and Europe than previously thought?

GIANTS IN TAMPA BAY, FLORIDA, 1528

In 1528, Pánfilo de Nárvaez and his surviving colleague Álvar Núñez
Cabeza de Vaca witnessed giants around the area of Tampa Bay, Florida.
Three hundred of their men went ashore, but only Cabeza de Vaca
and a handful of men survived the harsh jungle environment and the
consistent onslaught from native attacks. As the Spanish invaded, they
were outnumbered and outwitted by the locals and panic soon ensued.
Their ships left the ports early in the confusion and only around thirty
men survived, but Narváez was not among them. Cabeza de Vaca and

the remaining Spanish survivors were washed ashore near modern-day Tampa Bay.

> *"All the many Indians from Florida we saw were archers, and, being very tall and naked, at a distance they appear giants. Those people are wonderfully built, very gaunt and of great strength and agility. Their bows are as thick as an arm, of eleven or twelve spans long, shooting an arrow at 200 paces with unerring aim."* [19]

The remaining Spanish quickly formed an expedition to reach a Spanish settlement in Mexico and regroup there, thinking it was only a few miles away. However, after a series of battles with hostile Indians they ended up rafting their way into southwestern Texas.[20]

Traveling west along the Colorado River, de Vaca and the survivors of this disastrous expedition were the first Europeans to see a bison, and the first to travel from the East Coast to the West Coast of America.

Harassment by these robust warriors continued, so Narvaez decided to head south for the Gulf Coast and escape by the sea. Arriving there after much hardship, he and his men constructed five crude boats in order to search along the coast for a Spanish settlement. Unfortunately, a sudden, fierce storm caught them some distance from land. The high winds drove all the boats, with all their men aboard far out to sea. All were subsequently lost except Cabeza de Vaca and three companions who managed to reach the shore. They walked across Texas and Northern Mexico, finally reaching the Pacific coast where they linked up with Francisco Vazquez de Coronado in 1541, who had his own tall warrior stories to tell.[21] De Vaca returned to Spain and published his account, which was a bestseller of its time. In it there are references to their encounters with giants.

A few miles south of Tampa Bay, several skeletons were unearthed near Longboat Key that may show that the Spaniards' eyewitness

Álvar Núñez Cabeza de Vaca

31

accounts have some truth to them.

> *"According to Spanish historians, the Indians encountered in this region were quite tall. Historian Karl Bickel tells of finding two skeletons on neighboring Longboat Key, one seven feet, the other eight feet tall. At least one complete skeleton from Snead Island, with other Indian artifacts, now rests in the Smithsonian Institution."* [22]

In 1942, Bickel published the book *The Mangrove Coast* that gives a history of the west coast of Florida, beginning with the chronology of native tribes before the Spanish invasion. In 1940, Karl and Madeira Bickel purchased a 10-acre site off Bay Shore Drive that included the soon to-be-named Madeira Bickel Indian Mound. They donated it to the state to ensure it would be preserved.

CORONADO'S AND ALCARON'S GIANT DISCOVERIES, 1540

In 1539, an expedition led by Francisco Coronado was on a quest to discover the legendary *Seven Cities of Cibola*, an Aztec city that was said to be fabulously rich, with gold and treasures beyond any man's wildest dreams. Whilst searching for what today we call *El Dorado,* they ran into

"Coronado sets out to the North". Oil painting by Frederic Remington.

several tribes of Indian giants near Mexico's present-day border with California and Arizona. The expedition was documented by Pedro de Castaneda who accompanied Coronado and wrote the complete account of the adventure.

Their journey began in Mexico City, heading west towards the Pacific coastline with around three hundred Spaniards and eight hundred Indians. As they approached the coast, they redirected north and traveled through the areas now called Sonora and Sinaloa. Meanwhile, Coronado's associate Hernando de Alarcon set sail along the coast so they could align with the expedition members who were on foot. Coronado then sent out one of his team to rendezvous with the ship:

> *"Don Rodrigo Maldonado, who was captain of those who went in search of the ships, did not find them, but he brought back with him an Indian so large and tall that the best man in the army reached only to his chest. It was said that other Indians were even taller on the coast."* [23]

This particular giant was later revealed to be part of the Seri tribe, inhabitants of Tiburon Island.

Hernando de Alarcon   Salina, Kansas burial pit postcard.

Soon after this, whilst trying to establish contact with Alarcon, Captain Melchior Diaz took a group of men and guides out toward the north and west in search of the sea coast and the ships:

> *"After going about 150 leagues, they came to a province of*

exceedingly tall and strong men—like giants." [24]

These were later found out to be a Yuman tribe called the Cocopa, who were huge and went about mostly naked:

> "*When they carry anything, they can take a load of more than three or four hundredweight on their heads. Once when our men wished to fetch a log for the fire, and six men were unable to carry it, one of these Indians is reported to have come and raised it in his arms, put it on his head alone, and carried it very easily.*" [25]

By the time they reached the coast, where the Indians said they had seen the ships, they were already on their way back to Mexico. However, Alcaron, the captain, changed his mind and headed back north and soon came unexpectedly upon the San Gabriel, loaded with provisions for Coronado.

Adding a third ship to the mission, and after nearly losing all three ships in the murky shallow waters, they made it to the mouth of the Colorado River, the first westerners to explore this area. They dropped anchor and took two smaller boats to fight against the powerful current. They then headed into uncharted territory:

> "*...thus began the historic first voyage by Europeans up the Colorado River among the tall Yuman peoples who lived along its banks on either side.*" [26]

Alarcon and his men soon came upon about two hundred and fifty tall Cocopa warriors standing on the banks, ready to attack them. But the captain, by making hand signals of peace and offering gifts, won them over. Further upstream, thousands of giant Indians were witnessed with bows and arrows that he described as:

> "*large and well formed, without being corpulent. Some have their noses pierced, and from them hang pendants, while others wear shells... All of them, big and little, wear a multi-colored sash about the waist; and tied in the middle, a round bundle of feathers hanging down like a tail.... Their bodies are branded by fire; their hair is*

34

banged in front, but in the back it hangs to the waist." [27]

Alarcon and his men made it as far as the southern edge of the Grand Canyon. He is almost unique among the conquistadores in that he treated the Indians he met humanely, unlike many of his colleagues:

> *"The Indians had an experience they were never to repeat: they were sorry to see these white men leave."* [28]

DE SOTO'S ENCOUNTERS WITH GIANTS, 1540-41

Whilst the survivors of Narvaez's crew were making their way across the country, and Alcaron was making friends with giants, another Spanish explorer, Hernando De Soto, sailed nine ships into Tampa Bay that ignited one of the most fascinating stories between the Native Americans and the Spanish.

In the early spring of 1541 De Soto's army travelled from Florida to Middle Georgia. Some of the officers immediately noted that the peoples in that region were more advanced culturally than other Indians they had encountered, and were mostly around one foot taller than the Spanish (5 ft 4 was the Spanish average at the time). These were the Okonee and Tamatli tribes of the

Hernando De Soto

Muskogean Culture, who in turn were ancestors of the Creek Indians. The Spanish named them 'Los Indios Gigantes' (The Giant Indians). De Soto's chroniclers wrote that some 'Great Suns' (Chief Priests) of these provinces were seven feet tall. Their vast territory extended from Tampa Bay north to the present Jacksonville area and west to the Aucilla River, which runs along the eastern border of modern Jefferson County and empties into the gulf.[29]

For protection the Conquistadors took these chiefs hostage and called them 'guests.' De Soto also required the natives to furnish him with porters. The Indians' reaction to this policy varied. After some reluctance, the cacique of Ocala, "*an Indian of enormous size and amazing strength*,"[30] finally agreed to become De Soto's 'guest'. Vitacucho, the cacique in the neighboring province of Caliquin (present-day Alachua County), consented only after his daughter fell into De Soto's hands. But even while being detained, Vitacucho and his tall warriors secretly managed two uprisings. Copafi, the cacique of the Apalachee around Tallahassee, described as "*a man of monstrous proportions*,"[31] refused even to meet with De Soto, but a party led by the governor himself finally captured the giant and brought him in without much trouble because they had kidnapped his daughter.

Hernando De Soto's meetings with giants continued as he pushed further inland. After a winter break at Ambaica Apalachee, he moved through the country with more than six hundred men and two hundred horses, traveling through northern Florida, southern Georgia, and western Alabama, meeting many tribes along the way.

Rodrigo Ranjel, De Soto's private secretary wrote a diary detailing the expedition. The territory they were exploring was ruled by the giant

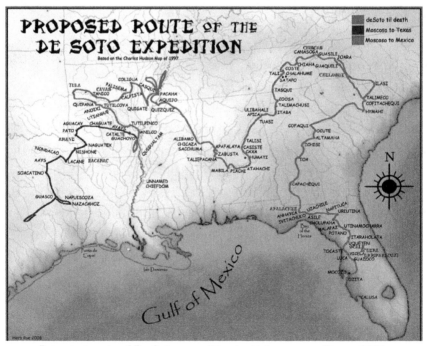

Proposed route of De Soto expedition by Heironymous Rowe, 2008.

Native American chief Tuscaloosa and upon the conquistadors' arrival, the chief's eighteen year-old son fiercely approached De Soto's cavalry. Ranjel writes:

> *"Seeing him we paused, dumb with amazement. For, though but a youth...he towered on high. A great-limbed giant: heads of tallest men reached only to his breast."*

After a three-day march De Soto and fifteen soldiers entered Tuscaloosa's village and discovered that the chief was even more enormous than his son and turned out to be the tallest and most handsomely shaped Indian they saw during all their travels. His physical measurements, writes Garcilaso de la Vega, who accompanied De Soto:

> *"...were like those of his son, for both were more than a half-yard taller than all the others. He appeared to be a giant, or rather was one, and his limbs and face were in proportion to the height of his body. His countenance was handsome, and he wore a look of severity, yet a look which well revealed his ferocity and grandeur of spirit. His shoulders conformed to his height, and his waistline measured just a little more than two-thirds of a yard [wide]. His arms and legs were straight and well formed and were in proper proportion to the rest of his body. In sum he was the tallest and most handsomely shaped Indian that the Castilians saw during all their travels."* [32]

Artists impression of the rather tall Tuscaloosa, with De Soto.

After a few days of watching colorful war dances, and Tuscaloosa completely ignoring the Spanish visitors, De Soto took the chief by the hand, and they walked together with him to the piazza. There they sat on a bench and talked for several minutes. Tuscaloosa was persuaded to join De Soto on their quest towards Mobile. However, owing to the cacique's huge size and immense weight, no horse was able to bear him. They eventually found a packhorse accustomed to heavy loads that was strong enough to carry the chief. But when he mounted the horse, Tuscaloosa's feet almost touched the ground. This description accords with Garcilaso de la Vega's statement that the chief stood half-a-yard taller (1.5 ft) than the tallest Spaniard. Though no one recorded Tuscaloosa's actual height, these two descriptions suggest he was between 7 and 8 feet tall.

Whilst trekking towards Mobile, two of De Soto's soldiers disappeared and the scouts returned to warn De Soto. Meanwhile, a rebellion was forming, and hundreds of Indian warriors hid within the town in anticipation. De Soto stood strong, and approached the town and its high walls. A welcoming committee of painted warriors, clad in robes made of animal skins and headpieces with vibrantly colored feathers, came out to greet them. Some young Native American maidens followed, dancing and singing. De Soto entered the town with a few of his most trusted soldiers, along with Tuscaloosa and the chief's entourage.

The Spaniards stood in a piazza, surrounded by a stream of foreign colors and fluttering sounds, but noticed around eighty houses within the village. Several of them were described as large enough to hold at least one thousand people. Unknown to De Soto, more than two thousand Native American warriors hid behind the walls. After some of the chiefs from the town joined him, Tuscaloosa withdrew from De Soto. With a severe look, he warned the governor and his soldiers to leave immediately. De Soto tried to regain custody of the chief, but a tussle between a Spaniard and an Indian chief ignited an all-out battle. Under a barrage of arrows, De Soto and his men retreated from the village. They regrouped, and made a plan of attack. When they gained entry to the village, they killed the chief's giant son, set fire to the buildings, and massacred around 2,500 of the city's inhabitants. Only 18 Spanish soldiers fell.

Despite the death of his son and the overall carnage left in the wake of the battle, Tuscaloosa escaped. Riding deep into unknown lands, De Soto and his men marched to capture him, but the great chief disappeared with twenty bodyguards, and the pursuing Spaniards found only abandoned cities with massive mounds.

During the mid-20th century, archaeologists found numerous large skeletons ranging between 7 and 14 ft in height in royal burials at Ocmulgee National Monument and Etowah Mounds National Historic Landmark (see pages 220 and 244). Both these town sites were ancestral to the Creek Indians, so the stories of the Spanish are quite plausible. Creek men today, especially in northern Alabama and Georgia, tend to be exceptionally tall.

FRANCIS DRAKE AND THE CALIFORNIA GIANTS, 1579

Elizabethan Naval Commander, Sir Francis Drake landed on the coast of Virginia, near the mouth of the James River in 1577 as part of his famous circumnavigation of the globe (1577-1580). He named the region Virginia in honor of Queen Elizabeth I, then explored the Chesapeake Bay for a few weeks. He then led a part of his fleet's crewmen on horseback and foot along the James River for 10 days until they reached the summit of a mountain, where they could see a vast

Portrait of Sir Francis Drake. Frontspiece to his nephew's *The World Encompassed* (1628)

valley covered in grasslands and fields. Drake's memoir states that this valley was densely populated by agricultural Indians, who were peaceful and culturally advanced.

He was part of the team involved in the discovery of the coast of Upper California, which was named *New Albion*. After experiencing the Patagonian Giants a year earlier, and spotting a few more on his famous voyage, Drake sailed northwards along the West Coast of the Americas.

Drake receiving the Crown from the Hioh, or King of New Albion. From David Henry's,
An Historical Account of All the Voyages Round the World (Cotsen Collection).

After moving up and down the North American coastline, he ended up in the vicinity of San Francisco Bay, where he remained for over a month (June-July, 1579). Here he worked on his ship and made contact with the Indians who were fascinated by the strange white men who had arrived in their territory.

Francis Fletcher, Drake's chronicler of the voyage, says the local chief was "*a man of large body and good aspect,*" and even placed his own crown—a headdress of feathers—on Drake's head and encouraged him to exercise dominion over their land. He also describes these Indians as a tall people with herculean strength:

> "*Yet are the men commonly so strong of body, that that which two or three of our men could hardly bear, one of them would take upon his back, and without grudging carry it easily away, up hill and down hill an English mile together.*" [33]

SANTA CATALINA ISLAND, CALIFORNIA, 1602

Although Santa Catalina Island had been visited by Don Juan Cabrillo in 1542, no detailed accounts of the inhabitants were given, apart from that the island "*had a large and vigorous population.*"[34] It was 58 years later that Spanish explorer Sebastian Vizcaino, the man who gave the island the name *Santa Catalina,* visited the island with chronicler, Father Torquemada. On the second day of their stopover the Spaniards found "*a level prairie, very well cleared, where the Indians were assembled to worship an idol which was there.*" Torquemada describes the center of the temple as being "*formed by a large circle of long stones pointing upward toward the mid-day sun,*" in the center of which was the idol that "*resembled a demon, having two horns, no head, a dog at its feet and many children painted all around it.*"[35] This megalithic complex was described as being two miles wide, and was part of a major ceremonial area to worship the Tongva deity Chinigchinich; a kind of 'sun-god.'

Catalina could have been the ceremonial heart of this ancient tradition, that, as we'll see later, could have gone back as far as 8,300 BC (See *Further Afield* chapter). Tantalisingly, the only graphic representation of the site was a simple circle drawn by him on a map, but this map is no longer in existence. Nor is the temple, as it disappeared in the ensuing decades thanks to the Spanish Christians: "*The early mission fathers sent an expedition to the island to destroy a so-called temple in which the natives worshipped.*"[36] A brief description of the islanders was given, although no mention of 'giants' was forthcoming:

> "*Torquemada considered the natives of Santa Catalina a superior race and in advance of the natives of the mainland in every way. The women were attractive, had fine eyes, and were modest and decorous, while the children were described as 'white and ruddy.*'" [37]

Over 3,000 skeletons were unearthed by Ralph Glidden on the Channel Islands in the 1930s including some that were of very large proportions.

JOHN SMITH AND THE VIRGINIA GIANTS, 1606
The History of Virginia, The Southern Literary Messenger *Vol 5, 1839, pg. 789*

The following account is about the famous Captain John Smith's encounter with immense natives in the early 1600s. From the article:

"Captain Smith's General Historic. Vol. 1, p. 120 gives an account of a prodigious giant tribe of Indians, the Susquesahanocks, whom he met at the head of the Chesapeake Bay. This relation has been rejected as incredible. Monumental evidences have, however, within the last age, come to light, which would seem to confirm the existence of such a race of giants. Human bones of extraordinary size, thigh bones three feet in length, and skeletons seven feet in length have been discovered on Flint Run in the county of Shenandoah, on Hawksbill creek, Tuscarora creek and on the South Branch of the Potomac."

The finds continued in the general area for the next 100 years after these accounts, including the unearthing of 7 to 8 feet tall skeletons which were at one time on display at the Maryland Academy of Sciences, with skulls of *"unusual size"* and thigh bones *"as thick as those of a horse."*[38] The following account is from Smith's diaries:

"They measured the calf of the largest man's leg, and found it three quarters of a yard about, and all the rest of his limbs were in proportion; so that he seemed the stateliest and most goodly personage, they had ever beheld. His arrows were five quarters long [sic], headed with the splinters of a white Chrystal-like stone..." Also from Smith, *"Those are the most strange people of all those Countries, both in language and attire; for their language it may well beseeme their proportions, sounding from them, as it were a great voice in a vault, or cave, as an Echo."* [39]

The NASA website says the following about Smith's Map of 1612.

"Considering the crude navigational tools he had at his disposal, Captain John Smith's map of Virginia was amazingly accurate."[40]

The Susquehannock on the map is the one Smith described above. Note the description: *"The Susquesahanocks are a gyant people & thus atired."*

The following is an abstract from Dr. Marshall Becker's paper.

Becker is a senior fellow of anthropology at the University of Pennsylvania:

"When John Smith first contacted a group of Susquehannock in 1608, he described these people as "gyant-like." Direct confirmation of this observation can now be provided through studies of the long bones of a population which was part of the Susquehannock "confederacy." Recent excavations at a Susquehannock site on the South Branch of the Potomac River in Hampshire County, West Virginia, revealed portions of a palisaded village and associated features dating from the middle of the 16th century. This remnant of a flood-destroyed site yielded 13 relatively intact burials. Surface collection of skeletal material immediately downstream of the site after the flood, provided long bones from at least 18 other adults. Calculation of the stature of the individuals represented in this sample and comparisons with the other Native American populations of this period confirm John Smith's observations."[41]

There is no shortage of sources confirming Smith's claims, such as the work of noted archaeologist Donald A. Cadzow. Cadzow's involvement

John Smith's 1606 map showing a Susquehannock Male (upper right).
The map was created by cartographer William Hole.

43

The Sasquesahanougs are a Gyant like peo=ple & thus a=tyred

in 1932 at the Washington County, Pennsylvania find, included 48 very large skeletons, one of them being seven feet, five inches tall. A 1932 newspaper article[42] announced the intention to find a fort of the giant Susquehannocks. That prediction would be borne out in September of that year, with the unearthing of the aforementioned giant skeletons. In the *Baltimore Sun*, July 13th 1930, is found a report describing Cadzow's work at Safe Harbor, Pennsylvania titled *Science Uncovers Evidence To Support Captain John Smith's Yarns.*

An article from the *Syracuse-Herald Journal*, July 6, 1954 described tall Native Americans of the past in the Spanish Hill area:

> *"Historians describe them as giants and this has been borne out by the fact that skeletons seven and eight feet tall have been exhumed."*

Another report buried in a document from 1852, described a non-sensational account that further authenticated John Smith's claims:

> *"Human bones of extraordinary size- thigh bones three feet in length and skeletons seven feet in length have been discovered on Flint run in this county, on Hawksbill creek, Tuscarora creek and in Hardy county."* [43]

KILLED BY A GIANT INDIAN
Biography and history of the Indians of North America, By Samuel Gardner Drake, 1834

This fatal, yet amusing anecdote, tells the story of a 'giant-like' Indian killing an Englishman, with a friend who got warned not to retaliate:

> *"One William Hammond being killed 'by a giant-like Indian' near New York, about 1637, Capt. Gardener told Waiandance that he must kill that Indian; but this being against the advice of the great Sachem, his brother, he declined it, and told the captain that that Indian was a mighty great man, and no man dared meddle with him, and that he had many friends."*

JOHN LAWSON MEETS THE GIANTS, 1701

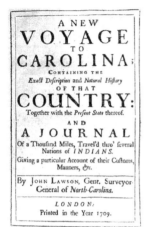

Englishman John Lawson explored 500 miles of the Carolinas in the early 1700s, and was the first to note that less than one in six Indians had survived the ongoing smallpox epidemic that lasted from 1650 to 1700.[44] The early Spanish explorers had spread numerous old-world diseases that decimated large swathes of Indians. Entire villages were decimated *"without leaving one Indian alive."* However, on his travels he did witness some larger than life natives in his book *A New Voyage to Carolina*:

"He was the tallest Indian I ever saw, being about seven-foot high, and a very strait compleat person, esteem'd on by the King for his great art in hunting." [45]

"The Indians of North-Carolina are well shap'd clean-made people, of diferent statures, as the Europeans are, yet chiefly inclin'd to be tall." [46]

THE COLORADO RIVER YUMANS IN 1775
With Anza to California, 1775-1776: The Journal of Pedro Font

This description of tall Indians comes from the journals of Pedro Font. Juan Bautista de Anza was a Spanish military leader who left Horcasitas (near present-day Hermosillo in Sonora) for Monterey, California in September 1775 with crew of 240 men. Their goal was to secure an overland route from the interior of Sonora, bring settlers, and affirm the Crown's claim to this outpost of empire at a time when England and Russia appeared to challenge it. Pedro Font was a dour, judgmental Catalonian priest loyal to the Church, unlike his captain who was a natural leader. However, Font's words caught our attention when researching this chapter:

"These Yumas, and likewise the Cajuenches and the rest, are

well formed, tall, robust, not very ugly, and have good bodies. Generally they are nearly eight spans high and even more, and many are nine and some even above nine, according to our measurements."

A 'span' is the width of an outstretched hand from thumb to little finger, and is rounded off to 9 inches, so 9 spans is around 81 inches or 6 ft 9 in.

HISTORICAL EYE-WITNESS ACCOUNTS, 1800S ONWARDS
Compiled by Ross Hamilton

The Osage Indians were originally located in Missouri near the Missouri and Osage rivers. They were first witnessed by French explorers around 1673. The Osage Indians were a seminomadic tribe and were known for gardening, hunting, and foraging. Warriors were very hardy and could travel 60 miles a day on foot. Eventually, they found themselves in the northwestern part of Arkansas. Regarding the Osage physicality is this passage from the diaries of Lewis and Clark:

> *"The Osage Nation of Indians live about two hundred miles up this (Osage) river. They are of a large size and well proportioned, and a very warlike people."* [47]

The early American writer Washington Irving said of the Osage:

> *"...the finest looking Indians I have ever seen."* [48]

In R. B. Marcy's *Exploration of the Red River of Louisiana in the Year 1852*, W.D.C. Armstrong enjoins similarly:

> *"Father Charlevoix in his Historical Journal of a Voyage Down the Mississippi says 'The Arkansas are reckoned to be the tallest and best shaped of all the savages of this continent, and they are called, by way of distinction, the fine men.'"* [49]

From *An Account of Louisiana: Being an Abstract of Documents in the Offices of the Department of State and of the Treasury*, published in 1803, it reads:

"On the Missouri and its waters are many and numerous nations, the best known of which are the Osages, situated on the river of the same name on the right bank of the Missouri at about eight leagues from its confluence with it; they consist of one thousand warriors, who live in two settlements at no great distance from each other. They are of gigantic stature and well proportioned, are enemies of the whites and of all other Indian nations and commit depredations from the Illinois to the Arkansas. The trade of this nation is said to be under an exclusive grant. They are a cruel and ferocious race, and are hated and feared by all."

George Catlin's painting of Osage leader Tehong-tas-sab-bee, 1841.
Courtesy of the Caitlin Collection.

According to Catlin in his book, *Letters and Notes* (1841), the Osages were the tallest men in North America:

> *"Very few of the men, at their full growth...are less than six feet in stature, and very many of them six and a half, and others seven feet. They are at the same time well-proportioned in their limbs and good-looking."* [50]

Further reports of 'living giants' continued in other parts of the country. In Onondaga County, New York, however, there was one dead one too— killed by a gun-shot in 1849:

> *"On the late Dr. Western's farm could be distinctly traced the remains of a small fortification, with a burying place. One grave was opened, in which were the remains of thirteen men. One of the skulls taken from it had been perforated by a bullet, which was found within it. Another skull found within this grave was very much larger than its fellows; the under jaw would fit completely outside of a common man's, and it is said that the other bones were of corresponding gigantic dimensions."* [51]

This one comes from *Hardesty's History of Monroe County, Ohio* (1882):

> *"He further told me of the killing of a big Indian at Buckchitawa, about the time of the settlement at Marietta (Ohio). The Indians had a white prisoner whom they forced to decoy boats to the shore. A small boat was descending the river containing white people, when this prisoner was placed under the bank to tell those in the boat that he had escaped captivity, and to come to the shore and take him in. The Indians were concealed, but the big Indian stuck his head out from behind a large tree, when it was pierced by a bullet from the gun of the steersman of the boat. The Indians cried out Wetzel, Wetzel, and fled. This was the last ever seen of the prisoner. The Indians returned next day and buried the big Indian, who, he said, was twenty inches taller than he was, and he*

was a tall man. When Chester Bishop was digging a cellar for Asahel Booth, at Clarington, many years ago, he came across a skeleton, the bones of which were removed carefully by Dr. Richard Kirkpatrick, and from his measurement the height of the man when living would have been 8 feet and 5 inches. It is probable that these were the bones of the big Indian of whom the Indian at Jackson's told me."

This strange account comes from *A History of Pioneer Families of Missouri*, by William Smith Bryan, 1876, pg.101:

"It is not known for certain whether any of the Indians were killed in this battle or not but one of their chiefs, named Keokuk, a man of some distinction, was wounded and died shortly after. He was buried in the prairie, one and one-half miles northeast of the present town of Wellsville, in Montgomery County [Missouri]. In 1826 his remains were taken up by Dr. Bryan and several other gentlemen and upon his breast was found a large silver medal, containing his name, rank, etc. He was evidently a giant in stature, for the jaw bone, which, with several other bones of the body, are still preserved by Mrs. Dr. Peery, of Montgomery county, will fit over the face of the largest sized man."

Not only does it appear that a spiritual and warrior class of giants existed among Native Americans, but substantial evidence points to wars and conflicts thousands of years ago between the local tribes and a separate race of giants (See *Legends of the Tall Ones* chapter).

Finally, this is an account from an old settler about two miles from Ross Hamilton's house, in Madisonville, Ohio:

"Another incident of a later date took place east of Madison, when the victim was an Indian. West of Madison was a station known as Nelson's, where were horses pasturing. A party of Indians on their way toward the hills rode off with some of these, one of which was hoppled. Nelson and others of the fort made pursuit, but failed in overtaking any except

the one on the hoppled horse, whom Nelson shot when near the site of the present residence of Esquire Clason. There the Indian was buried, and the circumstance turned to account by naming the place Indian hill. Esquire Clason says that many years afterward the grave was discovered by accident and the jawbone secured as a relic in his family. Judging from the relic, he says, the Indian must have been a giant in proportions." [52]

REMARKABLE RACE OF POLAR GIANTS
The Virginia Enterprise, September 29, 1899
The Antarctic Circle and Patagonia

For the most recent evidence of 'living giants' that were actually photographed, we return to Patagonia and further south towards the Antarctic, with some remarkable pre-Photoshop era pictures of explorer Dr. Frederick A. Cook standing between two rather large individuals. He spent two years as surgeon and photographer for the Belgian Antarctic

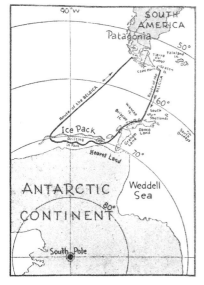

Expedition of 1897-99 (see map). This is just one of a number of photographs that were taken of the Ona Indians, who were possible relations of the Fuegians and Patagonians.

Dr. Cook is known to be 5 feet 9 inches tall,[53] so these taller than average Natives' heights can easily be estimated. On the left we have 6 ft 10 inches, and on the right we have 7 ft exactly. These two men are 19% and 20% taller than Cook. Micah Ewers did further analysis and deduced that Cook is 304 pixels, the giants 360 to 365 pixels or so. If we make Cook 5 ft 10 in his shoes, they become 6 ft 11 and 7 ft 1 respectively.

Cook also photographed a powerful 6 ft 6 Ona woman, as well as a 7 ft 2 naked male, that were published in 1938 in *Popular Photography Magazine*.[54] In the magazine he made it clear that some stood up to 7 feet 6 inches tall.

WILD SERI CANNIBALS
The Pittsburg Press, July 23, 1900
Tiburon Island, Gulf of California, Mexico

The sub-heading reads: "*Who Do Not Stop Growing Until Over Forty Years of Age... Giants in Stature and Wonderful Runners*." Tiburon Island was the last outpost of what the press at the time called 'savages'. In true warrior style, the Indians vehemently

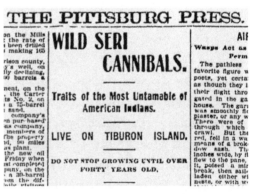

held their ground until the turn of last century, with witnesses describing them as extremely tall. Notably, the Smithsonian got involved:

> "*One of the most remarkable things about the Seri, said Prof W.J. McGee of the Bureau of Ethnology, to a Washington Post reporter, is that they seem to keep on growing all their lives. Whether this be in truth the case or not. I am sure that they continue to increase in stature until they are 40 years of age - certainly a very extraordinary phenomenon from a physiological point of view.*"

The article continues with admiration of their physical prowess, hunting skills, and ferocious nature, and they were described as slim of body, extremely agile, muscular, with very large hands and feet. How much longer they lasted in this primitive state is unknown, but W. J. McGee was making plans for them four years later. Not only was he involved in the purchase of the famous San Diego giant (see page 223), he wanted to exhibit some of the Seri Indians at the St. Louis World's Fair that opened in April 1904. He managed to persuade various other Native American tribal members to join in, including some (not particularly tall) Tehuelche Patagonians, but was unable to get the mighty Seri to attend. He basically attempted to represent *"family groups of pygmies and giants, showing the largest and smallest members of the human family."* [55] What is interesting though, is the fact that a Smithsonian anthropologist (who had recently resigned from the Bureau of Ethnology) was involved in showcasing living giants to the general public.

PATAGONIAN AND FUEGIAN.
Wood engraving of Patagonian and very tall Fuegian 1871.

We hope this selection of reports covering a 400-year period puts some perspective on this enduring mystery. Notable captains, military officers, Smithsonian ethnologists, and other high-ranking officials, have all reported seeing living giants with their own eyes. Even some early American presidents now have to be added to the list, as we'll see in the next chapter.

2

PRESIDENTS AND GIANTS

GEORGE WASHINGTON AND GIANT BONES, 1754-55

In Winchester, the most northerly town in Virginia, old legends talk about ghostly 7-foot-tall Indian warriors roaming the streets, most notably Piccadilly Street, that have even been witnessed in recent times and recorded by author Mac Rutherford. Jim spoke with the author to verify the following account from his book *Historic Haunts of Winchester* (2007), that discusses local giant lore and the relationship to President George Washington's discovery of very tall skeletons during the French and Indian War (1754–1763):

> *"The legend began hundreds of years ago. The first written report of such large Indians dates back to 1707, when Swiss explorer Louis Michelle visited the Shenandoah Valley. Local Indians who lived or hunted in the Winchester area, showed*

George Washington in
1772 at age 40.

54

*Michelle huge stones, thought to be sacrificial altars. He was
also shown burial mounds of ancient warriors known to have
been over seven feet tall. Michelle's diaries and maps relating to
his adventures in the Shenandoah Valley are currently stored
in the Royal Archives in London.*

*During the French and Indian war, the tale of giant Indians
was kept very much alive. Colonel George Washington, while
in command of the militia force in Winchester, directed the
building of Fort Loudoun to protect local citizens from attack.
While digging the Fort's foundation, a squad of Washington's
militiamen discovered Indian skeletons, Washington reported
that they were seven feet long."*

In 1754, Washington subsequently received title to 23,200 acres near where
the Kanawha River flows into the Ohio River, in what is now western West
Virginia. He also frequently bought additional land in his own name. By
1775, Washington had doubled the size of Mount Vernon to 6,500 acres,
and had increased its slave population to over 100. Part of Fort Loudon
remains today in Downtown Winchester and is open to the public as a
museum. The giant bones are not there.

ABRAHAM LINCOLN AND THE NIAGARA GIANTS 1848

Congressman Abraham Lincoln visited Niagara Falls in 1848 en route
from Boston to Chicago and delivered a speech while he was visiting the
area. Some strange comments came forth, hinting he knew about the
ancient giants:

*"When Columbus first sought this continent—when Christ
suffered on the cross—when Moses led Israel through the Red-
Sea—nay, even, when Adam first came from the hand of his
Maker—then as now, Niagara was roaring here. The eyes of
that species of extinct giants, whose bones fill the mounds of
America, have gazed on Niagara, as ours do now. Contemporary
with the whole race of men, and older than the first man,*

Niagara is strong, and fresh to-day as ten thousand years ago."[1]

Abraham Lincoln, aged 37, around the
time he made his speech

THOMAS JEFFERSON AND THE OSAGE INDIANS, 1804

In 1804 Thomas Jefferson met with Osage tribal leaders in Washington D.C. to discuss issues of land and trade. Jefferson was very impressed with the physical prowess of the Osage. Jefferson called their warriors "gigantic" – averaging well over 6 feet in height (One Osage chief was 7 feet tall and weighed 300 pounds). The following was described by Mrs. Margaret Bayard Smith (1778-1844) who was a close friend of Thomas Jefferson and chronicler of early life in Washington, D.C.:

> *"Tall, erect, finely proportioned and majestic in their appearance, dignified, graceful and lofty in their demeanor, they seem to be nature's own nobility."*

Had these people not been seen by the early French, the Jeffersonian Society, and others including the frontier painter George Catlin, we might today have no authentic record of their venerable lineage (see previous chapter).

Some believed them to be related to the old Cherokee gentry originating from Tennessee, who also tended to be tall, strong, and heavy. But the story of their origins reaches yet deeper into prehistory, as their tribal legend relates how they originated, in very ancient times, out of the Ohio Valley.

1788 miniature portrait of Jefferson by John Trumbull, aged 33   Silver peace medal given to an Osage chieftain by Thomas Jefferson

Thomas Jefferson was said to have opened an Indian burial mound on his estate, Monticello, in Virginia (no giants were reported). He also had an abiding interest in the ancient mound building civilizations. The following information from Professor J. Houston McCulloch shows Jefferson's interest in a very strange earthwork complex in Ohio called the Hanukkah Mound (Hanukkah is a Jewish festival):

> *"In an important new book entitled Jefferson and the Indians: The Tragic Fate of the First Americans, Anthony F.C. Wallace, University Professor of Anthropology, Emeritus, at the University of Pennsylvania, notes that in 1803, President Thomas Jefferson was impressed by William Lytle's early maps of the East Fork and Milford Works, and requested more information about 'Those works of Antiquity.'"* [2]

Jefferson's Presidential interest in these specific earthworks may explain why the Corps of Engineers would have taken the trouble in 1823 to map structures that had no conceivable contemporary military value. The fact that the 1823 map depicts precisely those earthworks surveyed by Lytle in 1803 strongly indicates that there was a more than coincidental link between the two surveys. There has been much speculation that the Lost Tribes of Israel made it to ancient America and blended with the Native peoples of the time. The controversial Newark Holy Stones, the Bat Creek Stone and the Hanukkah mound have all been pointed to as indications that this may have been a reality. The fact that Jefferson went well out of his way to have this site surveyed only adds to the mystery.

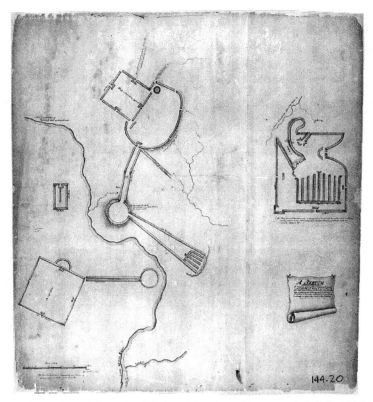

Hanukkah Mound Complex (National Archives Photograph RG77 144.20).

3

LEGENDS OF THE TALL ONES

"The Iroquois, the Osage, the Tuscaroras, the Hurons, the Omahas, and many other North American Indians all speak of giant men who once lived and roamed in the territories of their forefathers. All over what is now the U.S. are traditions of these ancient giants." [1]

Hundreds of stories describing giants exist within Native American folklore. Numerous authors and ethnologists collected their cultural legacy from interacting with the surviving Indians that chose to share this ancient wisdom, whilst some were fortunately recorded in the written form. Combined with the first-hand accounts seen in the previous chapters, these powerful and often startlingly realistic myths suggests that there is a coherent and vast amount of data on giant-lore. The authors thought originally when researching this chapter, due to the vastness of North America, we would only find vague and differing versions of the giants featured in their tales. What we quickly discovered, however, is that many of the descriptions and histories match up, and even provide glimpses of a lost historical timeline.

THE BEARDED GIANTS
The Firelands Pioneer Memoirs of Townships, November, 1858
Vermilion, Erie County, Ohio

This fascinating oral history not only talks about matter-of-fact giant bones being discovered in mounds, but the old stories say that some of the 'Tall Ones' had beards. This discovery is on the shore of Vermillion in northern Ohio, on Lake Erie:

> *"There are quite a number of mounds, in the township, where the bones, and sometimes the whole skeleton of the human race have been found. The bones and skeletons found are very large, and some of the inhabitants think they must have belonged to a race of beings much larger in size than the Indians found here by the first settlers....it was a tradition of the Indians that the first tribe occupying this whole country, was a black-bearded race, very large in size, and subsequently a red bearded race or tribe came and killed or drove off all the black beards, as they called them. The Indians found here by the first white settlers, belonged principally to the San-dusky, Tawa and Chippewa tribes."* [2]

Black-beaded giants getting killed off by red-bearded warriors!? This is very strange. Why such tales, if it was not a folk memory of some sort? We looked at a map of where Vermillion is in Ohio. It is a beach town, with direct water access to the copper mines of the Great Lakes.

THE GREAT PEACEMAKER, PASSACONEWAY

In the introduction to *A Tradition of Giants*, Ross Hamilton outlines the story of a great peacemaker from New England who stood seven feet in height during the 1600s. It is worth mentioning here in detail because not only was he a legendary figure and taller than average, he was also witnessed by the colonial settlers in the 1600s.

As well as being a powerful shaman of the Pennacook tribe, Passaconeway was one of the last kingly *Sachems* (Chiefs) of old, who eventually became *Bashaba* (Chief of Chiefs) in an effort to to bring together a multi-tribal confederation to defend themselves against the aggressive Mohawk nation. When he was nearing the end of his very long life (he was said to have lived to 120 years old), he traveled amongst

Indians and colonial settlers, and was revered by both during and after his life.

Legend states that he was so powerful, that he could make water burn, make trees and rocks dance, turn dried leaves back to green, and make living snakes out of dried snake skin.[3] One of his powers was to summon storms at will, and he even resorted to this when white settlers tried to arrest him. The intense rain and wind he manifested, gave him the time to flee into the forest.[4] Furthermore, traditions in Britain also tell of giants being able to control the elements, and even after their lives when their graves were disturbed, great storms would halt the progress.[5]

Passaconeway's powers also continued after his life. During his burial ceremony, a native witness told of his bright ascension over Mount Washington in New Hampshire, which was said to be Great Spirit's earthly abode.[6]

Although Passaconeway travelled widely around New England, his home base was in Lowell, Massachusetts. To this day, a controversial stone circle and a stone 'Beehive Chamber' reside in an area that was "*on the edge of an Indian reservation in 1659,*"[7] 20 years before Passaconeway's death, suggesting it could have been built by the Pennacook tribe. Hugh and Jim have both visited these sites. The connection between stone and giants does not end there. In these next examples, legends of giants made of stone, who also liked the taste of human flesh are described.

Left: 'Druid Hill' Stone Circle in Lowell. Right: Mount Washington, New Hampshire.

61

THE STONISH GIANTS & THE SHAWNEE
David Cusick's Sketches of Ancient History of the Six Nations, 1828

The Stonish Giants, sketched by David Cusick, 1828.

David Cusick was a Tuscarora artist and the author of the earliest known account of Native American history and myth, written and published in English by an Indian. He was also the first to publish accounts of giants from the stories of the Indians, at a time when enormous skeletons were being reportedly discovered across the country. His description and corresponding illustration of the infamous 'stonish giants' was further researched and published by Henry Schoolcraft in 1846.

Notes on the Iroquois, Henry Schoolcraft, 1846

Henry Rowe Schoolcraft was an American explorer and ethnologist noted for his discovery of the source of the Mississippi River and for his writings on the Native peoples of the North American Plains. He collected many myths from various tribes, most notably the Ojibwe, but this one was collected later in his life and describes the cannibalistic stone giants legend of the Shawnee, who were a nomadic tribe but centered around Ohio (where, incidentally, hundreds of giant skeletons have been uncovered):

> *"The country was invaded by a still more fearful enemy, namely: the OR-NE-YAR-HEG, or Stonish Giants. They were a powerful tribe from the wilderness, tall, fierce and*

hostile, and resistance to them was (in) vain. They defeated and overwhelmed an army which was sent out against them, and put the whole country in fear. These giants were not only of prodigious strength, but they were cannibals, devouring men, women and children in their inroads.

It is said by the Shawnees, that they were descended from a certain family, which journeyed on the east side of the Mississippi, after the vine broke, and they went towards the northwest. Abandoned to wandering and the hardships of the forest, they forgot the rules of humanity, and began at first, to eat raw flesh, and next men. They practiced rolling themselves in the sand, and by this means their bodies were covered with hard skin, so that the arrows of the Iroquois only rattled against their rough bodies, and fell at their feet. And the consequence was, that they were obliged to hide in caves, and glens, and were brought into subjection by these fierce invaders for many winters (or years).

At length the Holder of the Heavens, visited his people, and finding that they were in great distress, he determined to grant them relief, and rid them entirely of these barbarous invaders. To accomplish this, he changed himself into one of these giants, and brandishing his heavy club, led them on, under the pretense of finding the Akonoshioni. When they had got near to their strong hold at Onondaga, night coming on, he bid them lie down in a hollow, telling them that he would make the attack at the customary hour, at day break. But at day break, having ascended a height, he overwhelmed them with a vast mass of rocks, where their forms may yet be seen. Only one escaped to carry the news of their dreadful fate, and he fled towards the north."[8]

EXTERMINATION OF THE STONE GIANTS
Related by Mr. O'Beille, 1892

Further stories of the stone giants existed in the far west of the country and this oral history recounts their migrations towards the east, and tells how they were finally defeated:

> *"The stone giants, who principally inhabited the far West, resolved to come East and exterminate the Indians. A party of Senecas, just starting out on the war-path, were warned of their impending danger and were bidden to accept the challenge to fight the stone giants and appoint a time and place. This they did. At the appointed time the giants appeared at the place, which was near a great gulf. Then there came a mighty wind from the west which precipitated the whole race of giants down into the abyss, from which they were never able to extricate themselves, and the God of the West Wind was ever after held in reverence by the Senecas."* [9]

THE STONE GIANT'S WIFE

Further in the same text, another story tells of how a stone giant's wife sought help from another native woman. Whilst dealing with the game and animals her chief husband had been collecting during hunting, she was startled by hearing a woman's voice coming out of her wigwam. She looked in and saw a stone giant woman nursing the chief's child. *"Do not be afraid,"* said the giantess; *"come in."* As the wife sat down she told her that she had run away from her cruel husband who wanted to kill her, and that she wished to stay a while with the chiefs family. She had come from very far, from the land of the stone giants, and was very tired, and added that they must be careful what food they gave her. She could not eat raw meat; it must be well cooked, so thoroughly cooked, that she could not taste the blood, for if she tasted blood she might wish to kill them and the child and eat them. She knew that the woman's husband was a great hunter, and she knew that his wife brought in the game, but now she would be willing to go hunting instead.

After a while she returned, bringing in one hand a load which four ordinary men could not have carried. The terrified native woman cooked it and they dined together. As evening came on the stone giantess bade the woman go out and meet her husband and tell him of her visit; so she started, and the hunter was much pleased to hear of the help she had given.

In the morning, after he had gone on his hunting expedition, the giantess said, "*Now I have a secret for you: My husband is after me. In three days he will be here. We shall have a terrible fight when he comes, and you and your husband must help me to kill him.*"

Two days afterwards she said, "*Now your husband must remain at home, for mine is coming. But do not be afraid; we shall kill him, only you must help catch and hold him. I will show you where to strike him so that the blow will go right through to his heart.*" The hunter and his wife were both frightened at this, but she reassured them and they all three awaited the coming of the giant. So she placed herself in the entrance, and as he came in sight she was ready. She seized him and threw him on the ground. "*Now,*" she said, "*strike him on the arms, now on the back of the neck*"; and so he was finally killed. Then she said, "*I will take him out and bury him,*" which she then did.

She stayed a while quietly with the hunter and his wife, fetching in the game and being useful until they were ready to leave and return to the settlement. Then she said, "*Now I must go home to my people, for I need fear nothing.*" So she bade them farewell. And this is the end of the story of the Stone Giantess.

This story is very weird on many levels, as it has a matter-of-fact edge to it. It's particularly mythical, and shows a humane side to the female stone giants....as long as they are not fed raw meat!

These stories of the stone giants is a stark reflection of the tradition of the Mewuk Indians of California on the other side of the country.

STONE GIANTS OF CALIFORNIA
Ethnological Evidence that the California Cave Skeletons are not Recent
Science, New Series, Vol. 29, No. 751, May 21, 1909, pp. 805-806

The Mewuk Indians of the western slopes of the Sierra Nevada in Northern California have a legend of a cannibalistic 'rock giant' (another name for stone giant) who once dwelt in the caves on their lands:

"These Indians believe the caves to be inhabited by a stone giant, whom they call Chelalumche, who salliees forth at night in search of food. He preys, by preference, on people, but when he cannot get people, takes deer or other animals. He never eats his victims in the open but carries them into the caves and there devours them. Members of several subtribes have told me this, and have looked with horror on the suggestion that they or their ancestors might ever have put their dead in caves."

Chehalumche, the rock giant catching people to eat.

This comment was in response to the discovery of the Calaveras Skull that was discovered in February 1866. This has been dismissed as a hoax by archaeologists because it was found in a Pliocene layer, beneath a layer of lava dated to over two million years old. More recent remains have also been found in caves in the area, but the Mewuk rebuff the idea that they would bury their dead in the caves inhabited by giants. They say:

"Would you put your mother, or your wife, or your child, or any one you love, in a cave to be eaten by a horrible giant?" [10]

They claim that they never used this burial technique, so any remains must have been the result of the unfortunate victims of *Chelalumche*, the stone giant. Interestingly, there are no migration myths associated with the Mewuk, and the stories of the giant relate to a prehistoric era, long before the time of the modern Indians of that area. Other myths of

66

cannibalistic giants in the area include this next account.

Yayali the Giant
Miwok Myths, by Edward Winslow Gifford, 1917
UCPAE, Vol. 12, No. 8, pp. 283-338

Yayali also had a taste for human flesh.

> *"Where are you, grandchild? Where are you, grandchild? Where are you? Where are you? Yes. Yes. I am lost. Where are you? This way. Where are you, grandchild? Someone comes. Look out. Get ready. Prepare yourself, for Yayali comes."*

The story goes that the people broke cones from the tops of the pine trees and bundled these together. As Yayali started to climb the declivity where the people had taken refuge, they set fire to the bundles of pinecones and threw them into Yayali's burden basket. Yayali became so hot that he tumbled. *"Which way shall I fall?"* he asked. They told him to fall to the north. The giant met his death near Columbia, Tuolumne County. Nearby white rocks are reputed to be the bleached bones of the giant.

Another elaborate story relates that when he visited a local tribe, he overpowered them and killed and ate a man called Chipmunk. He then forced himself upon his terrified wife, but the wife hid the daughter she had with Chipmunk, and although the giant kept hunting humans and forcing his wife to eat the flesh of her kin, she secretly cooked and ate deer flesh, and gave that to her hidden daughter.

She eventually got pregnant, and gave birth to two giant sons, who she wanted to kill, but feared Yayali would seek revenge on her. Living in constant fear, she secretly spoke to her tribe, including Chipmunk's family, who decided to get some obsidian so she could cut his face and kill the giant and his children. They tricked Yayali and cut his head off, then cut up his body and hung the parts up on trees. Meanwhile, Yayali's brother's dreamt of their sibling and visited the tribe, not knowing he was dead. They heard the rumors of his human hunting prowess, so ate the meat on the trees. They then noticed their brother's dead head next to the spring, so retaliated and chased the woman, but she threw obsidian powder in their eyes, but they chased her to Chipmunks fathers home who was a shaman. They hid inside and called on the elements of wind, snow and hail, but the giants shouted loudly and were able to melt the snow. The shaman then called on the element of water and soon a flood came and drowned them. This was the end of their terrifying ordeal.

MORE CANNIBALISM!

Human flesh eating was not confined to just these previous examples. The Mi'kmaq Nation were a member of the Wabanaki Confederacy that controlled northern New England and the Canadian coastline including northeastern Maine.[11] This is from Mi'kmaq mythology recorded in 1809:

> *"We find records of horrible man-eating giants called Kookweijik; and another family of enormous beings called Ooskoon Kookwesijek—the liver-colored giants who return from their hunting expeditions carrying at their belts a string of caribou as easily as a Micmac could carry a string of rabbits. These tawny giants are friendly, as is shown by their dealings with a party of Micmacs recorded in Legend XVII; the party had been lost in a fog for several days in or near St. John Harbour, and afterwards held their powerful deliverers in faithful remembrance..."* [12]

To this we might add this from the Hotcâk tribe from the Lake Winnebago area of Wisconsin. These giants also had a taste for torso:

> *"Not only are the Giants by nature man eaters, as their Hotcâk name Wángerútcge reveals, but male Giants are as tall as trees, four times the height of a man. On the other hand, Giant women, who are particularly noted for their beauty, are about the same size as humans."* [13]

Later on in the text it describes a modern 'attack' by one of the giants:

> *"There may be a few solitary Giants left, since in historical*

times an Ice Giant attacked a man on the Wisconsin River between Stevens Point and Wisconsin Rapids. It was only because he was carrying a powerful medicine with him that he was able to fend off his huge opponent until his friends could come to his rescue.

This was written in 1941. Others, however, say that this race of malignant man eaters disappeared completely around 1840 when the last of them was killed off by a Good Giant who reduced himself in size to live among the humans and bless them." [14]

Whether he actually ate the victim was not discussed, but it does hint that even into historical times, the giants may have existed in this area.

Indian Legends from the Northern Rockies
By Ella Elizabeth Clark, University of Oklahoma Press, 1966

The Kutenais tribe were based in northern Idaho and had multiple stories of giants in their myths, with quite a number who—you guessed it—munched on humans:

"...giants followed the big streams and that whenever Indians went to a big stream, giants killed them and ate them." [15]

William Gingrass, Clark's main Indian informant also said:

"My great-grandmother's uncle, once found the skeleton of a giant, buried in a sitting position, in a grave near (Lake) Superior." [16]

The 'Flatheads' of Montana were their neighbors and *"Fully half of the Flathead stories deal with these giants, and easily two-thirds mention them."* Here is one example:

"Their ancestors reported that there was a time when a large portion of the earth was inhabited by a set of giants, terrible men, who killed everyone they met with, for which they were called Natliskeliguten, which in the ancient language

*means killer of men; that Sinchlep [Coyote] in pity for the
smaller people, went through the earth, killed every giant,
and converted them all into large stones; and even of late,
when Flatheads in crossing the mountains saw a basaltic rock
standing upright on the top, they said to one another, 'Keep
aside, there is Natliskeliguten, killed by Sinchlep," and every
large piece of Silex they saw around was for them a fragment
of an arrow of the killers of men ...."* [17]

This reference to standing stones is fascinating, as we know that Native
Americans certainly worked with stone in many parts of the country
(see next two chapters). Stories like this tantalisingly hint that erecting
megaliths and mounds was part of an age-old tradition that continued
until relatively modern times.

This passage is from the chapter entitled *Myths of the Mountains*,
talking about the very early ancestors of the Indians near Mount Hood in
Portland, Oregon:

*"In those days the Indians were also taller than they are now.
They were as tall as the pine and fir trees that cover the hills,
and their chief was such a giant that his warriors could walk
under his outstretched arms."* [18]

THE WOMAN AND THE GIANTS
Legends of the Paiute, Nevada

This legend talks about cannibalistic giants and their relationship to the
origins of the Paiute tribe in the Nevada area. The significance of this will
become clear, because some astonishing mummified remains and artifacts
were discovered in the region that match many of the traits of this story:

*"There was a giant named Tse'nahaha who killed people just
by looking at them. He carried a large basket full of thorns on
his back and when he caught someone he would throw them
into the basket.*

Some Indians were playing a game in a house and were

*having fun. They had stationed a woman outside to watch
for Tse'nahaha. She heard him coming – he was talking and
singing to himself. She tried to warn people that he was coming
but they did not hear her. Tse'nahaha was getting closer and
the women became frightened and jumped into a pit and
pulled a basket over herself.*

*Tse'nahaha came up to the house and looked around. He
made a sucking noise and when he looked at anyone in the
house they died instantly. The others would see the dead
staring and ask what they were looking at, but then they too
saw Tse'nahaha and died. Soon all were dead and only a baby
was left sleeping. Tse'nahaha left.*

*The baby began to cry and it was almost daylight. The woman
left the pit and went in to the house but did not look at the
dead. She called to the baby and took baby away and set the
house on fire. She dug kani'd while the baby ate and slept.*

*Pu'wihi, another giant came along and picked up the baby.
He held the head between his second and third finger and
carried him to the woman. He asked where she was from and
she answered that she was from the house over there – the one
that has the smoke pouring from it. There are many people in
it. The giant turned towards the house and the woman was
frightened and hid.*

*When the giant returned and could not see her he became
angry. But he found the way she had jumped away from her
tracks and found her under a rock crying. It was too dark to
see and he decided to come back in the morning. He thought
he would make a fire and grind up the baby. He found a large
rock and ground up the baby and ate him. He lay there singing
and after awhile he went to sleep. The woman got up and
made another jump towards the east to her aunts house.*

*She was safe at her Aunts house and the giant could not see
the mark of her stick from where she jumped – because she
had jumped from a rock. This woman became the ancestor of*

all the Paiute Indians." [19]

Another similar legend was reported in 1891. It recalls:

> *"...an indian of giant stature, who gave them trouble. They say that the giant warrior came from the north. He took up his abode near Pyramid Lake, and made war on the Piutes, killing many of their men. The giant was finally slain by Piute David, who crept up behind him and drove a poisoned arrow into his back, between the shoulder blades."* [20]

Interestingly, it mentions giant footprints in the area that were still revered by the Paiute at the time, plus a giant's grave that was kept clear of vegetation by the tribe. They could be referring to a series of oversized footprints that were famously discovered in nearby Carson. These were measured at 18 to 21 inches long and dated to the Pliocene (approx. two million years old).[21]

THE RED-HAIRED CANNIBALS OF LOVELOCK CAVE
Nevada

The Paiute (also spelled *Piute)* covered a huge area through Nevada, Utah, Idaho and California. The Northern Paiute resided around the now mostly dry Humboldt Lake near Lovelock, a small town about 80 miles north-east of Reno. Below is an excerpt from *Life Among the Piutes;* about a tribe of red-haired cannibals called the "Si-Te-Cah", written by Paiute activist and lecturer, Sarah Winnemucca Hopkins in 1882. It does not mention their size, but the first excavation in 1904 reported discovering an incredibly tall skeleton, with further accounts from 1911 onwards. This account has all the characteristics of the other man-eating giant legends:

> *"Among the traditions of our people is one of a small tribe of barbarians who used to live along the Humboldt River. It was many hundred years ago. They used to waylay my people and kill and eat them. They would dig large holes in our trails at night, and if any of our people travelled at night, which they*

did, for they were afraid of these barbarous people, they would oftentimes fall into these holes. That tribe would even eat their own dead – yes, they would even come and dig up our dead after they were buried, and would carry them off and eat them. Now and then they would come and make war on my people. They would fight, and as fast as they killed one another on either side, the women would carry off those who were killed. My people say they were very brave. When they were fighting they would jump up in the air after the arrows that went over their heads, and shoot the same arrows back again. My people took some of them into their families, but they could not make them like themselves. So at last they made war on them. This war lasted a long time. Their number was about twenty-six hundred (2,600). The war lasted some three years. My people killed them in great numbers, and what few were left went into the thick bush. My people set the bush on fire. This was right above Humboldt Lake. Then they went to work and made tuly or bulrush boats, and went into Humboldt Lake. They could not live there very long without fire. They were nearly starving. My people were watching them all round the lake, and would kill them as fast as they would come on land. At last one night they all landed on the east side of the lake, and went into a cave near the mountains. It was a most horrible place, for my people watched at the mouth of the cave, and would kill them as they came out to get water. My people would ask them if they would be like us, and not eat people like coyotes or beasts. They talked the same language, but they would not give up. At last my people were tired, and they went to work and gathered wood, and began to fill up the mouth of the cave. Then the poor

Sarah Winnemucca Hopkins

73

fools began to pull the wood inside till the cave was full. At last my people set it on fire; at the same time they cried out to them, "Will you give up and be like men, and not eat people like beasts? Say quick – we will put out the fire." No answer came from them. My people said they thought the cave must be very deep or far into the mountain. They had never seen the cave nor known it was there until then. They called out to them as loud as they could, "Will you give up? Say so, or you will all die." But no answer came. Then they all left the place. In ten days some went back to see if the fire had gone out. They went back to my third or fifth great-grandfather and told him they must all be dead, there was such a horrible smell. This tribe was called people-eaters, and after my people had killed them all, the people round us called us Say-do-carah [Si-Te-Cah]. It means conqueror; it also means 'enemy.'" [22]

Interestingly, Hopkins had evidence they existed:

"My people say that the tribe we exterminated had reddish hair. I have some of their hair, which has been handed down from father to son. I have a dress which has been in our family a great many years, trimmed with the reddish hair. I am going to wear it some time when I lecture. It is called a mourning dress, and no one has such a dress but my family." [23]

In 1904, 22 years after the publication of her book, a larger-than-life skeleton was reportedly unearthed in the area said to be 11 feet tall:

BONES OF A GIANT ARE DUG UP
The Evening News, January 14, 1904, pg.8
Winnemucca, Nevada

"Workmen engaged in digging gravel here uncovered at a depth of about twelve feet a lot of bones that once belonged to a gigantic human being. Joseph Rougon, who was in charge of the work, examined the bones and at once decided that they were those of a man or a woman. They were taken to

Dr. Samuels who examined them thoroughly and pronounced them to be the bones of a man who must have been nearly eleven feet in height. The metacarpal bone measure four and a half inches in length and are large in proportion. A part of the ulna was found which in complete form would have been between seventeen and eighteen inches in length. The remaining part of the skeleton is being searched for."

BONES OF A GIANT ARE DUG UP

Winnemucca, Nev., Jan. 15. — Workmen engaged in digging gravel here uncovered at a depth of about twelve feet a lot of bones that once were part of the skeleton of a gigantic human being.

Joseph Rougon, who was in charge of the work, examined the bones and at once decided that they were those of a man or a woman. They were taken to Dr. Samuels, who examined them thoroughly and pronounced them to be the bones of a man who must have been nearly eleven feet in height.

The metacarpal bones measure four and a half inches in length and are large in proportion. A part of the ulna was found which in complete form would have been between seventeen and eighteen inches in length. The remaining part of the skeleton is being searched for

In October 1936, the *Nevada State Journal* amended the size of the original 11 ft discovery:

"Many stories credited it with being 11 feet tall. The truth is that the figure, still with reddish hair on the skull, was 9 ½ feet in length." [24]

Entrance to Lovelock Cave. Courtesy of Ken Lund.

However, a certain institution from the East Coast got involved:

> *"The mummy is now in Washington D.C. It is the largest human specimen ever discovered."* [25]

Mummified bodies with red hair were reported discovered between 1911-12 in nearby Lovelock Cave, when guano businessmen discovered hundreds of artifacts encased in bird-poop. It got to a point where there were more artifacts than guano, so anthropologists were called in to take over. Within two years, over 10,000 artifacts had been recorded. Many showed signs of fairly advanced technology for the time. These included duck decoys, oversized sandals, stone tools and baskets, all dating back several thousand years.

Duck decoy discovered at Lovelock Cave.

Similar artifacts found in nearby *Hidden Cave* have been dated to 9,000 years old,[26] whilst in *Spirit Cave* two mummified bodies were discovered, with one of them dating to 9,400 years old, the oldest known in America and contemporary with Kennewick Man. Although the oldest official carbon-dating (of vegetation) found within Lovelock Cave is 2,740 BC,[27] could the red-haired tribe of Lovelock Cave be much older and possibly be the ancestors of their archaic Spirit Cave neighbors?

James H. Hart and David Pugh got the rights to dig and sell guano at Lovelock Cave in the fall of 1911, but when they started finding Indian artifacts they recalled that in the north-central part of the cave, at about four feet deep, *"was a striking looking body of a man 'six feet six inches tall.' His body was mummified and his hair distinctly red."* [28]

In the first year of mining some of the human remains and smaller artifacts were lost or destroyed. *"The best specimen of the adult mummies was boiled and destroyed by a local fraternal lodge, which wanted the skeleton for initiation purposes."*[29] We recently found out this was in fact the Fallon Fraternal Society[30] so it would be interesting to see if they have this on record. Other skeletons made their way to the Nevada State Historical

Society, but even in 1978, they excused themselves from investigation by saying "... *none of the institutions had any knowledge of the red-haired people's remains.*"[31]

Further accounts go into more detail. For example, the supposed discovery of another "...*skeleton of a man well over 6 ½ feet tall*" was announced in 1975.[32] This could well have been the one in possession of Clarence Stoker, who was said to have gathered a huge collection of artifacts and a skeleton between 6 and 7 feet tall in the 1960s. In the same article it mentions a curious 4-inch, donut-shaped stone "...*with 365 dots on the outside edge and 52 dots on the inside. It is unmistakably a calendar.*"[33] Further discoveries of incredibly large pestle and mortars were found in Lovelock Cave and the surrounding area, hinting that larger than average humans used them.

Pestle from Lovelock area.

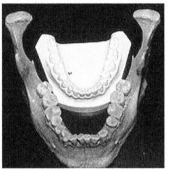
Jaw comparison.

Some fairly large skulls were also discovered, and four examples discovered by Stoker were still on display at the museum, but are now locked away in the basement. One of the jaws was photographed next to a cast of a modern human jaw that showed the difference in size. Micah Ewers calculated that it is between 12% and 20% larger than the control.

Our Very Oldest Inhabitant

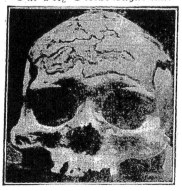

This photo was published in a newspaper in November 1914 showing an 11-inch-tall skull, which is considerably larger than a normal human skull.[34] *The Telegraph Herald* elaborated on the discovery the following month:

"*The human skulls which were strewn*

This skull of a protohistoric male was found in a commercialized Nevada cave. Its height is 11 inches. Native extraordinary size of eye sockets and abnormal teeth; other color details of skull differ from those of any now known today.

AMAZING DISCOVERIES FOUND IN HUGE CAVE IN NEVADA SEALED BY NATURE OVER 3,000 YEARS AGO.

*in great profusion about the floor of the cave show proportions
which indicate a race of men of great stature.*"[35]

Another skull was unearthed in early 1967 a few miles southwest of
Lovelock Cave. It was studied by anthropologists at Utah University
and published by Erik K. Reed who said *"The skull is large."*[36] He made
close comparisons to previously discovered skulls from the Southwest
to determine its age; one that was 6,900 years old, another 8,000 years
old, and one example *"undoubtedly much older."* It had a *"notably
strong browridge... strong nuchal crest...retreating forehead... massive
occipital torus or crest."*[37] It was classed among the *'Early Period Central
California material'*, which also have oversized occipital buns and glabella
prominences (crest between the eyes above the nose). Strangely, occipital
buns are a feature found in 81.8% of Neanderthal skulls but only in 60%
of upper Paleolithic skulls,[38] and it is rare among modern humans. Like
the skull at Spirit Cave, it had modern human features and red-hair.

Also found were a number of fiber sandals that were remarkably
large, with one reported to be over 15 inches (38 cm) in length that was
on display at the Nevada Historical Society's Museum in Reno in 1952.[39]
Micah Ewers, an Oregon based researcher got access to the artifacts at the
museum and confirmed that the shoe sizes include a 10.5 (US men's size);
a size 11 and size 12 and one set of size 15 sandals existed, that could have
fitted the feet of the 6 feet 6 inch tall gentleman snugly.

The traits of the red-hair, cannibalism and war-like nature of the
Paiute's mortal enemy spoken about by Sarah Hopkins was confirmed
from another source in 1913: *"...a tribe of cannibals, described by the
Paiutes as small of stature, having red hair and freckled faces."*[40] The "small
stature" does contradict the initial discovery of the taller than average
skeletons, but it is worth noting here as an anomaly.

Paiute traditions assert that the Si-Te-Cah practiced cannibalism,
and this may have some basis in fact. During the 1924 excavation of the
cave, three human bones were found just beneath the surface towards the
entrance of the cave: *"These had been split to extract the marrow, as animal
bones were split, and probably indicate cannibalism during a famine."*[41]

Their origins are still shrouded in mystery, but so are many of the tribes we've been looking at in this chapter. Red-hair and cannibalistic tendencies, and now, as with Spirit Cave Man, dating that goes back 9,400 years, there is clearly more to this area of ancient America than was once thought.

WAH-ZEE-YAH
Tales of Fort Snelling, 1849

The Sioux, who were based around Fort Snelling in Minnesota, have legends of the *Wetuc* or '*race of men who stood as tall as the tall trees*', as outlined in this account from 1849:

> "*Iron Members was going hunting, and when he was near Shah-co-pee's village, he met the Giant. He wore a three-cornered hat, and one side was bright as the sun; so bright one could not look upon it; and he had a crooked thing upon his shoulder... The Dahcotahs believe firmly the story of Iron Members. He was one of their wisest men. He was a great warrior and knew how to kill his enemies.*" [42]

HENRY ROWE SCHOOLCRAFT
The Scholar and the Giants

In the mid 1800's Henry Rowe Schoolcraft did a great deal to both further and hinder Indian traditions. He married a woman of native stock, with whom he collected hundred of myths from various Indian tribes, but unfortunately reported on the people in a general way thus:

> *The Indian has a low, bushy brow, beneath which a dull, sleepy, half-closed eye seems to mark the ferocious passions that are dormant within. The acute angles of the eyes seldom present the obliquity so common in the Malays and the Mongolians. The color of the eye is almost uniformly a tint between black and grey; but even in young persons it seldom has the brightness, or expresses the vivacity, so common in the more civilized races.* [43]

Whether this was the stance expected of him, or whether he had become grumpy in old age is unclear, but he did most of his good work long before the Smithsonian was formed. In 1822 Schoolcraft married Jane Johnston, part-Ojibwe, who had a vast knowledge of Ojibwe legend and history.

Later in life in 1846 Congress commissioned him to develop a comprehensive reference work on American Indian tribes. Schoolcraft worked for years on the history and mythology of the Indians and the findings were published in six volumes from 1851-1857.[44] His far-reaching books are often overlooked today, but one thing that did catch our attention was the fact that he believed the ancestors of the American Indians were responsible for the construction of the mounds, not a prehistoric white race, or some other exotic interloper. However, attributing the mounds to a mysterious foreign race is a tradition that comes up in various other myths from around the country collected by others (as we will soon see).

Henry Rowe Schoolcraft

Notes on the Iroquois, 1847

Schoolcraft shares their creation stories that includes this passage about some legendary giants:

> "By their earliest traditions, we are told that a body of the Ongwe Honwe, encamped on the banks of the St. Lawrence, where they were invaded by a nation few in number, but of giant stature, called Ronongweca." [45]

Further in the book, a tantalising glimpse may establish one of the reasons such large earthen and stone forts were built in prehistory:

"It is affirmed by their traditions, that, in the older periods of their occupancy of this continent, they were even obliged, or their fears suggested the measure, to build coverts and forts to protect themselves and families from the inroads of monsters, giants and gigantic animals....Such places would afford convenient shelters for their women and children." [46]

Does this suggest the great forts may have been constructed to protect the native inhabitants from marauding cannibalistic giants? Like any major architectural construction, there needs to be a collective reason and effort to go ahead with large projects (such as modern dams and power stations to supply energy today). This is also as good a reason as any, to protect one's tribe from the dangers of the outside world, including man-eating giants.

White Feather and the Six Giants
The Indian Fairy Book, by H.R. Schoolcraft, 1856

In Schoolcraft's 1856 work called *The Indian Fairy Book*, he reveals a further giant myth. It is a long and complicated adventure about a child whose family was killed by a tribe of giants. Six of these giants remained, and resided in a "high lodge" deep in the woods but eventually the boy fulfills a prophecy, goes through multiple challenges, and kills them all off. The giants even used magic to sneak in to the Indians village and disguise themselves as normal sized humans, and one of them even married one of the Indian women.

Schoolcraft's legacy is a national treasure that gives a portal in to the prehistory of the ancient Americans that has long since been lost.

VINE DELORIA JR.
Red Earth, White Lies: Native Americans and the Myth of Scientific Fact

Vine Deloria, Jr. (1933-2005) was a Native American scholar, theologian, historian, and activist, who collected many stories of giants in his decades of research:

> *"From talking with elders of several tribes, my understanding is that the Indians were and are describing people of more than average height. In fact, some elders as a routine matter have reported that the Indians themselves were much larger and taller."* [47]

In his classic book *Red Earth, White Lies: Native Americans and the Myth of Scientific Fact* (1997), it describes numerous legends of the Tall Ones, and challenges the way science is recorded and published, especially in relation to Native Americans. Ross Hamilton

Vine Deloria Jr.

worked closely with Deloria to uncover and rebuild the lost history of the great wars that took place between various tribes in prehistory, that we explore later in this chapter. One of the great warring tribes of North America were the Comanche.

THREE YEARS AMONG THE COMANCHES, 1859
Ten Feet Tall White Giants

Nelson Lee's detailed account of his life as a Texas Ranger, his subsequent capture by the Comanche people, and his escape through the mountains back to his colonial settlement, is a fascinating story that also demonstrates the inner workings of an Indian tribe who were changed forever by the interference of one white man. He came to admire some of his captors and even married a woman from the tribe. He learnt their myths and history and wrote about them in his 1859 book:

"Innumerable moons ago, a race of white men, ten feet high, and far more rich and powerful than any white people now living, here inhabited a large range of country, extending from the rising to the setting sun. Their fortifications crowned the summits of the mountains, protecting their populous cities situated in the intervening valleys. They excelled every other nation which has flourished, either before or since, in all manner of cunning handicraft—were brave and warlike— ruling over the land they had wrested from its ancient possessors, with a high and haughty hand. Compared with them the pale faces of the present day, were as pigmies, both in art and arms. They drove the Indians from their homes, putting them to the sword, and occupying the valleys in which their fathers had dwelt before them since the world began. At length, in the height of their power and glory, when they remembered justice and mercy no more, and became proud and lifted up, the Great Spirit descended from above, sweeping them with fire and deluge from the face of the earth. The mounds we had seen on the table lands were the remnants of their fortresses, and the crumbling ruins that surrounded us, all that remained of a mighty city. In like manner, continued The Rolling Thunder, the day will surely come when the present white race, which is driving the Indians before it, and despoiling them of their inheritance, and which, in the confidence of its strength, has become arrogant and boastful and forgotten God, will be swept from existence. For the Great Spirit is just—and as certainly as the rivers flow downward towards the salt sea, or the sun rises in the morning and sets at night, so certainly will He yet restore the land of their fathers to the red man, when the days of his affliction are passed." [48]

This powerful passage echoes the frustration of the Indians, who had to tolerate abuse and slaughter at the hands of the Western invaders, much like the way the giants of old treated them. Further accounts of 'fair skinned' giants are found in other parts of the country.

Tsul'Kalu' & the Cherokee Slant-Eyed Giants

In Jackson County, North Carolina, a series of 3,000 year-old petroglyphs are displayed on Judaculla Rock, a prehistoric monolith protruding from the ground, said to have been there long before the Cherokee arrived. Researcher Micah Hanks looked into the meaning of the strange carvings on the rock, most notably the handprint:

> "According to legend, this portion of the stone marks the place where an ancient Cherokee god of the hunt, known as Tsul'Kalu', had leaped from a nearby mountain, and landing within the valley below, had steadied himself against what is now Judaculla Rock".[49]

The name is also a reference to a race of giants who came from the west and interacted with the early Cherokee. James Mooney collected this story that was published by the Smithsonian in 1900:

> "James Wafford, of the western Cherokee, who was born in Georgia in 1806, says that his grandmother, who must have been born about the middle of the last century, told him that she had heard from the old people that long before her time a party of giants had once come to visit the Cherokee. They

Judaculla Rock in the 1930's with chalk fill to emphasise details.

84

were nearly twice as tall as common men, and had their eyes set slanting in their heads, so that the Cherokee called them Tsunil´ kalu´, "the Slant-eyed people," because they looked like the giant hunter Tsul´ kalu´. They said that these giants lived far away in the direction in which the sun goes down. The Cherokee received them as friends, and they stayed some time, and then returned to their home in the west." [50]

Some commentators suggest they could be describing Oriental facial features:

"In 1524, the Spaniard Giovanni de Verrazano, having explored parts of the eastern coastline, described the native people in the area of what was apparently aboriginal Lenape territory as having faces that tend to be broad, and large dark eyes, resembling the "Orientals." [51]

Cryptozoologists believe Tsul'Kalu may have been a version of Sasquatch,[52] because he was said to have lived in caves. Other stories say he cleared the side of a mountain to live there, and even had relations with a Cherokee woman. In this particular legend, it talks about how a mother wanted her daughter to marry a good hunter. Tsul'Kalu, a being of giant stature, started frequenting her home, but only by night bringing deer and other animals to eat. He always left before dawn, and appeared to have psychic abilities, as he always knew what the demanding mother wanted next—meat or wood. The mother demanded to meet her daughter's new husband, and when she did, she was terrified by his appearance. She fled, and the couple magically had a baby, that her family tried to get back, but Tsul'Kalu escaped and was never seen again.

Notice here that he only came out at night, as this echoes a later myth of the Cherokee, *the moon-eyed people.*

Remains of part of the wall at Serpent Fort.

The Moon-Eyed People & the Welsh Prince

In Fort Mountain State Park in Georgia, an ancient megalithic wall, shaped like a 1,000-foot-serpent has been linked to some very odd traditions of the Cherokee. These range from yellow-haired giants, to moon-eyed people, to Welsh princes from the 1100s. The yellow-haired ones were said to be an ancient race in the area before the Cherokee. Serpent Fort certainly looks like it was constructed by giants, as it is estimated it once stood 18 feet tall; its purpose still unknown.

Another tradition states that a group of moon-eyed people lived in the area of Appalachia, until they were pushed out by the Cherokee. In a 1797 book by Benjamin Smith Barton, he says they were call moon-eyed because they saw poorly during the day.[53] Another story relates that they were wiped out when attacked on a full moon, because they almost went blind during the moon's maximum brightness.

Strangely one old story describes them as "*very small people, perfectly white*,"[54] so not giants at all. Numerous other legends were collected by James Mooney who described a "*dim but persistent tradition*" of a white race, who were responsible for building the sites such as Serpent Fort.

In an 1810 letter from Tennessee governor John Sevier, he described that in 1782 or 83 he was told a long-standing tradition by Cherokee Chief Oconostota, that white people had built the forts and were pushed away by the Cherokee, but also said they were called "Welsh" and had come from across the ocean with a captain called "Madoc". Sevier also believed that the alleged discovery of six skeletons in brass

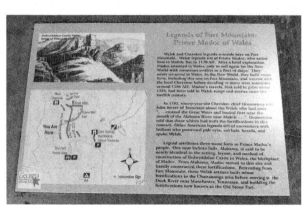

Legend of Prince Madoc of Wales on sign at Serpent Fort. (Courtesy of Doug Coldwell)

armor bearing the Welsh coat of arms discovered in the area was theirs.[55] Welsh tradition also stated that he did indeed exist and took ten ships across the ocean around 1170 AD. He even returned to Wales and made another journey back to America, never to be seen or heard from again. Even Queen Elizabeth I and John Dee used this as leverage to try and gain a foothold in America.

Madoc was said to have landed at Mobile Bay, Alabama and then sailed up the Alabama River to the area of several ancient earth and stone fortifications, including Serpent Fort. Could these really have been the yellow-haired or even moon-eyed people of legend? There is little evidence of this, but traditions like this persist throughout ancient America.

LIFE OF JOSEPH BRANT -THAYENDANEGA
Includes the Wars of the American Revolution
by William L. Stone, 1838

Thayendanegea, or Joseph Brant (1743 – 1807) was a Mohawk military and political leader, based in present-day New York, who was closely associated with Britain during and after the American Revolution. Due to this, he met many of the most significant Anglo-American people of the age, including both George Washington and King George III, and was an intellectual, peacemaker, and recorded some interesting myths of the origins of the Indians around Illinois and Ohio:

> *"A tradition, he said prevailed among the different nations of Indians throughout that whole extensive range of country, and had been handed down through time immemorial, that in an age long gone by, there came white men from a foreign country, and by consent of the Indians established trading houses and settlements where these tumuli are found."* [56]

Was this really Prince Madoc and the Welsh? Maybe. But there are traditions of fair-skinned tribes all over America, giant and small, some with blonde and red hair, sometimes with full beards (as we saw with the

Duhare of South Carolina), and some who carried all these traits. Unlike the moon-eyed people, these were said to be related to the Irish, not the Welsh.

THE GREAT PREHISTORIC AMERICAN WAR
Based on the work of Ross Hamilton

Many centuries ago, possibly as early as 1,500 BC, the Adena (originally known as the Lenni Lenape, and most recently the Delaware), moved en masse from an unknown area somewhere in the west of America toward the east. According to Choctaw tradition as conveyed by Vine Deloria Jr. to Ross Hamilton (in a personal communication), this was the time of the great Exodus. It is said the Lenape (Lenni Lenape) were seeking their ultimate destiny in a promised land:

> *"As the legend goes, these people found themselves at the shore of the Mississippi—the white man's enunciation of their Namesi Sipu, River of Fish. There they met up with the nation called Mengwe, who had come from a bit further north and closer to the northern source of the Namesi Sipu, perhaps the present-day Missouri, stronghold of the very ancient Siouan Language Group. It was a meeting of destiny, and was, at that time, a peaceful one."* [57]

The Lenape sent out their scouts across the river to further their advance into new territory, but they bumped into some larger than life characters. James Athearn Jones relates:

> *"They told that they had found the further bank of the River of Fish inhabited by a very powerful people, who dwelt in great villages, surrounded by high walls. They were very tall—so tall that the head of the tallest Lenape could not reach their arms, and their women were of higher stature and heavier limbs than the loftiest and largest man in the confederate nations. They were called the Allegewi, and were men delighting in red and black paint, and the shrill war-whoop, and the strife of*

the spear. Such was the relation made by the spies to their countrymen." 58

During his long years of research Henry Schoolcraft noted the persistent, recurring stories of this great prehistoric culture:

*"The oldest tribe of the United States, of which there is a distinct tradition, were the Alleghans. The term is perpetuated in the principal chain of mountains traversing the country. This tribe, at an antique period, had the seat of their power in the Ohio Valley and its confluent streams, which were the sites of their numerous towns and villages.... From the traditions of the Lenapees, given to the Moravian missionaries, while the lamp of their traditionary history still threw out its flickering but enlivening flames, the Alleghans had been a strong and mighty people, capable of great exertions and doing wonders."*59

John Heckewelder, assistant to the Moravian missionary David Zeisberger also wrote about the Alleghans:

"Many wonderful things are told of this famous people. They are said to have been remarkably tall and stout, and there is a tradition that there were giants among them, people of a much larger size than the tallest of the Lenape." 60

Eventually the Lenape and the Mengwe defeated the giant Alleghans, with the Lenape moving eastwards and the Mengwe moving northwards to the Great Lakes area. *"It is speculated that the Mengwe were of pre-Siouan origin, later combining with the pre-Iroquoian, St. Lawrence-Adirondack people to eventually (much later) evolve into the Iroquois."*61

The Adena flourished, and eventually (around 700 BC) moved further east. It is estimated that around 40 tribes of the eastern United States may have Adena (Lenape) ancestry. Unfortunately the Adena lost their giant traits and many of their tall members joined the *Wolf Tribe* otherwise known as the Susquehanna:

"Tuscarora David Cusick (1780-1840) writes in 1825 that among the legends of the people of the ancient stock, there was

a powerful tribe called Ronnongwetowanca. They were giants, and had a "considerable habitation." The giants were said to have had a "silly" mode of attack, waiting until their intended victim was not expecting anything—just as the Allegheny were reported to have done. After a time, and having endured the outrages of these giants, it is said that the people banded together, and through the final force of about 800 warriors, successfully annihilated the abhorrent Ronnongwetowanca. After that, it was said that there was no great tribe of giants. This was supposed to have happened around 2,500 winters before Columbus discovered America, i.e. around 1000 BCE— the time the archaeological Adena seem to have commenced their appearance in the Ohio Valley. Admittedly, this date is a crucial reference, practically standing alone when searching for specificity in the chronology." [62]

This great battle, that some researchers say was a near genocide, becomes evident when looking at skeletal discoveries in mounds and on ancient battlefield graveyards. Throughout the Ohio Valley and as far west as New York there are accounts of mounds that have hundreds of skeletons piled in them, often with broken bones and battered skulls. Is this the evidence of this great war that took place thousands of years ago in America, between the Adena and the giant Allegheans? Heckewelder writes:

> *"Having thus united their forces, the Lenape and Mengwe declared war against the Allegewi. And great battles were fought, in which many warriors fell on both sides... An engagement took place in which hundreds fell, who were afterwards buried in holes or laid together in heaps and covered over with earth."* [63]

Examples of this practice include H. H. Blackstone, a resident of Charleston, West Virginia in 1878, who opened a mound and found hundreds of *"bodies had been thrown promiscuously into one common grave,"* some that were *"eight feet in height."* [64]

In Indiana, further evidence of a great battle was unearthed in a mounds that *"...were so full of bones as to warrant the belief that they originally contained at least one hundred dead bodies; children of different ages, and the full grown, appeared to have been piled together promiscuously..... their possessors were men of gigantic stature.*"[65]

Ross Hamilton details these ancient wars that shaped ancient America in *A Tradition of Giants*, but when the skeletal evidence starts to match up with the Native legends, it is time to start taking these seriously.

Ross also noted that the aspect of stature seems to have been deliberately protected through selective rites, with the taller, stronger males honored through ascension to positions of social leadership, as in this example:

> *"The chiefs of the province of Chicora, a portion of what is now South Carolina, were famous for their height, which was supposed to prove their royal blood."* [66]

BUFFALO BILL AND THE GIANT BONE
The Life of Hon. William F. Cody, Known as Buffalo Bill; The Famous Hunter, Scout and Guide. An Autobiography, 1879.

To finish this chapter we have this strange account that occurred in 1871 in Wyoming, from the legendary Buffalo Bill:

> *"While we were in the sand-hills, scouting the Niobrara country, the Pawnee Indians brought into camp, one night, some very large bones, one of which a surgeon of the expedition pronounced to be the thigh-bone of a human being. The Indians claimed that the bones they had found were those of a person belonging to a race of people who a long time ago lived in this country. That there was once a race of men on the earth whose size was about three times that of an ordinary man, and they were so swift and powerful that they could run along-side of a buffalo, and taking the animal in one arm could tear off a leg and eat the meat as they walked."*
> *"These giants denied the existence of a Great Spirit, and when they heard the thunder or saw the lightning they laughed at it*

Buffalo Bill Cody, ca. 1875

and said that they were greater than either. This so displeased the Great Spirit that he caused a great rain-storm to come, and the water kept rising higher and higher so that it drove those proud and conceited giants from the low grounds to the hills, and thence to the mountains, but at last even the mountain tops were submerged, and then those mammoth men were all drowned. After the flood had subsided, the Great Spirit came to the conclusion that he had made man too large and powerful, and that he would therefore correct the mistake by creating a race of men of smaller size and less strength. This is the reason, say the Indians, that modern men are small and not like the giants of old, and they claim that this story is a matter of Indian history, which has been handed down among them from time immemorial.

As we had no wagons with us at the time this large and heavy bone was found, we were obliged to leave it."

The story got all the way back east to Yale College and one Professor Othniel Charles Marsh, head of the paleontology department, was sufficiently interested in the discovery to lead fossil hunting expeditions into the area later that year in search of remains of these giants. Unfortunately, there are no reports of him finding any.

We hope this small selection of Native American legends and stories gives some insight into the early inhabitants of this continent. When cross-referencing the stories we start to find unusual patterns emerging regarding the giants. These include red-hair, stone giants, cannibalistic tendencies, and fierce battles that took place millennia ago. With these legends in mind, the next chapter deals with the ancient mounds and reports of giant royal burials that have also become the stuff of legend.

4

GIANTS IN THE MOUNDS

"During the centuries of Indian domination in this country, the ancient earthworks were left undisturbed. The Indians had no knowledge of a preceeding race, and they were not vexed by inquiring science as to the nature or origins of the mounds".[1]

Mound building began in the United States around 3400 BC with the construction of Watson Brake, Louisiana. The oldest of the Mound Builder cultures north of Watson Brake, in the Ohio Valley, was the Adena, who were said to be around from 1000 BC to 200 BC in an era known as the Early Woodland Period (in Kentucky from around 1200 BC)[2] but mounds and Adena type skulls have been found with much earlier dates.

The Adena lived in an area including parts of present-day Ohio, Indiana, West Virginia, Kentucky, New York, Pennsylvania and Maryland. The Hopewell were said to have existed between 200 BC and 500 AD during the Middle Woodland Period. The Late Woodland people, who included the Mississippian culture flourished from around 1000 AD to 1600 AD who were in the same general area but went further south and west along the Mississippi River. The Fort Ancient culture (1000 to 1750 AD) built huge hill-top forts throughout Ohio. However, these sweeping generalizations do not give justice to vast and complex civilizations that may have been around for a lot longer than history books will allow.

SERPENT MOUND, OHIO

The Great Serpent Mound is a 1,370 ft long prehistoric effigy mound located near Peebles, Ohio. It is on the edge of a plateau that sits on the southwest side of a meteor impact crater. It is 4.5 km across and has powerful magnetic and gravitational anomalies contributing to it, going deep into the earth, even as far as the mantle. These anomalies cause all sorts of weather fluctuations and earth energy effects in the form of *earth lights*. As with many other mound sites (such as Grave Creek Mound and Cahokia), Serpent Mound was built upon a powerful magnetic anomaly created by this prehistoric impact.[3]

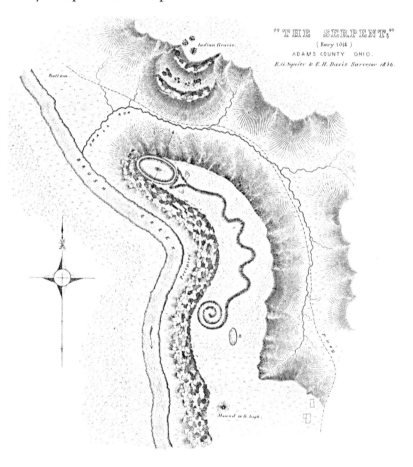

For a long time conventional archaeology dated Serpent Mound to the Late Woodland period of 1,070 AD, but this is now almost universally disputed with recent radiocarbon analysis putting it at around 321 BC[4] (one year after the death of Aristotle). This puts it in the realm of the Adena who were present in the area at this time. The so-called Fort Ancient culture may have helped to maintain the site, but were not the original builders.

Hugh met up with Ross Hamilton and researcher Jeffrey Wilson at Serpent Mound in September 2012 to explore the site and get a sense of what was once going on there. Jeffrey and Ross took Hugh up to the edge of the crater to see the panoramic view of the surrounding landscape, with local residents telling them about the strange weather patterns that affect this area.

View of Serpent Mound looking towards its head.

The coils of the serpent are aligned to the two yearly equinoxes and solstices; a subject both Hugh and Jim had a chance hear about at a lecture by Ross and Jeffery at the Megalithomania Conference in Connecticut in October 2011. They showed Archimedean, Euclidian, and Pythagorean geometric principles embedded in Serpent Mound and the earthworks of the Ohio Valley. Ross has written several books about Serpent Mound including *Star Mounds: Legacy of a Native American Mystery* (2012), where he makes the case that a massive terrestrial zodiac once existed on the ground with the great serpent as the middle of it. A similar zodiac is thought to exist around the legendary Glastonbury in England:

> *"Viewing it as though it were in the sky as a centerpiece of a living solar system, we may begin to grasp the nearly superhuman effort put into the planning and execution of the stunning organization of temple-like structures surrounding it, spanning no less than three states including Ohio, Indiana and Kentucky."*[5]

The proposed Ohio Valley mound and star correlations, by Ross Hamilton.

Jeffrey Wilson has been analyzing LIDAR surveys of the Ohio landscape and it has helped him discover many secrets invisible to satellite photography. Most notably, were the 'plumes' or feathers that are on either side of the Serpent's neck (LIDAR is a remote sensing technology).

Just prior to 1891, Professor Frederic Ward Putnam opened one of the burial mounds on the property of the Great Serpent Mound. This account describes an Adena male, six feet in length:

> *"Several peculiarities of this skeleton are worthy of notice. It was that of a well-developed man…and probably about 25 or 30 years of age, he never had any wisdom teeth, and a search in the maxillary bone of one side showed that there was no wisdom tooth forming in the jaw. With this exception, he had a fine set of teeth, and still embedded in the premaxillary bone is a partly formed left incisor tooth. No corresponding formation can be seen on the opposite side of the suture, and this is probably a super-numerary tooth, although the small size of the lateral incisors is suggestive of their being persistent first teeth. As is often the case in skulls of this race, the crowns of the incisors are distinctly folded."* [6]

This indicates that a second-row of teeth could have been forming when he died, suggesting he was an adolescent and may have grown much taller.[7] We explore this phenomenon in the *Double Rows of Teeth* chapter. Very close by this mound was another burial apparently of greater antiquity than the Adena era, more typical of an archaic period trench interment:

> *"The grave had been, all unwittingly, partly over an ancient grave of particular interest. This older grave had been made about five feet deep in the clay, and was about nine feet long and five wide. A pavement of flat stones was placed over the bottom, and on them, at the south side…were the fragments of a skeleton. The pieces of skull found at the southeastern corner of the grave were twice the usual thickness."* [8]

Putnam, perhaps fearing professional criticism, never openly writes of very tall skeletal remains, although he apparently unearthed them as shown in this old postcard (see overleaf). Since Putnam did all the known excavation work at Serpent Mound, it is assumed this is one of his exhumations. It clearly states it was from Serpent Mound on the postcard, but there is still debate as to where this photo of a 7 ft skeleton was actually taken. Notice that the legs are cut off at the knee's, so is "7 ft" what we actually see, or is it an estimation if he had his lower legs and feet attached?

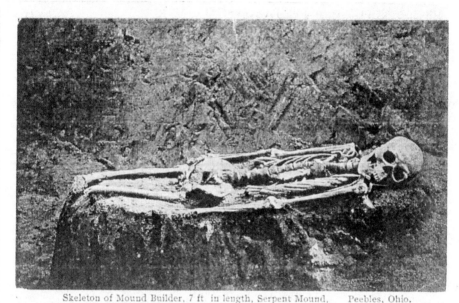

Skeleton of Mound Builder, 7 ft in length, Serpent Mound, Peebles, Ohio.

Postcard of 7 ft skeleton said to be taken at Serpent Mound, courtesy of Jeffrey Wilson.

If this was not taken at Serpent Mound, where was it taken? Was it perhaps the one in this following account?

GIANTS OF OTHER DAYS:
RECENT DISCOVERIES NEAR SERPENT MOUND, OHIO
New York Times, March 5, 1894

"From the Indianapolis Journal. Farmer Warren Cowen of Hilsborough, Ohio, while fox hunting recently discovered several ancient graves. They were situated upon a high point of land in Highland County, Ohio, about a mile from the famous Serpent Mound, where Prof. Putnam of Harvard made interesting discoveries. As soon as the weather permitted, Cowen excavated several of these graves. The graves were made of large limestone slabs, two and a half to three feet in length and a foot wide. These were set on edge about a foot apart. Similar slabs covered the graves. A single one somewhat larger was at the head and another at the foot. The top of the grave was two feet below the present surface.

Upon opening one of the graves a skeleton of upwards of six feet was brought to light. There were a number of stone hatchets, beads, and ornaments of peculiar workmanship near the right arm. Several large flint spear and arrow heads among the ribs gave evidence that the warrior had died in battle.

In another grave was the skeleton of a man equally large... Several pipes and pendants were near the shoulders. In other graves, Cowen made equally interesting finds. It seems that the region was populated by a fairly intelligent people, and that the serpent mound was an object of worship. Near the graves is a large field in which broken implements, fragments of pottery, and burned stones give evidence of a prehistoric village."

Newark & Chillicothe Earthworks, Ohio

The Newark Earthworks in Newark and Heath, Ohio, consists of three sections of preserved earthworks: the Great Circle Earthworks, the Octagon Earthworks, and the Wright Earthworks. The largest and most impressive earthworks in North America, this complex contained the largest earthen enclosures in the world, being about 3,000 acres in extent. The Newark Site still exists and is maintained as part of a golf course. The circle is 20 acres with 8-foot high walls and a 5-foot moat, the Octagon is an amazing 50 acres. Dr. Ray Hively and Dr. Robert Horn from Earlham College discovered lunar alignments at the site while researching it in the 1980s.[9] The Newark circle and octagon is aligned to lunar standstills, it measures aspects the 18.61 year metonic cycle of the moon, is considered twice as accurate as the astronomical measurements of Stonehenge, and predicts eclipses.

The Newark site was once believed to be connected to a sister site in Chillicothe, Ohio. The Great Hopewell Road was 60 miles long and headed south west. However this is disputed due to new studies carried out by two archaeologists, who LIDAR scanned the entire area.[10] However, there was once a six-mile stretch of earthwork banks projecting from Newark in the same direction, which probably confused the theory.

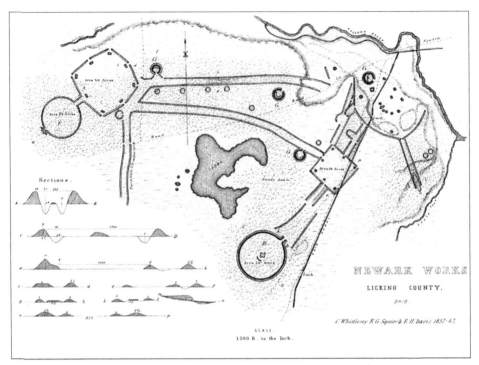

Above: Newark Works by Squier and Davis. Below: View of the main Newark circle.

This site also measured the metonic cycle, predicted eclipses and measured the suns setting and rising points at the solstices. Researcher Joseph Knapp has determined that Chillicothe was utilized for lunar observations between January through June each year because the Newark horizons blocked the best views of the moon. However in July through December, Newark's circle and octagon offered the best place to view the movements of the moon. Hively and Horn estimated that it took over 100 years of careful observation prior to constructing the earthworks. This research has revealed that the prehistoric cultures in the area had advanced scientific understanding as the basis of their complex construction.

Hugh visited both these sites in September 2012 and was impressed by the precision shaping of the earthworks, the accuracy of the circles, and the sheer immensity of some of the henges and ditches. The second circle at Newark resembles Avebury in England with a similar bank and ditch system, and like the great stone circles of Britain, it feels like it was designed to be there for eternity. Although no giants have been reported from this particular site, strikingly similar earthworks near Chillicothe have yielded some skeletons of rather tall stature, discovered (again) by Dr. Warren K. Morehead:

A SKELETON IN ARMOR
Wichita Daily Eagle, November 17, 1891, pg.2
Chillicothe, Ohio

"Dr. Warren Morehead and Dr. Cresson have opened up the most interesting prehistoric relic yet discovered in America on a farm seven miles west of here. They exhumed the massive skeleton of a man encased in copper armor from a long mound. The mouth contained pearls of large size but much decayed. At the side of the skeleton was another skeleton supposed to be that of a woman. The discoverers think they have found the king and queen of the Mound Builders."

Further gigantic skeletons were reportedly uncovered in the vicinity of the geometric Liberty Earthworks, a few miles southeast of Chillicothe. An account of the unearthing of three unusually tall skeletons is given:

AMERICANS SEVEN FEET
The Daily Newburgh Journal, October 26, 1898, pg.1
Liberty Earthworks, Southeast of Chillicothe

"There have been unearthed at Chillicothe, Ohio, three monster skeletons. They were found in the neighborhood of what was at one time one of the most important earthworks of the mound builders. The skeletons, which were those of men over seven feet in height, were found in various postures and it is supposed they fell either defending or attacking the earthworks and were buried with military honors."

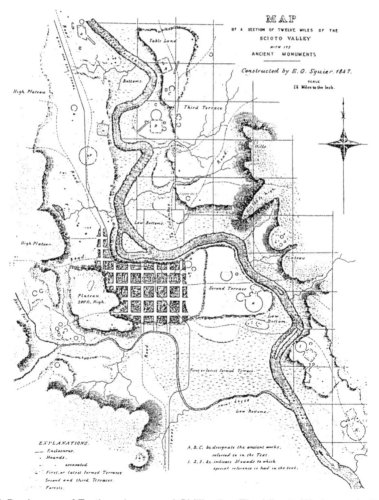

Squier & Davis map of Earthworks around Chillicothe. The Liberty Works are bottom right

MIAMISBURG MOUND
Montgomery County, Ohio

Miamisburg Mound is believed to have been built by the Adena Culture, anywhere between 1000 to 200 BC. It served as an ancient burial site, and has become perhaps the most recognizable historic landmark in the area. It is the largest conical burial mound in Ohio, once nearly 70 feet tall (the height of a seven-story building) and 877 feet in circumference; it remains virtually intact from its construction perhaps 2500 years ago. Excavations conducted in 1869 revealed details of construction suggesting the Adena culture built the mound in several stages. The excavators found a layer of flat stones, overlapping like shingles on a roof, at a depth of 24 feet below the surface.

Old illustration of Miamisburg Mound.

The mound also once had a stone facing. Monuments like Miamisburg Mound may have been used as cemeteries for several generations, and also marked the boundaries of tribal territories.[11] The stone facing must have been extremely impressive but many of these ancient structures were pirated for building materials by settlers.

Hugh visited Miamisburg in September 2012 to take a look for himself. On a hunch, he drove to the local town before visiting the mound site and discovered that the local Historical Society was open that day. He got talking with the members who were present that day, and Hugh had

Miamisburg Mound today.

the honor of being the first Englishman to grace their office! He enquired about the mounds in the area and found out that the entire town was once part of a greater mound complex that covered many square miles. Hugh was shown old records and local histories, before getting on to the controversial subject of unusually large skeletons.

Most of the Historical Society members had heard about the giants, and one of them ran off into another room and dug out a green photocopied booklet that had a full account of the excavations, titled *Brief Historical Background of Miamisburg Indian Mound*. Strangely, the booklet was produced by Monsanto, the genetic engineering giants, who were involved in nuclear weapons research during the second world war. The 'Mound Laboratory' was completed in 1948 and the site chosen *"because of the major Indian Mound which is adjacent to the Plant site."* Hugh purchased a copy for $3.00.

During the Second World War the plant made plutonium detonators for nuclear weapons, carrying out work that was *"very classified."* The plant had a small army of security guards and was surrounded by chain fencing and razor wire. When the Cold

The $3.00 booklet from 1975.

War ended, the plant discontinued the detonator work, but it continued to make nuclear power generators for space probes.[12] Beginning in 1960, the facility released radioactive tritium into the air and contaminated the soil with plutonium-238, which is said to have triggered the higher-than-average cases of cancer in the local community, with an estimated 90% of households contracting some type of cancer from the 1960s onwards.[13] It was not until 1993 that a 'clean-up' was carried out, but obviously this was too late for many of the locals.

So back in May 1975 the *Explosives Safety Engineering Conference*, organized by Monsanto Research Corporation was taking place and the *Brief Historical Background of Miamisburg Indian Mound* document was handed out to the attendees. The lengthy account it contains is from *The Miamisburg News* from April 29th 1920, covering the full history of what happened at the site from the early 1800s to the 1869 excavation. These following segments are from the booklet:

> "In the year 1814 or 1815, Jacob Gebhart commenced tunneling upon the northeast side of the Mound, at a point between the base and the top, nearly midway." Interestingly it continues, "ashes and charred remains of wood were discovered, a hollow sound peculiar to all artificial structures of this character, which followed the stroke of the pick, frightened the inquisitive explorer, and he abandoned his scheme."

It was not until 1839 that another attempt at excavating the mound took place. Ross Hamilton had previously visited the local library and uncovered the original entry describing what happened:

The Historical Collections of Ohio
R977.1-H83, Miamisburg Public Library, 1848

"Regarding the great Miamisburg Mound, in 1839 a man named Lewis received permission from the owner of the work, Dr. John Treon to excavate. Digging into the top of it, he uncovered a few bones at about 10 or 12 feet from the surface when he became frightened by a hollow sound off his pick. He

stopped the work there, but the bones were preserved by Dr.
Treon, and were of enormous size, a jaw [bone] slipping easily
over those of the largest man, flesh and all."

The booklet goes on to describes how the local landscape had an artificial lake that stayed full all year round; a forest had been cleared, and that the mound "*was originally composed of sun-dried brick, made of clay taken from the excavation which formed this pond."* Further evidence of giants were also uncovered:

"*A pioneer relates that whilst plowing in a field adjoining it,*
many years ago, he discovered a grave of extraordinary size,
which proved by actual measurement to be not less than ten
feet in length. Upon one occasion, after a heavy storm had
swept over the vicinity, a massive oak tree was up-rooted and
from its bed came up a gigantic skeleton complete. Owing to
some neglect, however, it was not preserved."

The article emphasises that the bones and relics discovered within the mound and surrounding area had a "*remarkable state of preservation."* The article continues:

"*The vicinity abounds with evidence of the existence of a*
mammoth race, skilled in the art of war and much further
advanced in civilization than any of the Indian tribes of which
we have authentic knowledge."

Described are numerous artistically fashioned artifacts such as pipes, pounders and war axes that are "*so ponderous that none but giant arms could have wielded them."*

In July 1839 a group of local citizens was formed to explore the mound in a professional manner. A weekly report was published in the *Miamisburg Bulletin*, until a lack of funds brought the work to an end. However it was such big news that a local reporter was invited to the excavations, so the story got out to various newspapers.

Jim uncovered this further account that summarises the story of what was discovered.

THE DAY THEY OPENED THE MIAMISBURG MOUND
Dayton Daily News, February 23, 1932

"At a distance of eight feet below the surface and directly west of the line of excavation the workmen came upon a human skeleton, entombed in a sitting posture and facing due east.... Wood, stone, charcoal and ashes were unearthed and carefully preserved with the human bones, which were of unusual size."

Once again it is mentioned that the skeleton was buried in a sitting posture facing east like so many other accounts. Frustratingly this is one of hundreds and hundreds of these accounts, that you essentially have to throw out as a researcher because they don't give exact measurements. It is obvious to anyone however, that if you are saying unusual size and greatly exceeding normal height you are talking about very, very large bones.

Thankfully, we have an accurate account a half-a-mile down the road from Miamisburg that was first recorded on December 23rd 1898, and published on Christmas Day in *The Courier-Journal*, Louisville, with the headline: *Skeleton of Giant That Antedates Adam*. Further newspapers altered the headline, but repeated the same discoveries. It was reported in multiple other sources as well, including this thorough one, that included illustrations of the skeleton and skull:

BONES OF PREHISTORIC GIANT FOUND NEAR MIAMISBURG.

The Middletown Signal, January 17, 1899

"The skeleton of a giant found near Miamisburg is the cause of much discussion not only among the curious and illiterate but among the learned scientists of the world. The body of a man more gigantic than any ever recorded in human history, has been found in the Miami Valley, in Ohio. The skeleton it is calculated must have belonged to a man 8 feet 1 ½ inches in height. It was found within a half mile of Miamisburg in a locality which contains many relics of the mound builders. Edward Gobhart and Edward Kauffman discovered it while

107

they were working in a gravel pit. Kauffman struck a hard substance with his pick and examining it found it to be a skull. When they unearthed the whole skeleton and realized its size they were aghast. The skeleton is of prehistoric age, being fossilized, Its giant proportions present a puzzling problem to the archaeologists. The old theory of tradition that there were giants in early days of the earth has long been discredited. It is a fact, generally agreed, that prehistoric men were little, dark, monkey-like, hairy creatures, considerably smaller than those of the present day. The prehistoric giant seems evidence of the opposite state of affairs. He is clearly a man and a very well proportioned one as to his limbs. The prehistoric giant must have had a head not differing greatly from a gorilla. In stature, he was far bigger and also better formed...The jawbones are intact and show that their possessor was patterned in the most powerful fashion. The teeth are models of strength and beauty of form.

Skull of Prehistoric Man Found in Miami Valley, Closely Resembling Gorilla's Skull.

Dr. Harlan, a dentist, of Miamisburg, examined the teeth and declared them to be as fine a specimen as he had ever seen. Other doctors have also examined the teeth and the skeleton. The body was not the only relic of interest to those engaged in scientific research found in the pit. A small flat stone about three inches long and two inches wide was discovered in the opening. It lay within a few inches of the skull of the prehistoric man, as the local examiners insist the find should be termed. Through one end of the stone had been drilled a small hole, possibly intended to be used as an opening for the fitting in of a handle. It is pointed out by those who have had their theory of the species of the discovery questioned that the stone, so evidently the work of human hands, clearly indicates that the skeleton was that of a man and not of a mammoth monkey. The bones have been placed on exhibition and many are the curious sight seers who have passed in wonder before them. It is claimed by residents of the Miami valley that a prehistoric race once inhabited the region and erected the largest mound in the country."

GIGANTIC SKELETON OF PREHISTORIC AMERICAN FOUND IN MIAMI VALLEY. GREATER THAN ANY RECORDED GIANT.

Once again the jaws were massive, the teeth perfect, and the skull showed many anatomic anomalies. None other than Professor Thomas Wilson, the Curator of Anthropology for the Smithsonian, said the following about the find:

"The authenticity of the skull is beyond any doubt. It's antiquity unquestionably great, to my own personal knowledge several such crania were discovered in the Hopewell group of mounds in Ohio, exhibiting very monkey-like traits. The jaws were prognathus (projecting beyond the face) and the facial index remarkably low. With these remains we found thousands of objects illustrating the extent of prehistoric commerce in this country; shells from the southern Atlantic coasts, mica from Virginia, copper from Lake Superior and volcanic glass from the Rocky Mountains."

The article then lists "authenticated giants" of modern times and puts this giant skeleton on the list.

Miamisburg Mound is located in a strange landscape. The town is recovering from nuclear leaks that caused much harm to many of the local residents. However, it is supposed to be fairly safe for a quick visit, and is one of the most impressive mound sites in North America.

GRAVE CREEK MOUND
Moundsville, West Virginia

Grave Creek Mound, like Miamisburg, is very similar to Silbury Hill in Wiltshire, England and is officially the largest conical mound in America. It is located in Moundsville, West Virginia, and the nearby Kanawha Valley has hundreds of similar earthworks to explore.

Old illustration of Grave Creek Mound, Moundsville

In early September 2012, Hugh drove to the border of West Virginia through Wheeling. As he approached Moundsville, it suddenly started raining heavily and a lightning storm erupted right over the town. Hugh felt it was some kind of warning, or even a strange welcome to the land of

110

the giants! After a nights sleep at the Wheeling Motel, he drove through the backstreets of Moundsville and discovered a monolith lying recumbent on the side of the road that may have once been part of this greater ancient complex.

Grave Creek Mound is the largest conical mound in North America, with a famous haunted prison directly behind it. The mound is 70 feet tall with a diameter of 295 ft, weighing in at 60,000 tons, and was part of a wider complex of mounds,

Recumbent monolith at Moundsville

octagonal earthworks, and stone towers up on the bluffs overlooking the river. This would have been a clear warning for those entering this territory by boat or land.

The mound once had a moat or henge around it that would have made it look a lot like Silbury Hill. The first excavation took place in 1838 and yielded two skeletons, the female wearing copper arm rings, and buried with various ornaments including the tiny Grave Creek Tablet.

Grave Creek Mound as it looks today, with Hugh in the foreground.

Strange energies, ghostly sightings, men in black, and even *Mothman* type hauntings have been reported around the mound, with a prison built right next to it that has become a paranormal hotspot. Television programs have used it for ghost-hunter shows and it is said that the ghosts of inmates who have died there are often seen in the prison. A notable example is the 'shadow man', who was spotted and photographed by several people and even responded to human interaction.[14]

Hugh felt as sense of that power on the night he arrived, when he was surrounded by a sudden onset of lightning and thunder, an often occurring phenomenon when investigating the graves of giants.

SKELETONS IN MOUND
Charleston Daily Mail, October 22, 1922

Here we have the most well-known report about the giants of Grave Creek Mound, discussing the female skeleton 7 ft 4 inches tall, and a male 8 ft tall, plus the mention of the jawbone fitting over the face of a local resident. However, this was 84 years after the original discovery:

> *"Archaeologists investigating the mound some years ago dug out a skeleton said to be that of a female because of the formation of the bones. The skeleton was seven feet four inches tall and the jawbone would easily fit over the face of a man weighing 160 pounds. Seventeen hundred ivory beads, 500 seashells of an involute species and five copper bracelets were found in the vault. The beads and shells were about the neck and breast of the skeleton while the bracelets were upon the arms. There was also taken from the mound the skeleton of a man eight feet tall. There were no ornaments beside it. These skeletons were sent to the Smithsonian Institution in Washington."*

This next article was published 64 years after the initial discovery

The Hawaiian Star February 13, 1902, pg.6

"When the excavations were made three skeletons were found directly in the center but raised a view feet from the level of the

surrounding land. One of the skeletons had belonged to a male human being about eight feet high, one a female and one a child. There was also in the rude chamber a tablet of stone, upon one side of which were hieroglyphics, which is now in the Smithsonian Institution at Washington."

Unfortunately there is no sign of any skeletons any more as it states the Smithsonian got involved. But did they really? As we dug deeper into the records, an earlier description of the discoveries emerged in a letter to the editor of a newspaper. This was only 40 years after the initial discoveries (see on right).

The first reported incident of finding taller than average skeletons was put forward by Peter B. Catlett, who lived in Moundsville and said he was present at the excavation in 1838. It was on 6th May 1876 when he was answering queries from P.P. Cherry about the Grave Creek Tablet. He said:

Moundsville, 1873.

Mr. Editor:—This city derives it name from one mysterious mound, situated in the centre. The mound is composed of soft, brown clay, similar to that foudd in an excavation about ¼ mile distant, from which it is supposed to have been transported. The level surface of the surrounding country, together with the two skeletons and many comminuated bones found in its centre prove the mound to be artificial. One of the skeletons is reported seven feet high. An excavation to the centre of the base and from thence to the top enabled us to (approximately) measure its dimensions, namely: base, diameter 250 ft., top, diameter 60 ft., increased by leveling process by some dancing party; their platform (now covering the tunnel) is unsafe to "trip the light fantastic toe" upon. The present height is about 17½ ft. Before the leveling, from 10 to 25 ft. higher.— The great antiquity of this mound is proven by a live oak tree, within ten ft. of the top, 4½ ft in diameter. The sides of the mound are covered with trees, beech, locust, oak, hickory, &c. A delightful breeze fans its brow. Two questions arise: Who built this mound? For what purpose? The skeletons found therein seem to answer the last at least partially. It was a royal cemetery similar to the Egyptian Pyramids. The first question remains a mystery unsolved. ITINERANT.

"....the engraved stone was found in the inside of a stone arch that was found in the middle of the mound, and in that stone arch was found a skeleton that measured seven feet and four inches. When the bones were placed upon wires, I took the lower jawbone and put it over my chin and it did not touch my face..."[15]

This was 38 years after the initial discovery, but the 1922 account seems to be using this as its basis, only that one has an 8 ft skeleton added to the description.

Andrew Collins carried out some research into the claims that actual *giants* were discovered and sent Hugh this following matter-of-fact account from when the mound was first excavated by A.B. Tomlinson's grandfather. Here are some highlights from the lengthy letter:

"Prompted by curiosity or some other cause, on the 19th of March, 1838, we commenced an excavation in this mound.... At the distance of one hundred and eleven feet we came to a vault that had been excavated in the natural earth before the mound was commenced.... In the upper vault was found one skeleton only, but many trinkets, as seventeen hundred ivory beads, five hundred sea shells of the involute species, that were worn as beads, and five copper bracelets that were about the wrist bones of the skeleton. There were also one hundred and fifty pieces of isinglass (mica)... The skeleton first found in the lower vault, was found lying on the back, parallel with and close to the west side of the vault. The feet were about the middle of the vault; its body was extended at full length; the left arm was lying along the left side; the right arm as if raised over the head, the bones lying near the right ear and crossed over the crown of the head. The head of this skeleton was toward the south. There were no ornaments found with it. The earth had fallen and covered it over before the ceiling fell, and thus protected it was not much broken. We have it preserved from the inspection of visitors; it is five feet nine inches high; and has a full and perfect set of teeth in a good state of preservation; the head is of a fine intellectual mould; whether male or female cannot be ascertained, as the pelvis was broken."

Stone tower up on the bluffs above the river in Moundsville. Part of the greater Grave Creek complex.

He concluded with this matter-of-fact statement:

> "There is nothing in the remains of any of these skeletons which
> differs materially from those of common people."

The controversial Grave Creek Tablet was said to have been found in the mound in 1838, and the account above shows a facsimile drawing of it. We explore the mystery of the tablet more deeply in the *Curious Artifacts* chapter.

The Grave Creek Tablet.

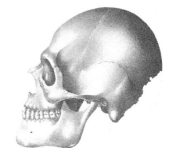

Female skull found in Grave Creek Mound.
From *Crania America* by Morton.

The intrigue and convoluted arguments make this case a tough one to crack, as clearly two different people are reporting two different sized skeletons, who both claim to have been involved in the original excavation in 1838. One that is of normal height, and another at 7 ft 4 inches. We have put all the evidence we can find in this investigation, but are at a loss to reach any final conclusion, although the sheer amount of giant skeletons discovered in mounds in this area does strengthen the argument for at least one giant skeleton being discovered in the enigmatic Grave Creek Mound.

Moreover, 176 miles southwest of Moundsville, an 8 ft skeleton was reported with similar grave goods to Grave Creek that we examine in the *Curious Artifacts* chapter. Meanwhile, here are some more 7-footers.

ARE BONES OF GIANTS:
MOUNDBUILDERS HAD PECULIAR HEADS
The Afro American, December 5, 1908, pg.2
Friendly, West Virginia

This report surfaced later in 1908 describing a mound in Friendly, West

115

Virginia, which is around 56 miles southwest of Moundsville on the way to the Marietta earthworks.

> "Prof. E. L. Lively and J. L. Williamson, of Friendly, have made an examination of the giant skeletons found by children playing near that town. The femur and vertebrae were found to be in a remarkable state of preservation and showed the persons to be of enormous stature. The skeletons ranged in height from 7 feet 6 inches down to 6 feet 7 inches. The skulls found are of peculiar formation. The forehead is low and slopes back gradually, while the back part of the head is very prominent, much more so than the skulls of people living at the present day. The legs are exceedingly long and the bones unusually large. The finding of the skeletons has created a great deal of interest and the general impression is that the bones are the remains of the people who built the mounds, the largest in the country being located at Moundsville, Marshall County."

Friendly residents Lively and Williamson were both real people and respected members of their community. J. L. Williamson held the office of Member of the Board of Education and the County Board of Review. The unusual nature of the skulls is discussed, as is frequently the case in these reports. West Virginia certainly has quite a few giant skeleton reports, and although the legendary giant discoveries from Grave Creek Mound were not quite what any budding giantologist would hope for, the local area was certainly a hub of taller-than-average Mound Builders. The similarity of the reports may have mixed things up over the years, especially if the geography of the area is not fully comprehended and understood. Further discoveries were made in this part of West Virginia, including this account from Dr. Donald Dragoo.

Cresap Mound
The Work of Donald Dragoo, 1959
Northern West Virginia

In 1959, Dr. Donald Dragoo, the curator for the *Section of Man* at the

Carnegie Museum unearthed a 7 feet 2 inch skeleton during the complete excavation (obliteration) of the Cresap Mound in Northern West Virginia, 6.5 miles south of Grave Creek Mound. Dragoo classified the massive jawbone he found there as the "Adena Jaw" and reported the following:

> *In all respects the Cresap Mound skeletal material conforms to the physical type of the Kentucky and Ohio Adena mounds previously described by Snow.*" [16]

The physical type of material Dragoo refers to are massive jawbones, unusually thick skulls, robust and massive frames indicating profound muscularity:

> *"This individual was of large proportions. When measured in the tomb his length was approximately 7.04 feet. All of the long bones were heavy and possessed marked eminences for the attachment of muscles.*" [17]

Dragoo published a photo of the actual skeleton in his book so there is no doubt it was authentic. Dragoo joins many other university-trained anthropologists and archaeologists who discovered over seven-foot skeletons in burial mounds, often with anatomical anomalies.

A few of the professionals reporting these skeletal finds were Dr. Walter B. Jones, Moundsville Alabama (7 ft 6 and many 7-footers), Dr. Forrest Clements Head of Anthropology at the University of Oklahoma (six 7 ft skeletons). Dr. Donald A. Cadzow Cambridge University (7 ft 5 in skeleton found in Pittsburgh with many other large skeletons with anatomic anomalies reported). Dr. Byron Cummings, head of the archaeology department at the University of Arizona, considered the *Dean of Southwestern Archaeology* (Several over 8-footers). Thomas Wilson, Curator of Prehistoric Anthropology at the Smithsonian (Verified an 8 ft skeleton with massive jawbone and other anatomic anomalies). W. J. Holland, curator of the Carnegie Museum (unearthed an over 8 ft skeleton in Pennsylvania as reported in many scientific journals including Scientific American).

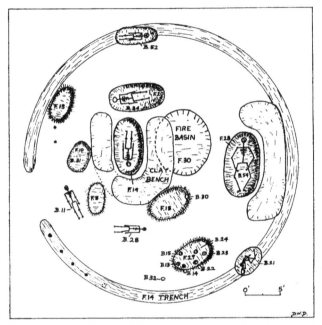

Ground plan of Cresap Mound showing clay floor level and
below. The 7.04 ft skeleton is on the right.

7.04 ft skeleton discovered in Cresap Mound.
The top part of the skeleton was burnt.

118

THE DOVER MOUND

The Dover Mound. by William Snyder Webb, Charles Ernest Snow.
University of Kentucky Press, 1959, pg.31
Kentucky

Anthropologists William Webb and Charles Snow unearthed a 7-foot skeleton at the Dover Mound, Kentucky in 1952 during a University of Kentucky sponsored dig. Like the Don Dragoo report, this account occurs in the 1950s and is reported by a highly respected professional.

The Dover Mound, before and after excavation.

MARIETTA EARTHWORKS

The Fostoria Review-Dispatch, July 25, 1901, pg.2
Marietta, Washington County, Ohio

Marietta is a beautiful town that was built over a geometric mound complex that had great 'squares' and 'circles', now hidden within the foundations of the town. Said to be a Hopewell site (c.100 BC) and located at the

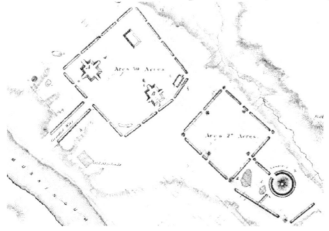

Squier and Davis survey of the Marietta earthworks.

confluence of the Muskingum and Ohio rivers, it consists of flat-topped 'cross' mounds, similar to step pyramids in Mexico. One of them now acts as the foundations of a library. The greater squares are at most 1500 ft wide.

In the modern graveyard are the remains of a mound that appears to be the axis-mundi of the complex. It has a deep henge around it showing a subtle and sophisticated side to the Mound Builders of the area.

The mound in the cemetary at Marietta.

Around the town are numerous banks and earthworks that are the last remnants of this site. It was here that Ross Hamilton, in *Star Mounds: Legacy of a Native American Mystery*, noted that the constellation Centaurus had half of its stars overlay the entire site, much like Orion mirrors the three pyramids of Giza, Egypt (as discovered by Robert Bauval).

In 1901, a very tall skeleton was discovered within the earthworks:

> *"Workmen, while engaged in excavating on upper Fourth Street, Marietta, unearthed what seems to be the remains of a prehistoric age. The bones, which are remarkably well preserved, are of abnormal size, and, as close as can be reckoned, the individual in question must have been measured at least seven feet in height. Experts are of the opinion that he belonged to a tribe of Mound Builders, whose earthen works appear at Marietta in a number of places."*

Beehive Stone Mounds
The Smithsonian Institution Bureau of Ethnology Report, 1890-91
Patterson, North Carolina

The Beehive Stone Mounds found in this tumulus are remarkably similar to stone cairns found up and down the east coast of New England. In this case, however, there just happened to be a *"not less than 7 feet high"* skeleton found in the mound:

> *"...located on the farm of Rev. T.F. Nelson, in the northwest part of the county, and about a mile and a half southeast of Patterson. It stood on the bottom land of the Yadkin, about 100 yards from the river, and was almost a true circle in outline, 38 feet in diameter, but not exceeding at any point 18 inches in height. The thorough excavation made, in which Mr. Rogan, the Bureau agent, was assisted by Dr. J.M. Spainhour, of Lenoir, showed that the original constructers had first dug a circular pit about 38 feet in diameter to the depth of 3 feet and there placed the dead, some in stone cist and others unenclosed, and afterwards covered them over, raising a slight mound above the pit. A plan of the pit, showing the stone graves and skeletons as they appeared after the removal of the dirt and before being*

disturbed, is given in figure. 207......No. 16 was unenclosed "squatter" of unusually large size, not less than 7 feet high when living."

Moundville, Alabama
The Tuscaloosa News, February 23, 1930
Moundville, Alabama

Here we are informed of the unearthing of artifacts and skeletons from the famous Moundville Mississippian site in Alabama (not to be confused with Moundsville, West Virginia). Moundville was the location of a sophisticated and thriving culture from 1000 AD until 1450 AD. Dr. Walter B. Jones, who led the excavation announced from his office that one of the skeletons was 7 ft 6 inches, with many others well over 6 feet tall. Jim called the museum that houses the skeletal remains and when he asked about the giant skeleton he was told by the curator, "*...well, except it didn't happen.*"

Jim explained that Dr. Jones made this announcement, who in 1930 was joined by curator William L. Halton, Assistant curator David de Jarnette, and Topographer Carl T Jones all from the Alabama Museum

Old postcard of Moundville, showing in-situ skeletons in top corner.

122

of Natural History in the excavation. Jim asked how could it be that all these men could sign off on such an outrageous claim. He was then told that there was a persistent mythology in the earlier part of the century and this surely was the reason for this account. Jim then asked but how could the highly competent and respected Dr. Jones incorrectly measure and report such a finding, and was once again reassured that someone from Princeton has studied the remains and there were no giants.

Jim then pointed to the next account from the *Tuscaloosa News* in 1976, that reports that Dr. Jones was made an honorary citizen of Moundville. An awkward silence ensued and the conversation came to an abrupt end. Anyway, by the end of his career Dr. Jones was made Director Emeritus of the University of Alabama Museum of Natural History.

> *"Jones' early discoveries uncovered facts about Indian settlements of West Alabama before recorded history, A race which he says were giant people from 6 and a half to 7 feet tall. It was Jones and Jones alone who realized the significance of the discoveries at first."*

The Moundville Rattlesnake disc, discovered at the site.

MOUNDVILLE
by John H. Blitz, 2008, pg.8

In this modern guidebook to the site, an account is given of Sheriff Hezekiah K. Powell unearthing a nine-foot skeleton from the mounds in Carthage, Alabama. We are told that the skeleton eventually made its way to the Smithsonian Institution. Blitz states that:

"Powell finding a giant was not exceptional. People were digging up giants all across rural America, in keeping with the scriptural wisdom that 'There were giants in the earth in those days.'"

Although Blitz wrote an entire book on Moundville, he never mentioned that Dr. Walter B. Jones, who led the excavation at Moundville announced from his office that one of the skeletons unearthed was 7 ft 6 inches, with many others well over 6 ft.

Right: Letter that was included in local newspaper describing witnessing giant skeletons at the museum and speculating on their origins.

ORIGIN OF MOUNDVILLE INDIANS

Editor, The News:
    Recently we visited Mound State Monument at Moundville in Hale County.
    It wasn't our first visit, but this time we noticed that some of the skeletons belonged to very tall people, possibly all males. One or two must have been seven feet tall. Our observations of the area and the mounds and the size of the skeletons confirmed two of my pet theories about the mound builders, and maybe three.
    I have made a fairly thorough study of the Alabama Indians for several years, and my first conclusion concerning the place from whence they came was, and is, that they did not come from Alaska. But since the Mormon Baker crossed the Pacific ocean from South America to Honolulu, I am more convinced that ever that the Indians of Alabama came by one of two routes: either they came from India by way of the many islands in the Indian and South Atlantic oceans, upon rafts similar to the one Baker used to cross the Pacific, or they were Polynesians and came by way of the Mediterranean through the Straits of Gibraltar.
    I am more sure that they came by boats, and that they were propelled by oars, but if not, then surely by rafts. But they definitely did not come by way of the Bering Sea straits and Alaska. They have no traits or resemblance to the Mongolians who are claimed to be the ancestors of the Eskimos. Their stature is definitely taller and larger than the Eskimos or Mongolians.
    It is more probable that they came from Polynesia and were temple worshipers and built the great mounds wherever they settled. Possibly they were sun worshipers. The South American Indians and Central American Indians all displayed by their buildings and temples and handiwork more intelligence than the Mongolians ever manifested; so did the Polynesians.
    The Cherokees and Creeks were intelligent, kind, happy and industrious, many tales to the contrary notwithstanding. I think it most probable that they were in the Western Hemisphere long before the Mongolians crossed the Bering Straits. It is my opinion that the Indians had been in Alabama and living in the Warrior River valleys as many as six to ten thousand years before Moses wrote about Adam and Eve.
    There is abundant evidence that there were giants among them, for our histories tell us that the famous Creek Indian Chief Tuskaloosa was seven or eight feet tall. There were giants — whole families of giants — in the Euphrates valleys, and they were capable of swimming a hundred miles.
    The Moundville park is so interesting that I could not resist the temptation to write about it and its former residents, for they built those great mounds by carrying baskets of earth, and I think it was year by year at the time of the green corn feast.
                                    P. E. DAY
50 University Lane

124

Spiro Mound, Oklahoma

The Spiro mound (Craig Mound) in Oklahoma is an elongated earthwork that appears to be four mounds next to each other, but joined together. The highest part, which contained the 'great mortuary' was 33 ft high and the full length of the quad-mound was 350 ft long. It was originally excavated in 1933, when commercial diggers calling themselves the *Pocola Mining Company* acquired the lease for them to 'dig'. From 1933 until 1935 Pocola employees dug haphazardly into the burial mound.

Excavation In the summer of 1935. From left to right: John Hobbs, unknown worker, W. Guinn Cooper and Billy Vandagriff. Photo from the collection of Dr. Robert E. Bell, from *The Spiro Mound: A Photo Essay* by Larry and Christopher Merriam.

They destroyed about one-third of the mound and sold thousands of artifacts made of stone, copper, shell, basketry, and fabric to collectors throughout the world. Dubbed the "King Tut of the Arkansas Valley" by the Kansas City Star in 1935, the site yielded artifacts in greater numbers, in better preservation, and showing more elaborate artistic, sophisticated decoration than any other Mississippian site. Continuing destruction convinced the Oklahoma Legislature to pass a licensing requirement for the protection of the site, and in November 1935 the Pocola Mining Company finally closed the site down when their lease ran out. Below is a matter-of-fact report of what was going on there at the time:

The Herald Journal, August 26, 1934, pg.2

"Indian relics estimated to be from 600 to 2000 years old and including the thighbone of a giant brave are being taken in large numbers from a burial mound 4 ½ miles from here. The Pocola Mining Company, composed of six Arkansas and Oklahoma men, is in charge of excavations, begun last February. Although it is a private enterprise, each item taken from the mound is catalogued and photographed and careful records are being kept of the disposition of the artifacts, human bones, beads of wood and stone, pearls and large conch shells. Situated in the middle of a field near the Arkansas River, the mound is approximately 100 feet long and 40 feet high at the peak. It is of sand, making digging comparatively easy. Excavations about 20 feet deep have been made. Among the treasured finds is a large femur, indicating its owner must have been about nine feet tall. Bones and skeletons of other human beings are of normal size."

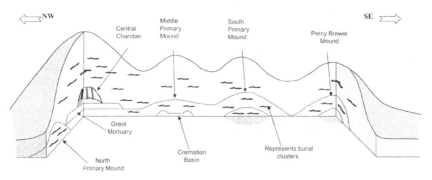

Image courtesy Larry and Christopher Merriam from *The Spiro Mound: A Photo Essay.*

This next extract is from the book *The Spiro Mound: A photo essay- photographs from the collection of Dr. Robert E. Bell.*[18] It was written down by W. Guinn Cooper of the Pocola Mining Company around 1936. Here it relates how they found one large skeleton at the site:

"He was better than seven feet tall. His jaw would fit around my face...He was more or less in pieces, we had to put him

together, you see. He was bound to be a giant. He said they did not dig in the level area around the mound. 'We'd just dig in the mound. We had our hands full there'. He said they didn't make any money out of the venture. 'No, we didn't, we were fighting to live. This was back in the great Hoover starvation period. The worst part of it and we were fighting to live.'"

Once again, the jawbone was reported to be so large that the finder could slip it over their face. This next remarkable discovery was analyzed by Ross Hamilton whilst researching *A Tradition of Giants*. We hand over to Ross for this next section:

Photo taken December 8, 1935, in J. G. Braecklein's Indian Store in Kansas City, Missouri. Photo from the collection of Dr. Robert E. Bell, from *The Spiro Mound: A Photo Essay* by Larry and Christopher Merriam.

SPIRO'S MAGNIFICENT MAN
N.A.I.R.C.A. Official Bulletin, 1936, by G.I. Groves and Allen Brown
Commentary from Ross Hamilton

The account following is a classic, because the rumor of its subject stayed around for many years after the fact of the bones' disappearance. It was reported that an eight ft skeleton in full armor had been discovered at

Spiro, Oklahoma, and had been rumored taken surreptitiously by the Smithsonian. As it turned out, the skeletal remains were not in full armor, but rather fully armed; and its mummy was simply ignored until someone noticed it was gone. Who, we wonder, snatched it, for what purpose, and where is it now? The author, G.I. Groves says his organization, the North American Indian Relic Collectors Association, is the first to invest in preparation and publication concerning the discovery and excavation. He claims that the information in the bulletin had been collected from various sources, including personal visits to the Mound, and interviews with various persons (He must have talked with the younger members of the Pocola Mining Co., as he calls them 'boys'). The bulletin includes a very early photograph of the Craig Mound with trees growing on it, that some describe as three feet in circumference (see pic on earlier page). The bulletin includes a story of one of the bodies found in the Mound which we had never heard anywhere else:

"Of the skeletal material, only four or five good specimens were found. One remarkable mummy was 8 ½ feet in length. He had been cremated to such an extent that the flesh was charred, and remained in that condition throughout the ages. Across the breast of this mighty warrior were seven large bows, three stone pipes, forty war points, and four eight-inch spears. No beads were found on this body. At the time of this discovery, little attention has been paid the excavation of this mound. The mummy was moved into the only tent available. A few neighbors marveled at the remains, but no museum authorities or archaeologists were interested enough to investigate. After occupying for several weeks the only shelter available, it was moved to the rear of the tent to make room for more valuable relics, and left to the ravages of the elements. In a few weeks, it had disappeared."

CAHOKIA, ILLINOIS

Cahokia Mounds State Historic Site is located on the site of an ancient Native American city (c. 600 - 1400 CE) situated in southern Illinois between East St. Louis and Collinsville. The park covers 2,200 acres or about 3.5 square miles, and contains about 80 mounds, but the ancient city was actually much larger. In its heyday, Cahokia covered about 6 square miles and included about 120 man-made earthen mounds in a wide range of sizes, shapes, and functions. Monks mound is the largest earthen pyramid ever built in ancient America, standing 100 feet high it has a base of 14 acres, one acre larger than the great pyramid of Giza. It required 22 million cubic feet of soil brought from over a mile away to create the four-stepped pyramid.

Aerial view of Monks Mound, Cahokia.

CAHOKIA-THE GREAT NATIVE AMERICAN METROPOLIS
by Biloine Whiting Young and Melvin Leo Fowler, 2000, pg.26

The authors describes how in 1891 the Reverend Stephen Peet wrote about his visit to Cahokia:

> *"There are also vast quantities of bones hidden beneath the surface and one can scarcely strike a spade through the soil without unearthing some token of the prehistoric races. Mr. Ramey, the owner of the mound, speaks about digging in one part of the*

129

field and finding heaps of bones eight feet deep and says that the bones are everywhere present. The workmen who were engaged in digging ditches for underdraining had a few days before came upon large quantities of pottery and skeletons of large size but had carelessly broken them instead of preserving them."

Another interesting Cahokia account comes from the *Saint Louis Dispatch* in 1906.

"A Mr. Hill who once lived upon it, while making excavation near the northwest extremity, uncovered human bones and white pottery in considerable quantities. The bones, which instantly crumbled to dust on exposure to the air, appeared larger than ordinary, while the teeth were double in front as well as behind."

AZTALAN, WISCONSIN
New York Times, August 10, 1891

Aztalan in Wisconsin is another Mississippian culture settlement that flourished during the 10th to 13th centuries. The indigenous people constructed massive earthwork mounds for religious and political purposes. They were part of a widespread culture with important settlements throughout the Mississippi River valley and its tributaries. Their trading network extended from the Great Lakes to the Gulf Coast, and into the southeast of the present-day United States.

The pyramid-like mound at Aztalan, Wisconsin.

Although the relationship is not well-understood as of yet, Aztalan is believed to have been intimately connected to the enormous Mississippian urban center of Cahokia, approximately 310 miles to the south, along the Mississippi river and its tributaries. Some things mentioned in the article were as follows: a large-sized skeleton being unearthed; at the side of the body was found a curiously carved pipe, in the shape of a human head with peculiar characters cut on the sides. Near the right hand was an axe of banded slate in the form of an ancient double-edged battle axe. We also read that another skeleton was unearthed of a person who must have been a giant in his day. Beneath the hand was an axe, finished with great skill and very nicely polished and grooved, which weighed five pounds. Many implements of copper, consisting of beads, disks, spears, arrows and axes, were found. Some of these appeared to have been cast, others were hammered into shape and contained nuggets of silver imbedded in the sides. All were tempered by some unknown process. The author of the article ended it with a moment of sobering reflection:

"While scientific men have long been aware of the existence of these wonderful works, nothing has been done in the way of obtaining an accurate description or of obtaining a better knowledge of them. Every year the plow is laying them low and persons ignorant of their value in the eyes of science are destroying not only the mounds themselves but also the relics contained in them and in a few years they will have disappeared entirely."

There is certainly a case to be made that the Native American Mound Building cultures had an unusually tall royal ruling class that were oftentimes buried in these impressive structures. The authors have run down several accounts to their source, but although one or two came to a dead-end, the others are simply matter-of-fact reports that are getting harder to ignore. The sheer number of these accounts, reports from university-trained professionals up and into the 1950s, and at least 17 reports of 7-foot and taller skeletons listed in Smithsonian ethnology reports testify to the validity of this theory.

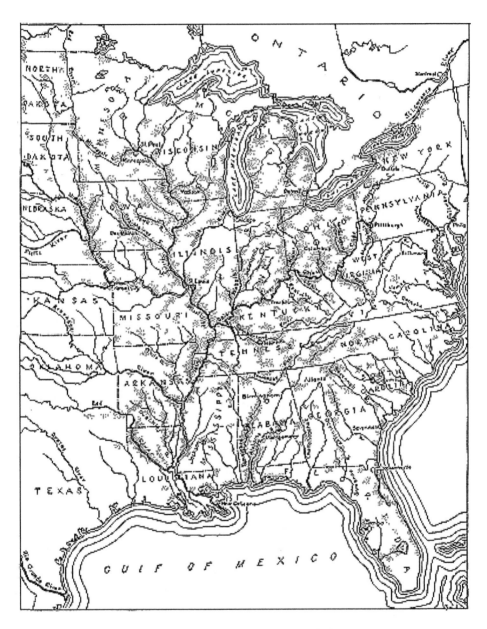

Distribution of mounds in eastern North America.

5

GIANTS OF NEW ENGLAND

Continuing on from Jim's introduction, here is a comprehensive selection of accounts from the states of New England that also give some background information on the megalithic structures and stonework that have very controversial origins. New England is more famous for the unusual stone chambers, thousands of miles of walls, and the occasional stone circle or dolmen. To find so many accounts of giants across its beautiful landscape, going back deep into prehistory, provides an enchanted glimpse into what was once there. As we see in the *Early Accounts* chapter, New England was a thriving Native American metropolis, even in to the 1900s. Our survey begins in New Hampshire.

NEW HAMPSHIRE

HUMAN SKELETON, 7 FEET IN LENGTH
The Plough Boy and Journal of the Board of Agriculture
Volume 2 , J.O. Cole, 1821 pg 239
Portsmouth, New Hampshire

This very early account from New Hampshire describes "*a human skeleton, 7 feet in length*" and emphasises the mystery of the double sets of teeth when it says: "*...the upper jaw had double teeth all around.*" This account is included in full in the *Double Rows of Teeth* chapter.

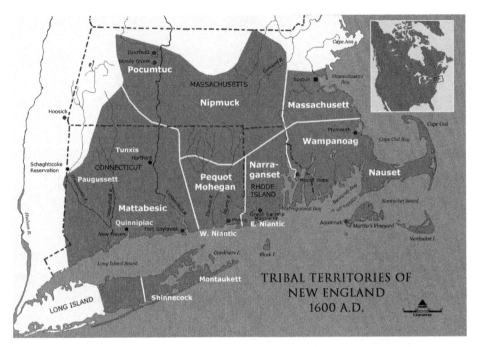

Above: Map of New England circa 1600 showing tribal territories and modern states. Below: Chamber at *America's Stonehenge* in Salem, New Hampshire that may date back to 2000 BC From William Goodwin's *Ruins of Greater Ireland in New England*.

Guide to the White Mountains and the Lake of New Hampshire.
Tripp and Osgood, 1850, pg. 17
Moltonborough, New Hampshire

"A skeleton was exhumed in this town (Moltonborough) some 30 years ago, of almost fabulous proportions. It was buried in a sandy soil, on the shore of the lake, near the mouth of a small river. It was apparently the skeleton of a man some seven feet high - the jaw bones passing easily over the face of a large man."

This account was verified when Jim and Hugh visited the Bellows Falls Historical Society in Rockingham. It was listed in an old booklet called *Sites in New Hampshire,* and added that *"Nearby was a cromlech of smooth gray stones not commonly found in the area, of dimensions suggesting another giant burial under it"* (from the notes of poet John G. Whittier). This is a rare and rather tantalising connection between the stone sites of New England and the giants.

INDIAN GRAVES IN CONCORD, N.H.
Boston Medical and Surgical Journal, Vol 53 1856, pg. 456
Concord, New Hampshire

A report from New England that discusses skeletons; *"one very large"* and *"The skull is very thick, the teeth in both jaws are entire, and all of them double."* This is also featured in the *Double Rows of Teeth* Chapter.

Indian Graves in Concord. N. H.—In excavating recently, says the Congregational Journal, for a cellar of a new house, a few rods west of the dwelling of Richard Bradley, Esq., at the north end of this city, nine skeletons of Indians have been exhumed in a space about ten feet square. They are supposed to be the remains of some of the ancient Pennacooks who once inhabited this region, and probably have been buried at least a century and a half. Among these were skeletons of six children, three of whom were around that of an adult, supposed to be their mother, and one very large, measuring six feet and three inches. The bones of this giant were of remarkable preservation. The skull is very thick, the teeth in both jaws are entire, and all of them double. The skeletons were found enclosed in bark, in a sitting posture, with some of their long, black hair still preserved. The bones of the children were much decayed. Dr. William Prescott, of this city, has preserved the largest skeleton, which may be seen in his cabinet.—*N. Y. Observer.*

Massachusetts

Gigantic Skeleton of an Indian
The History of Western Massachusetts, Vol II,
by Josiah Gilbert Holland, 1855, pg.364
Gill, Massachusetts

This account indicates a likely trade or visitation with the ancient copper miners of Michigan:

> *"Mr. J. D. Canning has in his possession a broken pipe and a copper tomahawk, which were unearthed, together with the gigantic skeleton of an Indian, by Mr. Horace Burrows and others, a few years since, while repairing the highway in the river district. The skeleton soon crumbled. The copper tomahawk doubtless belonged to a warrior renowned in his day and race, and was probably brought from the region of Lake Superior."*

Gleason's Literary Companion, Vol. 5, 1864
Hadley, Massachusetts

> *"An Indian skeleton of immense size was recently discovered three feet under ground near Fort River Hadley, Massachusetts. The bones were so far decomposed that most of them crumbled upon exposure to the air. Some of the doctors think that the Indian was not less than seven feet high and one hundred years old when he died."*

An Indian Tomb Unearthed
The New York Times, December 21, 1891
Saugus, nr. Boston, Massachusetts

"An Indian sepulcher has been unearthed on "Fish Marsh", in

Saugus. The tomb was about seven feet below the surface and it contained the skeleton of a man of enormous proportions, which crumbled to dust upon exposure to the air. The body was buried in a sitting posture, facing the east. Beside the skeleton were found a pipe, a tomahawk blade an arrowhead, an ax and a cylindrical shaped stone. Near the grave an underground passage has been discovered. Excavations are being made for the purpose of exploring the passage. The discoveries were made by workmen who were excavating for building purposes."

Left: Illustration of Phaeton or Cannon Rock, Lynn, Mass. Is this a prehistoric dolmen?

Below: Cannon Rock today from a different angle, with wood and concrete supports.

This fascinating account also has a 'megalithic' connection, as it is very close to Cannon Rock, a perched boulder that could also be a prehistoric dolmen. Joseph Henry, a 19th century scientist and the first director of the Smithsonian Institution, made a visit to what was then called Phaeton Rock in 1859. He wrote in a letter dated August 18th:

"It came from Canada and lodged in its present elevated position during what is called the drift period and was probably transported through the agency of ice."

However, when looking at the delicately poised position of the thirty ton slab on three smaller stones, leaning precariously over a steep bluff, perhaps our friend from Fish Marsh may have been involved, as hundreds of legends in Britain and Europe propose that giants were involved with constructing these types of dolmens. Today, it is supported by wooden blocks and concrete in car tires. A similar, but a larger dolmen resides at North Salem, New York, just outside the local fire station.

A History of Deerfield By George Sheldon, Volume 1. 1895 pg.78

"One of these skeletons was described to me by Henry Mather who saw it, as being of monstrous size - the head as big as a peck basket, with double teeth all round" (see Jim's introduction for full account).

HUGE JAWBONE
The New England Magazine, Vol. 16, 1897, pg. 546
Edgartown, Martha's Vineyard, Massachusetts

"The spot where the village of Edgartown stands today was at that time an ancient Indian burial ground. In one case, a huge jawbone of a man was dug up out from the ground, larger than that of any man at the present time, so large that it could be placed against the face of an ordinary man and entirely surround his jaw."

History of the Town of Middleboro, Mass. Thomas Weston, 1906, pg. 400

"His height must have been at least seven feet and eight inches."
(see Jim's introduction and *DRT* chapter for full account)

MARTHA'S VINEYARD
The Story of Martha's Vineyard by Charles Gilbert Hine, pg.136, 1908

"Some 15 years ago the skeleton of an Indian Giant in almost perfect preservation was dug up in the same locality [Cedar Tree Neck] the bones indicated a man easily six feet and a half possibly seven feet high. An unusual feature was a complete double row of teeth on both the upper and lower jaws."

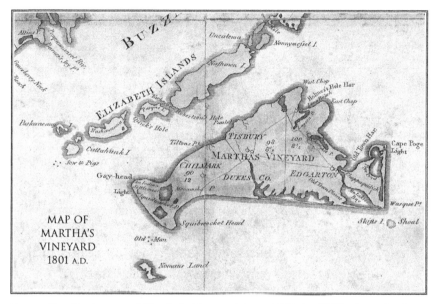

Above: Carelton's map of Martha's Vineyard from 1801. In 1897 a huge jawbone was found in Edgartown. The giant skeleton was reportedly discovered at Cedar Tree Neck near Tisbury. Below: Dolmen overlooking ocean in Chilmark, close to the where the giant was unearthed.

INDIAN SKELETONS WERE EXHUMED
The History Of Montague, Massachusetts
by Edward Pearson Pressey, 1910, pg.61
Montague, Massachusetts

"Indian skeletons were exhumed on L street at the Falls in 1873. And on the opposite shore Mr. Smith dug out seven skeletons in a sitting posture, each about seven feet in stature. When the Millers Falls trolley road was being excavated, north of Lake Pleasant, several skeletons were discovered, indicating regular burial."

CONNECTICUT

History of the Colony of New Haven, 1838, pg.126
New Haven, Connecticut, circa 1650

This obscure account was a footnote at the bottom of a page in tiny text in a town history of New Haven. It was not sensational, just another matter-of-fact account of a giant skeleton being dug up by the new local residents, who had come over from England building their properties in the mid 1600s. Daniel was the son of Thomas Buckingham, who was one of the first settlers in the area:

"The house of Daniel Buckingham, Esq, stands on one side of this burying-ground. In digging the cellar of the house, a number of skeletons were exumed [sic], one of which was near eight feet in length. They were buried in a horizontal position, and appeared to have been laid out on a bed of charcoal, and covered with the same."

United States Register, by Francis Vincent, 1860, pg.75
Hartford, Connecticut

"The Skeleton of an Indian, who when alive was over seven

feet tall, has been dug up in Hartford. An Earthen jug, some wampum, and glass beads, were found with the bones."

History of Norwich, Ct. 1866, pg.535
Norwich, Connecticut

"In preparing for the foundation of this house, a Gigantic Indian skeleton was exhumed and many rude stone tools and arrow heads thrown up."

THE GRAVE OF A GIANTESS
The New York Times, May 13th, 1888
Norwalk, Connecticut

This eccentric account in *The New York Times*, gives information on a legendary non-Indian giantess who lived recently in New England:

"There is a grave in Pine Island Cemetery that is no less than 10 feet long. It is that of Mrs. Mary Titus, a widow, who was laid to rest there on Feb. 5, 1769, a little over 119 years ago, in the nintieth year of her age. Tradition has it that Mrs. Titus was a giantess, which fully explains the enormous length of her grave. It is situated in a remote corner of the large burying ground, and its existence had been almost forgotten. A few days ago it was discovered by some city people visiting here."

A PETRIFIED GIANT DUG UP
The Evening Times (Washington D.C.), September 16, 1897, pg.4
New Haven, Connecticut

What they meant by "petrified" is unclear, but it could be a very rare example of mummification in the North East of America, or it could simply be a natural process.

"Italian Laborers Unearth a Stone Man Eight Feet long. Two

Italians, while digging yesterday on the premises of Deputy Sheriff Arthur Plumb, near Trumbull Church, discovered a petrified giant. Before Plumb lived upon the place it was occupied by Birdseye Plumb, who died many years ago. He used to tell his children of a giant named Christian Peterson, a Swede, who died 150 years ago. When the petrified giant was unearthed the traditions of the old town were recalled, and Sheriff Plumb says that this stone giant is no doubt the petrified remains of Christian Peterson. Sheriff Plumb said he would present the stone figure to the Fairfield Historical Society."

A PETRIFIED GIANT DUG UP.

Italian Laborers Unearth a Stone Man Eight Feet Long.

New Haven, Conn., Sept. 16. —Two Italians, while digging yesterday on the premises of Deputy Sheriff Arthur Plumb, near Trumbull Church, discovered a petrified giant. Before Plumb lived upon the place it was occupied by Birdseye Plumb, who died many years ago.

He used to tell his children of a giant named Christian Peterson, a Swede, who died 150 years ago. When the petrified giant was unearthed the traditions of the old town were recalled, and Sheriff Plumb says that this stone giant is no doubt the petrified remains of Christian Peterson. Sheriff Plumb said he would present the stone figure to the Fairfield Historical Society.

The story was reported again on September 23rd in *The Beaver Herald*.

SKELETON OF GIANT:
FARMER UNCOVERS RELICS OF OLD CITY
The Evening News, Jan 3, 1901
Shideler, nr. Hartford, Connecticut

"An entire skeleton of an Indian giant has been dug up, together with many other human bones, curious copper and stone implements and crude ornaments. The thigh bone of the giant's skeleton is twice as large as that of an ordinary man."

142

SKELETON OF GIANT

FARMER UNCOVERS RELICS OF OLD CITY.

Hartford, Conn., Jan. 31.—Numerous relics of a destroyed Indian village have been found on the farm of John A. Gray, near Shideler, this county.

An entire skeleton of an Indian giant has been dug up, together with many other human bones, curious copper and stone implements, and crude ornaments.

The thigh bone of the giant's skeleton is twice as large as that of an ordinary man.

The relics were found in a gravel pit at a depth of twenty feet.

People in large numbers are flocking to the scene of the discovery.

Farmer Gray believes that a vast treasure of gold will be found and he is guarding his property.

The relics were found buried under 20 feet of gravel. It is also reported that people in large numbers were flocking to the scene of the discovery. Some of the first accounts of giant skeletons Jim uncovered were on the Connecticut River: Gill, Northfield, Deerfield, Hadley, and Montague, Massachusetts, suggesting they lived by this waterway for many thousands of years.

YALE PROFESSORS TAKE CHARGE OF SKELETONS
The Providence News, May 13, 1904
Shelton, Connecticut

This skeleton was sent to the prestigious Peabody Museum in New Haven, Connecticut.

"Dr. H. B. Ferris, professor of Anatomy, Dr. George McCurdy, professor of anthropology and T. A. Bostwick, in charge of the Peabody museum, all of Yale, have been here and boxed up the skeletons of Indians found in an excavation in a mill yard recently. One of the skeletons is that of a man six feet 8 inches tall. It will be articulated if possible."

Further skeletons were also discovered including "*those of a man and woman with arms interlocked as if they had been buried in close embrace.*" The female skeleton also wore a necklace of an unrecognisable metal. What eventually happened to these skeletons is unknown, but considering the infamous *Skull and Bones Society* is based in this college, one has to wonder.

Rhode Island

Eight Foot Giant
Burrillville: as it was, and it is, by H.A. Keach, 1856
Burrillville, Rhode Island

"In 1836, Capt. Samuel White, in excavating beneath his wood house, found the remains of a human skeleton of proportions altogether unlike our modern inhabitants. He called several of his neighbors to view it, and among them was Doct. Levi Eddy. The body was lying upon the side, with arms folded, head bent forward, and the knees drawn upward. It was exhumed, the bones were put together, and all parties were surprised at its gigantic height. After surveying it awhile the Doctor exclaimed, 'He was a bouncer! he must have been as much as eight feet high.'"

Indians Were Very Tall
A History of Gloucester, Rhode Island by Elizabeth Perry, 1886
Gloucester, Rhode Island

This is another account of a skeleton of enormous size found in the area of the Nipmunck and Narragansett tribes (although this could be the same as the above account as these town are very close to each other).

"Some vestiges of these tribes still remain...a human skeleton was found several feet below the surface of the ground. When the bones were put together it measured eight feet. Some of these Indians were very tall."

Roger Williams and the Narragansetts. 19th-century engraving, after a painting by A. H. Wray

144

Vermont

History of the Town of Rockingham by Lyman Simpson Hayes, pg.338
Bellows Falls, Rockingham, Vermont, 1907

"...a remarkable human skeleton, unmistakably that of an Indian, was found." (see Jim's introduction for full account)

Maine

Monmouth Giant Seven and a Half Foot Skeleton
History of Monmouth and Wales, Maine, Harry H. Cochrane, 1894, pg.9
East Monmouth, Maine

"Not many years ago, a massive Indian skeleton was exhumed at East Monmouth. By proceeding carefully, the entire frame was unearthed. It proved to be that of a giant, measuring almost seven and a half feet in height. The skull is said to be as large as a common iron tea kettle."

A History of Swan's Island, Maine
by H.W. Small, M.D., 1898
Hocomock's Head, Swan Island, Maine

"In these ancient shell heaps have been found, by men of our present day, flint arrow heads and hatchets which must have taken much skill and patience in making. These must have been their implements used in hunting and perhaps in warfare. The promontory where the light-house stands, near the entrance to Old Harbor, is called Hocomock, a name given to it by the Indians long before the white men came. It may have been their name for this locality. Near to Hocomock Head is a point of land extending into the harbor, called Burying Point. A large number of Indian skeletons were unearthed by the plow. They were found most plenty near the Middle Head and near the

'Carrying-Place', which places were their burying-grounds. The skeletons were found just beneath the turf and were of large size, showing a race of much larger stature than the Indian of today. This tribe made irregular visits to the island for many years after the white settlers came, but of late, since their number has so decreased, they have ceased altogether."

SKELETONS OF GIANT RED MEN
The Lewiston Evening Journal, July 25, 1907, pg.2
Bath, Maine

James Perkins

"It is likely that the visitors of the Tercentennial, either at Bath or at Popham, may have the privilege of seeing skeletons of two of the magnificent specimens of physical manhood such as the American Indian of the days Sebenio, Samoset, Nahanada and Sansoa really were. Which, being interpreted, is that when James Perkins dug the cellar of his house at Popham Beach, on the knoll next north of the Riverside Hotel, the skeletons unearthed, who were, in life from six to seven feet in height, giants in fact. Mr. Perkins took the jaw bone of one of these Indians and placed it on his own face. It completely encased his jaw and he is a pretty good sized man. Mr. Perkins gathered all the bones of these two skeletons together and placed them in a barrel and reinterred them so. It is proposed to dig up the barrel and have the bones set together to illustrate what manner of inhabitants Weymouth and Popham discovered in the earliest years of the 17th century when they arrived in this section of Maine."

The fact that these giant remains are still buried would make for an interesting investigation, but would he really make up stories of giant skeletons? If so, for what gain? Captain James E. Perkins was born in 1867 and grew up in Popham Village. He was also an accomplished portrait photographer and the Penobscot Museum has 530 glass plate negatives of his work. Perkins was keenly interested in the history of Maine and had a love for his community. He passed away in1935.

Unearthed Skeleton with Indian Arrow in Skull
October 17, 1912
Kennebunkport, Maine

"Three skeletons, believed to be those of early American settlers, were unearthed here by workmen leveling some land near an old fort erected during the war of 1912. Two apparently were victims of Indian massacres or wars. Embedded in the skull of one of the skeletons was an Indian arrow. The tip of the skull of the second was chipped off cleanly as if done by a tomahawk held in a well trained hand. The third skeleton was that of a man 7 feet tall. It is believed that the bodies were buried in an old cemetery on this spot and that the graves were covered over by earth thrown up when the fort excavations were being made."

Old Postcard of Indian Stone Mound at Westfork, Maine.

147

6

ANATOMIC ANOMALIES

Hundreds of reports across the United States demonstrate some very unusual anatomical features. These include macrocephalic (large) skulls, double rows of teeth, elongated craniums, powerful jaws, and even horned skulls. In this chapter we will go through these anomalies case by case from official Smithsonian reports, newspaper articles, to letters and journals from doctors and respected members of the local community. Obviously there are earlier references in the Native American oral tradition, and some even described by the early American presidents. This first account describes a skull six times larger than average!

GIANT'S SKELETON

Dayton, O., Nov. 25.—The skeleton of a human giant was found in the gravel pit east of the city by W. C. Fry, the owner of the pit. He found it measured about nine feet in length. The skull was six times larger than that of the average Caucasian. Professors Metzler and Foerste of the Steele High school believe the bones are those of a member of the primeval race.

Mansfield Daily Shield - Nov 25, 1904

In the first part of this chapter we will examine a few of several hundred reports that say the jaw could fit over the face of a normal sized man, or even put their entire head easily within these massive skulls, creating a 'Skull Helmet'! But first let's take a look at one of the consistent anomalies that has been noted across North America, that has been labeled "The Adena Jaw."

THE ADENA JAW

Reconstruction of a massive jaw fitting over the face of a man.

POWERFULLY BUILT INDIVIDUALS
The Work of Don Dragoo

Charles Snow and William Webb unearthed the "7-foot" Kentucky Giant at the Dover mound (carbon dated to 2,650 years old) in 1951. The Carnegie Museum's Don Dragoo also unearthed giant skeletal remains in the late 1950s. Dragoo was directly affiliated with the Carnegie Museum of Natural History in Pittsburgh from the years 1952-1977. He is considered the last of the great Adena scholars and by the end of his career was named curator of the Carnegie's Section of Anthropology. In discussing these honored dead and referring to this taller Adena stature, he says in his *Mounds for the Dead* (1963):

> *"Two outstanding traits have been noted repeatedly for this group. One is the protruding and massive chin often with*

149

prominent bilateral protrusions. The second trait is the large size of many of the males and some of the females. Not only were these Adena people tall, but also the massiveness of the bones indicates powerfully built individuals. The head was generally big with a large cranial capacity." [1]

Dragoo named the anatomic anomaly of a massive jaw, the "Adena Jaw" after the Adena Mound Builder civilization, he also mentions the "massiveness" of the bones, a recurrent theme in these giant finds.

A HISTORY OF THE VALLEY OF VIRGINIA
by Samuel Kercheval, Charles Faulkner and John Jacob, 1833, pg.59
Shannondale Springs, West Virginia

A few of the notable points from this document from 1833 mention an enormous jawbone dug up with the teeth in a perfect state of preservation. A skeleton of *"unusual"* size with a 3 ft thigh bone and massive jawbone that *"would pass over any common man's face with ease"* were reported. A 7ft skeleton was also mentioned. If measured correctly, a 3 ft thigh bone would make this gentleman ten or eleven feet tall. Only a few eleven-footers have been reported (see *Curious Artifacts* chapter for another one that tall).

AN INDIAN MOUND OPENED
The Grange Advance, October 15, 1873, pg.4
Arcadia, Minnesota

Another burial mound, another giant reported, another jawbone large enough to fit over a large man's face:

"A few days ago the men engaged in building the road bed of the Green Bay and Winona railroad struck an Indian mound near Arcadia.... The skeleton of an Indian was found of such dimensions as to indicate that the frame must have been that of a giant. The jaw bone easily enclosed the face of the largest

laborer to be found on the work. The thigh bones were more like those of a horse than of a man, heavy and remarkably well preserved. A number of Mexican coins were also found. The unusual size of the skeleton has excited considerable interest and the curiosities will be carefully preserved for exhibition."

A GIANT IN STATURE
A History of the Pioneer Families of Missouri, 1876, pg.101
Montgomery County, Missouri

This report is fascinating because the classic traits described are actually those of an Indian chief who died in the early 1800s, suggesting their lineage continued up to recent times. In describing a local Indian war, the history book mentions that:

> *"...one of their chiefs, named Keokuk, a man of some distinction, was wounded, and died shortly after. He was buried in the prairie...of the present town of Wellsville, in Montgomery County. In 1826 his remains were taken up by Dr. Bryan and several other gentlemen....He was evidently a giant in stature, for the jaw bone, which, with several other bones of the body, are still preserved by Dr. Peery, will fit over the face of the largest sized man."* [2]

History of Kentucky, by Lewis Collins, 1877

Remarkably, there are four separate accounts of giants unearthed with jawbones that fit over the finders face, buried obscurely in Collins *History of Kentucky*. We don't imagine that these farmers from the 1800s were all contacting each other to get in on the same hoax. After reading through all these accounts in the same publication, one has to ask some big questions:

Page 107: *"On the farm of Judge T. C. Carson, 7 miles below Morgantown, are several mounds - one 8 or 10 feet high, covering between a quarter and half acre of land. No bones have been found in it; but from a smaller one, a number of bones belonging to a giant race have been taken - jaw bones which would go over the whole chin of a man and teeth correspondingly large; the teeth remained sound but the other bones crumbled on exposure to the air. In Saltpeter cave, in the Little Bend of Green river, a number of such bones were found."*

Page 524: *"Ancient Cemetery - A Race of Giants. On five high points on Caldwell Campbell's farm and on a farm of Samuel and Walker Mason, adjoining 8 miles SW of Richmond, are burial grounds of pre-historic inhabitants - in all embracing 3 acres. On one part, about one and a half acres, have been discovered the skeletons of giants - the femur, tibia, skull and inferior maxillary bones so large, when compared with the size of the late John Campbell (himself 6 feet 4 inches in height), as to indicate a race 7 or 8 feet high. John Campbell slipped the jaw-bone of one entirely over his own, flesh and all."*

Page 666: *"A Giant—Early in 1872, in prospecting coal in Ohio County, out a mile from Rockport, the complete skeleton of a human body of gigantic size was found, 6 feet below the surface. The lower jaw-bone, when fitted over the lower portion of a man's face in the party of explorers, completely covered it: the thigh bone, from the hip-bone to the knee, was 42 inches long and the fore-arm bone from wrist to elbow measured 22 inches. This would indicate a giant over 10 feet high."*

Page 722: *"Antiquities—A Giant. From a mound on the farm of Eden Burrows, near Franklin, were exhumed, in May, 1841, at a depth of over 12 feet, several human skeletons. One, of extraordinary dimension, was found between what appeared to have been two logs, covered with a wooden slab. Many of the bones were entire. The under jaw-bone of one was large enough to fit over the jaw, flesh and all, of any common man of the present day. The thigh-bones were full six inches longer than those of any man in Simpson county. Teeth, arms, ribs, and all,*

*gave evidence of a giant of a former race. Around his neck was
a string of 120 copper beads, and one bead of pure silver."*

These are great examples of obscure references to giants and large jawbones
fitting over someone's face, buried deep in historical documents. These
are observations, often by regular people unburdened by having to make
evidence fit a particular theory. Giants are mentioned as matter-of-fact
as how many cows Mr. Johnson had on his farm—without fanfare, just
simply stating what is seen before ones eyes—reported in every corner of
the country for over 100 years.

PREHISTORIC GIANT
The Evening Bulletin, March 21, 1882, pg.3
Manchester, Ohio

Another report from Ohio, who may be leading the league in giant reports:

*"A few days ago, some boys digging in an earth mound a short
distance above Manchester, Ohio, brought to light a human
skeleton in a good state of preservation, that measured over nine
feet in length. The head was of an enormous size, the jaw-bone
fitting loosely over the head of a large man. To what race of the past
these remains belong and from whence the race came or where
they went must forever remain a mystery. The discovery of the
bones has created a sensation and is attracting much interest."*

Pioneers of the Western Preserve by Harvey Rice, 1883, pp.172-174
Conneaut, Ohio, 1800

This is a very interesting account that also speculates as to the origins of
the giants in North America:

*"In excavating some of these mounds in the year 1800, human
bones of gigantic proportions were discovered in such a state of
preservation as to be accurately described and measured. The
cavities of the skulls were large enough in their dimensions to*

receive the entire head of a man of modern times and could be put on one's head with as much ease as a hat or a cap. The jaw-bones were sufficiently large to admit of being placed so as to match or fit the outside of a modern man's face. The other bones, so far as discovered, appeared to be of equal proportions with the skulls and jaw-bones, several of which have been preserved as relics in the cabinets of antiquarians where they may still be seen... The gigantic dimensions of these bones refute the idea that they were descended from any of the European continent, but indicate that there was in the early ages a race of giants on the earth, who have long since become extinct."

GIANTS SKULLS AND MIGHTY JAWS FROM TWO STATES
The New York Sun, December 15, 1886, pg.4
Illinois and Florida

Reported are two separate accounts from different states on the same day, and they both happen to describe the same anatomic anomaly:

"A mound near Liverpool, Illinois., was recently opened and several skeletons of very large men were found. The skulls were so large that they would go over an ordinary man's head, covering it to the shoulders. There was also found a small steel anvil, perfect in form and so hard that a file made little impression on it. Also a set of false teeth, of copper and ivory, large enough for a giant and of excellent workmanship."

The second account reads as follows:

"Henry Gwaltney dug into a mound near Wakulla, Fla. recently and found a skull that must have belonged to a giant. The under jaw was particularly large, being twice the size of an ordinary man's and none of the teeth was missing from either jaw but one showed signs of decay."

Giant false teeth of copper and ivory, skulls so large they go over an

154

ordinary mans head, and a giant jawbone twice the normal size. These are certainly worthy of further investigation.

NINE FEET TALL
The Sunday Vindicator, Sep 12, 1897, pg.9
Connersville, Indiana

This one from Indiana is of a 9 ft skeleton. It is reported that *"the femur bone is a yard along."*

NINE FEET TALL

Was This Man Whose Skeleton Was Found in Indiana.

Connersville, Ind., Sept. 11.—While Sexton Charles Rieman was digging a grave in the city cemetery he came upon the skeleton of a monster man. It had been buried in a sitting posture with the face to the east, and was only about three feet below the surface. The remains indicated that the being of which this was once a part, was a veritable giant, probably nine feet in height. The femur bone is about a yard long, and the massive under jaw is much larger than that of an ordinary man. It is supposed that the bones are those of an Indian or Mound Builder.

REMARKABLE SKELETON
The Omaha Daily Bee, December 25, 1897, pg.6
Southeast Iowa

The article reports the opening of a burial mound in Southeastern Iowa in which many artifacts and a giant skeleton were found.

"One remarkable skeleton was dug up by myself and another man. It was that of a giant, being over seven feet six inches in height. An idea of the size of this man may be gained by the

length of his shin bone. I stood it on the ground at my heel and it reached about two inches above my knee joint, being twenty-five inches in length. The only part of the skeleton we were able to take away was the jawbone. Everyone who has seen it says it is the most massive jaw ever seen by them. It measures from the top of the front teeth to the lower edge of the jaw bone one and three quarter inches. Around the lower edge it measures six and a half inches across the jaw from the two tips is five and a half inches. It has a remarkably perfect set of teeth."

Dug Up A Skeleton Eight Feet Long
The Washington Post, December 4, 1898
Londonderry, Ohio

At four feet below a gravel bed an 8-footer with prominent features on the skull, was found holding some interesting artifacts:

"a dozen darts of the finest workmanship" were discovered. *"The skull was a third larger than an average human skull, and the lower jaw was abnormal in size and thickness."*

A Prehistoric Giant
Daily Public Ledger., September 27, 1894, pg.3
Diamond Lake, Cass County, Michigan

A controversial 11 ft giant skeleton was reported in Michigan 1n 1894:

"The bones of the skeleton are well preserved. The lower jaw is immense. Any ordinary jawbone fits inside with ease."

This was later expanded upon in *The Bruce Herald, Volume-XXX-Issue 3044, March 10, 1899* with further details about artifacts and other mounds opened. As Jim was checking the records for the Diamond Lake area, he found an 8-footer discovered in *The History of Lake County, 1902*:

"Samuel Miller, who has resided in the county since 1835, is

authority for the statement that one skeleton which he assisted in unearthing was a trifle more than eight feet in length, the skull being correspondingly large, while many other skeletons measured at least seven feet."

ANCIENT MYSTERY REVEALED - UNEARTHING OF A PREHISTORIC GIANT
Evening Times, September 8, 1899
Akron, Ohio

A 10 ft skeleton found in Akron, Ohio, that once again had a massive jawbone: *"the lower jawbone of such proportion as to easily fit over the outside of the jaw of the largest modern man."*

ANCIENT MYSTERY REVEALED.

Unearthing of a Prehistoric Giant Near Akron, Ohio.

AKRON, Ohio, Sept. 8.—A find of incalculable value to science has been made at a stone quarry three miles northwest of the city. The find consists of skeleton of a gigantic man, believed to have lived in prehistoric times, and relics of a time when civilization was just beginning to dawn. In clearing away refuse quarrymen found the almost complete skeleton of a man. The skull was entire and the lower jawbone of such proportion as to easily fit over the outside of the jaw of the largest modern man. Ribs were found and also fingers and the larger pelvis bone, which was broken in two.

It is believed the man must have been at least ten feet in height. In addition to the remains of the human being there were found deer antlers, bears' claws, many kinds of teeth, remains of foxes and several lower jawbones resembling those of a wolf. Pieces of very rude pottery were scattered about and a mortar and pestle were found.

FIERCE GIANT LIVED IN CUYAHOGA COUNTY
The Stark County Democrat, December 12, 1902
Cuyahoga County, Ohio

"Evidence has just been secured which positively shows that the Cuyahoga valley was once inhabited by a giant race of

157

people. E. B. Howe, station agent at Ira... has unearthed a rare collection of implements... The find consists of a portion of man who, when in life, was over eight feet tall. The jawbone is fully twice as large as an ordinary human being's jawbone. Near the skeleton was also found a stone ax weighing 14 pounds, rare copper beads and fine specimens of copper wedges and decorated pottery. Howe has in his possession 1,500 stone implements."

OLD PREHISTORIC GIANTS FOUND
Pittsburgh Press, September 13 and 14, 1932
Finleyville, Pennsylvania

This story was also picked up by *The New York Times* on September 14th. A highly detailed account is given of the find, including a map of where the dig site was with photos. We are told that the unearthing of prehistoric giants found near Finleyville has focused the interest of scientists the world over upon a wooded hillside near Pittsburgh.

Fisher examining huge ...... found in the rock-lined burial ......

158

Excavators led by State Archaeologist D. S. Fisher unearthed 49 skeletons from a burial site in Washington County, Pennsylvania. Archaeologists were amazed at the excellent condition of the teeth. The largest skeleton was a *"giant"* nearly 8 feet high. It measured 89 inches from feet to skull and measured 26 inches across the chest. In the article there is a photo of Fisher examining *"huge bones"* and also a photo of some of the teeth. One female skeleton was noted for having *"huge"* teeth, all the skeletons had *"massive jaws"* and *"strong"* teeth. State archaeologist Fisher remarked, *"never in all my finds have I seen strong, well preserved teeth such as these."* Fisher's men also had to protect the site as there were hundreds of onlookers.

Jim found an article about another of Dr. Fisher's finds a year later in *The Pittsburg Press,* September 7th, 1933:

> *"G.S. Fisher of Finleyville, state archaeologist and discoverer of many relics that have found their way to the Smithsonian Institution in Washington D.C. already has unearthed 13 skeletons."*

This story continued in *The Pittsburg Press* Oct 7, 1932 page 7, where we find the following reported one month after the initial find:

> *"The highly regarded Dr. Donald A. Cadzow is making the trip to the capital with all the skeletal remains from the dig, including a giant 7 feet 5 inches tall."*

Cadzow was a former Cambridge University and British Museum Ethnologist and Archaeologist. As stated in the previous news report, Fisher, the State Archaeologist had the bones at his workshop in Finleyville from the September dig. In fact every detail carries over correctly from story to story.

Gigantic Skulls

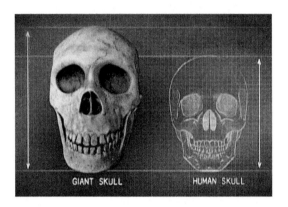

Jim and researcher Micah Ewers have come across references to 25 to 32 inch circumference skulls pulled out of mounds in the Ohio Valley. There is also a reference to a 40 inch circumference skull discovered in West Virginia (see page 183). This is twice the size of a normal human skull. The Smithsonian have also released accounts of skulls well beyond the normal scope of humans.

The 1873 Smithsonian Annual Report[3] discusses a skull from Anna, Union County, Illinois, said to have been of *"36 inches circumference"* that was discovered in a mound, and that *"parts of the skeletons found"* were *"very long."* Thirty six inches is enormous because a normal man's head is a hat size between seven and seven and a half, or 22 to 23 inches circumference, with flesh (or 20 to 21 inches without flesh). If such a giant's skull was in symmetric proportion to his body frame—as even the pathological giants in European medical studies conform to—then this skull may have pertained to someone between 9 and 12 feet high. (this account is also in *The Smithsonian Files* Chapter).

A Giant Exhumed
New Orleans Commercial Bulletin, May 7, 1852, pg.1
Shippingsport, Kentucky

In this early report that came about because of flooding between his two mills, Frank McHarra reported finding a giant skeleton that he estimated would have been upwards of 7 ft tall.

"The skull was of immense size, with unusual high cheek bones - a sure indication of the Indian race."

> A Giant Exhumed '—A day or two since Frank McHarra, found the remains of what is supposed to have been a gigantic Indian, near his mill at Shippingsport. The high water had caused the bank of the river to cave in, and while he was digging away a spot between the two mills, the bones were discovered. He had them carefully removed, and judging from the length of the thigh and leg bones, and other portions of the skeleton which were placed together, it must have been a man upwards of seven feet in heighth. The skull was of immense size, with unusual high cheek bones—a sure indication of the Indian race. An antique fashioned jug, made of earthenware, decorated with shells, was found alongside the bones. A year or two since, a quantity of human bones was found in the same vicinity, and it is supposed that a century or two since the spot was an Indian burial place.— *Louisville Courier, 24th ult.*

A Remarkable Skeleton Unearthed
The Public Ledger, August 25, 1870
Janesville, Wisconsin

"Several days ago, as some laborers were digging a foundation for a barn on the grounds of Mr. Stanley, in the town of Janesville, they unearthed a human skeleton of enormous size. It was found in a sitting posture, and is in a fair state of preservation. The skull measured thirty-two and a half inches in circumference, and the thigh bones forty-four and half inches in length. Dr. Townsend examined the remains shortly after they were exhumed and gave it as his opinion, that when living, the man must have been not less than thirteen feet in height. It was immediately sold for $10,000."

So if the story is true, who is shelling out $10,000 in 1870 dollars (equivalent to $180,000 today) for a 13 ft skeleton? This report raises another intriguing aspect of this phenomenon: How many giant skeletons and bizarre artifacts might have ended up in the hands of private collectors? They must have really wanted that skeleton, and we wonder, do they still have it?

GIANT HUMAN REMAINS FOUND
The New York Times, May 22, 1871
Kern County, California and Jeffersonville, Kentucky

Next to the Kern River a grave was dug that yielded a remarkable skeleton. The first part of this account described it as being 7 ft 5 inches tall with a cranium so large that *"a full-grown person placed his head inside the skull."* The Jeffersonville skeleton was said to be nearly 12 ft tall with a 3 ft thigh bone.

PRE-HISTORIC MOUND BUILDER IS SHOWN AS NINE-FOOT GIANT IN WOODEN MODEL
Randolph Register, September 21, 1938
Cattaraugus County, New York

At the Cattaraugus County Museum in New York exists evidence of an ancient race of giants of a different sort. The museum houses wooden replicas of two Mound Builders unearthed at the Cowan farm on Conewango Road in the county. Charles Huntington claims he was present when the skeletons were unearthed in 1876 and secured the exact measurements made by Dr. Franklin Larkin and Dr. T. Apoleon Cheney to be the basis for the wooden models. Mr. Huntington's replicas are of a 9-foot man and an over-7-foot female. Sharon Fellows of the museum sent us the images of the models, a newspaper account of the find from the *Randolph Register*, and contact information for the grandson of Mr. Huntington.

Jim spoke with Joanne Huntington, the wife of Charles Huntington's grandson. She told us Charles was an extremely bright and competent inventor who was driven by what he claims to have witnessed to create a memory of this incredible fact. The account from the *Randolph Register* states that the original bones crumbled to dust, but noted:

> *"One of the hunters, Jeff Darling told Mr. Huntington that the jaw bone was so large that when it was held to his face there was room for both his hands between his jaw and that of the skeleton."*

Once again this anatomic anomaly appears. We decided to read through

Pre-Historic Mound Builder is Shown As Nine-Foot Giant in Wooden Model

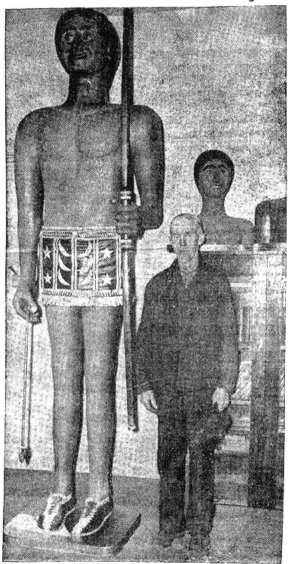

Charles Huntington of East Randolph poses here with the model of the giant pre-historic man which he has just completed. Since Mr. Huntington is of average height, the relative size of the mound builder is clearly shown. The model was built life-size, according to measurements taken by Mr. Huntington when a mound on the Conewango Road was opened 62 years ago.

Brought back from the obscurity of untold ages, a giant, nine-foot man has been modelled in wood by Charles Huntington of East Randolph.

This model is based upon an image which has been forming in Mr. Huntington's mind since the day, 62 years ago, when he witnessed the exhuming of the skeletons of pre-historic mound builders at the N. E. G. Cowan farm on the Conewango Road. Measurements which he secured at that time form the basis upon which the model was constructed.

Carefully cutting and shaping the wooden sections and continually checking them with measurements secured so many years ago, Mr. Huntington has painstakingly assembled the figure in such a way that it seems to be formed from one piece. The man has been clothed with a loin cloth and moccasins and armed with a huge bow and arrows tipped with genuine arrow heads.

The full length model was preceded by three bust-length models, two of them being reproductions based upon skeletons of a man and woman found at Moundsville, West Virginia, and the third based upon the skeletons found on the Cowan farm.

Cheney's Figures Quoted

When several of the persons who saw these earlier figures expressed disbelief that such large human beings had ever roamed the woods and fields of this vicinity, Mr. Huntington wrote to Albany for verification. He received a letter from C. A. Hartnagel, assistant state geologist, giving figures reported by T. Apoleon Cheney, a Randolph man, who was present at the time the mound was opened. Mr. Cheney's figures checked with those which Mr. Huntington had used. As an example of the remarkable size of the skeletons, the measurements of the os-femur, or bone between the ankle and knee, was 28 inches in length. The facial angle of 73 degrees and the high forehead would indicate a large degree of intelligence.

To provide a background for his pre-historic man, Mr. Huntington has laid out a group of paintings, several of which have been completed. One of the pictures depicts the mound on the Cowan farm as it was before it was opened.

Since Mr. Cowan had married one of his cousins and Mr. Huntington frequently visited them, he had often seen the mound in its original

(Continued on Page Three)

the *History of Cattaraugus County*,[4] knowing that these giant skeleton reports never happen in isolation. On page 13 we found this:

"A remarkable characteristic of these skeletons was their enormous proportions. The skull of one of these skeletons would fit loosely on my head; a rib bone would pass round me from spine to colon, a thigh bone reached from my knee to the upper part of the hip-bone; and the sub-maxillary would incase [sic] my jaw like an easy-fitting mask. The teeth were enormous especially the molars. An attempt was made to preserve portions of these remains, but by exposure to the atmosphere they crumbled to a fine powder. These people must have been at least 8 feet high, with other proportions corresponding."

The included newspaper article also says the following,

"Brought back from the obscurity of untold ages, a giant, nine-foot man has been modeled in wood by Charles Huntington of East Randolph. The model is based upon an image which has been forming in Mr. Huntington's mind since the day, 62 years ago, when he witnessed the exhuming of the skeletons of pre-historic mound builders at the N. E. G. Cowan farm on the Conewango Road. Measurements which he secured at that time form the basis upon which the model was constructed... When several of the persons who saw these earlier figures expressed disbelief that such large human beings had ever roamed the woods and fields of this vicinity, Mr. Huntington wrote to Albany for verification. He received a letter from C. A. Hartnagel, assistant state geologist, giving figures reported by T. Apoleon Cheney, a Randolph man, who was present at the time the mound was opened. Mr. Cheney's figures checked with those which Mr. Huntington had used. As an example of the remarkable size of the skeletons, the measurements of the os-femur [sic], or bone between the ankle and knee, was 28 inches in length. The facial angle of 73 degrees and the high forehead would indicate a large degree of intelligence."

164

A Giant Skull Found
The Omaha Daily Bee, May 25, 1882, pg.1
Red River Valley, Illinois

A giant skull is reported being found in the Red River Valley:

"The only deposit yet found of this extinct race in that region is a skull of immense proportions, a singular formation. It has been turned over to a historical society for examination. The skull is a perfect specimen and shows conclusive evidence of a race of giant natives."

A Giant Skull Found.

National Associated Press.

CHICAGO, May 24.—A St. Paul special reports a remarkable find of relics of mound builders in Red River valley. The only deposit yet found of this extinct race in that region is a skull of immense proportions a singular formation. It has been turned over to a historical society for examination. The skull is a perfect specimen, and shows conclusive evidence of a race of giant natives.

Must Have Been Goliath
The Providence Evening Press, September 13, 1883, pg.4
Barnard, Missouri

This report is a12-foot example from Missouri. We looked into the reality of this account and found that J.H. Haley was a real person and gave a speech near to this area in 1917.[5] However, whether he measured this skeleton correctly is unknown, as a 12-foot skeleton and a 40 inch circumference skull are both well beyond the normal range:

"Hon. J. H. Haley, a well known and reliable citizen of Barnard, Mo., wrote to the St. Joseph Gazette the particulars of the discovery of a giant skeleton four miles southwest of that place. A farmer named John W. Hanson found the bones protruding from the bank of a ravine that has been cut by the action of the rains during the past years. Mr. Hanson worked several days unearthing the skeleton, which proved to be that of a human being, whose height was twelve feet. The head through the temple was twelve inches; from the lower part of the skull at

the back was fifteen inches and the circumference forty inches. The ribs were nearly four feet long and one and three quarter inches wide. The thigh bones were thirty inches long and large in proportion. When the earth was removed the ribs stood up high enough to enable a man to crawl in and explore the interior of the skeleton, turn around and come out with ease. The first joint of the great toe, above the nail, was three inches long and the entire foot eighteen inches in length. The skeleton lay on its face twenty feet below the surface of the ground and the toes were imbedded in the earth, indicating that the body either fell or was placed when the ground was soft. Some of the bones crumbled on exposure to air but many good specimens were preserved and are now on exhibition at Barnard. Medical men are much interested. The skeleton is generally pronounced a valuable relic of the prehistoric race."

THE SKELETON OF A GIANT
The Oswego Times and Express, November 12, 1883, pg.1
Kingwood, West Virginia

"A human skull was unearthed here which measures 40 inches around the forehead. The skeleton is supposed to have been 14 feet high."

As we discussed in the previous account from Missouri, 40 inches around the forehead is is at least twice the girth of a normal human skull. 14 ft is also outrageously tall. However, the skeleton's height looks like it was just an estimate based on the size of the skull.

TEN TO FIFTEEN FEET TALL SKELETONS
History of Dearborn and Ohio Counties Indiana, 1885, pg.584
Whitewater, Ohio

"There is a large mound in Mr. Allen's field about twenty feet

high, sixty feet in diameter at the base, which contains a greater proportion of bones than any one I ever before examined, as almost every shovel full of dirt would contain several fragments of a human skeleton....We examined from fifteen to twenty. In some, whose height were from ten to fifteen feet, we could not find more than four or five skeletons....We found several skull, leg and thigh bones, which plainly indicate their possessors were men of gigantic stature. The skull of one skeleton was one-fourth of an inch thick; and the teeth were remarkably even, sound and handsome, all firmly planted. The fore teeth were very deep and not so wide as those of the generality of the white people. Indeed, there seemed a great degree of regularity in the form of the teeth in all the mounds."

The measurements of "ten to fifteen feet" are most likely an exaggeration, but we decided to include this story as it gives fascinating anatomic details.

BONES OF ANCIENT GIANT
The Branford Oregon Opinion, January 14, 1913
Ellensburg, Oregon

L. L. Sharp, the chief at the local land office considers the finding of a skeleton *"at least 8 feet high to be one of the most interesting anthropological finds in the Northwest."* Mr. Sharp also notes:

> *"The head is one of the most remarkable I have ever studied among prehistoric skulls. It is massive with enormous brain space."*

Bones of Ancient Giant

Amazing Discovery In Oregon Is of Great Interest to Anthropologists.

The discovery of the bones of a human giant at Ellensburg is one of the most interesting anthropological finds

other system of interment. I cannot think it possible that a human being of the advanced stage indicated by this great skull could have existed at the period when the shale was formed."—Portland (Ore.) Telegram.

The article goes on to give more detailed anatomical descriptions such as *"the forehead slopes down"*, *"the cheekbones are not high, like those of the Indian"* and it had a *"well rounded space at the back of the head."* Jim also uncovered an earlier version of this story from 1912.[6]

   A year earlier in the same area, 11 giant skeletons with double rows of teeth were reported (see next chapter).

GIGANTIC SKULL POSES PROBLEM
The Spokesman-Review, July 21, 1936, pg.10
San Bernardino, California

"Deputy Coroner E. P. Doyle asked scientific help today in identifying a mysterious human skull one and a half times the size of a modern man's. With other portions of a skeleton the skull was unearthed by a steam shovel operator here. It has a huge prognathus jaw, high cheek bones and jutting teeth in the upper jaw. The relics which included several vertebrae, a leg bone and three finger bones, were in a stratum of hard-packed rock eight feet underground."

BEACH GIANT'S SKULL UNEARTHED
BY WPA WORKERS NEAR VICTORIA
San Antonio Express, January 7, 1940, pg.68
Victoria County, Texas

In 1939 a skull was unearthed that was believed to be the largest skull in the world, as it was twice the size of a normal human cranium. Several large human bones were also unearthed at the site. Marcus S. Goldstein, the physical anthropologist in charge of the find was formerly an aide to Dr. Aleš Hrdlička of the Smithsonian.

"Twice the size of the skull of normal man, the fragments were dug up by W. Duffen, archaelogist, who is excavating the mound in Victoria County under a WPA project sponsored by the University of Texas. In the same mound at the same level, a normal sized skull was found. The pieces taken from the mound were reconstructed in the WPA laboratory under supervision of physical anthropologists."

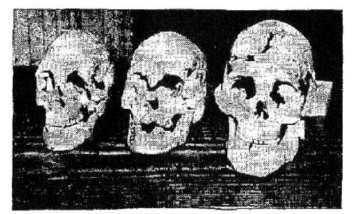

GIANT SKULL—Believed to be possibly the largest found in the world, the human skull shown on the right was recently unearthed in Victoria County by Texas University anthropologists. The other two are of normal size.

Goldstein wrote:

"A couple of unusual crania were unearthed at Morhiss Mound in Victoria County. One of these, although much mended and its base quite warped, is nevertheless obviously a skull of extraordinary size, in many respects larger than any yet reported. The possibility of abnormality, perhaps an endocrine disturbance, arose immediately, but the largeness of the skull seems to be symmetrical, the hand bones do not show the 'knobbing' typical of acromegaly, Moreover, other crania from the same site approximate the skull in question. Hence, it is my opinion that this exceptionally large skull was not the result of endocrine pathology." [7]

Horned Skulls

Perhaps the strangest anatomic anomaly reported are those skulls found with horns. Even today there are people alive who have strange protrusions from the forehead called *Cutaneous horns*.[8] There have been a small number of reports in America, but it is the one allegedly photographed at Sayre, Pennsylvania (see photo below) that we investigate first. Several newspapers reported on this controversial discovery. Here is one of the printed headlines:

FIND HORNED MEN'S SKULLS.

Remarkable Discovery by Archaeologists in Susquehanna Valley.

One version of the story is here in full from *The New York Times*:

SCIENTISTS UNEARTH RELICS OF INDIANS WHO LIVED 700 YEARS AGO
New York Times, July 14, 1916
Sayre, Pennsylvania

"Professor A. B. Skinner of the American Indian Museum, Prof. W. K. Morehead of the Phillips Andover Academy, and Dr. George Donohue, Pennsylvania State Historian, who have been conducting researches along the Susquehanna have uncovered an Indian Mound at Tioga Point, on the upper portion of Queen Eathers Flats, on what is known as the Murray farm, a short distance from Sayre Penn., which promises rich additions to Indian lore. In the mound uncovered were found

Horned skull linked with Sayre story.

170

the bones of sixty-eight men which are believed to have been buried 700 years ago. The average height of these men was seven feet, while many were much taller. Further evidence of their gigantic size was found in large celts or axes hewed from stone and buried in the grave. On some of the skulls two inches above the perfectly formed forehead, were protuberances of bone. Members of the expedition say that it is the first discovery of its kind on record and a valuable contribution to the history of the early races. The skull and a few of the bones found in one grave were sent to the American Indian Museum."

However, there is some intrigue to explore first, as there is no mention of a 'horned skull' in any of the archaeological reports from any of the three excavators. These are only in the newspaper reports. Professor A.B. Skinner, who was one of the archaeologists conducting the dig, quickly wrote an editorial to *The New York Times* explaining that not only were all the skeletons of normal size but that there were deer antlers buried at the heads of the skeletons. Someone in the crowd yelled that they have horns (below is corroboration of his exclamation in a later book).[9]

MURRAY]   *ABORIGINAL SITES IN AND NEAR "TEAOGA"*   205

in ingenious fashion by its owner. It was not three-fourths of a yard long like those Captain Smith admired which were evidently effigy pipes, as he said, "They had a bird or deere or some such device at the great end, sufficient to beat out one's brains." While the writer was present one of the men in working a grave exclaimed, "There are horns over his head!" Mr. Skinner said that indicated chieftainship. Later this was found to be a bundle burial, completely covered with antlers of Virginia deer. A passing visitor, however, heard the exclamation and attempted to verify it by interrogating a fun-loving Maine workman, and the story grew and was printed from coast to coast that one or more skulls had been found with horns growing from the forehead!

Not that we thought Satan and his minions were buried in a Pennsylvania mound, but this is a cautionary tale not to believe everything that is written.

Somewhere along the line, however, a controversial photo emerged of a horned human skull. Its origins were for a long time a mystery, but over the years has become *attached* to this Sayre story, mainly thanks to the internet. We asked researcher Micah Ewers to investigate where the image came from and he eventually found that the skull was acquired in 1959 by the *Surnateum: Museum of Supernatural History*. Here are the details of the specimen:

Inv. SDD/pe-92464

Exorcist's basket and horned human skull. Acquired by the Surnateum in 1959. Origin: France (1920-1940).

It was looked at in detail by their experts who tantalisingly concluded:

"Although we thought that the object had been cleverly manufactured, an analysis has demonstrated that the horns are genuinely part of the skull. An in-depth examination and X-rays leave no room for doubt: the skull is not a forgery." [10]

We follwed up by writing to the curator of the museum who contradicted what was written on the website. He said:

"The horned skull is a skull made for a cult to Pan during the XVIIth century (Painswick). It's perfectly made, but I don't believe in the existence of horned humans, so it's certainly a fake (but a real cult object)." [11]

Whether this skull is genuine or not remains to be seen, but it certainly has no connection to the Sayre story.

THREE GIANT SKELETONS
The Hocking Sentinel, April 28, 1898
Toledo, Ohio

Here is another news account that describes short horns on skulls:

"Workmen in the employ of the Ferguson Construction Company excavating for the Toledo and Ottawa Beach Railroad, a little beyond the city limits of Toledo, Ohio, unearthed three skeletons, evidently relics of some great race, as they were about seven feet in length. Just where the ears should be on the head are singular bony protruberances which curl forward. The finds were made in solid yellow clay about eight feet below the

surface. The cut is through a large mound, not half of which has yet been torn up. Several stone tomahawks of large size have been picked up in the locality."

GIANT BONES UNEARTHED: HORNS ON THE SKULL
Minnesota News, December 6, 1905
Sulphur Springs, Indiana

In this fascinating account Alonzo Lewis discovered a giant that had horns coming out from above the ears; one of many found on his property. Here is the full printed account:

GIANT'S BONES UNEARTHED

Horns on the Skull of Skeleton Found in Indiana.

Journal Special Service.

Knightstown, Ind., Dec. 5.—Bones of a primitive giant have been unearthed by Alonzo Lewis, a farmer living near Sulphur Springs. The skeleton is more than seven feet in length and the skull has horns about an inch and a half long, projecting upward from a point just behind the ears. Several similar skeletons have been found here in the past few weeks. All the peculiar bones were found in a gravel pit on the Lewis farm.

Although these might well be hoaxes, numerous other reports of horned skulls have been found throughout America, but not from skeletons of a giant stature. For instance, at Silver Lake in Oregon in 1903, a skull was found buried in the lake's beach.[12] From 1910 to 1911 around 44 skeletons were unearthed in Tapango Canyon, California, *"each has a horn-like development three inches long."*[13] Finally, some 4 feet tall, powerfully built *"pygmie"* skeletons with *"long tails"* were found in a cave on Repmans Hill in Virginia by two boys. These had horns protruding above the temples on the skull.[14]

We will let the reader make of these reports what they will, but the elimination of corrupted stories such as the Sayre example helps clear the way for accounts that might have some basis in truth.

CRANIAL DEFORMATION

Altering the shape of skulls is a practice that has been around for over 4,000 years, most notably in Peru. However, it is also prevalent in Africa, Micronesia, ancient Egypt, and Central America. In North America it was a popular practice of the Chinookan tribes of the Northwest and the Choctaw of the Southeast. The infamous *Flathead Indians*, strangely, did not practice cranial deformation, but were given this name in contrast to other Salishan people who used skull enhancement to make the head appear rounder. Other tribes, however, including the Choctaw, Chehalis, and Nooksack Indians, did practice head flattening by strapping the infant's head to a cradleboard. The results are remarkably similar to thousands of skulls discovered in Peru. Interestingly, many of the South American examples have red hair and powerful jaws, like some of their North American counterparts. These examples below show a *Flathead* skull (top), and two images of *Chinook* Skulls with extreme deformation (bottom).

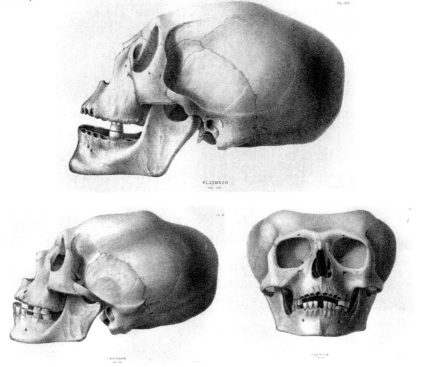

Chickasawba Mound, Arkansas
1877 - 1976

From 1873 Frank Lowber James prepared a large map of 35 townships in Mississippi County, Arkansas, that led to an interest in the ancient mounds. His first noted find was in 1875 and was recorded in the Smithsonian accession records. In November of 1877, James wrote to Joseph Henry, the first secretary of the Smithsonian Institution requesting funds to open the mounds in the area:

"It is the so-called Great Chickasawba mound, where for 10 acres, a spade can scarcely be thrust without turning up human remains, and those too of a most interesting and valuable character. Not only are these scattered bones in great quantity, but entire skeletons of gigantic size are frequently found. I have seen several over 7ft, 6in, in height. In these cases the vases or urns buried with them are large in proportion. Many of the crania found there show signs of artificial flattening, some of them being pointed." [15]

In 1901, Curtis L. Little gained permission to excavate the site further:

"The skeletons are very large and tall. One femur bone was unearthed that measured 29 inches in length. The skulls are extremely large, the jaw of one is such size that it would slip over my own and have considerable space to spare, being able to insert my first 3 fingers under the cheek bones. The skulls slope back considerably and the frontal bones are very flat." [16]

A 29-inch femur suggests a skeleton over 8 ft tall, much taller than the previous descriptions. Soon after this impressive discovery the area became 'open season' and most of the site was destroyed. In 1976 a 7 ft skeleton was unearthed whilst digging the basement for a house nearby. [17]

THE MUMMY OF A CLIFF DWELLER FOUND
The New York Times, March 8, 1896
Prescott, Arizona

This account was sent to Jim by researcher Gary David, who has written extensively about the accomplishments of Native civilizations in the American Southwest. The photo is of Montezuma Castle National Monument, located near Camp Verde, Arizona which features well-preserved cliff-dwellings.

Old photo of Montezumas Castle.

They were built and used by the pre-Columbian Sinagua people, northern cousins of the Hohokam around 700 AD. The structure is five stories high and took about five centuries to complete. It was occupied from approximately 1100-1425 AD, and occupation peaked around 1300 AD. However, they also had unusual burial practices and strange skulls:

> *"The mummy of one of the ancient cliff dwellers of Arizona, the first of undoubted authenticity ever discovered, has been found by a hunter well known in Northern Arizona, John McCarty...*
> *The body is that of a male and is of unusually great stature...*
> *In the skull, however, lies the element of greatest interest. The formation is entirely different from that typical of the ancient*

dwellers in the valleys of Arizona. The valley dwellers were Toltecs of almost Caucasian cranial features. The skull of the mummy, with forehead retreating from the nose and large rear development, is of the Aztec type. The teeth are entire and well preserved and protrude as in the same canine tribe. As the mummy showed signs of disintegration, McCarty has given it a coat of varnish, preparatory to placing it in an air-tight glass-covered box."

HUGE JAWBONE AND CRANIAL DEFORMATION
The History of Cape May, by Lewis T. Stevens, 1897, pg.11
Cape May, New Jersey

"A skull was exhumed which must have belonged to one of great age, as the sutures were entirely obliterated and the tables firmly cemented together. From the superciliary ridges, which were well developed, the frontal bone receded almost on a direct line to the place of the occipital and parietal sutures, leaving no forehead and has the appearance of having been done by artificial means, as practiced at present on the Columbia among the Flat Heads. A jaw-bone of huge dimensions was likewise found, which was coveted by the observer; but the superstitions of the owner of the soil believing it was sacrilegious and that he would be visited by the just indignation of Heaven if he suffered any of the teeth to be removed, prevailed on us to return again to its mother earth."

Drat, that fellow should have risked going to hell and saved the jawbone. But not just the jaw, as this skull shows clear signs of cranial deformation.

The St. Johns Herald, January 6, 1900
Apache Country, Arizona

"At a depth of 20 feet, large slabs of stone were encountered; there were three of them. When thee slabs were removed, three

177

cemented vaults contained three mummified skeletons. Two of the skeletons are 7 ½ feet long and one 8 ½ feet long. She brought with her the head and the neck of the largest skeleton. The head is very large; the jawbone will fit on the outside of the jaw of a living man with a large head; the teeth are massive and over an inch in length; the forehead is low; ears and mouth very large; top of the head runs up to a peak. One of the giants had two flint arrowheads buried in his skull. The teeth of the head brought away, contained pieces of dried flesh, which pronounced to be that of a human being, showing that the giants were cannibals."

This also again points to the ancient enemy of Native Americans, an enemy frequently described in the oral traditions of many tribes (see *Legends of the Tall Ones* chapter for more examples).

Snake priests out at sunrise to hunt for ceremonial snakes on first day of
Snake Dance Ceremony at the pueblo of Oraibi, Arizona,1898

GIANT SKELETONS IN THE GRAVEL PIT
The Daily Press, August 3, 1905
Dayton, Ohio

The sub-headings stated: "*Had great length of arms,*" and "*Skull long and narrow, indicating cranial deformity.*" This is a good example of classic cranial enhancement, but as for the arms, that's just weird:

"...several giant skeletons having been unearthed...the skeleton being remarkable for the great length of the arms... Attorney T. B. Herman, Republican candidate for city solicitor, was present when the find was made. He was with [Warren K.] Moorhead when the latter opened the mounds in Ohio and later claimed that the skeleton in Edgar's pit in no way compares with those of the mound builders. The skeleton is believed to be that of an Indian or other aborigine further removed in the scale of mankind. The skull was long and narrow and indicating a decided cranial deformity."

GIANT SKELETONS IN THE GRAVEL PIT

Dry Bones of Man of Abnormal Size Unearthed by Workman Near Dayton.

HAD GREAT LENGTH OF ARMS

Had Probably Been in Earth for Centuries as Bones Crumbled When Air Struck Them—Skull Long and Narrow, Indicating Cranial Deformity—Not Mound Builder.

SKELETON OF A GIANT FULLY EIGHT FEET TALL
El Paso Herald, April 19, 1915
Silver City, New Mexico

A report of the unearthing of a giant skeleton from New Mexico with cranial deformities is given:

"A peculiarity of the forehead is that it recedes from the eyes like that of an ape. The similarity is still further found in the sharp bones under the eyes. The skeleton was found encased in baked mud, indicating that encasing the corpse in mud and baking them was the mode of embalming."

It also points out that the cliff dwellers lived in the same area as giants. Were these cliff dwellings built to keep them safe from these invading titans?

"It is rather peculiar that less than 30 miles from where this skeleton was found and located on the Gile river are the former houses of a tribe of small cliff dwellers. The existence of these two races so near together form an interesting topic."

179

FINDS SKELETON OF ANCIENT MAYA INDIAN
The Chester Times, November 2, 1925, pg.3
St. Joseph, Missouri

A skeleton unearthed in Missouri is thought to be Maya because of the curious skull:

> *"A skeleton, seven feet two inches long, believed to be that of a member of the ancient Maya people, has been found beneath a creek bed near Fairfax, Mo., Frank Plumb, student of Anthropology, announced yesterday. The low, slanting skull, Mr. Plumb said indicated Maya origin, as it was the practice of this people to flatten the foreheads of their infants."*

A more detailed account is found in *The Miami News* page 30 on the same day, describing another elongated skull that was unearthed:

> *"Anslem Schumacher of Maryville, archeologist, discoverer of Indian graves and relics, who went to view Mr. Plumb's discoveries, also found a skull similar to that found by Mr. Plumb."*

EXPEDITION STARTS TO BRING SKELETON FROM CAPE FLORIDA
Florida-Miami News, June 9, 1936
Cape Sable, Florida

This account describes the unearthing of an 8 ft tall skeleton. The skull was identified by Karl Squires as being three quarters of an inch thick; twice the thickness of a normal skull. Some other anomalies were noted:

> *"The peculiar shape of the bones brought immediate attention and the remainder of the skeleton was unearthed. Eyes and ears of the early Floridian were set unusually high in the head which had a protruding chin and a receding forehead."*

In the next chapter we will look at the most strange and controversial anomaly reported—double rows of teeth.

Above: Elongated skull found at Puma Punku in Bolivia.
Middle: Selection of deformed skulls from the highlands of Peru.
Bottom: Olmec skull on display at Xalapa Museum, Mexico.

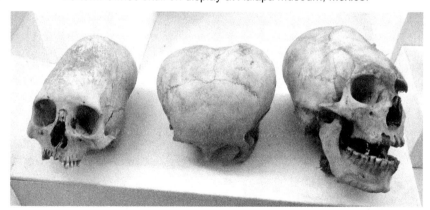

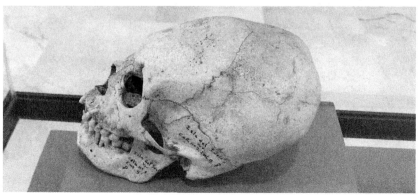

Painting by Paul Kane, 1848, showing a Chinookan child in the process
of having its head flattened, being held by an adult who has already
been through the process.

7

DOUBLE ROWS OF TEETH

"...in the time of Hadrian the Emperor (76 AD-138 AD), there was raised from the earth, in a place called Messana (Carthage), the body of the giant called Ida, who was twenty feet in length and who had double sets of teeth or two rows of teeth still standing completely preserved in his head or in his gums." [1]

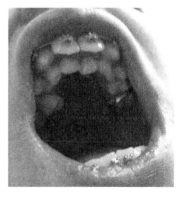

One of the strangest anatomic anomalies we find widely reported is *double rows of teeth* (DRTs). Huge jaws and perfect teeth—often found with no decay—are reported in dozens of accounts, suggesting they either had good dentists or it was a genetic trait. But it's the supernumerary teeth that appear in a much higher frequency than normal. In this chapter, we will look at several reports of double rows of teeth, supernumerary teeth (extra single teeth) and even one report of a third set.

Hyperdontia is a medical condition that is an infrequent developmental anomaly that can appear in any area of the dental arch and can affect any dental organ.[2] Adults have 28 teeth that can increase up to 32 to include the 'wisdom teeth' (third molars). As we'll see in these accounts, this number was sometimes much higher when a greater height was involved, but even today there is no clear reason why they occur. Hugh met up with a dental anthropologist to analyse these accounts, who was so blown away by these reports that she described it as being as rare as "*a race of three armed people.*"

In *The Natural History of the Human Teeth* (1803) Joseph Cox describes an interesting abnormality that may give a clue to why this phenomenon occurs:

> "*The lateral incisors grew in line even with supernumerary teeth, behind the central incisors and cuspidati, and so formed a second row. This was the most conspicuous deformity of the teeth I ever saw, for the mouth could not be opened to speak without completely presenting them to view.*"[3]

He goes on to describe another variant where extra teeth had "*pushed*" through that "*produced an appearance of a double-row*".

Harold T. Wilkins, in his book *Secret Cities of Old South America* (1952) also describes this phenomenon. First he speaks of a skull found in California, "*an amazing human skull of giant size with a double row of teeth*" (which is probably the Lompock Rancho case we examine in this chapter), but then he writes the following: "*A truly amazing corroboration of the dentition of these antediluvian giants of Ancient America is found in the Hulin section of the Berakthoth, of Babylonian Talmud, were it said the Giants, before the Great Deluge, had numerous rows of teeth. The Old compilers of the Hulin can hardly be said to have heard of this California find!*"[4] It looks like Wilkins must have got his information from the *Jewish Encyclopedia*, 1906, where it says: "*Some of these giants had feet 18 ells in length,*[5] *and the same length is given for the thigh-bone.*[6] *Numerous rows of teeth are also ascribed to them.*"[7]

We decided to look in more detail at this old Babylonian Talmud, which is a huge voluminous work written in the Chaldaic language about two thousand years ago, that does mention this phenomenon along with giants before the great deluge. For example: "*Who hath ever laid open the front of his garment? or who can penetrate into his double row of teeth.*"[8] It goes on to talk about Og, King of Bashan, who was a known giant: "*...his teeth bent themselves upon one side and upon the other*", suggesting his teeth jutted out like fangs or tusks. Another unusual description may also be referencing double rows of teeth: "*Thy teeth are like a flock of* *well-selected sheep, which are come up from washing, all of which bear twins....and none is barren among them."*[9] In the Benson *Commentary of the Bible* it discusses this passage explaining that the mention of twins *"...seems to denote the two rows of teeth: and none is barren among them — Not one tooth is lacking."*[10] The jury is out if this does mean double rows of teeth, but it at least may indicate the connection

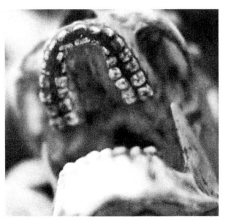

Reconstruction of set of double teeth in a giant skull.

between giant people in biblical times and the supernumerary peculiarity.

Please take a look at these accounts and make up your own mind, as these clearly show a mystery of the giants that is yet to be solved. Then we'll delve into the arguments for and against DRT connection to giants and get the view of a dental anthropologist from New York University.

Indian Graves in Concord, N.H.
Concord, New Hampshire, 1856

An early report from New England states: *"The skull is very thick, the teeth in both jaws are entire, and all of them double"*(see also page 135).

The Cardiff Giant Outdone:
Alleged Discovery of a Giant in The Oil Regions
Oil City Times, January 6, 1870
West Hickory, Pennsylvania

This report originally came from the *Oil City Times* in 1870 and underneath the immense armor, it revealed some startling anatomic oddities:

> *"They exhumed an enormous helmet of iron, which was corroded with rust. Further digging brought to light a sword which measured nine feet in length."*

185

The report continued that they had discovered:

"...a well-preserved skeleton of an enormous giant.... The bones of the skeleton are remarkably white. The teeth are all in their places, and all of them are double, and of extraordinary size."

The Cardiff Giant Outdone—Alleged Discovery of the Skeleton of a Giant in the Oil Regions.

The Oil City *Times* of Friday is responsible for the following:

On Tuesday morning last, while Mr. Wm. Thompson, assisted by Robert R. Smith, was engaged in making an excavation near the house of the former, about half a mile north of West Hickory, preparatory to erecting a derrick, they exhumed an enormous helmet of iron, which was corroded with rust. Further digging brought to light a sword which measured nine feet in length. Curiosity incited them to enlarge the hole, and after some little time they discovered the bones of two enormous feet. Following up the "lead" they had so unexpectedly struck, in a few hours' time they had unearthed a well-preserved skeleton of an enormous giant, belonging to a species of the human family which probably inhabited this and other parts of the world at that time of which the Bible speaks, when it says: "And there were giants in those days." The helmet is said to be of the shape of those found among the ruins of Nineveh. The bones of the skeleton are remarkably white. The teeth are all in their places, and all of them are double, and of extraordinary size. These relics have been taken to Tionesta, where they are visited by large numbers of people daily. When his giantship was in the flesh he must have stood eighteen feet in his stockings. These remarkable relics will be forwarded to New York early next week. The joints of the skeleton are now being glued together. These remains were found about twelve feet below the surface of a mound which had been thrown up probably centuries ago, and which was not more than three feet above the level of the ground around it. Here is another nut for antiquarians to crack.

This is the tallest skeleton we have in this book! It was estimated to be 18 feet tall, and the bones were being prepared to be sent to New York. Clearly, however, this could be an exaggeration, as 18 ft is unheard of in the historical record. Interestingly the discovery was reported to be buried 12 feet below a mound, so it could suggest a deep antiquity, however tall he was.

THE REMANS OF A GIGANTIC RACE
The Ohio Democrat (Logon, Ohio), June 10, 1893
Vasa, Minnesota

Twenty-three-years later a report from Vasa, Minnesota revealed another report of double rows of teeth:

"The remains of a gigantic race of extinct human beings have been discovered near Vasa, Minn. Each had double teeth in front as well as in the back part of the jaw."

THE ABORIGINES OF MINNESOTA
By JV. Brower, AJ. Hill and TH. Lewis. pp.215-216, 1906-1911
Delano, Minnesota, 1878

In *The Aborigines of Minnesota* it states that while digging Howard Lake mounds, some decayed bones were discovered:

"According to the Delano Eagle, June 13th 1878, one of the mounds on the south side of Twelve-Mile creek, about three miles from Delano, was explored by a party of young gentlemen. At the depth of five feet they found two human skeletons, the size of which indicated sons of Amalek. The bones were in the last stages of decay. One thigh-bone measured 20 inches in length and was proportionately large. The teeth were still sound, and double all round, though not of large size, but worn flat from long use".

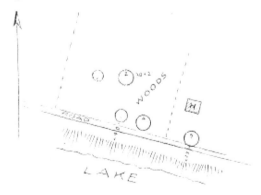

Early map of the Howard Lake mounds.

Further skeletal discoveries were made nearby:

"The lower jaw-bones were large, the teeth, so far as found, all double, the brow considerably receding backward."

187

TAKEN FROM MOUNDS
ON STARVATION POINT.
1867.

Skulls and bones from a nearby mound in Minnesota showing
receding foreheads and powerful jaws, 1867

DOUBLE ALL THE WAY AROUND
History of Medina County, 1881
Medina County, Ohio

Nine human skeletons were found when Albert Harris was digging the foundations of his house. In describing the tomb he said:

> *"It looked as if the bodies had been dumped into a ditch. Some were buried deeper than others,, the lower one being about seven feet below the surface. When the skeletons were found, Mr. Harris was twenty years of age, yet he states that he could put one of the skulls over his head, and let it rest upon his shoulders, while wearing a fur cap at the same time. The large size of all the bones was remarked, and the teeth were described as 'double all the way around.'"*

SKELETON OF A VERY LARGE PERSON, ALL DOUBLE TEETH
Ironton Register, May 5, 1892
Proctorville, Ohio

This tantalising report not only mentions a giant skeleton, but suggests an ancient, sophisticated settlement once existed in the area:

188

"Where Proctorville now stands was one day part of a well paved city, but I think the greater part of it is now in the Ohio River. Only a few mounds, there; one of which was near the C. Wilgus mansion and contained a skeleton of a very large person, all double teeth, and sound, in a jaw bone that would go over the jaw with the flesh on, of a large man; the common burying ground was well filled with skeletons at a depth of about 6 feet. Part of the pavement was of boulder stone and part of well preserved brick."

OFFICIAL SMITHSONIAN REPORT
Annual Report of the Smithsonian Institution, 1875, pg.392
Amelia Island, Florida

This Smithsonian report also describes double rows of teeth, well-preserved canines, and even evidence in one account, of triple-rows of teeth. This was far away from the mound cultures of the north. In early 1875, Augustus Mitchell, M.D., of Saint Mans, Georgia, was collecting specimens for ornithology in Florida to escape the cold winter. He excavated a mound on the southern end of Amelia Island, that was 15 feet high and about 30 feet in diameter. On one of the skulls he discovered he carefully examined the teeth and made some fascinating comments:

"A bi-section of some of these teeth showed the dental nerve to be protected by an unusual thickness on the surface of the crown. Not one carious (decayed) tooth was found among the hundreds in the mound.... In some the second set was observed; while one jaw had evident signs of a third set."

Further in the report, but slightly off-topic, was his amazement of another find:

"I came upon the largest-sized stone ax I have ever seen or that had ever been found in that section of the country."

Directly next to it was a well-preserved cranium, but it unfortunately turned to dust within two hours of him piecing the skeleton together.

However, he confirmed the size of the skeleton:

"According to the measurement of the bones of this skeleton, its height must have been quite 7 feet."

RELICS OF PAST AGES
Clinton Mirror, April 28, 1900, pg.7
Eagle City, Ohio

A giant skeleton was unearthed from a mound on the banks of the Iowa River, near Eagle City, that was once displayed in a shop window in Eldora:

RELICS OF PAST AGES.

Iowans Interest Scientists by Their Discovery of a Skeleton on the Iowa River Banks.

"The skull is very large and thick, full a quarter of an inch. A set of almost round double teeth are remarkably well preserved. They are yellow with age, are perfect in shape and appear to have been double, both above and below."

Dr. Morse's only explanation of its true height was this: *"The femurs are very long, showing a giant in stature."* He also emphasised:

"Dr N.C. Morse, a prominent physician, who examined the skeleton, pronounced it that of a person who had evidently been trained for athletics, as the extremities were so well developed."

HUGE SKELETONS
Historical Collections of Ohio, Vol. 2, 1908. pg.350
Noble County, Ohio, 1872

This matter-of-fact historical account of a skeleton *"at least eight feet in height"* describes *"double teeth in front as well as in back of mouth and in both upper and lower jaws."*

Huge Skeletons.—In Seneca township was opened, in 1872, one of the numerous Indian mounds that abound in the neighborhood. This particular one was locally

NOBLE COUNTY.   351

known as the " Bates" mound. Upon being dug into it was found to contain a few broken pieces of earthenware, a lot of flint-heads and one or two stone implements and the remains of three skeletons, whose size would indicate they measured in life at least eight feet in height. The remarkable feature of these remains was they had double teeth in front as well as in back of mouth and in both upper and lower jaws. Upon exposure to the atmosphere the skeletons soon crumbled back to mother earth.

A HISTORY OF MORROW COUNTY
Volume 1, 1911, pg.14
Morrow County, Ohio

In this account, an intriguing comment caught our attention:

"During the centuries of Indian domination in this country, the ancient earthworks were left undisturbed. The Indians had no knowledge of a preceeding race, and they were not vexed by inquiring science as to the nature or origins of the mounds."

Although no DRTs are mentioned, the account recalls 'extra' teeth:

"In 1829, when the hotel was built in Chesterville, a mound nearby was made to furnish the material for the brick. In digging it away, a large human skeleton was found, but no measurements were made. It is related that the jaw-bone was found to fit easily over that of a citizen of the village, who was remarkable for his large jaw. The local physicians examined the cranium and found it proportionately large, with more teeth than the white race of today."

RACE OF MEN WERE GIANTS
The Cambridge Sentinel, Volume IX, Number 40, July 20, 1912
Craigshill, Ellensberg, Washington

This report appeared in *The Cambridge Sentinel* in July 1912.[11] It describes the unearthing of 11 giant skeletons from a cement rock formation over which was a layer of shale. As well as stating one of the jaws had *"two rows of teeth in the front upper jaw"*, it also describes the jawbones as *"so large they will go around the face of the man of today."* We also see a description of an elongated

RACE OF MEN WERE GIANTS

Bones Recently Found Show Gigantic Stature and a Low Order of Intelligence.

Eleven skeletons of primitive men, with foreheads sloping directly back from the eyes, and with two rows of teeth in the front upper jaw, have been uncovered in Craigshill at Ellensburg, Wash. They were found about twenty feet below the surface.

skull: *"The sloping skull shows an extremely low order of intelligence, far earlier than that of the Indians known to the whites."*

The report also states that *"The femur is twenty inches long, indicating, scientists say, a man eighty inches tall"* (nearly 7 feet). It emphasised that J. P. Munson was a professor of biology who lectured before the International Biology College in Austria the previous year.

BAPTIST CHURCH - NEWTON CORNER
The History of Middlesex County, Ma. Volume 2, 1880, pg.243
Newton, Massachusetts

Baptist Church, Newton Corner. — Public worship was first held by several members of Baptist churches residing in Newton Corner, in the village hall, in the spring of 1859. The church was organized June 7, 1860, with twenty-one members. The church edifice was built on the corner of Washington and Hovey streets, in 1864. Five Indian skeletons and several ancient copper coins were turned up by the laborers in digging the cellar for the building. The remains were found in different parts of the ground, about two feet below the surface. This spot was probably once the seat of an

Indian settlement, and here they buried their dead. The jaw of one, which was in perfect preservation, with the full number of teeth, and double all round, was placed in the box which was sealed and deposited under the corner-stone. The coins, it is said, are believed to have been made during the reign of George I., bearing the date of 1720 or 1729. There were also two or three arrow-heads.

"Five Indian skeletons and several ancient copper coins were turned up by the laborers in digging the cellar for the building. The spot was probably once the seat of an Indian settlement and here they buried their dead. The jaw of one, which was in perfect preservation, with the full number of teeth, and double all round, was placed in the box, which was sealed and deposited under the corner stone."

We investigated this account as part of the *Search for the Lost Giants* TV show, but came to a dead end due to the fact that the church has been demolished and is now the site of a car dealership, so getting to that box is now impossible.

A HISTORY OF DEERFIELD, MASSACHUSETTS
By George Sheldon, Volume 1. 1895, pg.78
Deerfield, Massachusetts

This 8-footer is covered in detail in the *Giants of New England* chapter:

> *"...monstrous size—the head as big as a peck basket, with double teeth all round."*

A HISTORY OF JEFFERSON COUNTY
by Franklin B.Hough. 1854, pg.12
Rodman, Jefferson County, New York

Two reports on consecutive pages give accounts of large skulls with double rows of teeth. On the farm of Jacob Heath, near Rodman in Jefferson County, the local history book stated:

> *"Under the roots of a large maple tree was dug up the bones of a man of great stature, and furnished with entire rows of double teeth."*

A HISTORY OF JEFFERSON COUNTY
by Franklin B.Hough. 1854, pg.13
Watertown, Jefferson County, New York

This account gives details of a great battle that must have taken place, because the skeletons were found scattered in ditches defending an oval enclosure:

> *"Among these bones were those of a man of colossal size, and like nine-tenths of the others, furnished with a row of double teeth in each jaw."*

It also noted that the site could be very ancient:

"There is said to have been found at this place by excavating, hearths, or fire places, with bones of animals, broken pottery, and impliments of stone, at two different levels, separated by an accumulation of earth and vegetable mould from one to two feet thick, as if the place had been twice occupied. So great has been the length of time since these bones have been covered, that they fall to pieces very soon after being exposed to the air."

FULL SET OF DOUBLE TEETH
Onondaga, By Joshua Victor Hopkins Clark- 1849. pg.83
Syracuse, New York, 1819

In this diary of Victor Hopkins Clark, he discusses how the town of Syracuse was built over the Salt Springs Reservation, when the land was divided up in 1794. A feud ensued with a neighboring tribe and the superbly named '*Handsome Harry*' was the last native to fall. "*He was counted the handsomest man in the nation*" they said.

"Several skeletons were found...one of extraordinary size...The skull was comparitively large, and the jaws were surrounded with a full set of double teeth, all around. They were perfectly sound, covered with a beautiful enamel of the most perfect whiteness."

SYRACUSE—JOSHUA FORMAN.   83

Near the west bank of the creek, was an extensive Indian burying-ground, where skeletons have frequently been disinterred, and are occasiouly to this day—two having been exhumed during the past year. At the time the west locks were constructed at Syracuse, in 1819, over one hundred were taken up. In excavating the canal for the red mill, on the east bank of the creek, several skeletons were found. In 1843, one of extraordinary size was disinterred ; one of the lower bones of the leg being set beside the limb of a tall man, reached far above his knee. The skull was comparitively large, and the jaws were surrounded with a full set of double teeth, all around. They were perfectly sound, covered with a beautiful enamel of the most perfect whiteness. Such occurrences are not uncommon, at the several Indian burying grounds throughout the county.

194

A Giant Unearthed at Bowling Green, Measures Nine Feet in Length
The Daily Leger, Noblesville, August 16, 1902
Noblesville, Indiana

This report reveals more double rows of teeth. It reads:

"The skull measures almost 12 inches in diameter, and there are two distinct rows of teeth in the massive jaw....The bones were at first thought to be the remains of some giant Indian, but the shape of the head is not, the shape of the skull peculiar to Indians."

There is something else here rather strange too:

"The bones of the toes and fingers are remarkably well preserved and appear to have something resembling claws attached."

It is now clear why the discoverer *"...who, terrified at his find, ran, breathless, to the nearest farmhouse and notified the neighborhood."*

Double Both Front and Back
Logansport Pharos Tribune, June 19, 1912
Lake Cicott, Indiana

Charles Milton discovered a skeleton whilst digging sand around Lake Cicott. It was thought to be an area inhabited by Indians. The account states:

"The jaw bone is almost twice as large as that of the ordinary person. One peculiarity about the jaw is the fact that the teeth are double both front and back."

12-Foot Giant in California
The Native Races of the Pacific states of North America, By Hubert Howe, 1875
Lompock Rancho, California, 1819 (and/or 1833)

Hugh investigated this famous report back in November 2008, by visiting the area of the actual ranch it was discovered on.

195

"In 1819 an old lady saw a gigantic skeleton dug up by soldiers at Purisima on the Lompock Rancho. The natives deemed it a god, and it was reburied by direction of the padre." [12]

This short report re-emerged with a broader range of details in 1833 and now various authors and websites repeat the same story. It goes something like this:

Soldiers digging a pit for a powder magazine at Lompock Rancho, California, hacked their way through a layer of cemented gravel and found a 12 ft sarcophagus. The skeleton of a giant man about twelve feet tall was found inside. The grave was surrounded by carved shells, huge stone axes, two spears and thin sheets of porphyry (purple mineral with quartz) covering the skeleton. These were covered with unintelligible symbols. He had a double row of teeth, both upper and lower. The soldiers consulted a local tribe of Indians, who after going into trance, exclaimed they were geographically displaced Allegewi Indians from the Ohio Valley area. When the natives began to attach some religious significance to the find, authorities ordered the skeleton and all the artifacts secretly reburied.

This version of events was published in 1979 in *Giants: The Vanished Race of Mighty Men* by Roy Norvill; in 1978 in *Sowers of Thunder* by Anthony Roberts, but the original citing came from *Gods, Demons and UFO's,* by Eric Norman (aka Warren Smith), in 1971. Due to the confusion over this Jim located the following article that clarifies the original report from 1819:

"During the summer of 1862, a respectable old lady, a native of California, who resides not far from the Mission of La Purisima, in Santa Barbara county, informed us that shortly after she was married, her husband, who was corporal of the soldiers kept at the mission about 1819, was with his men doing some work about a well near the old mission of the same name, now situated on the rancho called Lompock-which was destroyed

by the great earthquake of 1812, when at San Juan Capistrano was also tumbled down, burying some fifteen people in the ruins. In the progress of their labors they disinterred a human skeleton of immense size, which fact getting wind among the Indians of the mission, they came down in excited crowds to the soldiers and begged them to desist, as the bones were those of whom they considered Gods, which, when disturbed, would work ruin and destruction on all the country around. Seeing the trouble going on, the Padres came among them and made the soldiers replace the bones from where they were taken and forbade their being troubled afterwards." [13]

The Indians mentioned here are the Chumash, who used to call the area "Lum Poc" meaning "stagnant waters" or "lagoon." In 1837 it was in the hands of the Mexicans, but in 1846 the US gained control of the area, and by the Second World War it was starting to be used as a military base. So the ranch is no longer a ranch. It's currently the Vandenburg Airforce Base and you are not allowed inside, especially if you are looking for a 12-foot -tall giant skeleton.

GREAT CAVES—SKULLS WITH DOUBLE ROWS OF TEETH
The Scientific American, Volume 6, 1862, pg.227
Channel Islands, California

The Scientific American.

NATURAL CURIOSITIES OF CALIFORNIA.

GREAT CAVES—SKULLS WITH DOUBLE ROWS OF TEETH.—
The Indian skulls with double rows of teeth are said to have been found not only abundantly on San Clemente Island caves, but also often still on the neighboring Island of San Miguel, the San Bernardo or Juan Rodriguez of Cabrillo. Obsidian and all species of silicious stones and rocks are exceedingly abundant in all portions of the Californias, Arizona, New Mexico and Utah, as well as of Mexico, and were used by the Indians for various and useful purposes, as knives, razors, swords.

The Scientific American reported on numerous finds on the islands off the coast of California:

> *"The Indian skulls with double rows of teeth are said to have been found not only abundantly on San Clemente Island caves, but also often still on the neighbouring Island of San Miguel, the San Bernardo or Juan Rodriguez of Cabrillo."*

The dating of these finds is said to be in the region of 3,362-8,000 years.[14]

MARTHA'S VINEYARD
The Story of Martha's Vineyard by Charles Gilbert Hine, pg.136
Martha's Vineyard, Massachusetts, 1908.

On the opposite side of the country we find a similar account from 1908 on a remote island off the southeast corner of Massachusetts:

> *"Some fifteen years ago the skeleton of an Indian giant in almost perfect preservation was dug up in the same locality; the bones indicated a man easily six feet and a half, possibly seven feet, high. An unusual feature was a complete double row of teeth on both upper and lower jaws. After all the bones were removed the place was carefully dug over, but no implements were found, a singular fact, as the Indians were supposed to always bury their implements with the dead."*

SKELETONS OF A GIANT RACE FOUND NEAR POTOSI
Urbana Union, February 16 and Dubuque Times, Jan 5, 1870
Potosi, Wisconsin

> *"The evidence appears to be pretty well settled that this whole Western country was once inhabited by a race of beings of gigantic stature, which were not only hardworking, industrious fellows, but well up in many of the fine arts....One of them was found to be seven and a half feet and the other eight feet in length. The jaws of each were filled with double rows of teeth,*

while the cheek bones were very high and prominent."

DRILLED SKULLS AND DOUBLE ROWS OF TEETH
American Antiquarian Vol. XII, No. 1, January 1890
Detroit, Michigan

This account contains a rare report of trepanning performed on human skulls. Although widely used in ancient Peru, it is not often reported in North America:

"At one time or another, remains of some forty individuals have been discovered in various excavations....At a depth of two feet, five skulls were found, lying in a circle, facing the center. Within this circle were ashes and charcoal, evidence of fire; but the bones were not all burned... Of these five skulls three were perforated, and perforated not with a single hole like those found by Mr. Crillman, but with three like the one from Saginaw to which he refers in the passage quoted. The three holes are drilled directly on top of the skull, are arranged in the form of a triangle and are a half an inch or so apart. In diameter they range from one third to one half inch. The two unperforated skulls are smaller and more delicate than these three and were evidently skulls of young persons or females. On the perforated skulls two had 'double teeth' in front. Mr. Bates says the third may have had also. (He is no longer in Detroit and some uncertainty exists in the matter.) The dentition of the other two skulls is normal."

REMARKABLE HUMAN SKELETON
History of the Town of Rockingham, Vermont, 1907, pg.338
Bellows Falls, Rockingham, Vermont

Jim and Hugh investigated this giant report from Vermont as part of *Search for the Lost Giants* TV show. In this local town history, the author re-tells the story of the discovery of a giant when they were digging the ground to lay down rail tracks for the Cheshire Railroad in the mid 1800s:

"When the earth was removed from the top of the ledges east of the falls a remarkable human skeleton, unmistakably that of an Indian was found. Those who saw it tell the writer the jaw bone was of such size that a large man could easily slip it over his face, and the teeth, which were all double, were perfect."

Unfortunately, they were mysteriously lost:

"This skeleton was kept for many years deposited in the attic of a small building on the north side of the Square. This building was then occupied by Dr. John H. Wells' office and drug store and stood where the Italian fruit store now does. When the building was rebuilt a decade ago or more the bones disappeared."

As part of our investigation we visited the ancient burial site at Bellows Falls which is now an abandoned rail yard. One of the strange synchronicities that occurred when we examined the area was the profusion of ancient Native American petroglyphs evident on large rocks on the water's edge, that date back at least hundreds, or maybe thousands of years. They consist of multiple abstract faces carved by the Abenaki Indians, with one that is much larger than the others, and appears to have unusual teeth. Is it the first depiction of a 'double row of teeth'? (see image below).

Bellows Falls petroglyphs. Does the face on bottom right depict double rows of teeth?

200

The petroglyphs have been damaged over time, but some still exist. We climbed down to see them close-up, but some are now partly buried under rocks. Many of them can be safely seen from the bridge at Bellows Falls. We were able to find a further lithograph from Henry Schoolcraft sketched around 1860 that shows some of the original forms.

Left: Henry Schoolcraft's Lithograph. Right: Bellows Falls petroglyphs today.

We also talked to members of the Bellows Falls Historical Society (see p.202) and were allowed to search through the hand written notes of Lyman Simpson Hayes who would write the *Town History of Rockingham* in which he describes the unearthing of the giant skeleton. In his notes, which were the last draft before he created the final Town History, Hayes had inserted an "all" to accentuate the point that "all" the teeth of the giant skeleton were indeed double, as can be seen below.

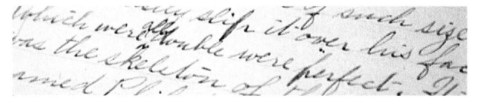

The skeleton was of the Native Chief Philip, who was known to have been of exceptional stature in life and was killed by rifle fire in a battle on August 17, 1755, as noted by John Kilburn. The Natives took the body of Philip and buried it under a flat rock so the white men could not find it. A hundred years later when the Cheshire Railroad was being built, the skeleton was unearthed by accident.

The skeleton was then wired together in the office of Dr. John H. Wells and kept there. We found the old office of Dr. Wells and learned

Lyman Simpson Hayes

from the Town History of Walpole that a Dr. Robbins also shared the office and practice with Dr. Wells. Dr. Artemis Robbins was reported to have then given the skeleton to his family. Dr. Robbins later invested all his savings in railroad stocks that became worthless and died destitute.

We were able to track down the last living relative of Dr. Robbins who was Caroline Wellington Johonnet, who once lived in Newton, Mass. The Census records we found indicated that she was still living at the house at least as late as 1945.

We traveled to the house in Newton, but the family who now resides there did not know much about Caroline but remembered that there were two old pictures in the basement. They showed us them and Hugh noticed faint writing on them undetected by the current owners. The pictures were family portraits of the Robbins as "Robbins" and "Johonett" were written plainly. This was indeed the last residence of the family. We then asked the homeowner if there was anything strange in or around the house that would indicate that a skeleton was placed there. We were told that a strange 8 x 4 foot stone build-out existed in the basement. We went downstairs and hammered away at the wall to see into the space and found that nothing was left in there. Oddly, a good portion of the space had been mortared after the fact and it appeared that something was removed from the area. That was the end of the road for our investigation but this is one of the most compelling accounts we have looked at. This was not a

After hammering at the wall Jim checks to see if there is a giant skeleton in the cavity.

hoax and in fact the skeleton in question belonged to a known giant Native who had double rows of teeth. This is a fascinating story of a skeleton wired together in the office of two prominent physicians but unfortunately now lost.

FOUR VERY LARGE SKELETONS
Niles' Weekly Register, Volume 21, 1822, pg.128
Mason County, West Virginia

This is one of the earliest reports of double rows of teeth, that comes from the Niles' Weekly Register, (originally cited in the Kenhawa Spectator). It describes a discovery of *"Four very large skeletons."* It goes on to say:

> *"The bones were perfectly sound, and much larger than common, and more especially the skulls, which can be very easily slipped over the largest man's head. The upper jaw bone has one row of double teeth all around, and the under jaw two teeth only on the left side, and no sockets whatever in the rest of the bone were provided by nature for more."*

DOUBLE TEETH ALL AROUND
The Plough Boy and Journal of the Board of Agriculture
Volume 2, J.O. Cole, 1821, pg.239
Portsmouth, New Hampshire

This early account of a 7-foot giant emphasises that *"the upper jaw had double teeth all around."*

> A late Portsmouth paper says that in digging a cellar, near that place, a human skeleton, 7 feet in length, was dug up. The skull was very thick, and the upper jaw had double teeth all around. The bones were about 2 feet below the surface, and without a coffin. A few days after, another was discovered. They are supposed to be the remains of two of the natives.

CAHOKIA GIANTS
The Saint Louis Dispatch, 1906
Cahokia, Illinois

This report is repeated from the *Giants in the Mounds* chapter, but worth putting in here to emphasize that the mound/pyramid builders were connected to this phenomenon:

"The bones, which instantly crumbled to dust on exposure to the air, appeared larger than ordinary, while the teeth were double in front as well as behind."

THE STRANGE STORY OF BENJAMIN BUCKLIN
Rhode Island, 1676

Jim and Hugh investigated the strange story of Benjamin Bucklin in episode 6 of *Search for the Lost Giants*. Bucklin was a giant colonial soldier with double rows of teeth who was killed in a battle along with eight other soldiers nearly 350 years ago. Here is the story.

The Nine Men's Misery monument marks the place where on March 26, 1676, nine Rhode Island soldiers, including Benjamin Bucklin, were killed by Native Americans in King Phillip's War.

King Philip, the chief of the Wampanoag tribe of the Rhode Island/ Massachusetts area of New England, initially succeeded in the battles with the colonists. One of the most disastrous military battles for the colonists was called Pierce's Fight, in which most of the colonial soldiers of Pierce's command were killed.

A group of nine of the soldiers escaped the original Indian ambush, but were separately later captured, tortured, and killed. Benjamin Bucklin was one of the nine who were killed. The nine bodies were found a day later by a military burial mission working on burying the remains of those killed the day before. The remains were buried on the spot on which they were found, a rise of land in a swampy area. Because of the gruesome nature of the torture indicated by the state of the bodies found by the burial mission, the site became known locally as the Nine Men's Misery.

The Nine Men's Misery monument in Cumberland is located in a quiet, dark, uninviting place in the woods, near a former monastery that now has been replaced by a public library. The monument—piles of stones cemented together with a cement pillar next to the stone pile, and adorned with a plaque—sits on top of a hill in what in 1676 was a swampy area. But what was discovered there sheds a new light on the mystery of double rows of teeth and the origins of this genetic trait.

204

Through interviews and library research in the Rhode Island area, we were able to help unravel this story. Here are a few of the numerous accounts we found in the records, of the exhumation of Bucklin and the fact that he had double rows of teeth.

PROVIDENCE JOURNAL
by James Whitney, Wednesday, January 20, 1886

"When the Whipple estate was in the hands of Mr. Whipple's father-in-law, Elisha Waterman, Esq. a strange incident occurred in relation to the nine men's grave. It was either during, or shortly after the Revolutionary War. Some Providence gentlemen, led, it is said, by Dr. Bowen, went up to the place and dug open the grave. They had already stretched three of the skeletons upon the ground ere they were discovered. When the Cumberland people found out what was going on, a hue and cry being raised, and the farmers assembling from all the region round, the cessation of the robbery was compelled, the disinterment being regarded as a first-class outrage...One fact was settled by the disinterment, and that was the identity of the men themselves who were buried. One of the skeletons dug up was of extraordinary size, and by the fact of it's having a double set of teeth, was recognized as that of Benjamin Bucklin (Buckland), of Rehoboth. It is assured thus that the men were from other colonies than that of Providence."

Dr. Bowen specifically exhumed Bucklin's skeleton and verified its enormity and the fact that he had double rows of teeth. If there is any doubt that Bucklin possessed this anatomic trait, here are a few more accounts we found.

HISTORY OF ATTLEBOROUGH
John Daggett, 1894, pg.115

"...I have seen no notice of this in history, but as to the main fact there can be no doubt. The bones of these men were disinterred (not many years ago) by some physician for anatomical purposes, and were found nearly perfect. But the

people in the vicinity insisted upon their being restored, which was accordingly done. One of the slain was ascertained to be a Bucklin, of Rehoboth, from the remarkable circumstances of a set of double front teeth, which he was known to possess."

He goes on to state in finer detail the unfolding mystery and confirmation of what was witnessed.

"....The fact that the medical students, from curiosity or to verify the tradition, or other motives, did visit the spot and exhume the bodies, and prove their identity by that of Benjamin Bucklin (or Buckland), of Rehoboth, from his unusually large frame and "double set of teeth all around," has also been substantiated. What is still more remarkable than the discovery of the letter, the author met a physician soon after the publication of this history, in 1834, who took pains to state that he had read the account of "Nine Men's Misery," and was able to testify that it was substantially correct, as he was one of the "medical gentlemen" present, and aided in the exhumation and finally examined the bones. Having this statement directly from his own mouth, it is personal knowledge of the event, so far as this fact shows."

HISTORY OF REHOBOTH
Leonard Bliss, 1836, pg.198

"Mr. Daggett visited the spot a century and a half after, talked with the people then living in the neighborhood, and wrote the story. He describes the spot and the heap of memorial stones piled upon the grave. This must have been about 1830. Mr. Daggett in his manuscript told of the dis-interment and about the skull of Bucklin with double teeth, which was then exhumed. These teeth filled the jaws: there were no "single" teeth...In 1866 I myself visited the spot and saw it exactly as John Daggett described it: but it is all gone now, having been moved north not less than a mile."

206

Through communication with members of the Rhode Island Historical Society we were able to learn that in the 1920s, the Cistercian monks who lived on the land where the soldiers' remains were buried, did not wish to have unconsecrated remains on their property. They had the remains removed and given to the Historical Society. We were told that the museum had a box with 9 skulls in it, including Bucklin's, for 50 years. Strangely, no photos were taken or records made of the skulls. The box of skulls was given to a Mr. Stephen Adams to be reinterred in 1976 for the 300th anniversary of the King Philip's War battle. It appears that the skulls were placed in the stone cairn at the Nine Men's Misery site. We attempted to gain access to the remains but the fact that it is the oldest Veteran's Memorial site in the country posed obvious problems. Maybe at some point we can view the remarkable skull of Benjamin Bucklin and have all the remains buried properly.

Jim with members of the Rhode Island Historical Society at *Nine Men's Misery*. Photo by Hugh Newman.

GIGANTIC SIZE AND STRENGTH
History of the Town of Middleboro Mass, Thomas Weston, 1906, p.400
Middleboro, Massachusetts

Strangely, this account is another case of a giant colonial soldier who fought in King Philips War as one of Colonel Church's scouts. Mr. Richmond of Middleboro was well known in his time for his enormous size, strength, fighting ability, and double rows of teeth:

207

"...A few years ago when the highway was straightened and repaired, remains were found, and he was re-interred. Afterwards, his body was exhumed in presence of Dr. Morrill Robinson and others to test the truth of the tradition as to his gigantic size and strength. When the skeleton was measured, it was found that the thigh-bone was four inches longer than that bone in an ordinary man, and that he had a double row of teeth in each jaw. His height must have been at least seven feet and eight inches."

WHERE IS THE JAWBONE OF FAMED JOE FOURNIER?
Owosso Argus Press, **February 8, 1972**
Bay County, Michigan

The last report of a giant colonist with double rows of teeth comes from the *Owosso Argus Press*, February 8, 1972. The article seeks to find the jawbone of the Famed Joe Fournier, *"who used to keep his teeth sharp by biting hunks out of bars in backwoods saloons."* Fournier is believed to be the model for the American mythological giant Paul Bunyan. Fournier was killed in a bar room brawl. The article goes on:

"Joe's skull, which housed his famed teeth, was bashed in by a single blow of a carpenter's mallet in 1875, ending a boisterous, battling career. One Adolphus "Blinky" Robertson was tried for the crime but was acquitted by a jury. One of the interesting parts of the trial was that Fournier's massive skull was introduced as evidence.

Old timers tell that the skull was for many years a prized exhibit in the Bay County Courthouse where its double thick bone and double rows of teeth were the marvel of all who saw it. The jawbone disappeared some time later and was subsequently reported at the University of Michigan dental school- where beginning students used to marvel at the crunch bicuspids. It also was reported in various museums and even in a couple of bars but no trace of its existence can be authenticated now.

*His association with the Paul Bunyan legends came about
because of a Detroit newspaperman, James T. McGillivray
had heard in his childhood of the great strength and fighting-
biting ability of Joe Fournier. McGillivray recalled campfire
stories in the woods of Northern Michigan about Joe Fournier*

*and his fighting prowess, especially
his legendary battle with Silver Jack
Driscoll. McGillivray was credited with
being the first to mention the name
Paul Bunyan in print, as he mentioned
it in his column Round River Drive, in
The Detroit News Tribune in 1910...
old timers in the area who were
interviewed recalled having heard
tales in their youth of Fournier's great
strength and his rumored affiliation
with the Paul Bunyan stories. Digging
into the story raised the question-but
did not answer it-where is the jawbone
of the famed Joe Fournier?"*

Illustration of Paul Bunyon

All three of these Caucasian men all had the same things in common,
great size, strength, fighting ability, and double rows of teeth. It would
seem illogical that numerous people would "*marvel*" at worn down teeth
or an extra tooth or two.

MEETING WITH DENTAL ANTHROPOLOGIST

Dr. Shara Bailey is a dental anthropologist based at New York University
(NYU). Hugh visited her as part of the TV series to discuss the phenomenon
of double rows of teeth. Before they met, Hugh sent her several accounts
from this chapter to examine. Dr. Bailey was intrigued by the many
accounts of duplicated tooth rows in North America. She explained that
single extra (supernumerary) teeth are rather rare, occurring in 1%-5% of
recent populations (but up to 10% in some isolated groups). More than

one extra tooth in an individual is even rarer. It is so unlikely to find full double sets of teeth in human jaws, that she compared it to finding "*a race of three-armed people*". She then explained that extra sets of teeth would require extra large jaws to accommodate them. This is most certainly the case as we saw in *The Adena Jaw* section of the previous chapter. However, making extra teeth is metabolically costly, she said, and was skeptical that it would occur so frequently, if at all.

Dr. Bailey showed Hugh photographs of individuals that had extra teeth: one from South Africa with an extra tooth (incisor) in the front and a mold from Melanesia that had extra bicuspids on either side of the lower jaw. However, Dr. Bailey said she had never seen a full set of extra teeth in her twenty years of studying dentitions from people from around the world.

She also found it interesting that many of the reports used the exact same language to describe the individuals, and also felt some reports may have had some errors. For example, several accounts of individuals with DRTs describe the teeth as very worn down. Dr Bailey showed Hugh a photo of how severe tooth wear can look like two sets of teeth to the untrained eye, because the roots show (there are two parts of the roots with each single tooth), therefore this is how this could have been interpreted.

However, in the account from Ellensberg, Washington, it clearly describes two full sets of teeth in the upper jaw (see pp.191-192).

Further investigation of the anomaly has revealed that 'heredity' could be the origin of this anomaly,[15] with research that links it to genetic throwbacks. It could simply be an ancient *anatomic deviation* that was known around the world in ancient times, and due to cross-breeding between different types of human, these strange traits then occur (this is explored further in the *Origins of the Tall Ones* chapter). Interestingly, there are numerous accounts of teeth being discovered that were in perfect condition, with no decay or dental problems. Even today, with all the discoveries in dental research, it is almost impossible to maintain perfect teeth, but they somehow managed it in ancient America as described in this account from 1910:

The Dental Summary, Volume 30, 1910, pg.7
Fenyville, Wisconsin

"C. H. Lawrence of Fenyville, Wis., has exhumed some bones of a prehistoric race from mounds near his home. One of the skeletons indicated a man eight or nine feet tall. Among the collection are three complete jaw bones, in each of which every tooth is intact and perfect, except that some are greatly worn, those in one jaw having been shortened to the level of the gums. The teeth in the larger inferior maxillary were in a perfect state of preservation, although the row of molars on the left side was considerably worn, indicating that their owner in life had chewed principally on that side. In none of these teeth are any cavities in evidence, which, together with the fact that none are missing, would indicate that the mound building age was a very poor one for dentists."

To further question the phenomenon, a 3,800 year-old skeleton was unearthed with 176 other bodies near the Central Valley town of Elk Grove in California, that showed signs of acromegaly (over-production of growth hormone), but rather than the teeth being more widely spaced apart (which usually happens with this condition) the skull exhibited:

"...a protruding brow, a lantern jaw, thick leg and arm bones, and teeth so crowded together that at one point they erupt in rows three deep." [16]

Skeptics might argue this is what could explain the DRTs in some of these accounts, but Dr. Eric Bartelink, a physical anthropologist at California State University said:

"Acromegaly has only been identified definitively at two other archaeological sites in North America...in the remains of a male buried in New Mexico about 600 years ago, and an unsexed 1,100-year-old skull found in Illinois." [17]

Bartelink noted that the skeleton was only 5 feet 5 inches tall, but the skull showed advanced signs of hyper-growth in the skull and teeth:

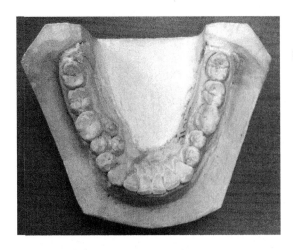

Mold from Melanesia showing extra bicuspids on either side of the lower jaw.

"In what seems to have been an unrelated condition, the man's right eyetooth also grew upside down, protruding through the bone of his face just under his nose." [18]

After looking carefully at all possibilities, the phenomenon of double rows of teeth could either be: 1) Literally two sets of teeth (double); 2) molars and premolars in the front of the mouth resembling 'double' teeth—an unusual anomaly in itself; 3) supernumerary teeth that are just occasional 'extra' teeth in the mouth, that could be seen as double sets of teeth, but not 'full sets'. 4) teeth so worn down that only the two roots exist that resemble two separate teeth.

Further investigation clearly needs to be carried out before we can understand the origins of these unusual traits. Some accounts could be due to the parlance of the time, but we do find it odd that double rows of teeth are so frequently linked with giant skeletons in the historical record.

Hugh discussing double rows of teeth with Dr. Shara Bailey.

212

8

THE SMITHSONIAN FILES

The Smithsonian Institution is continually linked to giant skeletons, or at least the lack of them. Dozens of reports end in something like this: *"The bones were shipped to the Smithsonian Institution for further study."*

In this chapter we look at giant skeletons that were sold to the institution, some that were simply given, and even Smithsonian reports of directly discovering them. Our favorite report is of the gentleman who refused to sell them a skeleton! The story of the Smithsonian is a remarkable tale that has become what some researchers describe as a "conspiracy."

The Institution was originally founded thanks to just over half a million dollars (equating to over $13 million today), donated by English scientist James Smithson (1765-1829). Due to his unusual will, his fortune ended up being given to the people of the United States in 1836 to found an institution *"at Washington, under the name of the Smithsonian Institution, an establishment for the increase and diffusion of knowledge."*[1]

The amount he gave to the US was around 1/66 of the United States' entire federal budget at the time.[2] President Jackson sent a diplomat to collect the money that consisted of 104,960 gold coins, but Congress decided to invest the money in treasury bonds issued by the state of Arkansas. The bonds became worthless after they defaulted. However, after much debate, ex-President John Quincy Adams persuaded Congress to restore the lost funds with interest.

James Smithson 1816.

Smithson's reasons for providing for a research and educational institution in a new country on another continent remains a mystery, as he never set foot in America. His bequest sparked widespread debate over what such a national institution might be. However, once established, *"the Smithsonian Institution became part of the process of developing the U.S. national identity."*[3] This is certainly the case, as early pioneers in the newly founded Bureau of Ethnology drove an agenda of *manifest destiny* and the new theory of *evolution*. They also exerted control over the prehistoric mounds, and all artifacts and skeletons discovered within them.

The Smithsonian Institution "Castle".

In 1864 the Smithsonian was established as a governmental trust to be run by a board and secretary. Curiously, it is neither governmental or private, sitting in a gray area.

The first major Smithsonian publication was created by Ephraim Squire and Edwin Davis. They were commissioned to describe, survey and illustrate the mound culture sites that were being quickly demolished by the incoming Europeans. Their incredibly popular book, published in 1848, did not mention giants, but it concluded that a prehistoric race, superior to the Native Americans was responsible for building the mounds. This became a contentious issue within the hierarchy of the Smithsonian over the decades, and was refuted by future Director John Wesley Powell, who was sympathetic towards the Native Americans due to his interactions with them over the years. Although the lost race theory was a popular one, it didn't succeed in becoming part of the new paradigm that the Smithsonian was building. To this day, it is official doctrine that the mounds were built by the ancestors of the Native Americans, and not a legendary lost race.

The publication caused quite a stir, as evolutionary theories and Manifest Destiny were being advanced by Lewis Henry Morgan, John Wesley Powell, and Otis T. Mason. These combined agendas would become the public norm, and influence how modern Native Americans were treated for decades to come.

> *"With land rights being one of the foremost issues facing lawmakers, having evolutionary theories that labeled the American Indian populations as savage would be seen as a pivotal breakthrough in addressing and advancing a Manifest Destiny agenda, along with a host of other scientific, government, and social ethnological issues."* [4]

In 1879 John Wesley Powell founded the Bureau of Ethnology in a new format. It was set up to be a storehouse of records and artifacts relating

to Native Americans, and to transfer archives, records and materials relating to the North America Indians from the Interior Department to the Smithsonian Institution. An annual budget of $25,000 was granted, with $5,000 given to the newly formed *Division of Mound Exploration,* much to Powell's discontent. As a firm believer in the Native origins of the mounds, he wanted to keep any research ethnological, not intrusive, but agreed to comply with the bill.

John Wesley Powell, who lost his arm in the Civil War, was a famous

John Wesley Powell with Paiute Indian.

geologist and explorer (of Grand Canyon exploration fame 1869-1872). His interest in history and archaeology stimulated his vision to create the nation's ultimate storehouse and research agency. The first annual report was published by the Smithsonian in 1882, under the guidance of Powell. That same year he appointed Cyrus Thomas as the Director of the Division of Mound Exploration.

Cyrus Thomas

Thomas was also quietly a believer in the legendary lost race theory, as by then hundreds of reports of giant skeletons, strange artifacts that appeared to have come from other countries, and sophisticated astronomy, geometry, and mathematics were being revealed from the earthworks, regardless of any Smithsonian involvement. The question of who the original inhabitants of North America were did not leave the spotlight for too long.

Thomas' organisational skills were put to use in coordinating the field workers who would go across the country collecting data, artifacts, and most importantly to our investigation, skulls and skeletons for research and display at the Smithsonian. Many of these discoveries were documented in the Annual Reports that we explore later in this chapter.

> *"These [Smithsonian] men were in every valley, on every hill, north and south. They let nothing escape."* [5]

He outlined his intentions clearly. The primary goal being:

> *"1. To make a collection of skeletons, especially crania found entombed in the mounds or graves."*

Cyrus Thomas soon came round to Powell's views of Native American origins, but this may have also been the trigger for *"the Smithsonian to quash all evidence that showed that the mound builders were related to any other culture on any continent."*[6] They also ignored any suggestion of 'diffusionism', the school of thought that believes throughout history there has been worldwide contact via the oceans and trade routes. Isolationism became the norm, where it is believed to have been isolated from any influence of overseas navigators, or even neighboring tribes.

Aleš Hrdlička

In 1910 the Smithsonian hired the most infamous figure in its short history to be the curator of the Division of Physical Anthropology. Aleš Hrdlička was involved in the Eugenics movement, a pre-Nazism philosophy funded by the Rockefeller Foundation.[7] His influence overpowered many contemporaries who were afraid to challenge the paradigm he was enforcing. We discuss Hrdlička further in the chapter, but his draconian zeal, combined with his racist denial of culturally advanced Native Americans did not help the image of the Smithsonian in the following decades.

Author David Hatcher Childress first raised the alarm that something was not right within the Smithsonian in 1993 with his controversial article entitled "Smithsoniangate."[8] It outlined many non-giant related artifacts discoveries at ancient sites, that were never heard of again. These included the lost Egyptian artifacts that were said to have been discovered in the Grand Canyon in April 1909 with numerous other discoveries. Online skeptics have ridiculed this article as the genesis of the Smithsonian conspiracy theory, but as we delved into these upcoming accounts, we quickly found it may prove to be relevant to giantology.

A probable urban legend, first written and published by Childress in his article, stated something quite strange and disconcerting, but could it really be true?

> *"In a private conversation with a well-known historical researcher (who shall remain nameless), I was told that a former employee of the Smithsonian, who was dismissed for defending the view of diffusionism in the Americas (i.e. the heresy that other ancient civilisations may have visited the shores of North and South America during the many millennia before Columbus), alleged that the Smithsonian at one time had actually taken a barge full of unusual artifacts out into the Atlantic and dumped them in the ocean."* [9]

Before we started this investigation, the Smithsonian was simply just another historical institution that everyone loved, looked up to and that had some nice museums. However, as we uncovered more and more accounts, it quickly became clear that the Smithsonian collected and received thousands of artifacts, treasures, sizeable skeletons, and amassed an impressive knowledge of America's earlier inhabitants. If there is no 'conspiracy', then where are all these relics now, and why do they deny they received them? Does the scene of the crated-up artifacts in *Raiders of the Lost Ark* hold any truth? Ross Hamilton tackles this ongoing issue:

> *"Combing through the Museum's old Annual Reports has been an education, raising a number of questions regarding the modern Smithsonian's repeated denials of specific, albeit lacking-in-detail nineteenth century finds. Interestingly, there were few or no such denials until the tenure of Aleš Hrdlička, early twentieth century head of anthropology at the Museum. Thus an important—perhaps pivotal question is raised: Why would this gentleman discount the existence of relics carefully recorded in the field reports of his predecessors John Wesley Powell and Cyrus Thomas? Was Hrdlička simply an apologist ignorant of his own reliquary's contents, a rank materialist who had not taken time to search the collections, or was there something darker creeping insidiously into American anthropology at the highest levels in the early twentieth century?"* [10]

Hugh visited the Smithsonian Institution in Washington D.C. in late 2014 to take a look for himself. It is a sparse place, with very few artifacts or anything 'ancient' on display. It has a cold, unwelcoming atmosphere, and the workers there knew nothing of giant skeletons in their records, even though Hugh showed them several examples. Hugh simply saw an empty shell of what could have been one of the most important repositories of knowledge in the world.

It's not all bad though. Their recent court case against the federal government over Kennewick Man shows a shift within the ranks, and a new respect for the ancestors of this ancient land.

The authors are fascinated by these following accounts because they appear to reveal an unfolding agenda and deliberate suppression of what was really being discovered in ancient America, as well as a severe lack of respect for Native American burials. Other commentators deny there is any cover-up, so please take a look at the following accounts— firstly from newspapers—then from their own journals, to determine what really happened at the Smithsonian.

GIGANTIC INDIAN
The Weekly Democratic Statesman. Austin, Tex. April 12, 1883, pg.6
Bristol, Tennessee

This matter-of-fact account is made by John W. Emmert, who unearthed the controversial Bat Creek Stone at Bat Creek Mound in Tennessee (see *Curious Artifacts* chapter for the full story):

> *"Mr. John W. Emmert, employed by the bureau of ethnology of the Smithsonian Institution at Washington, has lately explored a mound at Bristol, Tenn., and secured some interesting and valuable Indian relics. Among other things in the mound was found the skeleton of a gigantic Indian."*

---

14 HUMAN SKELETONS
West Virginia: A Guide to the Mountain State, 1952, pg.448
Staunton Park, West Virginia, 1883

Originally in the same year as the above report, this account came out in the 1952 book *West Virginia: A Guide to the Mountain State*:

In STAUNTON PARK (L), a triangular park near the western end of the town, is a conical Indian Burial Mound, 175 feet in circumference at the base and 30 feet high. Ornaments, stone weapons, fragments of pottery, and 14 human skeletons—one more than seven feet long— were found when the mound was opened by the Federal Government in 1883.

MONSTER SKULLS AND BONES
The New York Times, April 5, 1886
Cartersville, Georgia

This news report from *The New York Times* describes how water receded from the Tumlin mound field (now called Etowah mounds) and revealed:

> *"...acres of skulls and bones. Some of these are gigantic. If the whole frame is in proportion to two thigh bones that were found, the owner must have stood 14 feet tall."*

Also found were ornaments of shell, brass, and stone. It was noted that "*A representative of the Smithsonian Institution is here investigating the curious relics.*" This fact was confirmed by its inclusion in The Smithsonian's Fifth Annual Report (1887). The Etowah Mound site is just south of Cartersville Georgia, and is a 54 acre site that was built and occupied in three phases from 1000 to 1550 AD. Etowah has three platform mounds and three lesser mounds. *Temple mound A* is 63 feet high with a base of 3 acres (pictured below) and overlooks Temple mound B. This is another wonderfully impressive site from the Mississippian era of the Mound Builders.

Illustration of the "Large Mound" at Etowah from
The Smithsonian's Fifth Annual Report 1887.

Jim uncovered further reports from this mound complex. Two speak of the Smithsonian's involvement. From the *American Antiquarian, 7:52, 1885*:

> *"On the stones which covered the vault were carved inscriptions, and these when deciphered, will doubtless lift the veil that now shrouds the history of the race of people that one time inhabited this part of the American continent. The relics have been carefully packed and forwarded to the Smithsonian Institute, and they are said to be the most interesting collection ever found in the United States."*

This final account comes from the *North Otago Times*, July 23, 1884, pg.2, and mentions a "9 ft 2 in" giant.

> H. R. Hazelton recently opened the large Indian mound near Cartersville, Ga. A layer of very heavy flagstones covered a deep vault, in which was found the skeleton of a man 9ft 2in in height, surrounded by seven other skeletons, apparently those of very young persons. The giant evidently had been a king, as his head was encircled with a copper crown. His hair, black as jet, reached to his waist but he had no whiskers. The bottom of the vault had first been covered with a thick matting of reeds and dry grass, over which were spread the skins of some wild animal. The under-side of the stones covering the grave are filled with deeply carved inscriptions. If it is ever possible to decipher these, Mr Hazelton thinks he will have something reliable in regard to prehistoric man in America.

These numerous accounts talk of giants with copper crowns, strange carvings and stone vaults from 130 years ago. It seems only obvious to ask where are they all now?

AMERICAN ANTIQUARIAN 1887
VOLUMES 9-10 , JAN. TO NOV. 1887, PG.176
Crawford, Minnesota

"At a depth of 14 feet below the surface, the workmen came upon the skeleton of a giant, in a tolerable good state of preservation, the skeleton was 8 feet 2 inches in length and measured 2 feet 2 inches across the pelvis... At another point, about six miles from where this skeleton was found, at the mouth of the Sioux Coulec one of the agents or employs of the Smithsonian Institute, at Washington, exhumed the remains of another skeleton the size of which was calculated to be about 9 feet in length."

It seems difficult to imagine putting the bones of a skeleton together and being several feet off in your measurement. Two feet two inches across the pelvis is enormous as well.

221

Indian Relics in West Virginia
The Baltimore Sun, Jan 23, 1889
Romney, West Virginia

This is another giant account from Warren King Moorehead who reported unearthing giant skeletons in several states. Although he did not actually work for the Smithsonian (as the report claims), he was often in contact with them during his archaeological explorations. During his time he was a household name, famous for his work at Cahokia, Etowah, the original Hopewell mound site in Ohio, Maritime Archaic burial sites in the northeast, and other well known digs.

> *"There has been a great deal of excitement here for several days over the discovery of Indian relics and remains by Warren K. Moorehead, of the Smithsonian Institution... Eleven skeletons were found in a space of 20 feet, one of them must have been the skeleton of a giant, as the lower jawbone was almost twice the ordinary size. The femur was 2 inches larger than a six foot man."*

Giants Roamed Southern State
Spokane Daily Chronicle, Jun 21, 1933, pg.35
Natchez, Louisiana, 1891

Another account revealing *"Skeletons of Indians estimated to be more than seven feet tall".* Another mention of Smithsonian involvement:

> *"A search for locations for study by members of the Smithsonian institution disclosed from 15 to 20 of the skeletons in a grave on a mound at Larte Lake."*

This account is from Catahoula Parish, Loiusiana which was also mentioned in the *12th Annual Smithsonian Ethnology Report* (1890-1891). This included a description of the Troyville mound site in Catahoula whose dimensions are impressive, consisting of a mile long earthen wall 7 to 8 feet tall, 20 to 25 feet wide, enclosed in an area over 100 acres. The large mound in the enclosed area was 250 feet long, 160 feet wide at the base, and before it was disturbed, it was 75 feet high. The oldest earthen mound construction started in Louisiana with the creation of Watson Brake in roughly 3400 BC.

BIGGEST GIANT EVER KNOWN
The World, October 7, 1895
San Diego, California

This fascinating discovery reports on a giant mummy found in San Diego, that is most likely a hoax. However, lets take a closer look as there is some intrigue and inconsistency with this popular story. This first report appeared in 1895 with the sub-headings *"Nine Feet High and Probably a California Indian. Measurement Well Authenticated. Other Big Men and Women of Fact and Fable Who Are Famous Types if Gigantism."* The report continues:

> *"The corpse of the biggest man that ever lived has been dug up near San Diego California. At all events there is no satisfactory record in ancient or modern history of any human being nearly so tall. The mummy—for in such a condition the remains were found—is that of a person would have been about nine feet high in life. This makes allowances for the shrinkage, which may be pretty closely calculated. As to the accuracy in the estimate there can no question, as the cadaver has been carefully inspected and measured by Prof. Thomas Wilson, Curator of the Department of Prehistoric Anthropology in the Smithsonian Institution, and by other scientists. The tapeline even now registers the length from heel to top of the head at eight feet four inches.... The body was found in a cave by a party of prospectors. Over the head are the remnants of a leather hood. The man was well advanced in years. It has been stated that the man must have surpassed in height any giant of whom there is an historical record."*

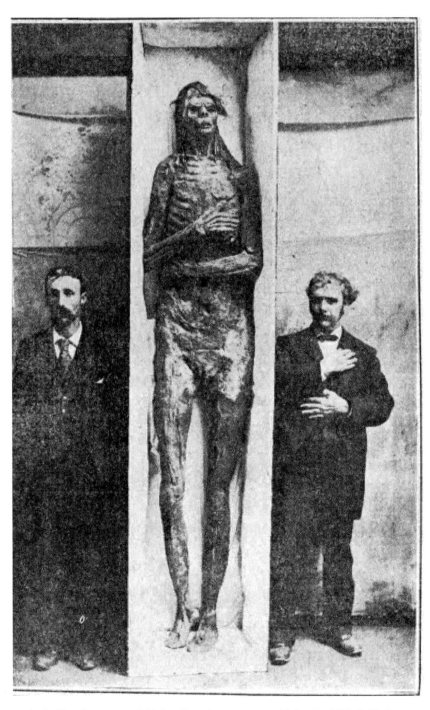

Left: The discoverer. Middle: The giant mummy. Right: Prof. W. J. McGee.

Thirteen years later—in 1908—when the mummy was being exhibited, the Smithsonian ran some tests and suddenly dismissed it as a hoax, saying it was made from "gelatin". The fact that it took that long, and after spending $500 to acquire it, plus the fact that it was *"carefully inspected and measured by Prof. Thomas Wilson, Curator of the Department of Prehistoric Anthropology in the Smithsonian Institution, and by other scientists"* thirteen years earlier does suggest there may be more to this story than meets the eye.

TALLEST HUMAN GIANT WHO EVER LIVED
The Salt Lake Tribune, June 7, 1908
San Diego, California

"The mummy of the 'tallest human giant who ever lived' was being shown at the Atlantic exposition while, a number of these Smithsonian scientists were there....The exhibitor agreed to sell it for $500 to the Smithsonian, which dispatched Mr. Lucas to the scene with, Prof. W. J. McGee. A piece of the giant's dried skin was removed and when tested In the chemical laboratory of the Smithsonian was found to be gelatin. Professor McGee Is shown on the left of the giant, In the accompanying picture, and the exhibitor who was perfectly Innocent of the fraud, is shown on its right."

So in 1908 the Smithsonian claimed that the find was a hoax. Interestingly, Aleš Hrdlička joined the Smithsonian in 1903, right inbetween the discovery and the final debunking. It is interesting to note that the Director of Prehistoric Anthropology, Thomas Wilson, and the ethnologist in charge W. J. McGee were both involved in this story, and were obviously keen to make sure the Smithsonian got it back to their headquarters at an immense cost ($500 in 1895 equates to $14,285 in todays money). But why would they bother doing that if it was simply a sideshow hoax? The strange twists, the Smithsonian involvement, and the immense amount of money spent on this makes this worthy of inclusion in this chapter.

BONES OF PREHISTORIC MAN: SKELETON OF GIANT FOUND IN A RUDE SEPULCHER ON PINE RIDGE
The San Francisco Call, August 22, 1897
Ukiah, California

A strange discovery was made while two men were hunting in a *"rudely excavated hole in a limestone rock."* Several very large bones were found that had been carefully placed there, and the remains were going to be sent to the Smithsonian. Whether they ever received them is unclear.

> **BONES OF PREH.STORIC MAN.**
>
> **Skeleton of a Giant Found in a Rude Sepulcher on Pine Ridge.**
>
> UKIAH, CAL., Aug. 21.—The discovery of the bones of a giant in a rudely excavated hole in a limestone rock on the western side of Pine Ridge has aroused considerable interest among local anthropologists. U. N. Briggs and Frank Patton unearthed the remains of what appeared to be a prehistoric man last week while out hunting on Pine Ridge. It being quite warm the hunters had sought a shady place at the base of a tall limestone cliff. They sat for an hour or so enjoying the soft breezes wafted from the valley beyond, and Briggs in poking around in a hole in the rock unearthed several bones. They appeared to be those of a human being. Upon closer scrutiny it was discovered that the cavity in which the bones had been deposited was evidently the work of human hands. The walls had been cut with a sharp-pointed instrument and the entrance to the tomb or sepulcher had at one time been closed up. The hunters examined the tomb closely and found a number of bones of the feet and hands and a portion of the skull. The remains will be sent to the Smithsonian Institution.

FINDING SKELETON OF GIANT
The Worthington Advance, November 18, 1897, pg.3
Ethnological work of the Smithsonian's Division of Eastern Mounds

This story from Iowa ran in *Barton County Democrat* and the *Nebraska Advertiser* on the 19th and 25th of the same month but the original report was from the *Evening Star*, December 16, 1893. This illustration accompanied all the reports.

FINDING SKELETON OF GIANT.

The longer article that this story is part of was describing the ethnological work of the *Smithsonian Institution's Division of Eastern Mounds*, and quoted the Director of the Bureau of Ethnology at the time, John Wesley Powell. This account joins at least 17 other accounts in the Smithsonian Institution's literature that reported over seven foot skeletons, that we will explore in the next section:

> *"It is officially recorded that agents of the Bureau of Ethnology have explored more than 2,000 of these mounds. Among the objects found in them were pearls in great numbers and some*

of very large size.. It is a matter of official record that in digging through a mound in Iowa the scientists found the skeleton of a giant, who, judging from actual measurement, must have stood seven feet six inches tall when alive. The bones crumbled to dust when exposed to the air. Around the neck was a collar of bear's teeth and across the thighs were dozens of small copper beads, which may have once adorned a hunting skirt."

Skull Given Museum: Archaeologist Presents Indian Relic to Smithsonian
The Washington Post, January 16, 1910
Vancouver Island, British Columbia

Captain Newton H. Chittenden, the famous ethnologist, archaeologist and explorer is the focus of this story. Chittenden spent 20 years devoted to ethnological research for the benefits of governments, society at large and accuracy in history. Here is a short biography of Chittenden:

"The first white man to explore the interior of the Queen Charlotte Islands, Captain Newton Chittenden was an American lawyer and lecturer who wrote both popular and governmental reports. He was a Union Calvary Regiment officer during the Civil War who was admitted to the Supreme Court. He also exhibited Indian and Inuit relics in Europe. These he collected while travelling 3,400 miles on burro and foot through the Southwest, Northwest Coast, and Central Plains."

SKULL GIVEN MUSEUM

--- · ---

Archaeologist Presents Indian Relic to Smithsonian.

BONES OF FLATHEAD CHIEF

Capt. Chittondon, of Santa Barbara, Cal., the Donor, Invaded Savages' Burial Ground at Night at Risk of Life—Has Refused Tempting Offers for Curio in the Last Twenty Years.

During his explorations for the government, Chittenden collected a massive skull of a giant. The way he obtained it is somewhat unorthodox, as he had to creep in to an Indian graveyard at night and steal the skull, before fleeing back to America. Although touted as a hero, he was simply a thief who stole the skull of an Indian chief. Not exactly what we would call 'archaeology' today. However, the skull was a classic elongated skull that had been deformed by cradle boarding. The tribe were still practicing the cranial deformation technique in the early 1900s.

The article states that he *"long treasured it as a priceless possession"* and the skull was *"of great interest to European anthropologists who examined it."* He was offered great sums to part with this skull but he ended up donating it to the Smithsonian Institution. Assistant Director of Anthropology Aleš Hrdlička when presented with the skull said it surpassed any previously in the institution. In the *Sausalito News* January 9th, 1904, Chittenden reports that he uncovered another over eight-foot giant in a burial mound in West Berkeley, California. He described the skull as huge and says *"I have no doubt that ages ago giants roamed around this country"*. It is then noted that he presented the skeleton to the Berkeley High School.

We find in the *Smithsonian's Annual report of 1911* noted on page 82 of their accession list: *Chittenden, Capt. Newton H., Brooklyn N.Y., Skull of Flat Head Indian, two head flattening pillows and the hunting shirt of a half-blood Cree-Indian* (51082).

REFUSES TO SELL SKELETON OF GIANT
Arizona Journal-Miner ,Oct 13, 1911, pg.3
Walnut Creek, Arizona

Refuses to Sell Skeleton of Giant reads this surprising headline. This gentleman decided against selling his discoveries to the Smithsonian, as he sought instead to give it to an Arizona Museum:

> *"Mr. Shoup was provided with photographic instruments and took several pictures. Mr. Shoup, of the Smithsonian, also desired to take it [the giant skeleton] back to Washington, but this request was held up by Mr. Marx stating that as the subject was found in the territory it should be kept there. Mr. Shoup* (and Mrs. Shoup of the Smithsonian) *was very much*

interested in those portions of the human frame that were intact, particularly the skull which indicated that the giant was of such abnormal size as to be beyond comprehension of that of a human being."

REFUSES TO SELL SKELETON OF GIANT

If authentic, one would assume that the photographs should still be in the Smithsonian records.

Burial Mound of Giant Race Holds Secret: Thighs and Skulls sent to the Smithsonian
St. Petersburg Daily Times, March 17, 1914, pg.38
St. Petersburg, Florida

In this account we read *"My friend with a full face of whiskers could easily slip the jawbone on and off quite easily."* Professor J. H. Pratt of the Southland Seminary reports finding bones of a 9-footer. He emphasises *"the extraordinary size of some of the skulls dug up."* Professor Pratt also worked at the University of North Carolina and wrote about the mineralogy in the state.

BURIAL MOUND OF GIANT RACE HOLDS SECRET

WAS UNEARTHED BY JOHN BETHEL AND COMPANION YEARS AGO

THIGHS AND SKULLS SENT SMITHSONIAN

Bodies Buried with Heads to North and in Tiers of Three—Too Badly Matted and Decayed for Reconstruction.

The discovery of an ancient burial mound on one of the keys near John's Pass is spoken of by John Bethel in his "History of Pinellas Peninsula," in the following language:

"While bunting on one of the keys at John's Pass before the war, in company with Anderson Wood, we came across what had once been a burial mound, but time, or possibly the gale of 1848 that made John's Pass, had worn it down when it swept over the islands.

"We would have passed it by unnoticed, as it had only the appearance of a ridge of sand and shell, had we not espied two human skulls and some bones. We concluded there were Indians buried there and that there might be some trinkets buried with them. So we returned to our boat and got a spade and hoe and went back and dug, but all we unearthed was bones. There appeared to be no trinkets with them. As far as we could tell, the bodies were buried three tiers deep, heads north and feet south. We tried to get a whole frame together to see the size of it, but the bones were so matted and so badly decayed that we could not do so.

Bones of Abnormal Size.

"Two of the largest bones, and the only two perfect ones we found, were a thigh bone and a jaw bone. Myself and partner each stood six feet, and if we measured the thigh bone correctly it was about two inches longer than ours. My friend, with a face full of whiskers, could slip the jaw bone off and on quite easily."

In the same chapter Mr. Bethel speaks of finding two petrified teeth were plainly visible, and the cups in them were very distinct. One of the teeth weighed two pounds, and the other one three-quarters. The pieces of ribs were large and flat, and those who saw them claimed they were from some family of the sea

Skull Found Indicates Previous
Floridans were Sizeable
Evening Independent, February 14, 1925
Boca Grande, Florida

Once again the Smithsonian is involved in the unearthing of a not-less-than 7 ft skeleton in a shell mound with an unusually large skull, that:

"...led to speculation over theories of giant race believed to have inhabited Florida before the coming of the Spaniard."

Large skeletons have been reported in shell mounds on both coasts of the US from Florida to Maine and up the west coast. Florida once had a massive shell mound 75 ft high and Maine once had a 30 ft high shell mound called the Whaleback Mound.

"The specimens are being prepared for shipment to the Smithsonian Institute which already has dispatched one unsuccessful expedition to Florida to excavate shell mounds on the west coast in search of proof of a giant race theory."

Not less than 7 feet, that sounds like a successful attempt to us.

Prehistoric Giants Taken from Mound
Pittsburgh Press, September 13, 1932
Near Finleyville and Canonsburg, Pennsylvania

"...49 skeletons found, one of a giant nearly eight foot tall, 26 inches across the chest. Some of the bones will be sent to the Smithsonian Institution in Washington for national study."

An Ancient Ozark Giant Dug Up Near Steelville
The Steelville Ledger, June 11, 1933
Steelville, Missouri

As part of the *Search for the Lost Giants* show, Jim and fellow researcher James Clary investigated the following account that had this sub-heading:

"Strange discovery made by a boy looking for arrowheads, gives this Missouri Town an absorbing mystery to ponder."

Highlights of the lengthy report are given:

"It all came about as a result of Billy Harman's hunt for arrowheads a few weeks ago. Poking about in Puckett's Cave... young Harman reached for something white in a hole in the ground and, to his vast amazement came up with a handful of human bones. Soundly startled, the 16 year-old lad put them down and dashed for home. Then, after gathering his courage and some reinforcements, he went back and proceeded to dig on the site of his discovery. From the ancient accumulation of ash and limestone debris he turned up the complete skeleton of an 8 foot giant. The grisly find was brought to Dr. R. C. Parker here and stretched out to its enormous length in a hallway of his office where it has since remained the most startling exhibit Steelville has ever had on public view... An appeal to Dr. Aleš Hrdlička, anthropologist of the National Museum in Washington and celebrated authority on primitive races is expected to help. Dr. Parker has written to him, offering to forward the skull or the whole skeleton, if necessary , for scientific study... Meanwhile, speculation is proceeding at a lively rate. The consensus of local opinion is that these prodigious bones are the remains of an Indian—maybe and Osage... A corner in the north wall, just within the entrance formed the giant's tomb. The body apparently had been placed in a kneeling position in a shallow grave... Some 13 years ago, Gorard Fowke, field explorer of the Bureau of Ethnology, Smithsonian Institution, spent several months investigating these cave-dweller remains... One of his most astonishing discoveries was evidence that these aborigines were cannibals, for along with the bones of animals, which they had used for food, he found also human bones, which had been cracked for the extraction of the marrow they contained. These people, he believed lived at least 1000 years ago."

Jim and James Clary found Puckett's cave and the general location where the 8-foot skeleton was removed along the north wall. They met with several relatives of Billy Harmon who all professed to the legitimacy of the find and also found where R. C. Parker's office once was, including running into an old timer who was a patient of Dr. Parker in his youth.

While reading through the microfilm at the Steelville library three reports of the find were uncovered including the photo that shows Les Eaton, a 6 ft man laid out next to the 8 ft skeleton in Dr. Parkers office.

The Steelville Ledger also reported that the skeleton was indeed packed up and shipped to the Smithsonian.

Photo of 6 ft tall Les Eaton lying next to the 8 ft skeleton in Dr. Parker's office.

GIANTS ARE NO MORE, DECLARES HRDLICKA
Berkeley Daily Gazette, March 12, 1934

GIANTS ARE NO MORE, DECLARES HRDLICKA

By United Press

In this news report we find the bold pronouncement from the Smithsonian's head of anthropology Aleš Hrdlička that *"Giants Are No More."* Hrdlička was named the first Director of Anthropology for the Smithsonian Institution in 1910. Although there were already many giant accounts in the Smithsonian's own Ethnology Reports (and other scientific journals of the time), we are told it was basically all a series of mistakes. In the article below he states:

> *"The finder makes a hurried comparison of the length of the fossil thigh bone with his own, and from this calculates the size of this hypothetical ancient giant. The person unfamiliar with human anatomy does not know that the upper joint of the femur is several inches higher than would appear from superficial examination of the living body."*

This explanation does not address the massive amount of reports that are well out of normal range: 26, 28 and 30 inch femurs, 28, 30, 32 and 36 inch circumference skulls are routinely reported. It has to be something else and certainly not an inability to understand how the femur fits into the upper joint, or how to run a tape measure around a skull.

Hrdlička had a couple of other controversial ideas; such as the following, printed in the *Science News letter*:

> *"the greatest danger before the American people today is the blending of the Negro tenth of the population into the superior blood of the white race."*[11]

Hrdlička was appointed to the *Committee on the Negro*, along with Earnest

234

Hooton and fellow pre-Nazi eugenist Charles Davenport. In 1927 their committee endorsed a comparison of African babies with young apes, in 1937 Hrdlička also published findings in his *American Journal of Physical Anthropology* to:

> "...prove that the negro race is phylogenetically a closer approach to primitive man than the white race."

Through cranial measurement, Hrdlička concluded that Native Americans along with African Americans were inferior to the white race. As geologist Kirk Bryan told his students during the reign of Hrdlička:

> "if you ever find evidence of human life in a context which is ancient, bury it carefully but do not forget about it." [12]

One of the reasons Hrdlička might have covered up or marginalized giant skeletal finds of Native Americans, is because it flew in the face of the field of Eugenics, which correlated cranial size with intelligence. Massive skulls were certainly not welcome additions to the debate.

Hrdlička also zealously believed there was no one inhabiting the US before 2000 BC and opposed anyone who questioned this, finally being forced to accept the Folsom finds from the New Mexico site. The Folsom site was excavated in 1926 and showed 23 bison had been killed using distinctive points called *Folsom points* between 8,000 and 9,000 BC. He called Louis Leaky a heretic to his face. He also may have taken the same approach to giant skeletal finds and inconvenient artifacts found in Native American burial mounds. He clashed with Warren K. Morehead who reported unearthing giant skeletons in West Virginia, Illinois, Pennsylvania, and Connecticut. Morehead's later writings showed he was becoming increasingly concerned about the plight of Native Americans. Hrdlička was not alone with his eugenist views at the Smithsonian, surrounding himself with many like-minded colleagues.

Obviously, anthropologists should not be tainted personally by this unfortunate dynamic, but hopefully they can re-evaluate evidence that may have been marginalized or excluded from their field.

GEORGIA'S SAND-DUNES YIELD STARTLING PROOF
OF A PREHISTORIC RACE OF GIANTS
The Portsmouth Times, July 28, 1936
Sea Island, Georgia

Even though Hrdlička pronounced *"Giants No More"* two years earlier, they just kept coming back to haunt him. In this account we are told that archaeologists were *"mystified at finding the skeletons of men who were seven feet tall."* In one photo Dr. Preston Holder points out the *"unusual characteristics"* of the skeletal finds. The article leads off by informing the reader of the following:

> *"Perhaps the discovery of dinosaur bones on the North American continent created no more sensation in scientific circles than the recent revelations of prehistoric man lately developed off the coast of Georgia."*

The Smithsonian Institution sponsored the work and the lead archaeologist was Dr. Preston Holder. Dr. M. F. Seltzer of the *United States National Museum* was dispatched to the scene and none other than Aleš Hrdlička examined some of the first skulls unearthed by Dr. Holder. The archaeologists used words like *"sturdy"* and *"brawny"* in describing the massiveness of the skeletal structure.

This particular dig was called *The Sea Island Mound Dig at Sea Island, Georgia*. It was a WPA (The Works Progress Administration) dig, sponsored by the Smithsonian and took place from May to June 1936 and February to May 1937. The WPA project numbers were 165-34-3338 and 165-34-8031. Jim read through several books including *The Georgia and South Carolina Coastal Expeditions of Clarence Moore* (1998), *A New Deal for Southeastern Archaeology* by Edwin Lyon (1996), and finally started to understand all this after reading *Shovel Ready Archaeology and Roosevelt's New Deal for America* by Bernard K. Means (2013). Jim could not find any mention of unusually large skeletons apart from in the original well-detailed article. The following is from *Shovel Ready Archaeology and Roosevelt's New Deal for America* :

"The history of New Deal archaeology on the Georgia coast has remained obscure, because the foremost archaeologist of the coast, Preston Holder, was not permitted to publish the major results of his excavations. His superiors at the Smithsonian Institution in Washington D.C., at the Oculmegee National Monument in Macon, Georgia and at the Works Progress Administration (WPA) offices in Savannah Georgia, did not allow him to publish his highly detailed progress reports and strongly discouraged and effectively prevented him from developing a Columbia University Dissertation on the entire Georgia coast." [13]

Although Dr. Holder, as well as Dr. Seltzer, and Dr. Hrdlička examined and commented on the evidence, we could find no mention of the giant stature of the skeletons after the initial report. This is in spite of photographs being taken at the site. However, we did find the following information regarding this episode. Kevin Kiernan, Professor Emeritus of English at the University of Kentucky in his paper, and Preston Holder on the Georgia Coast (1936-1938), informs us:

"Very little information is in print about Preston Holder's extensive, seminal, Works Progress Administration (WPA) era excavations of prehistoric and early contact Indian sites on the Georgia Coast, from Savannah to St. Simons Island, between April 1936 and February 1938. For reasons that remain obscure, his WPA supervisors in Washington (Smithsonian Institution) and Georgia did not permit Holder to publish his work-in-progress, discouraged the use of his results for his Columbia doctorate, and effectively hid his formal unpublished reports and relevant papers from scrutiny. In some cases, the supervisors expunged the reports and papers. Under his name, only one meager, two-page note, which was never intended for print publication, briefly describes five of the sites that he excavated in 1936 and 1937 on St. Simons Island." [14]

These are the words of a cautious and respected professor and look at the words he chose: *"reasons that remain obscure," "did not permit," "discouraged," "effectively hid," "expunged"* and *"never intended."* It should be noted that Professor Kiernan had many accolades and laureates.[15]

SMITHSONIAN GETS HUGE INDIAN SKULL
Rochester Journal, October 5, 1936
Aleutian Islands, Alaska

This is one of several giant finds that occurred in the Aleutian Islands of Alaska. They are a chain of 14 large volcanic islands and 55 smaller ones, forming part of the Aleutian Arc in the Northern Pacific Ocean, occupying an area of 6,821 sq miles and extending about 1,200 miles westward from the Alaska Peninsula toward the Kamchatka Peninsula.

Hrdlička personally unearthed this oversized skull two years after pronouncing *"Giants are no More."* Let us look at a quote from Ross Hamilton. who discusses Hrdlička in *A Tradition of Giants*:

SMITHSONIAN GETS HUGE INDIAN SKULL

By Associated Press,

WASHINGTON, Oct. 5.—After a Summer spent nosing around the Aleutian Islands, Dr. Alex Hrdlicka is home with a big head. In fact. the skull, which the Smithsonian Institution anthropologist picked up, once contained the largest human brain of record in the Western Hemisphere, Institution scientists say.

The skull, believed to have belonged to an Aleut who lived hundreds of years ago, had a brain capacity of 2,005 cubic centimeters. The average man has about 1,450 cubic centimeters and the average woman 1,300.

"It is hardly beyond the scope of an overly ambitious man and a cooperative (perhaps intimidated) staff to have cleaned house of a surplus of challenging artifacts in view of the political problems attending such evidence. Like the ecclesiastical editorship of the Constantine era, when a group of elite researchers believe themselves to be a sort of priestcraft charged with preserving the truth, much that would question their wisdom is inexplicably unobtainable. We do not know what treasures have laid in the private vaults of the Vatican, and a similar inscrutability is inherent with the Smithsonian. An institution selecting its executive staff by private appointment, we are left to assume the anthropology division of the National

Museum is one of the last good old boys clubs still influencing the national psyche in a questionable sense. We wonder why there is no one there to engage a whistle-blowing operation."

CAT. NO.	NAME	Skull (No lower jaw or face)
377,860	People	Aleut
	Locality	Kagamil Island, Alaska (Mummy caves)
ACC. NO.		
138,127	Collector	A. Hrdlicka
	How acquired	Coll. for Museum Date acc'd Feb. 4, 1937
ORIG. NO.	Where placed P.374 5- A - k ..	
	Remarks	Male Adult. Very large - capacity about 2,000 cc

B 1 - 2/3

Skeletal parts present:

	Rt.	Lt.		Rt.	Lt.			
Hum.			Fem.			Sternum.		
Rad.			Tibia			Ribs		
Ulna			Fib.			Sacrum		
Scap.			Innom.			Vert.	C	T
Clav.			Foot				L	
Hand								

U. S. NAT. MUSEUM   GPO 16—28000-1   DIVISION OF PHYSICAL ANTHROPOLOGY

Official Smithsonian catalogue card of skull that Dr. Hrdlička discovered in 1936

SMITHSONIAN AMAZED AT DISCOVERY OF 6 ½ -FOOT MUMMIES IN CAVES
The Washington Post, July 22, 1937
Sonora, Mexico

This is a teaser of a later chapter and is a very interesting story examining the explorations of Paxson Hayes in Sonora, Mexico, and the involvement of the Smithsonian:

"Paxson C. Hayes and Gerald C. Barnes....have found traces of an extinct race of Mexican giants... Smithsonian officials agreed Hayes and Barnes had something there, but weren't sure what it was."

The taller than average mummies are part of a controversial story we investigate fully in the *Giants of Sonora, Mexico* chapter.

239

The Largest Skull Ever Recorded Is Discovered by Archaeologist
The Washington Post, June 24, 1937
Potomac Creek, Stafford County, Virginia

A gigantic skull was found by archaeologist and presiding judge W. J. Graham of the United States Court of Custom and Patents Appeals. He found the enormous specimen in Stafford County, Virginia, the site of many other giant skeleton finds. All his finds were sent to the Smithsonian. Judge Graham was astounded after he saw it mounted and said, *"it looked almost as big as a watermelon."* This would be a correct assumption as it had a cranial capacity of 2100cc. The one on the left is an average human skull and the one in the middle, is *"above average."*

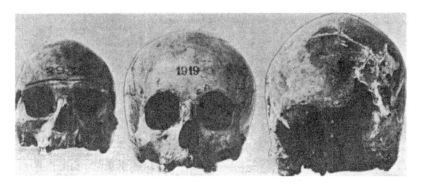

He also estimated that its owner must have had a hat size over eight. It was also recorded in the Smithsonian accession records as can be seen below:[16]

CAT. No.	NAME	Skull without Face (Very Large), mandible (frag)
378,138	People	Indian
	Locality	Potomac Creek, Stafford Co., Va.
Acc. No.		
144,975	Collector	Wm. J. Graham
	How acquired	Gift Date acc'd Aug. 17, 1937
ORIG. No.	Where placed	2-K
	Remarks	Adult Male.; macrocephalic (2100 cc); cast.

Skeletal parts present:

	Rt.	Lt.		Rt.	Lt.		
Hum. . .			Fem. . .			Sternum . . .	
Rad. . .			Tibia . .			Ribs	
Ulna . .			Fib. . .			Sacrum . . .	
Scap. . .			Innom. . .			Vert. . . . .C . . . . .T	
Clav. . .			Foot . .			L	
Hand . .							

ALEUTIAN GRAVE HOLDS BONES OF GIANT
Toledo Blade April 27, 1944, pg.8
Aleutian Islands, Alaska

The report describes the discovery of a giant *"at least seven feet tall."* The bodies were arranged in a geometric pattern like *"spokes of a wheel."* These finds may have a possible connection to this following story recorded by David Hatcher Childress about an episode in the Aleutians. This is an often-told tale about possible skullduggery:

"Ivan T. Sanderson, a well-known zoologist and frequent guest on Johnny Carson's 'Tonight Show' in the 1960s (usually with an exotic animal—a pangolin or a lemur), once related a curious story about a letter he received regarding an engineer who was stationed on the Aleutian island of Shemya during World War II. While building an airstrip, his crew bulldozed a group of hills and discovered under several sedimentary layers what appeared to be human remains. The Alaskan mound was in fact a graveyard of gigantic human remains, consisting of crania and long leg bones. The crania measured from 22 to 24 inches from base to crown. Since an adult skull normally measures about eight inches from back to front, such a large cranium would imply an immense size for a normally proportioned human. Furthermore, every skull was said to have been neatly trepanned (a process of cutting a hole in the upper portion of the skull). In fact, the habit of flattening the skull of an infant and forcing it to grow in an elongated shape was a practice used by ancient Peruvians, the Mayas, and the Flathead Indians of Montana. Sanderson tried to gather further proof, eventually receiving a letter from another member of the unit who confirmed the report. The letters both indicated that the Smithsonian Institution had collected the remains, yet nothing else was heard. Sanderson seemed convinced that the Smithsonian Institution had received the bizarre relics, but wondered why they would not release the data. He asks, "...is it that these people cannot face rewriting all the textbooks?"

241

SMITHSONIAN REPORTS

The following accounts are all official Smithsonian documents and reports of excavations from their series of annual reports.

The Fifth (1887) and Twelfth (1894) Smithsonian Annual Reports.
Both feature numerous giant accounts.

Annual Report of the Board of Regents of the Smithsonian Institution for the year 1873 (pg.418)
Anna, Union County, Illinois

This account from a burial mound in Illinois is truly remarkable. It was recorded by T. M. Perrin when excavating various mounds and earthworks in the area (see *Anatomic Anomalies* chapter for further details):

> *"The skulls are very large but fall to pieces on being exposed to the air. One skull was found that would have measured 36 inches in circumference."*

242

*Annual Report of the Board of Regents of the
Smithsonian Institution for the year 1875 (pg.392)*
Amelia Island, Florida

In this early Smithsonian report, there is a description of a giant skeleton being unearthed with an enormous skull, double rows of teeth and a giant axe (See earlier reference in *DRT* Chapter). Dr. Augustus Mitchell states:

> *"Anticipating a perfect specimen in this skull, I was doomed to disappointment; for, after taking it out of the earth and setting it up, so that I could view the fleshless face of this gigantic savage, in the space of about two hours it crumbled to pieces, except small portions. According to the bones of this skeleton, its height must have been quite seven feet."*

---

*Annual Report of the Board of Regents of the
Smithsonian Institution for the year 1877 (Pg.260)*
Kishwaukee Mounds, Illinois

In this official report it describes *"stone hatchets, axes, and skinning stones"* being found at the Kishwaukee Mounds in Illinois. However, a ten-pound axe is also discussed, followed by this:

> *"...but the largest one in this section is in Dr. Everett's collection. It weighs one ounce over 15 pounds; is of dark colour; the shape is artistic; the external boundary lines are all graceful curves. Only a giant could have wielded it."*

And:

> *"One of them was in the grave of a giant, for a large man could pass the jawbone around his face and the thigh bone was four inches longer than that of a man six feet two inches high."* (pg.274)

Further on we find:

> *"It was found lying in a grave by the side of a huge skeleton, much taller than the current race of men."* (pg.276)

Fifth Annual Report of The Bureau of Ethnology of the Smithsonian Institution 1883-1884 (Pub. 1887)

Thanks to authors Greg Little and Andrew Collins (*Path of Souls*, 2014), for researching these following accounts that mention *"large"* or *"extremely large skeletons"* in the Smithsonian's Fifth Annual Report:

Wisconsin. A large mound in Sheboygan County yielded a *"large"* skeleton (pg.19).

West Virginia. At the Smith farm in the Kanawha Valley, a *"large skeleton"* was recovered (pg.52). At a lower level in the same mound, another skeleton, 7 ft 6 in, was found (pg.52). Another mound (#7) in the same area yielded a 7 ft skeleton (pg.56). Two *"very large skeletons"* were found in the *Poor House* or *Institute Mound* (pg.57).

North Carolina. The *Nelson Mound* yielded a 7-foot skeleton (pg.62). The Jones Mound, not too far from the Nelson Mound, also yielded a *"very large"* skeleton (pg.67).

Georgia. Etowah Mound: A 7-foot skeleton was found(pg.98).

Cyrus Thomas concluded the report with an article called *Burial Mounds of the Northern Sections of the United States*, that showed a clear shift from his initial stance that a legendary lost race were responsible for the mounds:

"...there is nothing found in the mode of constructing these mounds, nor in the vestiges of art they contained, to indicate that their builders had reached a higher culture status that that attained by some of the Indian tribes found occupying the country at the time of the first arrival by Europeans." (pg.108)

This was the beginning of the end of the lost race discussion that had been going on for decades. Whether they related this to the stream of massive skeletons that were being uncovered is not clear, as further taller-than-average examples were continuously being unearthed and recorded, most notably in the *Twelfth Annual Report* of 1894, that covered excavations ranging from 1882 to 1891.

Twelfth Annual Report of the Bureau of American Ethnology of
the Smithsonian Institution, 1894 (pg.113)
Dunleith Mounds, East Dubuque, Illinois

The *Twelfth Annual Report* has become a mecca for giantologists, for reasons
that will soon become clear. John Wesley Powell summarized the intention
of the report when he wrote in the introduction "*The most important
question to be settled is, 'were the mounds built by the Indians?'*"(pg.21).
This one describes the opening of burial mounds in Dunleith, Illinois, that
was also reported on page 35 of the Fifth Annual Report:

> "*No. 5, the largest of the group carefully examined. Two feet
> below the surface, near the apex, was a skeleton, doubtless an
> intrusive Indian burial. Near the original surface of the ground,
> several feet north of the center, were the much decayed skeletons
> of some 6 or 8 persons, of every size, from infant to the adult.
> Near the original surface, 10 or 12 feet from the center, on the
> lower side, lying at full length upon its back, was one of the
> largest skeletons discovered by the Bureau agents, the length as
> proved by actual measurement being between 7 and 8 feet. It
> was clearly traceable but crumbled to pieces immediately after
> removal from the hard earth it was encased.*"

Twelfth Annual Report (pg.117)
Welch Mounds, Pike County, Missouri

> "*The earth of the main portion of this mound was very fine
> yellowish sand which shoveled like ashes and was everywhere,
> to the depth of from 2 to 4 feet, as full of human skeletons as
> could well be stowed away in it, even to two and three tiers.
> Among these were a number of bones not together as skeletons,
> but mingled in confusion and probably from scaffolds or other
> localities. Excepting one, which was rather more than seven
> feet long, these skeletons appeared to be of medium size and
> many of them much decayed.*" The report also stated "*Another
> was of extraordinary size.*"

Collins and Little spotted further mentions of "large skeletons":

Mississippi. In Union County at the Ingomar Mounds, a *"large skeleton"* was found (pg.273).

Georgia. At Etowah, the 7-foot skeleton described in the earlier Bureau report was again cited (pg.302).

Twelfth Annual Report, 1894 (pg.335)
Nelson Mound, North Carolina

"No. 16 was an unenclosed "squatter" of unusually large size, not less than seven feet high when living."

Two skeletons of *"large stature"* were found in the nearby Nelson Triangle (pg.336).

Twelfth Annual Report, 1894 (pg.362)
Long Island, Roane County, Tennessee

"The length from the base of the skull to the bones of the toes was found to be 7 feet 3 inches. It is probable, therefore, that this individual when living was fully 7 ½ feet high. At the head lay some small pieces of mica and a green substance, probably the oxide of copper, though no ornament or article of copper was discovered. This was the only burial in the mound."

Twelfth Annual Report, 1894 (pg.419)
Kanawha Valley, West Virginia

From a mound in the Spring Hill Enclosure, West Virginia it is reported:

"...among the decayed fragments of bark wrappings, lay a skeleton fully 7 feet long, extended at full length on the back, west."

Twelfth Annual Report, 1894 (pg.426)
The Great Smith Mound, West Virginia

On page 426 it describes the opening of a burial mound in Kanawha County, West Virginia by Professor P. W. Norris of the Smithsonian. This find was also reported in *The New York Times* and several other places:

> *"At the depth of 14 feet a rather large human skeleton was found, which was in a partially upright position with the back against a hard clay wall. All the bones were badly decayed, except those of the left wrist, which had been preserved by two heavy copper bracelets...Nineteen feet from the top the bottom of this debris was reached, where, in the remains of a bark coffin, a skeleton, measuring 7 ½ feet in length and 19 inches across the shoulders was discovered. Each wrist was encircled by six heavy copper bracelets."*

Fig. 299.—Copper bracelet from mound No. 21, Kanawha county, West Virginia.

Professor Norris' handwritten notes about the excavations at Smith Mound are included. The highlights of his original notes make clear matter-of-fact statements about giant skeletons. The authors acquired these notes thanks to researcher Josh McGraw's diligent efforts. We believe they are important because these were Norris' first impressions of the dig. Here are a selection of them that stood out:

> *pg.47: "Human skeleton - gigantic 1, large 1."*
> *pg.55: "...only nearly decayed fragments of a large human skeleton."*
> *pg.56: "Gigantic human skeleton (?)."*
> *pg.57: "...decayed skeleton (less the cranium which certainly had never been placed there) of a very large human being"*
> *pg.59: "The cranium (which is of the Peruvian type) together with the lower jaw are sent to the Bureau...was found a very large human skeleton too (?) decayed for excavation."*
> *pg.63: "...anything of interest save the (?) above mentioned which had been missed near the head of the giant."*
> *pg.64: "...the bones of the giant."*
> *pg.81: "2 very large human skeletons in a sitting posture."*

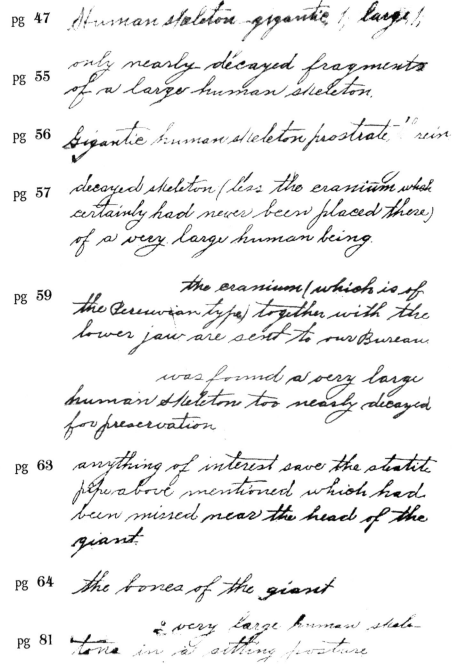

pg 47   Human skeleton gigantic (large (,

pg 55   only nearly decayed fragments of a large human skeleton.

pg 56   Gigantic human skeleton prostrate, rein

pg 57   decayed skeleton (less the cranium which certainly had never been placed there) of a very large human being.

pg 59   the cranium (which is of the Peruvian type) together with the lower jaw are sent to our Bureau.

was found a very large human skeleton too nearly decayed for preservation

pg 63   anything of interest save the steatite pipe above mentioned which had been missed near the head of the giant.

pg 64   the bones of the giant

pg 81   a very large human skele-ton in a sitting posture

Professor Norris' handwritten notes about the giants unearthed at Smith Mound.

Below are some further accounts from the *Twelfth Annual Report* collected by Little and Collins:

> **West Virginia.** "*Two very large skeletons*" were found in Mound 31 (Institute, or Poor House Mound) in the same grouping as described above (pg.432). "*Many large skeletons*" were found in rock mounds nearby (pg.436). In the nearby McCulloch Mound was another "*very large skeleton*" (pg.437). Another "*very large skeleton*" was excavated from Barboursville, Virginia (pg.440).

> **Ohio.** Stone graves near Ripley, Ohio, yielded two "*extremely large skulls*" and "*long femur bones*" but no complete skeletons (pg.453).

> **Coshocton County, Ohio.** A stone box grave with a 7 ft long skeleton was found (pg.458)

> **Pennsylvania.** The remains of one "*large size adult*" were found in McKees Rocks Mound (pg.495).

The report recorded over 40,000 artifacts and countless skeletal remains. Over 2,000 mounds were excavated during the timeframe of this report (1882 - 1891). Powell concluded "*the author believes that the theory which attributes these works to the Indians....to be the correct one.*"[17]

Although there are clearly numerous accounts of taller-than-average skeletons, neither Powell or Thomas (who wrote the concluding remarks in the 1894 report) mention them once. They are simply ignored. Why would they do this, especially at a time when hundreds of giant skeletons were being reported in American newspapers, in town and country histories, and by their own Smithsonian employees?

They also both dismissed any and every theory of overseas ancient cultures visiting America, and made a point to put an end to the lost race theory. It almost certainly appears they linked the giant skeletons with the enigmatic lost race that Cyrus Thomas had firmly believed in previously. Whether he simply came to his senses based on his years of research and analysis, or whether the particularly demanding Powell influenced him in some way, is not clear.

Some of these skeletons the Smithsonian discovered were remarkably tall (up to 8 feet), yet they have all gone missing or have since been taken away by NAGPRA. No matter what Powell or Thomas thought about these reports, it is very telling that they did not mention any of the taller-than-average skeletons in their final words.

These reports leave a very intriguing legacy for our generation to ponder. The written word constitutes a powerful record of what came before us, and for the directors of one of the worlds leading institutions to ignore or deliberately suppress their own writings and research, as well as the hundreds of news reports, leaves us to conclude that their were forces gathering at the national museum that signalled an end to the true legacy of ancient America.

U.S.N.M.—DEPARTMENT OF ANTHROPOLOGY—DIVISION OF PHYSICAL ANTHROPOLOGY

MUSEUM NUMBER	NAME _Skeleton_
_227508_	PEOPLE _Sioux, full blood_
ACCESSION NUMBER	LOCALITY _Indiana_
_42.109_	COLLECTOR _Dr. Wm. A. Collins_
ORIGINAL NUMBER	HOW ACQUIRED _Gift of the A.M.M_
_A.M.M.2136_	DATES _Jan. 7, 1904_ Skull 75-I
Put in Hooper case 10	WHERE PLACED _Laboratory_ Skeleton 77-C
	DIMENSIONS _Giant_
	REMARKS _Died in 1878, said to have been 8 feet tall; skeleton prepared by boiling. Male_

Example of a Smithsonian accession card of "Sioux, full blood" with dimensions as "Giant."

250

9

CURIOUS ARTIFACTS

Unusual artifacts were often reported along with giant skeletons all over North America. Extra large tools and weapons, tablets with peculiar writing, metal artifacts, mysterious ancient coins and medallions, and even an ancient gun. All these out-of-place-artifacts are described in the following accounts.

STRANGE INSCRIPTIONS

THE GRAVE CREEK TABLET
Grave Creek Mound, Moundsville, West Virginia, 1838

The Grave Creek Mound is discussed in detail in the *Giants in the Mounds* chapter. It was built by the Adena culture between 300-150 BC[1] and when the 62-foot mound was opened in 1838, a strange tablet with curious writing was said to have been unearthed with skeletal remains in a stone-arched vault. Various accounts report that giant skeletons were found.[2]

J. P. MacLean, best known for his 1893 book *The Mound Builders*, said this on the matter:

"It was in this vault that the inscribed stone was found on the 16th of the following June. From a letter written to Mr. P. P. Cherry, March 7th, 1878, by Mr.

251

Tomlison, it would appear that the stone was found at the end of a second drift which was excavated from the side of mound to the upper vault. After striking the second vault the men from the first vault drilled upward until the second fell to the bottom." [3]

MacLean included a letter dated June 19th 1879, from Colonel James E. Wharton, who was present when the stone was found:

"On going to the end of the drift we found some debris, and a man or two at work, and another...wheeling out the dirt that seemed to have fallen...We went out and lazily engaged in hauling over the dirt for curiosities, some few of which we found." [4]

The letter continues explaining that they carefully sifted through the dirt looking for artifacts, and a man who was working there handed them the tablet that was still covered in dirt. This obviously raises alarms as it was not clear if it was found that day. However, it was said to look worn and ancient and it was covered in mud, although the authenticity has been speculated upon ever since. Wharton had no doubt it was genuine:

"The letters were not all Phoenician, showing that the one who cut them had been long mingling with others, and his language had been corrupted. Whereas a fraud would naturally have copied all the letters from the published alphabet; the ornament on it is well proportioned showing that the maker was accustomed to seeing what he copied. There was no motive for the fraud, no one anywhere in the region who could have made it if he would, and few frauds of the kind have been heard of." [5]

Multiple suggestions of the inscription's origins have been put forward since its discovery,[6] but the initial interpretation of it being a corrupted Phoenician alphabet is intriguing. The Phoenicians were also known as the Canaanites, who originated in the area of modern day Syria, Lebanon and Israel. This ancient holy land was known for its historical giants, that we will take a look at in the final chapter.

Harvard epigrapher Barry Fell also suggested it was Punic (Phoenician), used along the Iberian Peninsula in the 1st millennium BC. It reads from right to left and translates as:

1. The mound raised-on-high for Tasach
2. This tile
3. (His) queen caused-to-be-made [7]

Fell explained:

"The alphabet of the tablet was deciphered by Spanish scholars, and published by English epigrapher D. Diringer in 1968. The basic language is Semitic, and all words occur in standard literary Semitic dictionaries." [8]

The original is now lost but there are some molds of it in the Smithsonian and one in the museum at the site in Moundsville.

A stone with similar inscriptions called the 'Wilson-Braxton Tablet' was discovered in 1931 in a stream bed in central West Virginia. It was originally thought to be of Viking origin, but Fell, using the same techniques he used on the Grave Creek Stone, with lettering found in standard Semitic dictionaries, translated it to read:

1. The memorial of Teth
2. This tile
3. (His) brother caused-to-be-made [9]

The Wilson-Braxton Tablet, discovered in 1931.

If these curious tablets are genuine, they leave some tantalising clues as to the origins of the Mound Builders.

THE BRUSH CREEK TABLET
Muskingum County, Ohio, Brush Creek Township, March 3, 1880

Thankfully this image is still in existence, for the original has gone missing. The following is a letter from the men who excavated the mound where the tablet and numerous skeletons were reportedly found. The content is carefully and thoughtfully documented and is the sworn testimony of the five men involved in the find. Ross Hamilton believes that the skeletons buried in the Brush Creek Mound were the truly ancient "Tall Ones" and that the out-of-place sugar-loaf-shaped mound quite possibly was one of the oldest in the country before it was destroyed. Ross also believes that the couples were the breeding elite and were ceremonially put to death by their own people, so they did not fall into the hands of an invading enemy - the Lenape.

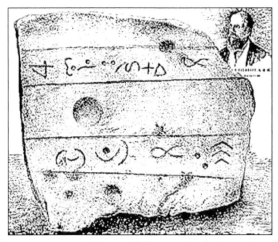

The now lost Brush Creek Tablet was found among skeletons measuring over 8 and 9 feet in length in Brush Creek Township, Muskigum County, Ohio, in the early1880s.

To Dr. F. T. Everhart, Historian

"Dear sir, on December 1, 1879 we assembled with a large number of people for the purpose of excavating into and examining the contents of an ancient mound, located on the farm of Mr. J. M. Baughman, in Brush Creek Township. The mound is situated on the summit of a hill, rising 152 feet above

254

the bed of the stream called Brush Creek. It is about 64 feet in width by about 90 feet in length, having an altitude of 11 feet 3 inches; is nearly flat on top. On the mound were found the stumps of 16 trees ranging in size from 8 inches to 2 and a half feet in diameter. We began the excavations by digging a trench four feet wide from the east side....At this juncture work was abandoned on account of the lateness of the hour, until Monday December 8th when it was resumed by opening the mound from the Northwest. When at the depth of seven and a half feet in the north trench, we came upon two enormous skeletons, male and female, lying one above the other, faces together, and heads toward the west. The male by actual measurement, proved to be nine feet six inches, the female eight feet nine inches in length. At about the same depth in the west trench we found two more skeletons, lying two feet apart, faces upward and faces to the east. These, it is believed were full as large as those already measured but the condition in which they were found rendered exact measurement impossible.

On December 22nd we began digging at the southwest portion of the mound, and had not proceeded more than three feet when we discovered an altar made of sand rock. The altar was six feet in width and twelve feet in length, and was filled with clay, and of about the same shape that the mound originally was. Immediately behind or west of the altar, were found three skeletons, lying faces upwards heads toward the south, measuring, respectively: eight feet ten, nine feet two and nine feet four inches in length. In another grave a female skeleton eight feet long and a male skeleton nine feet four inches long- the female the lowermost, and the face downward, and the male on top face upward, behind the site of the altar.

After proceeding about four feet, we found, within three feet of the top of the mound, and five feet above the natural surface, a coffin or burial case, made of a peculiar kind of yellow clay, the like of which we have not found in the township, consequently, we believe it was brought from a distance. Within the casket were confined the remains of a female eight feet in length...We have found 11 human skeletons in all... The above report contains nothing but facts briefly told and knowing that the public has been humbugged and imposed upon by archaeologists, we wish to fortify our own statements by giving the following testimonial. We the undersigned citizens of Brush Creek Township, having been present and taken part in the above excavation, do certify that the statements herewith set forth our true and correct, and in no particular has the writer deviated from the facts in the case. Signed Thomas D. Showers, John Worstall, Marshall Cooper, J.M. Baughman, S.S. Baughman, John E. McCoy."

This account is detailed with meticulous measurements of everything, including the skeletons. Ross Hamilton commented on this:

"At the bottom of the three-page account, the signature of six citizens was affixed in an affidavit verifying the truth, correctness, and non-deviation from the facts. It is quite possible that these people reported on something a bit rarer than ever expected. The mounded structure was possibly Archaic Allegheny." [10]

GIANT IN ANCIENT MOUND: CURIOUS RELICS OF PREHISTORIC TIMES IS FOUND IN THE TOMB
The Washington Post, June 23, 1908
Huntington, West Virginia

This caught our attention because it is in the vicinity of Grave Creek Mound in Moundsville and a similar inscribed tablet is mentioned. It also included copper bracelets found with a *"massive"* skeleton. Unfortunately the mound is now gone, and only the written word of what was reported still exists:

"The municipal authorities of Central City, four miles west of here, three weeks ago ordered the removal of a prehistoric mound from Thirteenth street. Today twelve feet above the base of the mound a gigantic human skeleton was discovered.

256

It is almost seven feet in length, and of massive proportions. It was surrounded by a mass of rude trinkets. Eight huge copper bracelets were discovered. Thus, when burnished, proved to be of purest beaten copper and a perfect preservation. Rude stone vessels, hatchets, and arrowheads were found with the skeleton. A curiously inscribed totem was found at the head of the skeleton. The Smithsonian Institution will be notified of the discovery."

DISCOVERY OF ANCIENT TOMB OF AZTEC MAN - REMARKABLE FIND OF ABORIGINAL GIANT
'Artisans and Artifacts of Vanished Races'
by Theophilus L. Dickerson, 1915, pg.151
Alcinda, Indiana

"Some workman while digging in a piece of hilly woodland discovered a curiously shaped stone that extended about four feet below the surface and bearing strange hieroglyphic characters. Curiosity prompted the workmen to remove this stone cover from the vault, which was found to be circular in shape. The stone cover was six inches in thickness. In the stone grave was the remains of a skeleton approximating the stature of a giant, and in primitive times no doubt he occupied a commanding position, judging from the care that had been given in building a stone sepulcher and the metal and stone ornaments found about this prehistoric human skeleton. The copper ornaments on this aboriginal giant almost cover the skeleton. The characters on the stone cover resemble the phonetic or queer hieroglyphic symbols on the stones of Aztec ruins in Mexico, Central America and Yucatan."

Virtually every report we have seen with strange hieroglyphic writing has also come with a report of a giant skeleton being found. We might surmise that the giants were affiliated with a literate mentality. It is a curious thing indeed.

Ancient Metallurgy

The Great Lakes area was once a busy copper mining area that goes back to at least 5000 BC.[11] It has been estimated that millions of pounds of copper ore was mined in the region, although most of it seems to be no longer be in North America. In this section we look at reports of metals being found with oversized skeletons, not only in the Great Lakes region, but across the country and even in Canada.

Inscribed Copper Breastplate
The Stark County Democrat, Ohio, May 14, 1874
Labrador, Canada

This account from Canada relays a tale of a stone cairn that yielded a brass shield and breastplate. The article reads,

"Dr. McHenry, of Quebec, who spent last summer in Labrador, writes to the Archaeological Weekly that he found many important evidences of the presence of the Northmen in that peninsula, on the banks of the river Moisie and in the regions frequented by the Nasquapee Indians. One cairn in particular, the stones of which were so heavy as to defy the assaults of

Embossed copper breast plate worn by the Timucua. circa 1562, Florida.

258

Indians or bears, he forced open with gunpowder, and found in it a gigantic human skull, breastplate and brass-bound shield. The breastplate, though much rusted, bore signs of an inscription or legend, failing to decipher which, he sent it to Copenhagen to see if it could be made out by the American archaeologists there."

GIGANTIC SKELETON OF A MAN
The New York Sun, August 27, 1891
Salt Lake City, Utah

This account yields another out-of-place-artifact from Utah:

"The gigantic skeleton of a man, measuring 8 feet 6 inches in height, was found near the Jordan River, just outside Salt Lake City last week. The find was made by a workman who was digging an irrigation ditch. The skull was uncovered at a depth of eight feet from the surface of the ground, and the skeleton was standing upright. The workman had to dig down nine feet in order to exhume it... A copper chain, to which was attached three medallions covered with curious hieroglyphics, was around the neck of the skeleton, and near it were found a stone hammer, some pieces of pottery, an arrowhead and some copper medals. Archaeologists believe that the original owner of the skeleton belonged to the race of the mound builders."

THE CATHOLIC CHURCH IN THE NIAGARA PENINSULA
by William R. Harris 1626 -1895, pp.19-20
Niagara, New York State

We are informed that Dr. Reynolds unearthed 20 skeletons *"one third larger than the Iroquois or Huron"*, 15 feet down at the head of the Gallops Rapids on the River St. Lawrence:

"Remains of earthenware, pieces of copper, and instruments of

259

*rude workmanship were ploughed up within the area...Some of
the skeletons were of gigantic proportion. The lower jaw of one
is sufficiently large to surround the corresponding bone of an
adult of our generation."*

We find the mention of a mound in Orleans County, New York that yielded:

*"...skeletons of giant size, pieces of pottery and earthenware,
covered with patterns in relief, wrought with great skill."*

We also are informed that in 1809, three and a half miles from Aurora,
New York, a copper plate that was sixteen inches long and twelve inches
wide was ploughed up:

*"Upon it were engraved characters extending its whole length,
which have not yet been deciphered."*

It even describes where they were mining for the copper:

*"In 1847, prospectors of the Minnesota Mining Company
discovered an abandoned mine, in which were found ladders,
masses of broken rock, tools and implements, proving that
the mine had been opened and worked by a race of men who
knew the value of copper for decorative, ornamental and other
purposes."*

CEREMONIAL AXES OF COPPER
Seip Mound and Hopewell Group, Ross County, Ohio, 1902

A large copper axe was unearthed at Seip Mound, Ross County, Ohio,
while an even larger example was found by Warren K. Moorehead at the
Hopewell Group site. They are generally believed to be ceremonial, rather
than practical. The Seip Mound axe weighed 27 pounds (12.25 kg) and the
larger one was 38 pounds (17.25 kg). Other examples were also discovered:

*"Many of these rare objects were found by Moorehead in the
central mound of the Hopewell Group, by the writer in another
mound of the same group, by Mills in the mound City Group,*

and by McKern in the Wisconsin Hopewell Mounds. Some of the longest of these measure as much as 18 inches, with a width of six inches or more." [12]

FIG. 85.   CEREMONIAL AXES OF COPPER

These immense specimens, like the huge ceremonial blades of obsidian, were not intended for utility purposes but were probably used in the ceremonial proceedings of the Hopewell peoples, being part of the paraphernalia of the priests and medicine men and displayed only on state occasions. They weigh 38 and 27 pounds respectively, the smaller one being from the Seip Group, Ross County, Ohio, while the larger specimen was found by Moorehead in the Hopewell Group. Scale, 1/8.

Mound Giants in Indiana Said to Antedate Indian
The News, October 23, 1925, pg.6
South Bend, Indiana

This account is about the unearthing of eight skeletons in a burial mound:

"The eight skeletons lay in circular formation, arranged like the spokes of a wheel, with skulls together. Copper breastplates, bands and other bits of armor adorned the skeleton of one man, who apparently had been of giant stature. Embedded in this skull was a beautiful chipped flint arrowhead."

Grove Vosburg, the 70-year-old farmer on whose land the burial mound

261

MOUND GIANTS IN INDIANA SAID TO ANTEDATE INDIAN

SOUTH BEND, Ind.—Eight skeletons, one of them clad in copper armor, and a hoard of rare war weapons and bits of personal adornment have been found in a mysterious mound on the farm of Grove Vosburg, near Walkerton.

Vosburg, a 70-year-old farmer, had long desired to know the secret of the mount, which according to local tradition dates back hundreds of years. Secretly excavating the pile of earth he came upon a strange burial place.

GIANT SKELETONS

The eight skeletons lay in circular formation, arranged like the spokes of a wheel, with skulls together. Copper breastplates, bands and other bits of armor adorned the skeleton of one man, who apparently had been of giant stature. Embedded in this skull was a beautifully chipped flint arrowhead.

The soft earth of the mound revealed other treasures. Three pounds of ore, believed to be either silver or white gold, lie with the bones. There were corroded copper bands, which antiquarians here believe were used to bind war clubs; two pipe bowls, one of smooth black stone and the other carved with the replica of a fantastic monster, were found.

The belief that the bones are not those of Indians, but belong to the ancient and little known race of mound builders has arisen because of the great size of the bones and the fact that skull formations are not those of Indian types. The skulls seem to have little forehead and the eye cavities are high in the head.

resided, had always wondered about its contents and secretly dug into it. Many intricate artifacts were found:

"Three pounds of ore, believed to be either silver or white gold, lie with the bones. There were corroded copper bands, which antiquarians here believe were used to bind war clubs; two pipe bowls, one of smooth black stone and the other carved with the replica of a fantastic monster, were found."

Once again the skulls were said to have been of a strange type with a *"little forehead and the eye cavities are high in the head"*.

Spokes of a wheel, strange skulls, copper armor and giant skeletons; our guess is that Mr. Vosburg was not spinning a tall tale.

This next account shows that the ancient giants also had a fondness for silver.

VERY OLD INHABITANTS
The Weekly Kansas Chief, October 29, 1874 pg.1
Battle Creek, Michigan

In this special telegram to the *Chicago Times* we have a strange account about a lost silver breastplate with unusual inscriptions, although this may well have been from early Spanish settlers, as silver was not mined or produced in America:

> "...twenty-two skeletons were found, sitting upright, face to
> face in a circle. A number of arrowheads, stone pipes and
> hatchets were found with the skeletons; also a silver breast
> plate covered with curious inscriptions. This plate was sold to
> a young man for $10, who has since moved away, and our
> archaeologists are now endeavoring to get trace of it... The
> most remarkable part of the discovery was the size of the
> skeletons. They were giants and averaged from seven to eight
> feet in height. The lower jaw of any of them could be fitted with
> the greatest ease over a man's face. The teeth were perfectly
> preserved and very large... Old settlers say that when they
> came into the country the Indians, although they had a burial
> place nearby, had no knowledge of these old mounds and said
> that they were built before the recollection of their forefathers."

OVERSIZED AXES

The following reports of gigantic axes are often considered to be ceremonial
objects, but the reality is that many show signs of wear, and are oftentimes
reported with enormous skeletons, suggesting they may have indeed been
wielded and used by these ancient giants.

A GIANT MUMMY :
THE BODY THAT OF A MAN EIGHT FEET TALL
L. A. Times, Nov. 7, 1896, pg. 1
Elkwell Creek, Kentucky

This rare giant mummy from Kentucky is reported along with a giant axe
found with the burial:

> "While digging a cellar near Elkwell Creek, John Winter
> excavated a giant mummy and discovered several interesting
> relics of great value. The find has created excitement here

263

*and crowds are flocking to the scene. The mummy is that
of a man of great stature, being over eight feet tall. It was
wrapped in a winding sheet of skins and carefully sealed in
a canoe shaped coffin. In a few minutes after being exposed
to the air, the mummy commenced to crumble away, but by
careful handling Winter has succeeded in keeping intact his
remarkable discovery. At the head of this prehistoric giant was
a tremendous stone ax, only such as could have been wielded
by a man of wonderful strength. It is a formidable looking
instrument and it is supposed that it was used as the giant's
weapon of war. In the coffin were a few pieces of what appeared
to be cooking utensils and a huge hollowed stone that probably
contained food for the dead. It held also a large, heavy spear
flint point and a shield made of skins. After removing the
mummy and coffin, Winter continued the search and a few
inches deeper discovered a handsomely carved pipe, an axe-
head of curious shape and several broken pieces of crockery.
Many of Winter's neighbors are digging up the ground around
the spot where the body of the dead man was found, in search
of additional curiosities."*

GIANT'S AXE
West Virginia Historical Magazine Quarterly, **March 17, 1902**
Charleston, West Virginia

This account describes the unearthing of a 7 ft 8 inch skeleton from the
Great Smith Mound in West Virginia by Professor P. W. Norris of the
Smithsonian Institution (see also on page 246). A 1902 letter in the *West
Virginia Historical Magazine Quarterly* not only speaks of the find, but also
the unearthing several years later of a giant axe that Mr. Roller connects to
the giant discovered years earlier. This letter describes the giant skeleton
find, as well as the huge axe.

Jim recently received an email from a woman called Sarah from
West Virginia, who emphasised that the people in this letter really existed

and were respected members of the community:

"Just a side note, both men in the letter you provided me were and still are very prominent and respected figures in Charleston."

GIANT'S AXE.

— — —

Charleston, W. Va., March 17, 1902.

Dear Mr. Laidley:

Some years ago when the Colonel Ben Smith mound was opened by Professor Norris, of the Smithsonian, he found the skeleton of a giant which measured seven feet eight inches in length.

This occurred about fifteen years ago. Now comes a sequel. A few days ago Joe Foster was ploughing near the mound and unearthed a stone axe. This axe is of granite, beautifully made and well preserved. It weighs *seven pounds eight ounces.* The largest ever found about here.

Dr. J. N. Mahan bought the axe, and has it in his possession. Could this have been the giant's axe?

Can't you get some of your correspondents to give an article on Indian axes, their history, sizes, &c.?

Very truly yours,

ROBERT DOUGLAS ROLLER.

To W. S. Laidley, Esq.

LARGEST AXE IN THE WORLD
The Archaeological Bulletin March/April, 1916 pg. 104
Collection of J. G. Braeklein. Des Moines River, Clarke County, Mo.

An incredible hand-axe weighing in at a staggering 33 lb and 10 ounces (15.5 kg) was discovered with numerous other artifacts. The axe certainly looks like it has been wielded and worn down over time, so whoever did this was clearly not someone of standard height and size.

The axe was discovered by a farmer boy near the mouth of the Des Moines River, Clarke County, Mo., with numerous other artifacts (see overleaf).

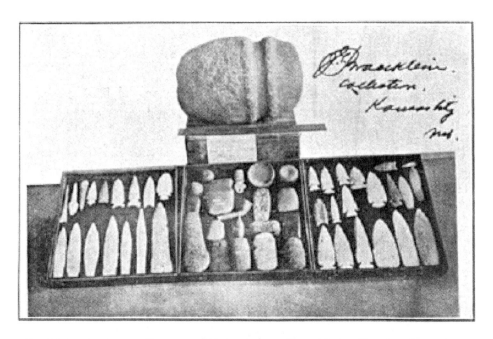

Specimens in the collection of Mr. J. G. Braecklein, Kansas City, Mo.
The large axe shown above is said to be the largest in the world---weighs
33 pounds and 10 ounces---was found about six years ago by a farmer boy
near the mouth of the Des Moines River, Clarke County, Mo.

Weapons and Tools

Ceremonial Blades of Obsidian and Quartz
Seip Mound and Hopewell Group, Ross County, Ohio, 1902

These huge blades were discovered in the Seip Mound and in the Hopewell
Group mounds in Ross County, Ohio. The obsidian blade could also be
a giant arrow head (discovered in the Hopewell Group) by Moorehead
in 1891. It's length is 17 inches. The smaller 13 inch quartz spearhead
was found at Seip Mound. Both were said to be *"ceremonial or sacrificial
offerings"*[13] (See images on next page).

FIG. 87. CEREMONIAL BLADES OF OBSIDIAN AND QUARTZ

Probably unique as to number, size, and the skill required in their production
are the ceremonial blades in the form of spearpoints and knives, taken from the
great central mound of the Hopewell Group by Moorehead in 1891. Over one
hundred of these ceremonial specimens, part of a ceremonial or sacrificial offering, comprised the find, the specimens ranging in size from 6 inches to 18 inches
in length. The specimen shown at the left, of obsidian, is over 17 inches long;
that at the right, of quartz, from the Scip Mounds, is 13 inches in length.
Scale, 1/3.

OUR OWN ARCHEOLOGY: A VALUABLE RELIC OF A
FORMER AGE FOUND IN NEBRASKA, AND WHAT IT TELLS
Boston Evening Transcript, June 12, 1906 pg. 2
(Originally from The Omaha World-Herald)
Florence, Nebraska

The article mostly discusses the finding of a stone spearhead considered
the most symmetrical and sophisticated ever found in Nebraska. Professor
Charles F. Crowley of Creighton Medical College determined it was made
of flint not found in that part of the country. The spearhead is described
as follows:

267

"The implement, which is seven and one-quarter inches long... and three inches wide...is considered to be the most symmetrical and the best made ever found in this state...One side of the stone is colored a lustrous cobalt blue, while the reverse is white. Held to the light it is of a beautiful translucent rose orange."

The article continues:

"An Omaha Archaeologist who has examined the implement declares it to be an arrowhead, and infers that it was probably used by one of the race of giants of which the legends of the Omaha tribe of Indians speak. One of the tribal secret societies which has existed far back in the history of the nation tells of a people who preceded them in this section of the world, the males of which were ten or twelve feet high. Some ancient mounds opened in this vicinity have shown skeletons between eight to ten feet long."

ANCIENT GUN FOUND
Newport Miner, March 17, 1910, pg.2
Lincoln County, Idaho

A rather interesting account is given that describes an ancient gun being found. Alternatively it could have been acquired from an early Spanish or European settler and the skeleton was not that old, or it is simply a story to sell newspapers. Who knows? Here it is anyway:

"...hidden in the deep recesses of a deep cave 25 miles north of Shoshone, Lincoln County in Southern Idaho, is the skeleton of a giant ten feet tall...discovered by a hunting party from this city. As corroborative proof the members are now exhibiting the rusty and time-worn barrel of what appears to be an ancient gun weighing between 25 and 30 pounds, resembling a flint lock rifle. This they say was picked up beside the skeleton. These bones will be taken out of the cave at the earliest possible date and carefully packed and forwarded to the Smithsonian Institute."

Just like Native American tribes across the country, the Shoshone have an oral history that speaks of giants. The Bruneau River in Idaho was named after a French fur-trader in the mid-17th Century. Near its headwaters is the legendary land of the giants who terrorized the Shoshone forefathers, frightening them from their ancestral hunting grounds. Present-day natives still refer to central Idaho's Sawtooth Mountains as the Coapiccan Kahni or Giants House.

Unique Chert Hoes
History of Franklin County, Indiana, Jacob Reifel, 1915, pg.548
Moraine, Indiana

This account is interesting because these hoes were found with a very tall skeleton:

"Unique Chert Hoes found in Moraine, Twelve feet below the surface, surrounding Skeleton of Prehistoric Giant, Height seven feet six inches. Seen in Museum of T. L. Dickerson, Brookville."

Unique Chert Hoes Found in Moraine, Twelve Feet Below Surface, Surrounding Skeleton of a Prehistoric Giant, Height Seven Feet Six Inches. Seen in Museum of T. L. Dickerson, Brookville.

Peculiar Gravel Mound in Henry County, Indiana
'*Artisans and Artifacts of Vanished Races*' by *Theophilus L. Dickerson,*
by Theophilus L. Dickerson, 1915, pg.153
Kennard, Indiana

This account stands out because it is a rare case of carved ivory, most likely from a prehistoric mastodon tusk. On page 153 of this fascinating book a very intriguing account from Indiana is found:

**PECULIAR GRAVEL MOUND
IN HENRY COUNTY, INDIANA**

THIS ISOLATED MONUMENT OF NATURE AT AN EARLY PERIOD
SURROUNDED BY WATER—TWO ROADWAYS FROM NORTH
AND SOUTH LEADING TO IT, MADE BY HUMAN AGENCY.
HUMAN SKELETON EIGHT FEET IN HEIGHT UN-
EARTHED TWELVE FEET BENEATH SUR-
FACE — EIGHTY-FOUR IVORY BEADS
FOUND IN IVORY SAUCER ON
THE BREAST OF GIANT.

When farmers and road builders were digging into the mound for glacial screenings they found the following:

"*After opening this deposit to a depth of 12 feet from the top of the mound they unearthed a human skeleton whose framework measured nearly eight feet in height. His skull would fit over the head of a large man: his jaws being massive and teeth in a perfect state of preservation. On the breast of this big chief was a saucer-shaped vessel of ivory, about six inches in diameter, containing 84 ivory beads, that must have been made from the tusks of a mastodon.*"

We finish this chapter with some beautiful stone pipes found in various mounds, illustrated by Squier and Davis. Many of these were found in the mouths of the buried giant skeletons and were clearly an important part of their lifestyle.

Selection of effigy pipes found in mounds from the Squier and Davis collection.

271

10

MYSTICS & SECRET SOCIETIES

One very interesting twist that occurred during the compiling of historic reports of giant skeletons, was finding that many esoteric sources spoke of the reality of giants and their connection to the lost continent of Atlantis. In the literature of the Freemasons, Rosicrucians and Theosophists giant skeletons were frequently mentioned, some that were given as proof of the existence of this lost landmass. Atlantis was said to be the original home of the esoteric mystery teachings that have been passed down through the ages and kept on record by these secret orders.

Further research led to discovering that two of the most gifted clairvoyants in human history both spoke of the reality of giants and their connection to Atlantis and North America. This is a very strange twist in an already intriguing mystery. The reality that a submerged continent did exist in the Atlantic, or one of the other many theorized locations, is beyond the premise of this book, so take a look at these accounts for yourself, and enjoy a rare glimpse into a secret world, a mystical realm where giants were said to have existed.

SKULLS OF GIANT CAVEMEN
The New Age Magazine, Volume 18, 1913, pg.207

This account from an Ozark cave in Arkansas is found in *The New Age Magazine*, given by the highly regarded reporter Victor Schoffelmeyer. *The New Age Magazine* was a Rosicrucian publication. Just like indigenous oral history, secret traditions of the Freemasons and Rosicrucians have been passed down through the generations in a thoughtful and meticulous way. Why would these fraternal orders whose rituals and symbolism are extremely precise, have their doctrines polluted with erroneous information? The reality is that both orders cite giant skeleton reports in their literature and use them as proof of a connection they had with a global maritime civilization that existed over 10,000 years ago—a lost civilization that is thought to be the mother culture where all the esoteric knowledge and symbolism they practice came from.

SKULLS OF GIANT CAVEMEN

many of these caves. At a depth of more than three feet he found the remains of several giant human skeletons, including an almost perfect skull which differed in many particulars from a modern specimen. When partly joined the largest skeleton was almost ten feet

In *Search for the Lost Giants*, Jim and his brother Bill investigated this account. The site of the cave mentioned had been flooded with the damming and creation of Beaver Lake. The U.S. Army Corps of Engineers constructed Beaver Dam during the years 1960-1966. Bill and professional scuba diver Mike Young dived into the lake and found a huge shelter cave believed to be the site of the skeletal finds. While a 70 ft stone wall was found at the entrance of the cave, showing likely human habitation, but

Mysterious underwater wall in cave discovered during filming.

no more clues were forthcoming. No more documentation describing the skeletal material or what happened to it could be found either. Further text from the original article reads as follows:

> *"While the historical features of the Ozarks held our attention, by far the most fascinating discovery was one made by an aged recluse and naturalist who for ten years had lived in a shelter cave near where we camped. "Dad" Riggins spent much of his time digging in the ashes which form the floor of many of these caves. At a depth of more than three feet he found the remains of several giant human skeletons, including an almost perfect skull which differed in many particulars from a modern specimen. When partly joined the largest skeleton was almost ten feet tall. "Dad" Riggins showed us hieroglyphics covering the Palisades thought to be thousands of years old."*

Victor Humbert Schoffelmayer (1878-1962) was a newspaper writer and agricultural authority educated at New Engelberg College, a Benedictine boarding school in northwest Missouri, and at Josephinium Technical College in Ohio. Later Schoffelmayer worked for Menger as a writer on the Southern Messenger. Beginning in 1905 Schoffelmayer was a reporter on a number of newspapers in Missouri, Kansas, Iowa, and Minnesota. He was the art and music critic on the Minneapolis Journal before he became editor in 1913 of the *Southwest Trail*. Working out of Chicago, he edited the publication at a time when there were few agricultural bulletins available. He and his wife, Carrie, traveled over 50,000 miles a year in a special railroad car, promoting farm machinery and distributing agricultural literature.

In December 1917 Schoffelmayer began working for George Bannerman Dealy as field editor of the *Semi-Weekly Farm News*, a subsidiary of the *Dallas Morning News*; soon thereafter he became their agricultural editor. During the 1920s and 1930s he authored four important books. One of these was *Texas at the Crossroads* (1935).

Schoffelmayer served as president of the Texas Chemurgic Council and as a member of the board of trustees for the Texas A&M Foundation and board of governors of the National Farm Chemurgic Council. He was a fellow of the American Geographic Society, a life member of the Philosophical Society of Texas, and a member of the Texas Academy of Science and *Sigma Delta Chi*, an honorary journalism fraternity. Mr. Schoffelmayer was quite the accomplished individual. In 1939 he was elected 'Man of the Year'—a man who also wrote about humans who were ten feet in height.

ROSICRUCIAN SCIENCE CONFIRMED
Mercury; A Rosicrucian Messenger of Constructive Philosophy, 1932, pg.205
Elrama, Pennsylvania

This next account is from the publication, *Rosicrucian Science Confirmed*, that discusses a skeleton *"nearly eight feet tall"* unearthed near Elrama, Pennsylvania. The account mentions that the Smithsonian Institution was reported to have received the remains. Bear in mind, this is the same discovery already featured in *The Smithsonian Files* chapter (p.231).

ROSICRUCIAN SCIENCE CONFIRMED

America as the Home of Antiquity: Campers, near Elrama, Pa., have dug up skeletons of human beings who lived in America *thousands of years* before the redmen. They were probably exterminated by invaders from Asia. Forty-nine bodies were uneartht near Pittsburgh, Pa., estimated to be 10,000 years old. One is of a giant nearly eight feet tall. The bodies will be reassembled at Finleyville and delivered to the State Museum at Harrisburg. Some are to be sent to the Smithsonian Institution at Washington, D. C.

The same account was reported in *The New York Times* and other sources. A 7 ft 5 in skeleton was the largest uncovered and the skeletons were reported by George S. Fisher Pennsylvania State Archaeologist to have massive teeth and jawbones. Several months later it was reported that University of Cambridge trained archaeologist Donald A. Cadzow accompanied the moving of the remains including the giant skeleton to Harrisburg where the Smithsonian took possession of them.

RAYS FROM THE ROSE CROSS
Rosicrucian Fellowship, Volume 7-8, 1917, pg.110

The following account was listed in the Rosicrucian publication, *Rays from the rose cross - a magazine of mystical light.* The same reference also appeared in the mystic Madame Blavatsky's book *Isis Unveiled.* Blavatsky is the founder of the Theosophist movement and once again giants and Atlantis are prominent themes in their belief system. Judge E. P. West who reported the startling find mentioned in the account was also noted in Smithsonian literature for his excavation reports from Missouri, but oddly this remarkable account did not make it into their official records.

Elena Petrovna Gan, a.k.a. HP Blavatsky (1831-1891)

"Judge E. P. West discovered a skeleton about 2 weeks ago and made a report to other members of the society. They accompanied him to the mound and took out the remains of 2 skeletons. The bones are very large—so large, in fact when compared with an ordinary skeleton on modern date, they appear to have formed part of a giant. The head bones, are monstrous in size. The lower jaw of one skeleton is in a state of preservation, and is double the size of the jaw of a civilized person. The thigh-bone when compared with that of an ordinary modern skeleton, looks like that of a horse."

BONE CAVE, TENNESSEE

The two following accounts are from the Bone Cave in Tennessee. Jim and Bill were able to investigate this personally during the filming of *Search for the Lost Giants.* They went hundreds of feet into the cave and verified the following account. They spotted torch marks that must have been from when it was originally investigated, and found the dates 1872 and 1899 carved deep in the cave along with some of the names of the explorers. They eventually made it into a passage filled with water and found a cavernous room at the end but could continue no further because of the high level of danger presented by rock falls, hypothermia and toxic air. The infamous 'dead house' was not quite reached. This flooded tunnel, however, was possibly connected to the Old Stone Fort, built roughly 2,000 years ago.

Side view of the "Bone Cave showing the entrance on the left, the first "vaulted space" and the proposed location of the "dead house" on the top right.

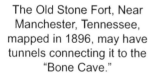

The Old Stone Fort, Near Manchester, Tennessee, mapped in 1896, may have tunnels connecting it to the "Bone Cave."

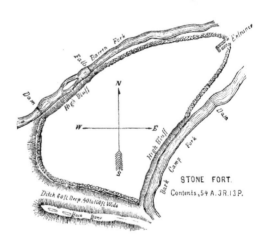

Mackey's National Freemason, Oct. 1872 to Sept. 1873, pg. 219

"A few days since some boys discovered an almost entire human skeleton of mammoth size. The bones of the forearm were nearly 20 inches long, while the bone of the lower part of the leg was longer than an ordinary man's lower limbs, foot and all. The jaw bone of this giant would slip over the face of an ordinary man."

The passage used by the Freemasons was originally reported in this newspaper account from earlier that year (in March 1872). It describes the investigation that subsequently took place that Jim and Bill used to navigate their way through the caves on their recent expedition. (Note: the repeated text has been removed but the rest of it is so fascinating we share it with you in full):

The Hartford Weekly Times, March 30, 1872, pg.2

"Near this city is a cave commonly known as "Bone Cave," from which have been brought, at various times, by boys and other persons who have tried to explore its hidden recesses, human bones of unusual size. The popular legends of the people are to the effect that it is somewhat connected with the people or race which created the "Old Stone Fort," which stands a short distance to the west of the town... Stimulated by these discoveries and a laudable desire to learn the secrets of this mysterious cavern, on last Thursday six gentlemen, including the editors of this paper, made this necessary preparations and started out to explore the "bone cave."

After an exhilarating walk of two miles through a clear bracing air, we reached the entrance of the cave, where divesting ourselves of our overcoats and lighting our torches, we entered one of the many passages, but after a short scramble we found further advance stopped by large pieces of rock that had fallen and blocked up the passage... Soon other members of the party came down and explorations commenced. We found ourselves in a vaulted chamber about twenty-five feet wide by sixty long. with passages leading in every direction. Following one, we rambled on for forty or fifty feet and then there appeared one of the most beautiful lakes we have ever seen. The water was clear and sweet and the ceiling over the water, studded with stalactites, reflected back the light from our torches like gems. We had no means of ascertaining the size of the lake, for the banks were perpendicular and it seemed like a pearl set in a bed of rocks. Another passage which was explored by B. F. Fleming was found to extend in a direct line toward the "Old Stone Fort."

This passage followed for a distance of nearly two hundred feet, when further progress was stopped by the passage being filled up with debris. This passage looks as if it had been cut from the solid rock by the hand of man and gives rise to the hypothesis that at some time, far back in the dark ages, this cave was used by a race of men—giants if you like—that built this stone fort and the mounds and that this underground passage led from the fort to the cave, a mile distant. After a good look at this part of the cave, we returned to daylight, having been underground three hours and traversing over a mile inside the cave. After partaking of a lunch sent us by a very hospitable lady whose name we have mislaid—but not her kindness—we had a short search in the tunnel known as the "Dead House." Here we found many bones but all in a state of decomposition and decay. This tunnel or chamber is coated with a soft, loose soil to a depth of a foot or more, into which one can plunge a stick with perfect ease, while all the rest of the cave is solid rock."

Left: Jim and Bill at the entrance to "Bone Cave." Middle: The first passage.
Right: Jim coming up for air at the furthest point, some 250 feet into the tunnels.

EDGAR CAYCE

Edgar Cayce (March 18, 1877 – January 3, 1945) was an American mystic who answered questions on subjects as varied as healing, reincarnation, wars, Atlantis and future events while in a trance. A biographer gave him

279

Edgar Cayce in October 1910

the nickname "The Sleeping Prophet." A nonprofit organization, the Association for Research and Enlightenment was founded in Virginia Beach to facilitate the study of Cayce's work. A hospital and a university were also established.

Among his 14,000 readings and 25 million words transmitted in a trance state, the clairvoyant Edgar Cayce gave 68 readings on the ancient American mound culture. These are discussed in Greg Little's excellent book *Mound Builders: Edgar Cayce's Forgotten Record of Ancient America*. The Cayce information often matches up with the research we have been carrying out for years. There are several mentions of giants in Cayce's readings. The following is a reading about a past life of a woman in Florida who was said to have been alive in the era of the Mound Builders. The Cayce language is a little strange but does makes sense:

"We find the entity was in the land of its present nativity, in what is now known as the southernmost portion - or in Florida; during those periods when there were those settlings from the Yucatan, from the lands of the Inca, from the Norse land, when there were the beginners of the Mound Builders and those that gathered upon what is now the east portion of Alabama and Florida - though it was quite different then in its structure, outwardly. The entity's sojourns then were with those of a race of unusual height, unusual proportions to what might be termed in the present." [1]

Edgar Cayce proclaimed in a trance state, among other things, that the Nile flowed backwards in the distant past, a fact verified by recent satellite imagery and that the *Essenes* had women in their ranks (announced before graves of women were discovered at Qumran). Cayce also gave several readings which mentioned giants. The following is from the Cayce Reading

No. 364-11: *"Please give a few details regarding the physiognomy, habits, customs and costumes of the people of Atlantis during the period just before the first destruction."* He replied:

> *"These took on many sizes as to stature, from that as may be called the midget to the Giants - for there were Giants in the earth in those days, men as tall as (what would be termed today) ten or twelve feet in stature, and well proportioned throughout."*[2]

It is telling that Cayce says that they are *"well proportioned throughout."* This phrase has been noted countless times in newspaper reports and town histories across America describing giant skeleton finds.

Rudolf Steiner

Mystic Rudolph Steiner also made mention of giants existing in Atlantis.

> *"Just at the time when Atlantis began to sink there was a great contrast between men who were good as to their qualities of soul, and were a race of little men, and the giant forms who were wicked and in whom everything turned to flesh."*

It is noteworthy that both Steiner and Cayce, just like H.P. Blavatsky, spoke of the existence of "little people" in Atlantis. In digging through historical documents searching for giant skeleton accounts we ran into countless reports of the skeletons of little people being exhumed from burial mound sites. Many accounts mention giant skeletons and little people reported to have been buried together as well. Native Americans, like indigenous peoples all around the globe, not only have oral traditions describing a race of giants in the past, but of a race of little people that is as intriguing as the countless giant reports!

Rudolf Steiner in 1892.
Etching by Otto Fröhlich.

11

CURSE OF THE GIANT HUNTERS

I t is widely believed by cultures worldwide that when an ancient burial place is disturbed, destructive energies can often be unleashed. While this assertion may seem fanciful to some, we give you several strange accounts from the *twilight zone* files to suggest that there may be some truth to this reality.

NAN MADOL, MICRONESIA

We start with Nan Madol and its mysterious megalithic ruins located on the tiny Micronesian Island of Pohnpei in the Pacific Ocean. Millions of tons of basalt blocks were transported here to build the site. According to

The prehistoric Micronesian city of Nan Madol - Basalt "logs" came from miles away.
(Courtesy of Dr. James P. McVey, NOAA Sea Grant Program)

Pohnpeian legend, Nan Madol was constructed by twin giant sorcerers Olisihpa and Olosohpa from the mythical Western Katau, or Kanamwayso. They were said to have built the site using levitation and hailed from an ancient advanced civilization that once existed in the Pacific, often called Lemuria or Mu. There are several historical accounts of giant skeletons being found in the area to support these legends.

THE BULLETIN OF THE AMERICAN GEOGRAPHICAL SOCIETY
Volume 1, 1859, pg. 133

"A narrow entrance has, however, been opened at the top, through which we descended, and found ourselves in a dark cell 8 feet deep, and 11 by 10 feet in length and breadth. The only light that reached us entered through the cracks between the long prisms laid across overhead. The foreigners told us that coral stones once formed a pavement on the floor of the vault, but within 10 or 15 years they have been torn up by visitors searching for relics. They say that in 1838, Capt. Chas. Coffin, of the ship Ohio, Nantucket, and Capt. E. B. Sherman, of the Marcus, Fairhaven, visited the vaults together, and took from it several human bones of gigantic size."

In episode 4 of *Search for the Lost Giants*, we explore the "giants curse" Jim's landlord, Al Pieropan, got in touch with us because he taught on Pohnpei for several years and heard many strange stories from the islanders. The Natives on the island viewed the burial place of the ancient giants with superstitious dread and would not visit the site. Al was even told by native friends not to eat any of the fruit he had taken from the site because it was cursed.

The following story has been also widely reported regarding mysterious Nan Madol.

In the early twentieth century, when the island was under German rule, Governor Victor Berg entered the sealed tomb of Nan Madol and opened the coffin of the island's prehistoric rulers. He reported finding skeletons of giants between two and three meters tall (7 to 9 feet tall). The next morning, on April 30, 1907, after a stormy night, Governor Berg died. The German physician serving on the island could not determine the cause of death. The natives were certain it was a curse that proves supernatural powers guarded the city of the dead.

Victor Berg did indeed die mysteriously at the age of 46. Rufino Mauricio, the only archaeologist on Pohnpei has dedicated his life to preserving the ruins: *"We don't know how they brought the columns here and we don't know how they lifted them up to build the walls, most Pohnpeians believe magic was used to fly them."*[1]

It goes on to tell that locals avoid the ruins believing it to be a place of supernatural dread. It has earned the awe of many archaeologists because the basalt walls were once up to 40 feet high and about 17 feet thick, made up of several million tons of basalt stone columns.[2]

David Hatcher Childress also reports that in the 1930s Japanese archaeologists unearthed bones of seven-foot men and found platinum coffins that were brought back to Japan and later destroyed in the Hiroshima nuclear blast![3]

CHEHALIS IS EXCITED: REPORTED DISCOVERY OF AN IMMENSE CAVE IN LEWIS COUNTY
Spokane Daily Chronicle, March 7, 1901
Tacoma, Washington

In 1901 a miner called H. F. Forrest reported finding a network of strange caves on the south side of Mount Rainer in Washington after removing a rock that he believed *"had been hewn by human hands."*[4] Forrest reported finding walls decorated with hieroglyphs and two stone tombs containing the remains of a 7 ft 10 inch man and a 7 ft woman. He claimed they were ornamented with engraved gold jewelry.

Forrest returned to Chehalis to share his story and attempted to interest others in joining him to further explore the caves. Forrest however, disappeared and was never heard from again. His belongings were later found in a hotel room that he was staying in.

CHEHALIS IS EXCITED

Reported Discovery of an Immense Cave in Lewis County.

TACOMA, Wash., March 7.—The town of Chehalis is excited over the reported discovery of an immense cave in the eastern part of Lewis county. Exploration was made a distance of five miles, revealing strange and wonderful sights. After entering a lower passage beneath the main cavern the explorer came to a subterranean lake. Upon the pebbled beach were found boats of ancient and strange make, some petrified, others partially so. In one of the small rooms of the first cavern were found the remains of two human beings, both giants in size; the man 7 feet 10 inches long, the woman a few inches less. Both bodies were reported either frozen stiff or mummified. Hammers and drills of brass were found. The elaborate work must have taken years and was apparently done ages ago by a prehistoric race.

80 STOCKTONIANS LEFT BEHIND IN SEARCH FOR 'LOST CONTINENT'
Stockton Record, June 18, 1934
Cascade Mountains, California

In 1934 mining engineer J. C. Brown who had worked for the *Lord Coudray British Mining Company*, reported an amazing find while working in the northern California section of the Cascade mountain chain. Brown described finding rooms cut out of the mountain of solid rock. He told of stone rooms with copper and gold plates on the walls with many having 'hieroglyphs' on them. Brown also claimed to have found one stone room that contained skeletons of immense size from 6 ½ to over 10 feet tall.

Brown went to Stockton, California and told his incredible story and convinced a local newspaper editor and museum curator that he was credible. An expedition was organized to explore the caves. As noted in the *Stockton Record*, 80 people were organized for the expedition. Before the trip started however, Brown went missing, never to be heard from again.

285

The residents were baffled with his disappearance and held an all-night vigil for him. It was noted that not only did Brown seem truthful and responsible but he had profited in no way from his claims.

Various News Articles on the disappearance of J.C. Brown

TRACES OF GIANTS FOUND IN DESERT
The Meriden Record, August 5, 1947, pg.2
Death Valley, California

Fast forward to 1947 and we learn of a reported discovery by retired physician Dr. F. Bruce Russell. Russell had claimed to have found 32 caves in the 180 square mile area of California's Death Valley and southern Nevada with a colleague, Dr. Daniel S. Bovee, who he had worked with on archaeological excavations in New Mexico several years earlier.

In early August of 1947, Howard E. Hill of Los Angeles, spoke before the city's Transportation Club and told a sensational story that described the original discovery of the first cave by Russell in 1931, when he fell in a mine shaft. His incredible story begins with the discovery of ancient mummies:

"...several well preserved mummies were taken Sunday from the caverns in an area roughly 180 miles square extending through much of Southern Nevada from Death Valley, California, across the Colorado River into Arizona."

Claims were made that bizarre artifacts of all kinds of an advanced and lost civilization had been discovered in these caves. Strange hieroglyphs were reportedly chiseled on polished granite, and odd symbols were noted.

"With Dr. Daniel S. Bovee of Los Angeles—who with his father helped open up New Mexico's cliff dwellings— Dr. Russell has found mummified remains together with implements of the civilization. Hill said in another cavern was found the ritual hall of the ancient people, together with devices and markings similar to those now used by the Masonic Order...He said the explorers believe that what they found was the burial place of the tribe's hierarchy."

He also reported several caverns that contained the mummified remains of 8 and 9 ft tall people.

After the Second World War, Russell and several amateur archaeologists incorporated *Amazing Explorations Inc.* with Howard E. Hill as their spokesman. The goal was to explore the site to prove his story once and for all. However, not long after this, Russell's car was found abandoned in Death Valley with a burst radiator and he was never heard from again.[5] Without Russell to guide them, later explorers were never able to find the entrance to the cave.

Discovery of an ancient civilization in the Colorado desert was reported Tuesday by Dr. F. Bruce Russell.   —AP Wirephoto

However, 15 years earlier a near identical report was published by Bourke Lee in his book *Death Valley Men* (1932).[6] In the chapter *Old Gold*, it describes a conversation he had several years earlier with a small group of Death Valley residents concerning some incredible caves they had discovered. The story closely matched Russell's discovery in 1931, so it could have been describing the very same discovery. The explorers who were called "Jack and Bill" told author Bourke Lee that the area was once underwater and claimed to have seen the remains of ancient docks. They could allegedly see the Furnace Creek Ranch far below them. They told Bourke Lee that they had brought some of the treasure out of the caverns and tried to set up a deal with certain people, including scientists associated with the Smithsonian Institution, in order to gain help to explore and publicize the city as one of the wonders of the world.

These efforts ended in disappointment because apparently a 'friend' of theirs stole the treasure (which was also the evidence) and they were scoffed at and rejected by the scientists when they went to show them the 'mine' entrance and could not find it. Lee never heard from them again.

Philip Rife also tells us in his book *The Goliath Conspiracy* that some possible corroboration of the men's findings comes from a Native American legend about Death Valley:

"When the world was young and the valley which is now dry, parched desert was a lush hidden harbor of blue water which stretched halfway up those mountains to the Gulf of California, it is said that the Havmusvus came here in huge rowing ships. They found great caverns in the Panamaints and in them they built one of their cities. Living in their hidden city, the Havmusvus ruled the sea with their fast moving ships, trading with far away peoples and bringing strange goods to the great quays said still to exist in the caverns. Then, as untold centuries rolled past, the climate began to change. The water in the lake went down until there was no longer a way to the sea. But as time went by the water continued to shrink, until the day came when only a dry crust was all that remained of the great blue lake." [7]

Now to turn the freak show factor up to 11, we bring in the story of mass murderer Charles Manson. Manson was arrested at the Barker Ranch near the Devil's Hole in the Wingate Pass area in 1969, the same location where reports of the lost cities came from. The Devil's Hole is a geothermal aquifer-fed pool within a limestone cavern. Manson believed the Devil's Hole site was a gateway to an underground ancient city that he would take his followers to in order to ride out the coming race war. He supposedly sat by the hole meditating for three days trying to figure out its mysteries.

And quite mysterious it is, two divers died there in 1967—their bodies never recovered. The hole is filled with caves that apparently connect to other sources of water in the valley, and it may be possible to travel from one to the other, though it would be a foolish journey. So foolish, in fact, that the hole is now fenced off completely.

All these accounts speak of artifacts of a vanished race and giant human remains. Is there really evidence of a lost civilization

Entrance to the Devils Hole.

to be found hidden in strange man-made caves in the western part of this country? Whether these stories are true or false, it is all intriguing and worthy of further investigation. Now it is time to step out of the twilight zone and explore the *Lost City of Giants* of Sonora, Mexico.

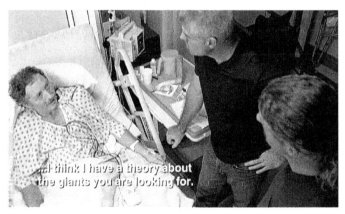

Researcher Terje Dahl may have got affected by the "curse of the giant hunters" when he tried to visit Catalina Island during the TV shoot. He came down very sick and was hospitalised. Pictured here with Jim and Bill Vieira.

12

GIANTS OF SONORA, MEXICO

The saga of the *Lost city of Giants* in Sonora, Mexico is one of the most intriguing that we have encountered to date. The story starts out with the investigations of Dr. Byron Cummings, the 'Dean of Southwest Archaeology'. Dr. Cummings was the highly respected head of the Archaeology Department at the University of Arizona.

Dr. Byron Cummings was Professor of Archaeology at the University of Arizona (1915 - 1937) and Director of the Arizona State Museum. Photo courtesy of Tad Nichols.

In 1930, Dr. Cummings was contacted by J. L. Coker, a miner who was working in the isolated Sonora section in Mexico. Coker reported unearthing skeletons averaging 8 feet tall with one of the bodies measuring 8 feet 3 inches in height. Coker also described one of the skulls he found as measuring more than a foot long and ten inches wide. These finds match the oral history of the Yaqui Indians who claim that a race of giants inhabited the area long ago.

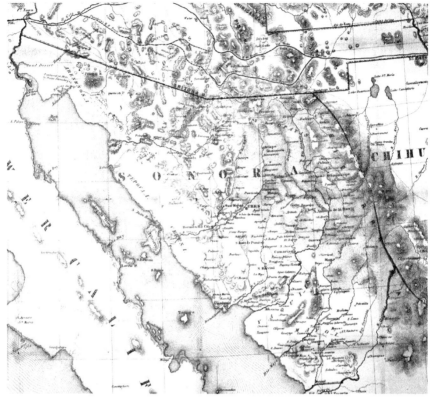

Old map of the Sonora region that stretches from Mexico into the US.

Dr. Cummings explained his findings in the *Border Cities Star,* Dec, 4, 1930 article. The headline read *Superstitious Natives Destroy Relics of Prehistoric Supermen*:

Superstitious Natives Destroy Relics of Prehistoric Supermen

Scientists Hope to Save Skeletons of Giant Men Found In Mexico and Prove That Humans Have Deteriorated Physically

"There have been past discoveries of single skeletons measuring more than the average height of present humans, but there never has been several found together so that the existence of a tribe or race of giants could be proven."

291

Also reported is Dr. Cummings asking the Science Service in Washington to aid the university in sponsoring the proposed expedition to Sonora, which he ended up leading. This was partly done to verify Coker's claims.

From the *Telegraph Herald* and *Times Journal,* Dec. 14, 1930 pg.1, is found an account of Dr. Cummings following up the discoveries of Coker several weeks later:

Uncover Bones of Race of Supermen

Giants Lived in Mexico
2,000 Years Ago

"Sayopa, Sonora, Mexico. Five large skeletons, the first evidences that a race of supermen once roamed this vast wasteland, were unearthed today by an international expedition of scientists. Working rapidly for two nights and a day, the little band of American and Mexican archaeologists unearthed the petrified remains of a youth 6 feet 8 inches tall, the skeletons of four other children of lesser stature and several jars filled with human ashes. The importance of these discoveries was the fact that they definitely established the scene of operations as a great burial ground, according to Dr. Byron Cummings, dean of the University of Arizona archaeology department and leader of the expedition."

It is reported that Dr. Cummings and Professor Manuel San Domingo, a Mexican Government scientist of Sonora, faced the fierce and superstitious Yaqui Indians at the burial place of the giants in Sonora. Despite the pleas of the scientists, the Yaquis smashed to pieces the giants' bones with their rifle butts:

"However, before the expedition could get properly to work, down swooped the Yaquis armed with rifles and knives. They fiercely bade the archaeologists quit or take the consequences. The Mexican professor tried in vain to placate the Indians. His remonstrances were abruptly shattered by a tough Yaqui brave who upraised a heavy rifle butt and battered the giant remains to pieces."

This story certainly does not end there and gets stranger in the years to come.

The American Southwest had always been a hotspot of giant skeleton reports, many times the accounts tell of strange caves and artifacts associated with a lost ancient race that possessed a high degree of technology. From the *Prescott Evening Courier* Dec. 11, 1930 pg.5, is a letter to the editor by a William Crocker. Crocker says the following about the expeditions to Sonora, Mexico:

"Nearly every issue of the papers during the last week has had something to say about an expedition going into Mexico to search for the bones of a race of giants. Why go to Mexico? Several years ago, Bill Singleton, a boss on the highway, told me while working on the road through Chino Valley some human bones were dug up which, when compared with those of the average man today, indicated they belonged to a race of men who measured between nine and ten feet tall. Jess Kiple at Pruchman's will verify this statement. Another interesting find in this section was one made several years ago between Dewey and Humboldt a new piece of road cut into an old burial ground. Del Daves, now dead, doing some digging there, found two skeletons lying side by side, each about 4 feet long and each having enormous heads. Beth Gray, a mining man of this section who saw the skulls, said they were so big that it would take a number nine hat to fit them."

So, what is going on here? Dwarves with huge heads, alongside giant skeletons being unearthed in Mexico by a team led by the prominent archaeologist Dr. Byron Cummings of the *University of Arizona*. Reports of giants (and little people) are in fact circulating all over the country, often times by respected scientists.

The story then continues with the following account reported in the *Telegraph-Herald and Times-Journal* four years after the initial report of giants made by Dr. Byron Cummings. In the Dec 9, 1934 article, Dr. Cummings announces finding the bodies of men and women in Yaqui country who were are all over seven feet tall in a perfect state of preservation. Dr. Cummings stated that the find was made by ethnologist Paxson C. Hayes of Santa Barbara, California:

> *"Traces of a lost race of giants, who wore oriental turbans and mummified their dead in a fashion similar to that of the ancient Egyptians have been found in the Yaqui Indian country in Sonora, Mexico. Other traces of the oriental origin of the ancient giants was reported by Hayes who declared he had found several tables buried near the mummies. These tables were of a size similar to those unearthed recently in the heart of the Gobi desert."*

Also reported in the *San Jose Evening News*, May 22, 1933, pg.38 is:

> *"Hayes spent four years excavating 34 mummies from one of the caves. Hayes brought back evidence of a civilization which may compel archaeologists to revise theories of the origin of the American Indian."*

Hayes' went on describe anatomic anomalies such as elongated heads and reddish hair:

> *"They have slant eyes and sloped foreheads...the hair, which is*

black, has a peculiar auburn tinge when examined closely."

Paxson Hayes' interest in the study of snakes is what initially brought him to the region, then Yaqui Indians told him of the location of the lost city and of a mysterious giant race. Paxson Hayes lived with the fierce Yaqui Indians of Sonora for seven years and became close to them and was accepted by them, which turned out to be the key to gaining access to the region.

Jim and his brother Bill had an opportunity to meet with Carlos Hayes, the son of Paxson, at his place south of Tucson, Arizona, to discuss his father's findings. Whilst filming *Search for the Lost Giants* Carlos informed them that the Yaquis are fiercely independent people who could never be controlled by the Mexican or US governments. His father earned the trust of the Yaquis and they allowed him to explore the vast caves of Sonora where he found the lost city of giants. Carlos theorized that the reason that many of these giant skeleton finds were not scientifically established is because native peoples did not trust the intentions of the interlopers who sought to desecrate sacred and ancient places.

Although Hayes was accepted by the Yaqui and allowed to explore the area, Dr. Byron Cummings was not. Therefore, the Yaquis smashed the giant skeletal remains to pieces after an ancient burial mound had been opened by mining engineers.

Then we have from the *Milwaukee Journal,* Mar 8, 1935, pg.8, the continuing story of Hayes and his explorations into Sonora. A Mr. Marshall, the author of the article from *The Detroit News* reports the following about this episode:

The Lost City of Giants
In Hills of Sonora, Mexico, an Explorer Has Found 34 Mummies, Each Over Seven Feet Tall

"While I was in Nogales, Ariz., six weeks ago, Hayes, the discoverer of the lost city, came out of the hills long enough to re-outfit, and to present competent, factual proof of the nature

of his discoveries, before returning to the site of the lost city, which is 11 days' muleback journey southward from Hermosilla, capital of Sonora. Hayes had pictures of the mummified bodies of members of the race of giants. Thirty-four mummies have been uncovered, and the smallest measured seven feet one inch in height. He had pictures of the ruins of the buildings and samples of the burial shrouds, all in a fair state of preservation. Confirmation of the prescience of the ruins of an ancient civilization in Sonora came two years ago. Since then Hayes' party has made seven expeditions into Yaqui country."

Paxson Hayes with head of giant mummy. The head is enclosed in a huge gourd. Official Press Photo no. 9614/ACME, 27th December 1935.

Nine months later we have the photo above and following description from the *San Jose News*, December 31, 1935 pg. 12:

"Paxson Hayes, explorer, studies the head of a giant mummy discovered by him in a deep cave hitherto unexplored regions of Sonora, Mexico. The mummified remains were of a race 7 ½

feet tall and preserved in excellent condition. Corn found with the mummies has been given to scientists."

Then a year later is found from the *Spokane Daily Chronicle*, January 9, 1936, pg.11:

"These crumbling ruins of a long-perished city, where mummified human forms revealed that seven-foot giants and three foot pygmies apparently lived together, were found by Paxson C. Hayes ethnologist, who has spent the last seven years exploring the upland wastes of northern Mexico. The architecture is of a type never before discovered, resembling that of cliff dwellings but with distinct Mongolian features. The strange civilization is believed to antedate that of the Mayans. Hayes plans an expedition for a thorough search of the huge caves in Sonora, 400 miles from Hermosillo City."

The story continues and we are informed from the *Berkeley Daily Gazette*, Jun 10, 1937, pg.1:

"The many reports of a race of "supermen" who once inhabited parts of the Mexican State of Sonora received new support today with the arrival of Paxson C. Hayes and C. G. Barnes both of Santa Barbara en route from Sonora to Washington. Bringing out of Sonora a Mexican boa constrictor and stories of mummified and skeletal remains of men and women from six feet and seven inches to eight feet tall, they announced they had discovered the district of "the lost city of Sonora." They planned to continue to Washington, for a conference with the Mexican Ambassador, Francisco Najera, to seek cooperation of Mexican scientists in exploration of the discoveries. Hayes was embroiled in a controversy with Dr. Roy Chapman Andrews of the Smithsonian Institute in Washington, in 1933, over the existence of the so-called "super-men" or race of giants. Reports of the existence of remains of a race of giants have been recurrent throughout the Southwest since before 1930.

Skeletons actually were found by a party headed by Dr. Byron Cummings of the University of Arizona, which indicated the existence of such a race, it was said. The Cummings expedition was driven out of Sonora by threats of an uprising of Yaqui Indians."

Regardless of the evidence presented, the Smithsonian did not seem to be overly interested in these finds for some odd reason. Dr. Cummings in fact, was very critical of eastern scientific institutions such as the Smithsonian. Not only did Dr. Cummings report finding giant skeletal remains but he was embroiled in a controversy when he discovered human remains with prehistoric animals which indicated a much greater antiquity for humans on this continent. Carlos Hayes informed us that his father lost his funding earlier on in his explorations but continued the rest of his life to bring this evidence to light.

Photo shows the ruins of Sonora, photographed by Paxson Hayes. Official Press Photo no. 9602/ACME, 2nd January 1936.

298

The saga of Paxson C. Hayes and fellow explorer Gerald C. Barnes continues as they arrive in Washington D.C. Reported in *The Washington Post*, July 22, 1937 is *"Smithsonian Amazed at Discovery of 6 ½-Foot Mummies in Caves."* We are informed of the following from the article:

> *"With several dozen snakes (all alive), and the burial robe of a prehistoric giant (quite dead), packed in their trailer, they stopped in Washington yesterday to promote interest in their unique fields of activity. Herpetologically speaking, their purpose in coming here from California was to present President Roosevelt with 15 Smoki snakes., 10 California and Mexican rattlers and an 8-foot baby Mexican boa constrictor, which was shedding. Marvin C. McIntyre received them at the White House, expressed gratitude and suggested the reptile house at the zoo as perhaps the best place for the snakes. Dr. Ernest P. Walker, assistant director of the Zoo, officially welcomed the snakes to their new home. That over, the visitors then dropped in at the Smithsonian Institution with the prehistoric burial robe and a four-legged stool, both of which they unearthed in a burial cave in northern Sonora, Mexico. The Californians explained that the cave, one of 18 they had discovered, contains well preserved mummies of a race which averaged over 6 ½ feet in height (previously reported up to 8 feet tall). The caves are scattered over an area of 450 square miles. Hayes who has just returned from his fifth expedition to the caves heard about their existence from the Yaqui Indians of Mexico."*

The article also shows a photo of Hayes, Barnes, and W. H. Blackburn, Head Keeper of the Washington Zoo, as they assist a Mexican boa constrictor. Jim found the following information in the *Annual Report of the Board of Regents of the Smithsonian Institution 1937* (pg.74), citing additions to their collections. *"Smoki People, through Paxson C. Hayes and G. C. Barnes, Prescott, Ariz., 5 Western bullsnakes, 2 red rattlesnakes, 2 Mexican rattlesnakes."*

In 1933, Hayes was already in a dispute with Dr. Roy Chapman

Andrews, a Smithsonian scientist, over reported giant skeletal finds. A logical guess is that they did not follow up on these finds either.

This final article from *The Deseret News*, Nov 9, 1950 pg.2, is the last mention we could find of this story after literally 20 years of descriptive articles filled with twists and turns.

A LAND OF GIANTS?

Mexico Cave Find Clue to Past Ages

This report is essentially a summation of the facts of the case, but also mentioned that some of the giant mummies had blond hair, although this is not mentioned in the earlier reports. Here are some highlights:

"When the bones of the mummies were laid out properly the various bodies measured from seven feet six inches in most cases up to the largest skeleton which was a full eight feet"

"The greatest mystery of Hayes' finds...were the saffron colored burial robes found on the giants. There may be a great historic

tale behind the powder-blue designs of latch hooks and pyramids that embellish the robes. Hayes thinks that the tiny series of white dots that recur throughout the robes are symbols of the ancient Indian time cycle..."

It is also mentioned that Hayes took the burial robes to the chiefs of the Seri Indians on Tiburon Island off the West coast of Mexico and they were as puzzled as him.

Explorer Paxson Hayes holds robe found in cave of Blond Giants.

Our guess is that none of the players in this lengthy story had any support for their stories or evidence, and probably ended up frustrated, resigned that closed mindedness may have undone the truth. In an effort to explain the reluctance that some professionals have to entertain theories outside of accepted paradigms, we quote from Thomas Kuhn's *Structure of Scientific Revolutions* (1962):

> *"Mop-up operations are what engage most scientists throughout their careers. This paradigm-based research is an attempt to force nature into the pre-formed and relatively inflexible box that the paradigm supplies. No effort is made to call forth new sorts of phenomena, no effort to discover anomalies. When anomalies pop up they are usually discarded or ignored. Anomalies are usually not even noticed and no effort is made to invent a new theory—and there is no tolerance for those who try."*

One of the giant mummies in the entrance of the cave. This mummy is 7 ½ feet tall. The cloth and rope is a variety never before seen. Official Press Photo no. 9613/ ACME, 27 Dec 1936.

The mysteries of Sonora do not end here though. In 2012 the following was reported:

> *"Excavation of an ancient burial site in South Sonora, Mexico, has revealed a series of skeletons with intentionally deformed skulls. Of the 25 sets of human remains found close to the Mexican village of Onavas, 13 had deformed craniums."* [1]

Image of elongated skull from Onavas, Mexico. Courtesy of *Mexico's National Institute of Anthropology and History* (INAH).

Carlos Hayes, the son of Paxson, told us that he would take us into Sonora to search for the lost city of giants when the time is right. Carlos (pictured below) is friends with the Yaqui Indians of the area, but at the time of filming there was a dangerous travel warning posted for the region, so that exploration is on hold....for now.

302

Paxson Hayes is pictured with some of the corn he
found in caves in Sonora. The corn was buried with
mummies 7 ½ feet tall, and originally believed by
Hayes to be 12,000 years old. Official Press Photo no.
LA330889/ACME. 30th Dec 1935.

LA 9513————————————————(LOS ANGELES BUREAU)
EXPLORER DISCOVERS ANCIENT TOMBS
LOS ANGELES, CALIFORNIA. PAXSON E. HAYES, EXPLORER, HAS
JUST RETURNED TO LOS ANGELES AFTER SEVEN MONTHS IN THE YAQU
INDIAN WILDS OF SONORA, MEXICO, WHERE AS A FRIEND OF
YAQUI CHIEFS HE MADE SEVERAL STARTLING SCIENTIFIC DISCOVERI
HE TELLS OF A CAVE 450 MILES INLAND IN THE SONORA MOUNTAINS
SAID TO BE LARGER THAN THE CARLSBAD CAVES OF NEW MEXICO,
AND IN THESE CAVES, HE SAID, WERE FOUND GIANT MUMMIES 7½
FEET TALL. CORN BURIED WITH THE MUMMIES HAS BEEN GIVEN TO
MEXICAN AGRICULTURE EXPERTS WHO ARE NOW TRYING TO GERMINATE
IT. SCIENTISTS OF SOUTHERN CALIFORNIA ARE ALSO TRYING TO
GERMINATE THE CORN. HAYES IS IN LOS ANGELES TO INTEREST
SCIENTISTS IN AN EXPLORATION VENTURE.
      PHOTO SHOWS ONE OF THE GIANT MUMMIES IN THE ENTRANCE
OF THE CAVE. THIS MUMMY IS 7½ FEET TALL. THE CLOTH AND ROPE
USED IN THE WRAPPING IS OF A VARIETY NEVER BEFORE SEEN.
EARS OF CORN FOUND WITH THE MUMMY HAVE BEEN TURNED OVER TO
AGRICULTURE EXPERTS. BUREAUS:
"YOUR CREDIT LINE MUST READ (ACME)" 12/27/35

Example of back of the press photos that the authors aquired. Credit: ACME

13

FURTHER AFIELD

Continuing from last chapter's investigation beyond the borders of North America, we tackle some intriguing accounts from Alaska, Hawaii, Canada and the California Channel Islands.

ALASKA

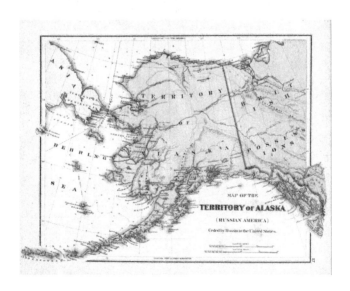

ALASKAN MUMMIES
The Dawson Daily News, August 20, 1901, pg. 23

We start with an account of giant mummies found in a cave in Alaska reported in 1901:

"On an island in Prince William Sound, Alaska is a wonderful cave, containing remains of a prehistoric race of Alaska Indians. The cave is guarded by an Indian tribe which inhabits the island...Two years ago a party of prospectors entered the cave and discovered a number of bodies laid away in niches of the rock. The party came out intending to explore further on another day but were notified by the Indians that they could not enter. The prospectors declared that the mummies of Indians were much larger than any living race of men, being seven and eight feet in stature. What is believed to be a mummy from the identical cave is owned by F. H. Baldie of Tacoma, whose wife is suing him for divorce. None outside of the family knew of his Alaska mummy until Mrs. Baldie scheduled it among his assets as worth $2,000, requesting half its value in cash."

A woman scorned will apparently force you to sell your *mummy*.

FIND THE REMAINS OF A GIANT RACE
The Spokane Press., November 16, 1908, Pg. 4
Fairbanks, Alaska

Seven years later during a mining operation in Alaska, A. R. Simpson reported finding a giant petrified human bone buried 52 feet deep in the earth. Simpson's wife, *"who is a woman of education and friends of Herbert Spencer and Thomas Carlyle in her youth, took up the work of learning the significance of the find."* Dr. W. R. Cassels of Fairbanks pronounced the bone to be undoubtedly from the leg of a prehistoric giant and others who have seen it agree with him. This and any others to be discovered were turned over to the Smithsonian Institution in the hope that they would conduct a further investigation (see news report and photo overleaf).

FIND THE REMAINS OF A GIANT RACE

BONE, THOUGHT TO BE TRACE OF GIANT RACE.

CANADA

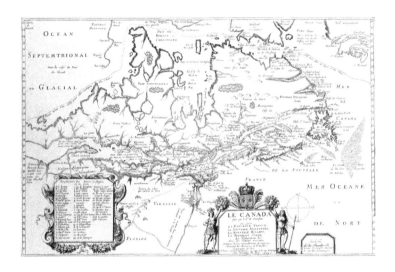

Indian Burying Ground is Found
The Border Cities Star, Sept. 5, 1934, pg.19
Simcoe, Ontario, Canada

W. Edgar Cantelon, curator of the Norfolk Museum of Arts and Antiquities announced the discovery that included skeletons measuring eight feet in height and large deposits of arrowheads, spears, drills, gorgets, wampum and pottery:

"Evidence showed thousands of persons lived in the district, he said, some of whom were extraordinarily tall. Skeletons measuring about eight feet in height have been unearthed."

William Cantelon was an artist as well as curator of the Norfolk museum, which still exists. By all accounts Mr. Cantelon was widely respected and beloved.

SKELETONS OF GIANTS - LOST CITY DISCOVERED
West Coast Times, Issue 1924, November 29, 1871
Cayuga, Canada

The report discusses a find made earlier that year on August 21st, and we have included the full story as it gives a fascinating insight into the lives of these Canadian titans:

"On Wednesday last, Rev. Nathaniel Wardel, Messrs Orin Wardell, of Toronto and Daniel Fredenburg, were digging on the farm of the later gentleman, which is on the banks of the Grand River, in the township of Cayuga. When they got to five or six feet below the surface a strange sight met them. Piled in layers, one upon top of the other, some two hundred skeletons of human beings nearly perfect—around the neck of each one being a string of beads. There were also deposited in this pit a number of axes and skinners made of stone. In the jaws of several of the skeletons were large stone pipes, one of which Mr. O. Wardell took with him to Toronto a day or two after this Golgotha was unearthed.

These skeletons are those of men of gigantic stature, some of them measuring nine feet, very few of them being less than seven feet. Some of the thigh bones were found to be at least half a foot longer than those at present known and one of the skulls being examined completely covered the head of an ordinary person. These skeletons are supposed to belong to a race of people anterior to the Indians. The pit and its ghastly

307

occupants are now open to the view of any who may wish to make a visit there.

There is not the slightest doubt that the remains of a lost city are on this farm. At various times within the past years the remains of mud-homes with their chimneys had been found; and there are dozens of pits of a similar kind to that just unearthed, though much smaller, in the place which has been discovered before, though the fact has not been made public hitherto. The remains of a blacksmith shop, containing two tons of charcoal and various implements, were turned up a few months ago. The farm, which consists of 150 acres, has been cultivated for nearly a century and was covered with a thick growth of pine, so that it must have been ages since the remains were deposited there. The skulls of the skeletons are of enormous size and are of all manner of shapes. The teeth of most of them are still in an almost perfect state of preservation, though they soon fall out when exposed to air. Some large shells, supposed to have been used for holding water, which were also found in the pit, were almost petrified.

A good deal of excitement exists in the neighborhood and many visitors call at the farm daily. The skulls and bones of the giants are fast disappearing, being taken away by curiosity hunters. It is the intention of Mr. Fredenburgh to cover the pit very soon. From the appearance of the skulls it would seem that their possessors died a violent death, as many of them were broken and dented. The beads are all of stone and of all sizes and shapes. The pipes are not unlike in shape the cutty pipes and several of them are engraved with dog's heads. They have not lost their virtue of smoking. Some people profess to believe that the locality Fredenburgh Farm was formerly an Indian burial-place but the enormous stature of the skeletons and the fact that pine trees of centuries growth covered the spot, go far to disprove the idea."

HAWAII

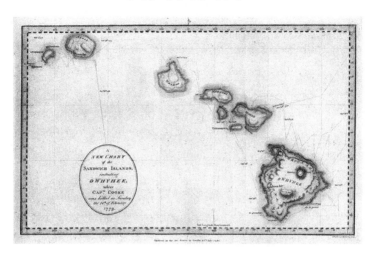

THREE SKELETONS OF OLDEN GIANTS ARE DISCOVERED
The Honolulu Star Bulletin, December 22, 1913, pg.2
Waimea, Hawaii

The Hawaiian Islands revealed this astonishing account:

"Three gigantic skeletons, unearthed a few days ago at Waimea, Hawaii have aroused intense interest among those who have heard of the unusual happening. The immense size of the skeletons confirm stories in Hawaiian legends of the great stature and tremendous strength of the men of old... John H. Wise, who has been at work in the Waimea homestead district on the homesteading project in which he and several other local people are interested, vouches for the correctness of the information, having personally inspected the skeletons and made rough but practical measurements of some of the bones. There is no question that the men living were well

THREE SKELETONS OF OLDEN GIANTS ARE DISCOVERED

Road-workers at Waimea, Hawaii, Dig Up Bones of Men Over Seven Feet Tall

LEGEND OF GREAT BATTLE BELIEVED NOW CONFIRMED

Story of Maui King Whose Bodyguard Fell on Invasion, Brought Back to Mind

*over seven feet high,' said Wise today. 'The leg bones for instance,
were far longer than that of any man of Hawaii today, so far
as we know.'*

*I am something over five-feet-ten in height and the leg-
bone, from foot to knee came halfway between my knee and
thigh. The bones were of immense size. The skulls were also of
great size... Perhaps unfortunately for scientific research, the
Hawaiians who were employed on the road-gang refused to
allow the skeletons to be taken away and they were reburied.*

*However, Wise says they can probably be secured in case
they should be desired for the Bishop Museum. He thinks
the ethnologists would find much interest in a study of what
were evidently physical giants... The bodyguard of the Maui
king according to the tradition, was composed of warriors over
seven feet and the tradition declares that every one of those
giants perished in battle and the point where the bodyguard
was destroyed, before the king and his followers fled, is said to
be about where the skeletons have now been found."*

This account lined up precisely with the oral tradition of indigenous
Hawaiians, right down to the location of the burial spot.

PREHISTORIC MEN 7 FEET TALL
The New Castle News, Friday, January 7, 1944, pg.6
Big Island, Hawaii

*"Beneath layers of lava and coral on the Island of Hawaii have
been found skeletons of prehistoric men seven feet tall."*

However, that is all that was reported so no further details are forthcoming.

THE BUTTON BOX: A DAUGHTER'S LOVING
MEMOIR OF MRS. GEORGE S. PATTON,
2005, pg.167, Mauna Loa, Hawaii, circa 1910

"The Parker ranch was on the mighty slope of Mauna Loa, the volcanic mountain opposite the Carter's house. One of the painolas told Ma that when he was a little child, one of his great-grandfathers had died and the family took him into the hollow cone for burial. There, by the light of torches, the little boy saw his ancestors, mummified by the airless dark, wrapped in their feather capes and lying in their great canoes. The paniola told Ma, that the bodies were of very tall men—giants. Ma was dying to see this but the cowboy told her that no one knew any more where the entrance to the cinder cone was. The people were afraid that strangers would enter the sacred place and vandalize it. They had hidden the tunnel.

Mr. Carter was very interested when Ma told him this story. He said he had known about it for forty years but had never known any of his Hawaiians to tell a stranger. However, he did know of a burial cave that she could see that might interest her and he arranged to have us taken there by a part-Hawaiian friend of his named Mr. White. Mr. White was very interested in the history of his people and was delighted to find someone else who shared his passions, so he took us to the Grave of the Common Dead near Hoonaunau. This cave was a broken lava tube, halfway up a crumbling lava flow, similar to a cliff. We had to get there by climbing a rope ladder. At the front of the cave, in the light, were recent burials—many in coffins and

A young Mr and Mrs George S. Patton on their wedding day, 1910.

311

a few wrapped in tapa cloth like their ancestors. Some of the coffins were open and we were fascinated by the skeletons.
I could have stayed there all day, but Mr. White wanted us to come inside. He had a lantern with him and we saw an extraordinary sight. The lava tube was larger as you got away from the sunlit entrance and on the floor were seemingly numberless skeletons laid out nearly side by side. The ones toward the front were about normal size, but toward the back of the cave they got bigger and taller. Mr. White took out a tape measure and, walking carefully around the bones, measured one fairly complete skeleton to show that it was more than seven feet tall. He said the ancient Hawaiians had been a race of giants."

The "Ma" referred to by daughter Ruth Ellen Patton Totten was the wife of World War II hero, General George S. Patton. The description given in the book matches in many respects skeletal finds from other parts of Hawaii such as the dead being buried in canoes and lava tubes.

THE SECRETS AND MYSTERIES OF HAWAII
by Chiles Pila, 1995, pp. 162-163

"At the north end of the Big Island, near the sleepy town of Hawi, is a large 750-pound rock in the middle of the road. It is about the size and weight of a General Motors V-8 diesel engine block. It was carried there by King Kamehameha all the way up from the floor of Waipio Valley. He used only his brute strength. King Kamehameha the Great was over seven feet tall and considered a god among men. King Kamehameha (1758 – May 8, 1819), conquered the Hawaiian Islands and formally established the Kingdom of Hawaii in 1810. Like many Native American rulers he was a giant in stature and possessed herculean strength."

The following is from *Hawaiian Folklore Tales* by C. Alexander Stames, 1975, pg. 79:

> *"Although King Kamehameha was reputed to be 7 feet 10 inches in height, 8 foot 3 inch skeletons have been unearthed on various parts of Hawaii."*

From *The Californian*, Volume 4, 1881, pg. 259 is found the following,

> *"John Li, was a native Hawaiian. Lot Pakee, the oldest, the mightiest and the grandest of the ancient line of chiefs, was Chamberlain. He was nearly seven feet high, of magnificent proportionate frame, had the strength of a Hercules and often in his early manhood had he performed prodigies of valor and surprising feats of athletic nature."*

It appears that a royal class of giants may have been a mainstay of ancient societies, sometimes almost up until the present.

THE MYSTERY OF THE
CALIFORNIA CHANNEL ISLANDS

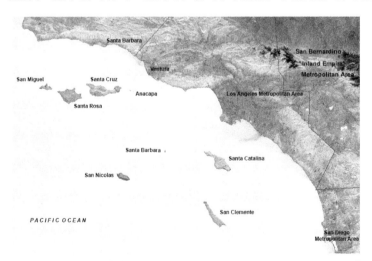

Map of the California Channel Islands. Giant discoveries have been made on San Miguel, Santa Rosa, San Nicolas, San Clemente and Catalina Island, as well as on the mainland.

313

The Channel Islands off the coast of California have turned up hundreds of controversial discoveries. Not only were giant skeletons reported, but also a prehistoric stone circle (see *Early Explorers* chapter) along with ancient carbon dating and evidence of red and blond cultures with "ruddy" skin. Numerous oversized skeletons, artifacts, and evidence of occupation going back as far as 40,000 years ago have been recorded on the islands.[1] The story is intriguing and controversial, and it stars amateur archaeologist Ralph Glidden and his bizarre museum on Catalina Island, but before the main act, a German naturalist got the story going in 1913.

STORY OF A SKULL, BURIED SIX CENTURIES, TELLS OF THE PERFECT AMERICAN
Pittsburg Press, July 20, 1913
Catalina Island, California

Dr. A. W. Furstenan reported unearthing an 8 ft tall skeleton with artifacts such as mortar and pestles and arrow heads on Catalina. He was told of a legend while in Mexico of a giant and noble race that lived on the Island, who existed long before the white man and had since vanished. Here he is pictured with one of the skulls:

Story of a Skull, Buried Six Centuries, Tells of the Perfect American

The Wonderful Discovery of Naturalist Furstenan of Denver, on Catalina Island—An Eight-Foot Giant Buried With His Life Treasures.

Denver, Colo., July 23—For six centuries an Indian sphinx sat buried in the sand on the shore of Catalina Island, off the coast of California, the with his treasurers in his lap. These were arrow and spear heads, curious wampum made of carved fish vertebræ, rude knives and needles,

Indians are Rising out of Legend
Ogden Standard Examiner, Sunday, November 10, 1929, pg.32
Santa Catalina Island, California

Amateur archaeologist Ralph Glidden unearthed and collected a total of 3,781 skeletons on the Channel Islands between 1919 and 1930. Working for the Heye Foundation of New York he claimed to have unearthed a 9 ft 2 in skeleton and several measuring over 7 feet:

"A skeleton of a young girl, evidently of high rank, within a large funeral urn, was surrounded by those of sixty four children, and in various parts of the island more than three thousand other skeletons were found, practically all the males averaging around seven feet in height, one being seven feet eight inches from the top of his head to the ankle, and another being 9 feet 2 inches tall."

AT RIGHT
This Skeleton of
a Man Who was 7 Feet 8 Inches
Tall Reposed Below the Tomb
in Which the Remains of 64
Children Were Found.

During the expedition to the interior of Catalina Professor Glidden collected the skeletons of 3,781 Indians. The largest he found was of a man 9 feet 2 inches tall. Practically all the male adults were of gigantic stature, averaging around 7 feet in height.

The skeleton in the picture is 7 ft 8 in example

315

THE INDIAN WAS THE LARGEST FOUND ON THE ISLAND
The L.A. Times, August 21, 1938, pg.3

The article is about the reported unearthing of another over 7 ft skeleton on Catalina Island by Ralph Glidden and Judge Earnest Windle:

> *"Glidden made the discovery, notified the judge, who joined him and wrote of it. 'The Indian was the largest found on the island' Windle says, 'Had he been alive today he would have worn a hat size 10 ½. He was seven feet two and one-half inches tall and must have weighed in the neighborhood of 300 pounds. His jawbone was so huge that the inside of it will fit easily, and leave room to spare around the outside of a normal person.'"*

GIANT'S BODY FOUND AT AVALON
The Indian Valley Record, May 13, 1937, pg. 2

This is a continuation of giant skeletal remains found in the previous report:

> *"Workmen excavating for a pipeline on Avalon's main street uncovered the skeleton of a giant measuring seven foot and three inches."*

CALIFORNIA
News of the Week

Giant's Body Found at Avalon
Avalon (Santa Catalina Island).— Workmen excavating for a pipe line on Avalon's main street uncovered the skeleton of a giant measuring seven feet and three inches. With the bones, believed to have lain there for centuries, was a perfect bowl and pestle.

Catalina Islander Magazine 1924 - 1937

Three articles from the *Catalina Islander* magazine from 1924, 1930, 1931 and 1937 shed further light on Glidden's discoveries. Even the famous author and mystic Arthur Conan Doyle—who wrote the Sherlock Holmes stories— is quoted speaking of Catalina Island and the seven feet tall skeletons.

This is from the *Catalina Islander* January 16th 1924:

> *"I have mentioned that an Indian graveyard was found upon the island. I had an opportunity of studying the photographs of the skeletons. One of them was a man seven feet in height, so they were clearly a very different race from those old savages whose stocky figures and gorilla-like skulls were being uncovered at that very moment at Santa Barbara..."*

In the *Catalina Islander* April 2, 1930 page 6 is found:

> *"Although the writer of this article visited many of the Catalina Indian town sites and burial places of the interior while Professor Glidden had done his excavation work during the past 17 years, a recent visit to the museum was very interesting... One of the skulls measured 26 ½ inches, and the body with it indicated that the man was fully seven feet in height."*

Indian Skeleton 7 feet, 2¼ inches high, with hands crossed and fingers over right eye.

The *Catalina Islander* November 18th, 1931 page 10:

> *"Before the advent of the white man, a tribe of Indians, recorded by Spanish explorers as 'white Indians' inhabited the island. Their complexions were ruddy and their skins almost as white as their own, according to the chroniclers. That they were a giant race is proved through recent excavations that have been made in ancient burial grounds which have brought to light skeletons of those early people, that measure from seven to nine feet in height."*

The report continues and speculates on their origins:

> *"Anthropologists believe that the Catalina Indians may have originated from certain Peruvian mountain tribes known to have been of fair complexion. Finds of some of the artifacts lend strength also to the theory that they may have been related to the Aztecs or the Mayas."*

Also from February 11, 1937, page 4:

> *"Recent excavations made on Santa Catalina Island by Ralph Glidden, curator of the Catalina Museum of the Channel Islands substantiated the historic references to a race of Indians of gigantic stature that once inhabited this island paradise. A great funeral urn fashioned out of stone, its rim decorated with four equi-distant circles of wampum is zealously guarded in a glass case in the Glidden Museum... Glidden found a man, probably a guard, that measured seven feet nine inches in height."*

The stone urn mentioned here weighs 134 pounds and was buried with the giant skeleton. It was described as *"fashioned as skillfully as though by modern tools instead of primitive implements."* The urn is still housed at the Catalina Island Museum.

In 1962, Philip K. Wrigley purchased Glidden's entire collection and donated it to the Museum. Due to NAGPRA, many of the Museum's American Indian remains are housed at the University of California and studied by archaeologists at the Fowler Museum.

Jim made contact with the assistant curator of the Catalina Island museum John Borrangina, who in March 2012 rediscovered Glidden's lost records, photos and field notes as reported in *The L.A. Times* after being stored away in the museum's attic for nearly 90 years.[2] All the photos have since been catalogued and numbered and have been analyzed by various researchers including L.A. Marzulli who believe some of the examples may be as tall as 8 ft 6 inches, fitting in with previous discoveries on the island.[3]

As part of *Search for the Lost Giants*, Jim and Bill Vieira visited Catalina to investigate the contents of the box, and indeed there were photos of hundreds of skeletons and skulls, excavations, artifacts, and burials. After carefully looking through everything at the museum and scanning the island from a bird's-eye view (thanks to a helicopter), they returned home with a bad taste in their mouths. Clearly Glidden had little respect for the sacred burials of this incredibly ancient culture and treated the bones and skulls as props in his bizarre and morbid museum.

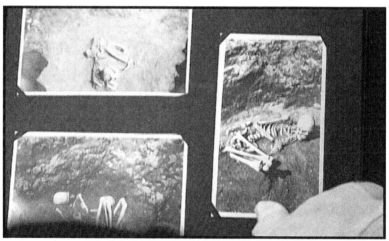

Various photos taken by Glidden rediscovered in
March 2012 by John Borrangina.

However, during their investigation of Glidden's records, the Vieira brothers did find an account of a 28-inch femur unearthed by Glidden on San Nicolas Island reported by the judge of Avalon, Earnest Windle. This would make the gentleman over 8 feet tall and the next account may point to the veracity of this discovery.

San Nicolas Island, California
The Evening Tribune, July 7, 1897, pg.3

"After nearly three weeks sojourn on the barren island of San Nicolas a party of relic hunters reached Long Beach, Cal. loaded with skeletons, skulls and ancient implements and ornaments of Indian tribes... There were 11 in the party which left Long Beach in the gasoline schooner San Clemente for San Nicolas Island, which lies 65 miles off the coast of Santa Barbara... The party found 87 skulls buried in the sand of the island but were only able to secure three entire... Positive evidence was found that the island was inhabited by two or more different races in the dim past, one of which was of great size, a peculiar characteristic being gigantic jawbones. Some of the specimens of the latter brought by the party are almost large enough to slip over the head of an ordinary man... Mr. Longfellow, one of the party, speaking of the trip said, "I am sure that two different races fought and died on the island, as most of the bodies were of moderate size while some were almost giants. The latter were always in isolated graves. We found many stone implements and weapons of stone but all are very crude and show almost no ornamentation."

Santa Rosa Island
The Native Races of the Pacific States of North America,
Hubert Howe Bancroft, 1875 - 1882, pp. 694-695

This account is also featured in *The Scientific American*[4] (also see *DRT* chapter). A Mr. Taylor heard from a resident of San Buenaventura that:

"...in a recent stay on Santa Rosa Island, in 1861, he often met with entire skeletons of Indians in the caves. The signs of their rancherias were very frequent, and the remains of metates, mortars, earthen pots, and other utensils very common. Extensive caves were met with which seemed to serve as burial

*places of the Indians, as entire skeletons and numerous skulls
were plentifully scattered about in their recesses. Further skulls
are also reported as having been found on the islands, furnished
with double teeth."*

Seven feet tall skeletons were reported (see image below), and some
startling carbon dating emerged putting these inhabitants back to over
7,000 years old.

FIGURE 23. Indian cemetery, Santa Rosa Island, containing abalone shells radiocarbon dated
at 7,070 years. Tops of skulls were painted red, several skeletons measured over seven feet
tall. Photo courtesy of Santa Barbara Museum of Natural History, 1959.

In 1941, Phil Orr of the *Santa Barbara Museum of Natural History* began
work on the island. In over thirteen years of work he excavated 180 sites,
and in 1959 at a place called Arlington Springs, he discovered something
that shocked the world.

Orr found a human femur, and believed the remains were those
of a 10,000-year-old man and dubbed him the "Arlington Springs Man."
However they were later believed to be female and she was renamed
"Arlington Springs Woman." After thirty years of matriarchal glory, she
became "Arlington Springs Man" again! Further tests showed that the
remains dated back 13,000 years,[5] making this potentially the oldest
known human skeleton in North America.

321

The March 2011 edition of *Science*, had this headline that confirmed the deep antiquity of these early inhabitants:

"Evidence for a diversified sea-based economy among North American inhabitants dating from 12,200 to 11,400 years ago is emerging from three sites on California's Channel Islands." [6]

Jon Erlandson, professor of anthropology and Director of the Museum of Natural and Cultural History at the University of Oregon said:

"The points we are finding are extraordinary, the workmanship amazing. They are ultra thin, serrated and have incredible barbs on them. It's a very sophisticated chipped-stone technology." [7]

This type of technology may indeed be related to some other sites of an even earlier age that we will explore in the next chapter. We will also investigate if this archaic human activity is related to the giant discoveries on the same islands. This lays down an intriguing possibility as to the origins of the North American giants.

Jim and Bill Vieira going through Ralph Glidden's records at the
Catalina Island Museum.

14

ORIGINS OF THE TALL ONES

The debate over the origins of the North American giants has been going on for nearly 200 years. Native American mythology, the latest scientific research, genetic data, and ethnological research is shedding light on these mysteries, and the enigmatic Denisovans, Nephilim, and visitors from other ancient cultures may have been involved. Extremely old skeletal remains and anomalies such as 250,000-year-old Hueyatlaco finds in Mexico (see page 350), as well as the mummified red-haired remains in Nevada, do pose a series of tantalising problems that any budding giantologist might ponder. North America has ample evidence of outside migration well before first contact over 500 years ago, but there is still a huge question mark over the origins of those mighty giants we have discussed in this book.

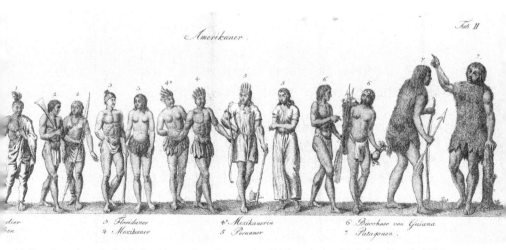

Native American height chart based on the work of Wünsch, by Christian Ernst, 1796.

323

In this final chapter, we will look at numerous theories as to where these giants came from, how they got so big, and why they are no longer with us. If we break down the hundreds of theories of who is proclaimed to have visited North America before the white man arrived, we are left with just a few examples that may be related to the Tall Ones. However, as Ross Hamilton, Vine Deloria Jr., and archaeologists such as Jeffrey Goodman point out, the origins of the Tall Ones might well have been within the confines of America itself, and there is evidence that they had protocols in place to maintain their elite status over multiple generations.

> *"The very tall native people recorded early in American history were said to be of a time-honored tradition of selective mating or marriage both fragile and in a stage of imminent collapse. The introduction of smallpox hastened things. Like European royalty, there apparently existed prescribed marital protocols among certain families. In the Eastern Woodland cultures of North America, there was an effort to preserve genetic lines sustaining, among other things, certain physical characteristics giving rise to a class of nobility over time. Long in political power, family members received chieftainships and the duties affiliated with seats of influence."* [1]

The unique traits of the Tall Ones were recognised by early societies and may have been seen as an important, possibly divine or royal bloodline they were determined to nurture and maintain. Even if this were the case, where they came from is another matter. Perhaps a good starting point would be to take a look at the early migrations of Native Americans to start to piece together the greater "giant" puzzle.

MYTHS AND MIGRATIONS

Creation myths and oral histories describing the migrations of certain tribes may be a factor in determining the origins of these mighty giants. For example, the Sioux, Iroquois and Cherokee all have creation myths, and all have stories of giants. Chief Attakullakulla's speech to the Cherokee Nation in 1750 said:

"We traveled here from the rising sun, before the time of the stone age man." [2]

The origin of the Iroquois has been lost in the depths of time, but during the 1700s their descendants related stories to Catholic priests that they came from the east after being destroyed by a great flood.[3] The possible relation to the legendary Atlantis will be expanded on later in this chapter.

> *"Native American traditions clearly narrate of very tall and impressively constructed men and women whose lives and deeds became the stuff of legends to the old tribal families. They were a royal class who were descended from a remotely ancient clan of spiritually realized stock such as the Cherokee Nunnéhi or the Choctaw Nahúlo."* [4]

Choctaw tradition states that the Lenape (the archaeological Adena) originated somewhere in the far west of the continent and migrated en masse towards the rising sun. Vine Deloria Jr. called it the *"great exodus"* (see *Legends of the Tall Ones* chapter). The Algonquin-speaking Lenape were also said to have come from the western part of America and migrated eastwards.

Modern scholars tell us that all of North America was considered to be called Turtle Island,[5] although in hindsight the Lenape may have been *seeking* Turtle Island, the land of their ancestors. This passage is from the oral history of the Iroquois:

> *"Sky Woman fell down to the earth when it was covered with water. Various animals tried to swim to the bottom of the ocean to bring back dirt to create land. Muskrat succeeded in gathering dirt, which was placed on the back of a turtle, which grew into the land known today as North America."* [6]

The Hopi believe they originated in America and are among its oldest inhabitants. There is an interesting passage in their elaborate myths that may also describe a so-called land bridge:

> *"Masaw told them that the northern area would be the back door to the new world, this new continent, and that in the*

future many people would come into this new land via this back door. But they would do so without Masaw's permission."[7]

Native Americans, however, as a general rule, oppose the land bridge theory as it does not reflect their ancient traditions passed down by their ancestors over many generations. Vine Deloria summarises the situation:

"Some tribes speak of transoceanic migrations in boats, the Hopis and Colvilles for example, and others speak of the experience of a creation, such as the Yakimas and other Pacific Northwest tribes. Some tribes even talk about migrations from other planets." [8]

THE BERING LAND BRIDGE

The migration from Asia over the Bering land bridge is the fixed scientific perspective regarding the origins of Native Americans. This, however, is now under intense scrutiny on many fronts. It was first proposed in 1590 by José de Acosta and has been widely accepted since the 1930s.

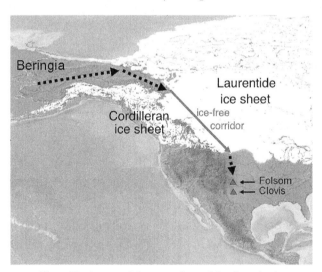

Theoritical map of the peopling of the America's.

Dr. Aleš Hrdlička of the Smithsonian was involved in championing the theory of the Bering land bridge as he was convinced all humans came from a common source that was not in America. Hrdlička was also fond of the theory of evolution, and as we know, was not interested in anything dating back beyond 2,000 BC until in 1927 his contemporaries pointed out that the Folsom Points were dated to around 8,000 - 9,000 B.C. (See *The Smithsonian Files* chapter). Soon after the land bridge theory was in full swing, a new theory emerged when 'Clovis' points were discovered in New Mexico. Over the next few years virtually all states had found Clovis evidence, so a neat and tidy theory that Siberian nomads entered America around 9,500 BC via the land bridge became the norm, and continued without much resistance from academia until the mid-twentieth century.

The Clovis Barrier (an invisible wall against new ideas, protecting the prevailing theory) held strong for decades, but when, in 1958, a discovery was made in Lewisville, Texas, with what appeared to be Clovis fluted points discovered in a layer that was at least 38,000 years old, the barrier crumbled. Then in 1997 Tom Dillehay discovered Monte Verde in Chile, with radiocarbon dates going back to at least 1,000 years before Clovis. This pretty much triggered the full collapse of the so-called Clovis Barrier. But more was to come.

Two Migrations Via the Land Bridge

There is now a theory that there were two migrations via the Bering land bridge. One at the very earliest time of around 20,000 years ago[9] and the "Amerind" (American Indian) migration was said to have come over at 9,500 BC. The humans who arrived at that time are said to be the direct ancestors of the North American Indian. However, it is very unclear who originally crossed the land bridge 20,000 years ago, but they may well have been the descendents of the mysterious Denisovans who were known to have existed in northern Siberia—which is especially interesting as their DNA has been found in some Native American populations. We will explore the connection to this culture soon, but whoever they were, it has been postulated that they may have had features resembling modern humans.[10]

As part of his research Dr. Dennis Stanford investigated the proposed area of Siberia that the original Native Americans were said to have come from, and also the area of the land bridge. He found no Clovis evidence whatsoever. Stanford is an archaeologist and Director of the

Paleoindian/Paleoecology Program at the National Museum of Natural History at the Smithsonian Institution. Along with Prof. Bruce Bradley, he is known for advocating the *Solutrean hypothesis*, which contends that stone tool technology of the Solutrean culture in prehistoric Europe may have influenced the development of the Clovis tool-making culture in the Americas. Therefore, they postulated that the Solutreans traveled across the Atlantic, hugging the ice-sheet until they reached America around 15,000 years ago.

Meanwhile, on the opposite side of the country, early travellers were settling in on the California Channel Islands.

WEST COAST SEAFARING ORIGINS

We have already seen that the Channel Islands may have had very early human occupation, which also suggests they were seafarers and proficient hunters, who we also know were fairly tall, with some reports suggesting a height of 9 feet 2 inches (see *Further Afield* chapter). Red and blond haired traits are also sometimes evident, not only on the coast, but inland such as in Nevada and the southwest states and even into Sonora in Mexico. The dating of the mummies and artifacts as far back as 9,000 BC do suggest that this area of North America was inhabited by taller than average people, with (some) red and blond haired tribes, with a robust Cro-Magnon skull type that has been compared to modern humans. The extremely ancient dates that are arising have consequently caused much controversy.

The proposed 12,200 year old discoveries on Santa Rosa Island are at least 1,000 years older than the famous Clovis Culture.[11] Their intricate stone tools show that they were a completely separate culture to the Folsom and Clovis. Radiocarbon dates suggest that prehistoric man also inhabited San Miguel, one of the Northern Channel Islands as long ago as 10,700 years. About 18,000 years ago these northern islands were connected to each other as one large island that scientists call *Santarosae,* with possible occupation as long ago as 40,000 years.[12]

Were these islands the origin point of the tribes that carried the 'giant' traits, and migrated east to flourish for the proceeding millennia? However, from where did these islanders originate?

Australasian and Melanesian influences are now thought to have occured in South America going back 23,000 years, and even as far back as 50,000 years. In 1999 Walter Neves studied skulls found in Brazil and concluded they were of Australian Aboriginal or Melanesian origin. In July of 2015 brand new research backed this up.[13] The 2015 paper hinted at multiple migrations, but confirmed that Native American DNA had some connections to these original sources.

Before we explore the deep antiquity of many of these potential ancestors of the giants, some discoveries further south along the west coast to Baja California may provide some clues.

BAJA CALIFORNIA AND MEXICAN ORIGINS

The western edge of America and the Southwestern states could have been influenced not only by incoming migrants from Australasia and Melanesia, and the large-statured Seri and Sonora tribes (that we discussed in the *Early Explorers* and *Sonora* chapters), but also by the taller-than-average Guaycura Indians of Baja California, who had distinct similarities to their giant Patagonian cousins:

"The Guaycura Indians were native to our area and as legend has it that, the men were used for procreation and the tribe was run by their Amazon Queen, Queen Calafia. Some schools of thought have it that after her, California was named. She was quite famous as evidenced by the use of her name 'Calafia' throughout Baja and Mainland Mexico. Also the Guaycura Indians were tall, over 6' tall and looked like no other Indian in any part of Baja or Mainland Mexico. There is no record of any Indian anywhere in the western hemisphere that has any likeliness to them. Due to the fact of their resemblances to the seafaring voyagers of the Pacific Islanders, and the similar latitude to the Hawaiian Islands, there is more than a possibility that they were direct descendants of Polynesian seafarers attempting to find the Hawaiian Islands that had blown off course and landed at southern Baja California and settling there. You will notice as you observe the local people

of the area you will see an amount of tall slender dark haired Indians, these are descendants of the original Guaycuras. By 1767, virtually all the Guaycura Indians in the area had died either of European diseases or in skirmishes with the Spanish."[14]

An area slightly further south is known today as San Jose del Cabo. It was originally inhabited by the Pericúes. Although the oldest Pericú remains are dated at 3,000 years old, archaeological evidence extends as far back as 11,000 years ago.[15]

"Their skull morphology and recent genetic studies led by Dr. Silvia Gonzalez strengthen the theory that the Pericúes did not originate in Northern Asia, where some experts believed Native Americans first came from. Instead, the Pericues are closer to the ancient populations of southern Asia, Australia, and the South Pacific Rim. The Peñon Woman discovered near Mexico City and dated at 12,700 - 15,000 years BP, among the oldest human remains recovered in the Americas so far, has similar cranial morphology to the Pericues. The same skull configuration is also found at Lagoa Santa in Brazil and in Patagonia."[15]

Are the Patagonians, who we know were giant in stature, of the same origins as the giants of the west coast of North America? Did they come

Martyrdom of Lorenzo Carranco, at the beginning of the Pericú Revolt in Santiago de los Coras de Añiñí, 1st October 1734. Notice the size of the Pericuan Indians.

330

from the same stock either by sea or the land bridge? With more scientific research being carried out, the more it looks like those with these traits were inhabiting the southern tip of South America, all the way up to North America.

> *"The distinctive hyperdolichocephalic (long-headed) skulls found in Cape Region burials have suggested to some scholars that the ancestors of the Pericú were either trans-Pacific immigrants or remnants of some of the New World's earliest colonizers."* [16]

Much like the mighty Patagonians, the Pericúes of Baja California were taller and stronger than the average Mexican and were noted for their strength and physique.

A DNA study that took place in 2004 concluded that the two oldest known Americans; Peñon woman (in Mexico) and Kennewick Man (in Washington) might have belonged to the Pericú tribe (or were at least distantly related) as their skull types are remarkably similar—long and narrow (dolicocephalic)—very different from classical Native American traits.

These surprising discoveries certainly suggest that sea-faring was a very ancient skill, as we have already seen on the California Channel Islands. The fact that all these cultures may have been exceptionally tall (based on the skeletal remains found on these Islands, and ancient legends), can no longer be ignored. The Pericúes were thus described:

> *"The missionary descriptions indicated that the men were naked and the women wore grass skirts, and they were very tall and slim."* [17]

They also used copious amounts of tobacco in their ceremonies, and their burial customs were deeply reminiscent of what we have seen in the burial customs of the mortuary mound-building giants all over North America:

> *"Gonzalez indicated that they had a complex burial system involving mortuary-like burial areas located both along the coast and in caves. She said they also used wooden spear*

*throwers, and likely painted bones with red ochre, as early
decorated shells and pearls have been found in Baja."* [18]

The report emphasised that there was *"very strong evidence that the first
migration came from Australia via Japan and Polynesia and down the
Pacific coast of America."* This is now backed up by modern science, and
they could well have been distantly related to the mysterious Denisovans.

DENISOVAN GENES IN AMERICA

The Denisovans are still a virtually invisible culture that could well be the
ancient ancestors of the Patagonians and the Pericú. We featured the
Denisovans in *Search for the Lost Giants* with researcher Terje Dahl. Author
Andrew Collins was the first to publish a detailed analysis of the mysterious
Denisovans and their possible traits relating to the giants of North
America.[19]

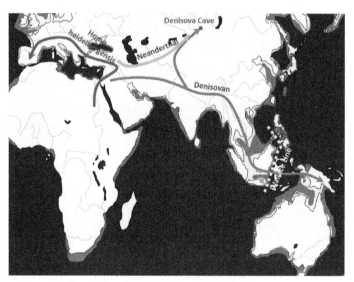

Spread and migrations of the Denisovans.

In 2008 Russian archaeologists found a fragment of a large finger bone
of a young female in a remote cave in the Altai Mountains of northern
Siberia. *"The single finger bone is unusually broad and robust, well outside
the variation seen in modern people."*[20] The cave and its contents were
originally dated to around 41,000 years old, but new results (published
in September 2015) stretch the dates back to between 50,000 and 170,000

years ago.[21] The original 41,000 year old discoveries included the finger bone, two teeth and a very interesting finely finished obsidian bracelet, like the world had never seen before. But crucially, the DNA analysis of the finger bone created a worldwide sensation and the discovery of a completely unknown extinct human species known as the *Denisovans.*

The two teeth that were discovered (from separate individuals) have got giantologists talking. The molars are much larger than normal, with one having a chewing surface twice that of a modern human.

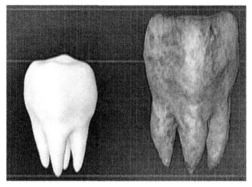

Above: Modern molar on left with width of 10.67 mm. The Denisovan tooth on the right with width of 14.7mm. Below: Photo of human molar compared to Denisovan tooth replica in Shara Bailey's office.

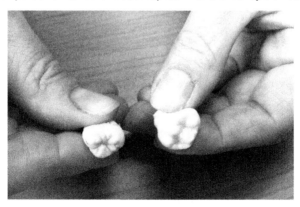

When the tooth was initially discovered, *Max Planck Institute* paleoanthropologist Bence Viola mistook it for that of a cave bear's tooth. Only when its DNA was tested was it confirmed otherwise. "*It shows you how weird these guys are,*" he said. "*...their teeth are just very strange.*"[22]

GIANTS IN SOUTH AFRICA

Andrew Collins also investigated a 400,000-year-old femur from a cave called the *Sima de los Huesos* ('Pit of Bones') in northern Spain. It belongs to an extinct species of hominin known as Homo heidelbergensis, who occupied Africa and much of the Eurasian continent between 800,000 and 200,000 years ago ('hominin' is defined as the group consisting of modern humans, extinct human species and all our immediate ancestors).

> *"...anthropologists have always considered that the closest ancestor to Homo heidelbergensis was the Neanderthal. Yet an examination of the mitochondrial DNA from the Homo heidelbergensis femur found in Spain revealed it to be much closer to that of the Denisovans."* [23]

This is intriguing because although they were on average no taller than 5 ft 10 in (170 cm), another branch of their population were much larger. Professor Lee R. Berger of the University of Witwatersrand has examined numerous fossil bones belonging to Homo heidelbergensis populations that inhabited South Africa between 500,000 and 300,000 years ago and has discovered that these were often over seven feet (2.13 meters) in height. Berger states:

> *"Everywhere we find them we find them enormous. These are what we call archaic Homo sapiens. Some people refer to them as Homo heidelbergensis. These individuals are extraordinary, they are giants."* [24]

This was further investigated by author Michael Tellinger who visited the university and met with Prof. Francis Thackery to take a closer look at the bone. It was discovered in the 1960s along with several other bones, at the Otavi Mountains in Namibia. There were more bones from the skeleton but these were never collected. Thackary emphasises that it is from an *"anatomically modern human"* or Homo sapiens, and who lived *"within the last 100,000 years"* (not 200,000 years as Berger suggested). He explained that *"In my experience having traveled through museums around the world, I have never seen a human femur this big."* He concluded that it was *"twice the size*" of a standard human femur.[25]

So here we have it! At last an academic—Professor Francis Thackery of the University of Witwatersrand—actually stating on camera that this femur is from a human being that was twice the size of a modern human. This would mean a height of between ten and twelve feet (which is way beyond the seven-foot height described by Professor Berger).

The discovery of a potentially twelve-foot tall Homo heidelbergensis specimen is compelling, because the Denisovans were their distant decendants. This basically means that Denisovans could well have been the same height as *Homo heidelbergensis*, especially when we consider the "robust" finger bone and the "large teeth" that have a chewing surface twice that of a normal human. So could this mean they were also 10 - 12 feet tall? Maybe not, but the evidence of these bizarre bones in Africa at least proves that giants actually existed on earth.

The discovery of a huge jawbone in the Penghu Islands off the coast Taiwan has also confirmed the existence of giants in Denisovan territory. Taiwanese fishermen may have uncovered from the sea floor, an unknown type of human that lived anywhere between 200,000 years ago and 10,000 years ago. "*Width of the bone at the lateral part of the mandible is 20.7 mm (0.8 inches) for Penghu, but on average 14 mm (0.55 inches) for fossil modern humans.*"[26] This is about a third larger than a modern human, so the owner of the mighty jaw could have been up to nine feet tall.

Considering Denisovans existed fairly close to here, we must consider this may be a significant discovery in relation to giant genes entering North America in the distant past, and may indicate they were indeed capable of seafaring. More research is currently being carried out, but until confirmed by science we can speculate that this is quite possibly the jaw of a Denisovan.

DOUBLE ROWS OF TEETH (PART 2)

Neanderthals occupied many of the same regions as the Denisovans, from Southeast Asia to as far east as the Altai Mountains of southern-central Siberia. There have been numerous reports of their skulls being found with *taurodontism,* a strange dental anomaly similar to some of those described in the *Double Rows of Teeth* chapter:

> *"Like hyperdontia, to which it is related, taurodontism is*
> *considered a genetic abnormality that results in the enlargement*
> *of teeth out of proportion to the roots of the jaw. The cause*
> *of taurodontism is not properly understood, and is explained,*
> *variously, as a genetic mutation, a pituitary malfunction or*
> *even an evolutionary throwback."* [27]

Most interestingly the Wikipedia page directly states that people suffering with this condition could have also had *"multiple teeth."*

Almost every member of the human population outside of Africa has one to four percent Neanderthal DNA[28] and the Denisovans are their close cousins.

> *"The current Melanesians, represented by the Pacific islanders*
> *of Papua New Guinea, and Aboriginal Australians, all show*
> *between four and six percent Denisovan DNA.[29] Other human*
> *populations, such as the Burmans, Malays, Han Chinese, and*
> *Polynesians, also have Denisovan DNA, but in far smaller*
> *quantities."* [30]

This is intriguing as this is the geographic region where the Denisovans and Neanderthals mated with Homo Sapiens, along with an unknown humanoid that Andrew Collins calls *Species-X* (not to be confused with *haplogroup X*, that we discuss in the next section). No doubt the gene pool became more complicated at this time in this area. Migration and mating were the favourite pastimes of the ancients so it could be that their genetic markers made their way over to America. Genetic throwbacks such as increased height, large teeth, supernumerary teeth, and powerful skeletal frames due to hybridization—all could have been a regular occurrence.

Collins speculates that the genuine accounts we cover in this book most likely refer to human or hominin hybrids who carry strong Denisovan-human or Denisovan-Neanderthal-human genetic markers. He also believes it is possible that the giants of North America contain DNA belonging to Species X, who are now believed to have bred with all three other sub-species—Denisovans, Neanderthals and archaic humans.[31]

This in turn may have caused various mutations. Interestingly, the "archaic humans" or "Cro-Magnon" (those skeletons discovered in Europe), were surprisingly tall, had massive jaws, high cheekbones and thicker skulls— traits of many of the North American giants—but where did they truly originate?

Double rows of teeth seem to be an indicator of something unusual hidden within the genes of the giants. As Shara Bailey, NYU dental anthropologist pointed out, the size of the head and jaw may be the genetic trigger for extra teeth to grow, as there is the *space* to do so. The temptation to simply ignore all the reports of DRTs and their possible connections to the ancient Denisovans and other ancient cultures around the world has to be challenged.

RED-HAIRED GIANTS

It has become known that the Neanderthals—who were breeding with the Denisovans in Siberia—routinely had red or auburn hair. Almost every member of the human population has 1% - 4% Neanderthal DNA. However, the Neanderthals were in no way giants. A mutation that may have resulted in red hair and light skin among Neanderthals has been discovered, according to the *Smithsonian Museum of Natural History*. Two Neanderthals—one from Italy and one from Spain—had a mutation in a gene controlling hair and skin color.

> *"The mutation changes an amino acid, making the resulting protein less efficient. Modern humans have other MCR1 variants that are also less active, resulting in red hair and pale skin. The less active Neanderthal mutation probably also resulted in red hair and pale skin, as in modern humans."* [32]

It is also known that South Pacific islanders are powerfully built and often taller than the world average. In addition, red-haired traits still exist in places such as Easter Island, Tonga and Vanuatu. The western edge of Peru and Chile has prolific evidence of red and auburn-haired tribes with extremely elongated skulls from remote antiquity. In fact some of the oldest mummies on earth were found in Chile, with the earliest example dating to a staggering 9,020 years old,[33] contemporary with Spirit Cave Man in Nevada (9,400 years old).

Further 'red-heads' have been found preserved in another way on the southeast tip of America. The Florida bog mummies were originally discovered in 1982 at Titusville, a few miles from Cape Canaveral. These submerged mummies also had red and auburn hair and were found in an incredible state of preservation. They were carbon dated to 8,280 years.[34] Although these inhabitants did not reach over 5 ft 8 in, at another site called Warm Springs in the city of North Port, some skeletons reached the height of 6 ft 2 in. The most compelling aspect of these discoveries is that intact brain matter was DNA tested and the Titusville mummy-genome contained haplogroup X, which is a distinct DNA marker originating from Europe and the Middle East.

EUROPEAN DNA IN AMERICA

Haplogroup X is particularly intriguing because not only is it present in 3% of Native Americans, in Europe and the Middle East 2% - 4% of people carry this gene, primarily in parts of Spain, Bulgaria, Finland, Italy and Israel.[35] Certain tribes in southern Siberia also carry the "X" type[36] (that has caused some confusion to academics regarding early migrations). It seems this particular gene may play an important role in understanding the origins of the giants in North America, especially migrations that came from the east. Archaeologists Robert L. Kelly and Dabid Hurst Thomas summed it up:

> *"Some geneticists and archaeologists suggest that haplogroup X points to an ancient migration from Europe, in addition to ones from Asia."* [37]

Haplogroup X is said to have entered America from the east as long as 34,000 years ago. At around 14,000 - 12,000 years ago they arrived in much greater numbers. This could well have been the Solutreans, mentioned earlier in this chapter, who have been put forward as some of the first explorers to enter America from Europe.

Haplogroup X was found in the Florida bog mummies (8,280

1870's photo of the tall Iroquois chief John Wampum

years old), but it is also found in tribes that once inhabited the northern tier of North America. A small amount is found among the Na-Dene-speaking Navaho, the Sioux and Yakima on the northwest Pacific coast, and Algonquian speaking tribes in the North East.[38] It occurs to a larger degree in the Oneota, Nuu-Chah-Nulth and Ojibwa of the Great Lakes.[39] Most of these tribes are affiliated with the Iroquois, although the origins and the language of the Iroquois Nation tribes are disputed by scholars. Some myths state they came from the northeast after a great flood destroyed their civilization in prehistory,[40] whilst a faction of the Iroquois say they came from within a 'sacred mountain' (personal communication between Chief Jake Swamp and Ross Hamilton). As we have seen from the historical record, most of these Iroquois tribes had giants among them.

MIGRATION FROM THE GREAT LAKES

There are some intriguing possibilities that these tribes around the Great Lakes region may have had members of exceptional height—and even had double rows of teeth—going as far back as 6,000 years. Tribes in the Middle Great Lakes/St. Lawrence culture area, from Southern Ontario, Southern Québec, and Southwestern New Brunswick between 4000 and 1000 BC, were taller than their neighbors. Men were around six feet (180.7 centimeters), while the women reached around five and a half feet (170 cm).[41] This was much taller than the local inhabitants of the area.

A strange twist in this story that Andrew Collins commented on was that over a period of one millenium, they actually increased in height. Now, they only grew on average one-inch during a one thousand year period, but this is still very interesting because it shows a trait of extreme growth that may show early evidence of genetic abnormalities, in addition to selective breeding, a custom that potentially continued into the mound building cultures of North America.

> *"The traditional belief that there were men of giant stature among the ancient Iroquois is apparently true. Archaeologically however the evidence no longer is available for study, and even if the Iroquois had knowledge of such remains, they likely would not relate their location."* [42]

Some of the taller-than-average people from the tribes around the Great Lakes were known to have had,

> *"...hyperdontia, or extra teeth... a genetic trait... biological..."* [43]

In the *Double Rows of Teeth* chapter, we discuss this trait found in skulls all over North America, and now we can see where it may have originated, but whether these were related to the Denisovans is unclear. However, these could well have been the Archaic Allegheny people who were known to be of giant stature and were said to come from this area.

KEEPING THE GENE POOL TALL

With all this human hybridization taking place in the distant past, genetic traits could have been formed by various mutations, generating extra sets of teeth, double-teeth, or extra single teeth, extreme height, and other anomalies associated with the American giants. The Archaic Allegheny people (whom Ross Hamilton calls the Allehana), could have been the early ancestors of the Mound Builders who carried these genetic markers with them and selectively bred to enhance and continue these traits. Such genetic throwbacks might be seen as a disadvantage in today's world, but in the ancient lands of North America these characteristics could easily have been revered by the giant elite. Perhaps it was for this reason they maintained the purity of their bloodlines by interbreeding only with others in the elite royal class—or those with these unique features. This would have improved the chances of the genes to become stronger and more consistent over time.

> *"...having a firm genetic base in the stature of seven feet, even*

*taller men possessing a healthy physicality may have lived
throughout Illinois, Indiana, Pennsylvania, etc."* [44]

Haplogroup X is not fully understood, as few tribes have been DNA
tested in North America. The proximity of where haplogroup X is found,
combined with the flood and migration myths already discussed in this
chapter, does open the door for another controversial theory.

THE GIANTS OF ATLANTIS

Did giant people once populate the mythical lost continent of Atlantis,
who then dispersed to multiple locations, including North America, after
a cataclysm? As mentioned in the *Mystics and Secrets Societies* chapter,
the Rosicrucian's, Freemasons, Theosophists, Rudolph Steiner, and Edgar
Cayce all spoke of the existence of Atlantis as an historical fact. Surprisingly,
they all asserted that giant humans were also part of the population of
the lost island continent. No 'lost continent' has been discovered as yet,
but many of Cayce's readings telling of giants entering North America do
sometimes correlate with what we have uncovered in this chapter.

> *"The geographical origin of haplogroup X is unknown, although
> it is found in areas around the Atlantic Ocean, where Edgar
> Cayce reports Atlanteans settled. When researchers from
> Trinity College tested individuals in Ireland for haplogroup X
> they discovered that the relatively isolated Irish on the far west
> coast of that country, closest to where Atlantis was, have the
> highest concentration of this type."* [45]

As we mentioned previously haplogroup X was said to have entered
America around 34,000 years ago and again at around 12,000 - 14,000
years ago. Edgar Cayce describes large numbers of Atlanteans leaving their
stricken land at roughly both these times:

> *"Scientists say haplogroup X may be of European origin. They
> are unwilling to designate Atlantis as a site of origin since it does
> not exist. It is very possible that when humans with haplogroup
> X genes departed from the central point of Atlantis, some went*

*to the American continent in the west and others traveled to
Europe. This would explain the striking similarities between
the tools and customs of the Solutrean people of southwestern
Europe and the Clovis people on the North America continent."[46]*

The astonishing thing about all this is that haplogroup X is found in, and
only in, the areas that Cayce claims that Atlantean refugees landed. It
sounds like science fiction, but there is no harder science that genetics. It
is worth noting that the Iroqouis tribes have been found to have up to 25%
haplogroup X. Author Greg Little tells us what Cayce had to say about the
Iroquois:

> *"Cayce indicated that the largest migration from Atlantis
> occurred just before 10,000 BC. The majority of these Atlantean
> survivors went to the Northeastern coastal areas of America
> and Canada becoming the Iroquois. It should be recalled that
> Cayce also stated that not all of the Iroquois were Atlantean.
> The Atlanteans migrating to the Americas merged with the
> people already present in America by that time. The Atlanteans
> became leaders of the tribes." [47]*

Another compelling piece of information comes from the Cayce readings

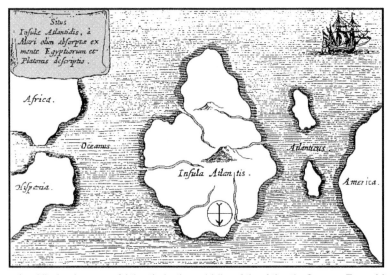

Athanasius Kircher's map of Atlantis in the middle of the Atlantic Ocean. From Mundus
Subterraneus 1669, published in Amsterdam. The map is oriented with south at the top.

342

regarding the Atlantean connection to the Mound Builders. Reading 3004-15, states the following:

> "There the entity was the priestess. And there may be seen some of those activities that are a part of the awareness to some in that land of Ohio, where there were those plans for such, in the mounds that were called the replica or representative of the Yucatan experiences, as well as the Atlantean and in Gobi land. All of these are as one consciousness in the entity's activity."

It is stated that many of the Mound Builder structures were representations of what once existed in Atlantis, used for ritual and ceremonial purposes. The southeastern section of the Portsmouth, Ohio earthwork (now destroyed), is a startling match of Plato's description of the central city of Atlantis.

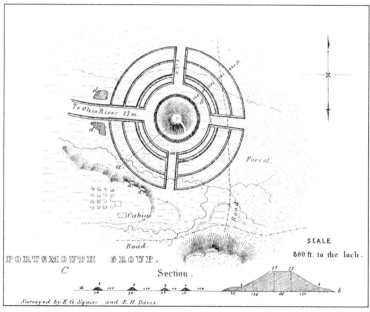

Portsmouth Works group C. Squier and Davis.

Cayce gave a total of 68 readings that had a connection to the Mound Builders. Here are two of his readings, showing the importance of the Ohio River Valley as the heart of the great mound building empire. From reading 3528-22:

"The entity was among those of the second generation of Atlanteans who struggled northward from Yucatan, settling in what is now a portion of Kentucky, Indiana, Ohio; being among those of the earlier period known as Mound Builders."

Reading 3393-29:

"Before this the entity was in the land east from the present nativity, or in the settlings in the land when there were the Mound builders in Ohio, Indiana, and the various groups that traveled through that land."

Edgar Cayce's information about humanity's past—which at the time was considered preposterous—is now being verified by science. Take, for instance, the ancient temple site of Göbekli Tepe in Turkey, which has been dated to an astonishing 9,600 BC. This date, coupled with the sophisticated construction, was considered unthinkable up until the time of its discovery in 1994.

This is also the area of the biblical 'Watchers' who were said to have overseen humanity and seeded a legendary race of giants called the 'Nephilim'. As haplogroup X has also been found in this area, this may prove fruitful for those that believe the so-called Nephilim made their way from the Bible lands to the coasts of North America.

Nephilim and Biblical Giants in America

Genesis 6:4: *"There were giants in the earth in those days; and also after that, when the sons of God came in unto the daughters of men, and they bare children to them, the same became mighty men which were of old, men of renown."*

This passage from the Bible is talking about the offspring of "sons of God" who are called the 'Nephilim'—offspring of the legendary 'Watchers' and human females. If you Google 'giant skeletons', more often than not the word Nephilim comes up, with webpages stating the giants of North America are in fact the very same giants featured in the Bible. Various authors such as Steve Quayle, Fritz Zimmerman, and L.A. Marzulli are convinced that the North American giants originated from the Middle East, or the 'Bible

Lands,' and they were pushed out by the warring Israelites spearheaded by Moses. These giants then fled and settled in America.

We are perhaps being too simplistic here, as all these authors and other giantologists who promote the idea of the Nephilim have actually carried out some very interesting research, but first, we must determine who exactly the Nephilim were.

The word Nephilim originally appeared in the Torah, or Hebrew Bible—our Old Testament—and roughly translates as 'Those who fell, those who came down, those who left one place to go to another.' It does not mean 'Fallen Angels.' The name is also used in reference to giants who inhabited Canaan at the time of the Israelite conquest according to Numbers 13:33.[48] Nephilim is also a general term used to describe multiple giant races and individuals in the Bible. For example, the Amalekites, Amorites, Anakim, Ashdothites, Aviums, Avites, Canaanites, Caphtorim, Ekronites, Emins, Eshkalonites, Gazathites, Geshurites, Gibeonites, Giblites, Girgashites, Gittites, Hittites, Hivites, Horim, Horites, Jebusites, Kadmonites, Kenizzites, Maachathites, Manassites, Nephilim, Perizzites, Philistines, Rephaim, Sidonians, Zamzummim, Zebusites and Zuzim.

There are also 22 individual giants mentioned by name: Adonizedec —King of Jerusalem; Agag—King of the Amalakites; Ahiman; Amalek; Arba; Beelesath; Gog and Magog; Gogmagog; Goliath; Hoham—King of Hebron; Horam—King of Gezer; Jabin—King of Hazor; Jobab –King of Madon; Lahmi; Nimrod; Og of Bashan; Ogias—Og's father; Perizzites; Sheshai; Sihon—King of the Amorites; Sippai and Talmai.[49]

Some notable giants include King Og of Bashan who was the last of the Rephaim (a Hebrew name for giants), and an Amorite King. He had a iron bedstead (or sarcophagus) measuring nine cubits in length and four cubits in width, which is 13.5 ft by 6 ft according to the standard cubit of a man, that would make him somewhere between 9 to 13 feet in height. Goliath and his three brothers of Gath, are known as sons of the Nephilim. After killing Goliath, David and his brothers hunted down Goliath's brothers and became the first literal *giant hunters* in history!

The non-canonical (Apocrypha) books of Baruch 3:22–28 and Sirach 16:6–9 indicate that giants (Greek; gigantes, gigantōn, respectively)

An old illustration of Og's gigantic bed.

previously lived in the land of Canaan before Moses conquered them.[50]

This is referring to when Moses was heading up to the "Promised Land" during the Exodus. They moved north along the west coast of Israel and up into Lebanon. They met with giants and eventually defeated them, but where did the giants find exile?

Ancient Babylon (and the area north of there) was the home of the Amorites, at least one of whom could be described thusly: *"whose height was like the height of the cedars, and he was as strong as the oaks."*[51] The idea that the Amorites were giants is supported by the report of the spies whom Moses sent through the land of Canaan. The Amorites were one of the groups they saw, and they claimed that *"all the people whom we saw in it are men of great stature."*[52] It is telling that in their response, Joshua and Caleb did not challenge the size of the land's inhabitants.[53] In Numbers 13:33 it stated:

> *"And there we saw the giants, the sons of Anak, which come of the giants [Nephilim] and we were in our own sight as grasshoppers, and so we were in their sight."*

The giants obviously were not wiped out by Moses and his army, as around 600 AD, further reports of over-eight-foot warriors emerged in the Greek histories citing King Nebuchadnezzar of Babylon in his campaign against Jerusalem:

> *"...killing a warrior who lacked only one palm's breath of five royal cubits."*[54] (This equates to 8 feet 4 inches).

Zimmerman's book *The Nephilim Chronicles: Fallen Angels in the Ohio*

Valley (2012), gives a lengthy argument that those driven out of the Bible Lands were the Amorites. This tall, megalith-building culture would have traveled along the Iberian Peninsula, up through Europe, and eventually become known as the *Beaker People*. After arriving in the British Isles, Zimmerman tells us they built hundreds of mounds and may even have built Stonehenge. They were skilled metal traders, and were on the hunt for tin in England. Somewhere along the line, they sailed to North America and into the Great Lakes area to mine copper. Some stayed, and this was the genesis of the North American race of giants.

Other authors skip the convoluted part about the Amorites and Beaker people and say they simply came straight over to North America (Marzulli, Quayle etc). Whatever the case, there are several accounts of giant skeletal remains and artifacts in the area of the "Nephilim" in the Middle East that we have in our records.

Skull-types get heavily investigated by Zimmerman who proposes that the classic Adena skull type: large jaw, high cheekbones, thick skull wall, and large features, are the same as the Amorites/Beaker People and later the Phoenicians. It's an interesting theory, as there are some similarities in burial customs, mound styles and skull features, but when put under scrutiny certain aspects fall short. However, the authors do recommend the book, as it has hundreds of giant accounts from all over the world and has been thoroughly researched.

L.A. Marzulli's books include *On the Trail of the Nephilim* (2013) and not only do the American giants get put forward as Nephilim, but the elongated skulls discovered in Peru do too—even though they are not giant in any way. He is looking for evidence in all parts of the Americas and suggests most megalithic structures and earthworks were constructed by these biblical giants (or Peruvian coneheads) emphasising that they were not Native American in any way.

Steve Quayle was the first modern author to propose that giants from all parts of the world are the offspring of the biblical giants. His enormous book is a thorough chronicle of historic and modern giants, and emphasises, like Marzulli, that they were responsible for worldwide megalithic construction. They were not particularly pleasant, and ruled various cultures often in a violent manner.[55]

Finally, a curious artifact was witnessed in 1877 that does suggest a direct connection to the Bible lands (that any Nephilim advocate should use as part of their evidence). After his surrender, Chief Joseph, a renowned Nez Perce leader handed over a small pendent to General Miles and after a few years it was inspected and turned out to be an ancient Mesopotamian cuneiform tablet. It was translated by Robert Biggs, professor of Assyriology at the Oriental Institute of the University of Chicago who found that it was a sales receipt for a lamb dating back to 2042 BC.

> *"The chief said that the tablet had been passed down in his family for many generations, and that they had inherited it from their white ancestors. Chief Joseph said that white men had come among his ancestors long ago."* [56]

Chief Joseph in 1877 and cuneiform tablet.

THE WATCHERS AND THE NUNNEHIM

The Nephilim and the Watchers from the Bible have their counterparts among the Algonquian, Iroquoian, and Siouan speaking peoples, and possibly the Muskogeon. The Native Cherokee *Nunnehim* (Nunnehi), and the Lakota *Watchers* are contained within the traditions of the great conclave of Native American culture. This stretched from the Dakotas across the Great Lakes to the eastern tribes and down to the Great South and the "Five Civilized Tribes." They all apparently have their *own* versions of the Watchers and the Nephilim.

The Nunnehim are believed to be the survivors of a great country in the ocean to the east. Their origins are said to be in the Atlantic basin going back many thousands of years. When the basin began to flood under the water of melting glaciers, these blessed people moved into the Americas as well as Europe and the Mediterranean, bringing with them the sacred spiritual technologies of the Antediluvian world. Many of them were said to have been giants in stature. Like the post-Atlantean legend of the Tuatha Dé Danann from ancient Ireland, they withdrew back into the hills and the subconscious mind, leaving their lands to Indigenous folk. The Watchers are the *wisdom keepers* among the Nunnehim. Lakota tradition to this day suggests that they have their lodges of habitation strategically placed in order to look out for, and to protect the Native Tribes. This tradition of the Nunnehi and the Watchers predates any known outside influence including the Nephilim of the Bible.

According to the traditions of the Cherokee, Choctaw, Chickasaw, Creek and Seminoles, the Nunnehi are revered as,

> *"...traditionalists, historians, artists and, musicians...they are able to physically alter their size and appearance."* [57]

AMERICAN GENESIS

One theory that usually gets overlooked in regard to the origins of the giants is the idea that they originated in America. Many Native creation myths allude to this. One example is in the writings of Tuscarora David Cusick in his book *Six Nations* (1825). He states that when the Great Spirit made the people, some of them became giants.

"It seems that the tall people at least shared the status of being the first inhabitants of Indian memory, and that the smaller-in-stature folk lived among or in proximity to them from remotely ancient times." [58]

Some of these creation myths may now have scientific discoveries to back them up as human remains and artifacts in the Americas are much older than originally thought.

"The Sandia Cave discoveries, along with the finds made at Hueyatlaco, Calico, and Toca da Esperanca, strongly suggest a human presence over 200,000 years ago in the Americas. This challenges not only the orthodox time estimate for the entry of Homo sapiens into North America (12,000 years ago) but also the whole picture of human evolution, which has Homo sapiens arising from Homo erectus in Africa about 100,000 years ago."[59]

Hueyatlaco in Mexico is famous because extremely ancient evidence of human occupation was recorded in the 1960s. Sophisticated stone tools and artifacts were dated to a quarter of a million years old by a team from the United States Geological Survey.[60] Inside Sandia Cave in New Mexico stone implements similar to Folsom points were discovered in 1975. However these were also dated to 250,000 years old. In Calico, Southern California, stone tools dating to 200,000 years ago were discovered in 1964. In Toca da Esperanca in Brazil, further discoveries were found to be of a similar age.[61]

Extremely ancient artifacts have been discovered all over the Americas, and human remains that go back even further have shaken the foundations of academia, and have raised serious questions regarding the origins of modern human beings. The most striking problem is that of modern-looking human skulls.

On December 1, 1899, Ernest Volk from the Peabody Museum of American Archaeology and Ethnology at Harvard University, discovered a fossilised human femur and two skull fragments in New Jersey. As these looked like they were from modern humans, they were analysed by our good friend Aleš Hrdlička from the Smithsonian who said *"The antiquity of this specimen must rest on the geological evidence alone."* The layer it was discovered in was later dated by the New Jersey Geological Survey (1987) to be 107,000 years old - 7,000 years before modern humans were said to have arisen in Africa.[62] Further examples include an anatomically modern human skull that was discovered in Buenos Aires in 1896. This was inspected by Hrdlička who admitted it was found in *"the upper-most portion of the Pre-ensenadean stratum."* This would date it 1 million to 1.5 million years old.[63] Hrdlička also inspected an atlas bone (from the top of the spine) that was also found in Argentina lodged in a layer 3 - 5 million years old. He concluded that it could not be ancient because it was from a modern human, disregarding the geological layer it was found in. He felt it was only worthy of being *"dropped of necessity into obscurity"* (much like his non-scientific analysis of the giants of North America!)

In 2002, scientists from Liverpool's John Moores University and Oxford's Research Laboratory of Archaeology dated a skull discovered in Mexico to about 13,000 years old. It was that of a 26 year old woman found in the suburbs of Mexico city that baffled the discoverers:

> *"...it is long and narrow and typically Caucasian in appearance, like the heads of white, western Europeans today."* [64]

As we have seen already, Peñon woman has been compared to the historic Pericú people of Baja California, who also shared similar physical traits with the Patagonians.[65] Is the human family tree, most notably in North America, more complicated than once thought?

> *"...it is probably no accident that some of our northeastern Indians have repeatedly been described as European in appearance."* [66]

Jeffrey Goodman Ph.D wrote the book *American Genesis*[67] and speculated that Homo sapiens sapiens actually *speciated* in the Americas and spread around the world from there. He indicated that our species is much older than is generally supposed, and outlines many of the accounts above. He even suggests migrations could easily have gone the *other* way across the Bering land bridge and to other parts of the world.

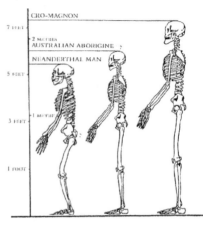

Cro-Magnon man in Europe suddenly appeared in the human timeline (around 45,000 years ago), with developed stone tools that are remarkably similar to many discovered in the Americas, despite the fact that the ones in the Americas were from a much earlier date.

Height comparison of Neanderthal, Aborigine and 7-foot tall Cro-Magnon.

Another intriguing aspect of his theory is the problem of Cro-Magnon-type skulls being discovered in America that date back to long before the emergence of Cro-Magnon man in Europe. These characteristics have also been noted in later giant skeletal remains in North America.

The use of the *Cro-Magnon* title is slowly being replaced by *Archaic Homo Sapiens* or something similar. This passage from Wikipedia summarises their impressive traits, although it fails to mention that they often exceeded seven feet in height:

> *"They are thought to have stood on average 176.2 cm (5 feet 9 ⅓ inches) tall, though large males may have stood as tall as 195 cm (6 feet 5 inches) and taller. They differ from modern-day humans in having a more robust physique and a slightly larger cranial capacity. The Cro-Magnons had long, fairly low skulls, with wide faces, prominent noses, and moderate to no prognathism. A distinctive trait was the rectangular eye orbits."*[68]

After thirty years of general academic denial of Goodman's work, German Dziebel—on his *Anthropogenesis* blog—has brought this theory back to life. Along with numerous other academics, he also hypothesises that humans originated in America, and not in Africa, and has evidence to back it up:

> *"While we don't have a single ancient DNA sample to ascertain whether modern African populations are directly related to ancient "anatomically modern humans" (e.g., Omo, Herto, etc.) and hominids in Africa, we do have ancient DNA data (X chromosome, autosomes, blood groups) that document matches between Neanderthal and Denisovan genetic variation, on the one hand, and modern humans in the New World."* [69]

Skulls that look remarkably similar to modern human skulls do completely twist the origins of Cro-Magnon man, as it was always thought he originated from the other side of the Atlantic Ocean.

> *"After speciation in the New World had occurred, early Homo sapiens sapiens colonized first Eurasia and then Africa replacing and admixing with local hominids."* [70]

But who were these people? In *America: The New World or Old?* (1990) Werner Muller suggests Cro-Magnon man left America and headed to Europe, a theory that neatly fits into their mysterious appearance in the human timeline. He argues the Salish, the Sioux, the Algonquian, and a mysterious white-skinned, bearded people that once inhabited the northern tier of North America may have been Cro-Magnon. The white race were not too friendly towards the other groups so many of them migrated south to avoid the white antagonists, although Muller hints that a climatic catastrophe may have caused this too. He states that the white-skinned people moved eastwards across the North Atlantic into what is now Scandinavia and Western Europe.[71] He dates this migration to around 44,000 years ago—very close to the proposed time of the sudden emergence of Cro-Magnon man in Europe.

Goodman argues that stone tools discovered in Spain and other parts of Europe were a style that was already fully developed in America dating back to 48,000 years ago. Del Mar Man (San Diego) was carbon dated to around this time and a skull from Sunnyvale, California was dated to 70,000 years ago. Both look surprisingly Cro-Magnon.[72]

"In the 1940s and 1950s, leading physical anthropologists such as Ernest Hooten of Harvard University, Carelton Coon of the University of Pennsylvania, and J. B. Birdsell of the University of California at Los Angeles broke with traditional views, suggesting that the first Paleo-Indians were not Mongolian but Caucasian." [73]

The term Caucasian does not just refer to white people. It includes populations of Europe, North Africa, the Horn of Africa, Western Asia, Central Asia, and South Asia. The term was used in biological anthropology for many people from these regions, without regard necessarily to skin tone. [74]

MEGAFAUNA AND THE GIANTS

The megafauna of North America included mammoths, mastodons, sabre toothed tigers, sloths, beavers, short-faced bears, lions, horses, bison, giant condors and other incredible beasts that thrived in America from from as far back as 2.5 million years ago to around 11,000 years ago. At Big Bone Lick in Kentucky numerous bones of mastodons *"with tusks twelve feet long,"* along with Clovis points dated to around 10,000 years old were discovered.[75]

An account of these finds from 1762 mentioned a tantalising legend of giants:

"No such creatures as these had ever been seen alive by the Indians, but legend said that they had once been hunted through the forests by men of gigantic stature and that when the last of these men had died, God had destroyed their mighty prey in order to protect the present race of Indians." [76]

Although in this book we have described great battles between the Indians and the giants, there may have also been a peaceful coexistence in archaic times where the Tall Ones were not only seen as gods, but were also extremely helpful to their shorter counterparts:

"It is said the thunderbirds once came to earth in the form of giants. These giants did wonderful things, such as digging the

354

ditches where the rivers run. At last they died of old age, and their spirits went again to the clouds and they resume their form as thunderbirds." [77]

The above legend may give some credence to many of the traditional stories and myths describing the first humans descending from the Great Spirit into human form.

Megafauna of North America to scale with human on bottom right.

This next account was a favourite of Vine Deloria's, who felt it was an important part of extending the history of mankind into the deep past. It recounts a giant human trying to kill a giant beaver in the Pacific Northwest. It reads:

> *"...there was a large man who chiseled for a large beaver. He worked in vain but he could not kill it... He cut the mother open, took out the young ones, and put them in the water... They say both the man and the beaver were giants."* [78]

Vine Deloria Jr. collected numerous accounts of megafauna in relation to giant humans that often ended with a "Higher Spirit" destroying the beasts, or at least driving them away.[79]

*"Giant men, quite often with white skin, are involved in about
20 percent of the big-animal stories that I have located."*[80]

Deloria goes on to emphasize that the giant men died out just before, or
at the same time as the megafauna[81] and that mammoths were herded like
cattle by the giants. This account comes from Mississippi:

*"There had likewise been a tribe of cannibals, who feasted on
the bodies of their enemies. They...were giants, and utilized the
mammoths as their burden bearers. They kept them closely
herded, and as they devoured everything and broke down the
forests, this was the origin of the prairies...this cannibal race
and the mammoth perished about the same time, by a great
epidemic."* [82]

Deloria emphasises that it was not due to malnutrition or disease, but
because of changes in the atmosphere:

*"Watching this process of downsizing, Indians may have felt
they were being saved by the Great Spirit....or they may have
attributed the demise...to an epidemic."* [83]

These discoveries listed above certainly paint a different picture of what
was going on in America during the late Pleistocene (and possibly post-
Pleistocene). Many of these oral histories hint that the giants were from
the earliest of times and that many of them died out in the time of the
megafauna extinction.

Later in this chapter we will look carefully at the *Younger Dryas
impact* of 12,900 years ago, as it was this cataclysm that is thought to have
wiped out the megafauna. This may have also caused the ice sheets to
melt, leading to extreme flooding, darkened skies and other devastating
phenomena lasted for over one thousand years.[84]

Y SCIENCE OF THE MOUND BUILDERS

liscoveries in the last decade suggest the Native
highly advanced in mathematics, astronomy,
d it has been recorded up to relatively recent

times that they were adepts of high magic and shamanic practice as evidenced in the knowledge of their *Manitou* principles (spiritual and fundamental life force). Stories suggest they could even control the weather and influence fertility and the growth of crops.[85] It has long been debated these are merely folk tales and not based in reality. However, there are numerous stories collected by Lakota Elder Vine Deloria that describe medicine men who could make corn grow before one's very eyes. These include stories from the Navajo, Zuni and Pueblo peoples. An interesting example is titled *The Pawnee Corn Growers* that was witnessed by a certain Major North and other white people in historic times:

> *"...a few kernels of the corn were buried in the loose earth... the soil was seen to move, and a tiny green blade came slowly into view. This continued to increase in height and size, until in the course of twenty minutes or half an hour from the time of planting, the stalk of corn was a foot or fifteen inches in height.... at this point Major North was obliged to leave the lodge, to take out a white woman who was fainting..."* [86]

From *The Andersen Intelligencer,* July 16, 1903, it was reported that corn was found in a Kentucky mound sealed in a jar. It was said to be buried 60 feet below the ground alongside a giant skeleton measuring 8 ft 6 in. It was planted and produced a good yield which was then distributed to other farmers by the finder.

This is one report that speaks of an enormous skeleton being buried

GREW IN SPITE OF AGE.

Corn Found In Indian Mound Planted and Proved Productive.

Floyd Tully of Stout, O., has received from a Clay county (Ky.) friend an ear of corn that has a history. It was grown from seed dug out of an Indian mound in that county, says the Cincinnati Commercial Tribune: The seed, which was 60 feet under ground, was in a jar, sealed, and was close to a skeleton that measured 8½ feet in height.

The corn was planted and proved a good yielder, and the ear presented to Mr. Tully was part of the product. Mr. Tully distributed kernels among his friends, who will plant them this year.

with corn that, when planted, was a very good yielder. Could this account be part of a greater story pointing to a lost ancient technique to imbue crops with these special characteristics?

Authors of *Seed of Knowledge, Stone of Plenty* (2005) John Burke and Kaj Halberg were for a long time intrigued by accounts of fertility and natural magnetism associated with the mounds of North America. During the 1990s they decided to investigate the secret energies hidden within ancient sacred sites using high-tech modern equipment to see if the earthworks and megalithic sites could somehow affect the fertility of seeds and grains. Their dedication to unraveling the truth paid off when they realised the mounds they tested charged-up seeds and grains to such a degree that the crops would have increases in yield, be more fertile, be frost and disease resistant, but most importantly to our research, be larger.[87]

They found that this exact same 'energy' also affects consciousness and can put one into an altered state, often at these megalithic or earthwork sites (and at vision quest locations). Extensive tests were carried out and their conclusions should have shaken the scientific world, but were quietly ignored by the mainstream and put on the shelf as 'fringe science.' However, it revealed the ancients had a secret energy science fully developed and possibly used for thousands of years previously. The mounds and megaliths may have had a very useful purpose—they were not just ceremonial, but designed to guarantee an abundant harvest in an age when crop failure was very common.

Further tests were also carried out by geobiologist Alanna Moore on her farm in Australia. She laid out multiple mini-stone circles and got amazing results.[88] The natural magnetic telluric currents organised themselves and created a force field that increased the health and vitality of her crops, again with increased size.

Could this work on a macrocosmic level where multiple sites spread out across an entire county would create what John Michell called 'The Enchantment of the Landscape'—a force field of higher consciousness and positive energy, that gave abundant health to all the crops, plants, animals and humans within it? Is it too much to consider that the ancient Mound Builders perhaps believed that what was increasing their crops in size, may have increased their own size?

ELECTROMAGNETIC ENERGIES AND GIANTISM

In a scientific paper published by Tsutomu Nishimura, Kaneo Mohri, and Masanori Fukushima of the Translational Research Center, at Kyoto

University, they pronounced that "*...exposure to an extremely low frequency electromagnetic field (ELF-EMF) was associated with an increase in animal body weight.*" They also suggested bones may increase in size over time:

> "*It is also possible that EMFs exert an effect on skeleton size via alteration of the proliferation and activity of bone cells. In support of this hypothesis, pulsed EMF stimulation has been used clinically for more than twenty-five years for the treatment of patients with delayed fracture healing and non-unions. Furthermore, a substantial number of in vitro studies have shown that EMFs have positive effects on the proliferation and activity of bone cells.*" [89]

Their most recent tests put forward the theory that "*the large body size of the dinosaurs was caused by ELF-EMFs generated by natural phenomena: geomagnetic storms, volcanic activity, earthquakes, or Schumann resonance.*" With so many Native American legends speaking of major cataclysms deep in prehistory, and events such as the *Younger Dryas Impact*, this data may also prove useful in understanding how natural phenomena affects the size of human and animal life.

Furthermore, the latitude of where the animals were living also had a direct effect on body size. The geomagnetic field of the earth is almost twice as strong at higher latitudes (nearer the North Pole), as compared to those at lower latitudes (nearer the Equator). Their research focused on,

> "*...the relationship between magnetic field (MF) exposure and animal body size because Bergmann's rule holds that organisms tend to be larger at higher latitudes.*" [90]

Bergmann's rule is an ecogeographic principle that generally states that populations and species of larger size are found in colder environments, and species of smaller size are found in warmer regions. The areas of latitude where the Patagonian and Onas giants once existed—at the southern tip of South America, and far north in the Canadian Lakes region, where there were humans who were growing one inch every thousand years—are two examples of where the Bergmann Rule may have been functioning. Being a giant may have been normal at extreme high and low latitudes.

"Our hypothesis is that, these changes in geomagnetic fields might cause organisms to grow in size.... These animals would gain a considerable amount of body size over generations, if their surrounding environmental MF and/or EMF become stronger."

They also demonstrated that DNA may be affected:

"...100 mT static magnetic fields have an effect on mitochondria; they found that energy activity and cell respiration in mitochondria that were exposed to a MF [magnetic field] increased by factors of 1.5 and 1.3, respectively, compared with the sham control group. It seems that mitochondria are activated by MF and thereafter provide more ATP [Adenosine triphosphate transports chemical energy within cells for metabolism] to some organelles in the cells of an organism. Promotion of ATP synthesis by a MF would provide the energy to maintain a larger body size. That is, organisms would be able to use magnetic energy as well as other forms of physical energy." [91]

Could this have somehow been known by the ancient shamans? Were mounds deliberately designed and constructed to replicate or enhance these energies—and even create an artificial 'growth' environment for the elite to live within?

This positive effect on the body and bones may also have had an effect on consciousness (as outlined by Burke and Halberg), so these fluctuations in the Earth's natural magnetic field could have been seen as having a *spiritual* effect, and places of natural magnetism could have become the locations where these mounds were built.

The elite, however, may have lost some of this knowledge over time and although the mounds still functioned as energy generators—even up to the present day—new farming techniques, religious practices, and an already large population were on the increase.

"Cultivating the ennobling principle of what is termed Orenda, Native American medicine traditions assert that the men of

old were far more robust and tireless. As late as just 5 or 6,000 years ago, a world tradition of very tall and strong people was alive and well, yet all gone now. Stories relating of such people permeate the Americas, a situation where they seem to have survived longer. Gradually losing the remarkably potent power associated with the Orenda principle, these people mainly came to a tragic end while the smaller-in-stature people, to whom they were directly related, were growing in number. The old order was gradually supplanted, succumbing to absorption or extermination. Going back before five and six thousand years however, and by the sparse or inferred evidence, the world was populated differently. Clans of very tall, physically robust, and otherwise gifted people had the rule." [92]

There may have been numerous external factors that stimulated growth in humans. However, the one factor that is often overlooked is the effect of carbon dioxide on life on Earth. Today we see the increase of CO_2 as a sign of impending doom, but in prehistoric America, scientists have speculated this may have been the missing component in understanding the increased size of megafauna, and quite possibly the mega-humans that we have been discussing.

In *A Comprehensive Theory on Aging, Giantism and Longevity* (1979), Donald Patten raises several essential questions about why the megafauna (and the coexisting giant humans) decreased in size so rapidly. He noted that gigantism occured across a great many species and the decrease happened quickly *"because of a radical change in environmental conditions."*[93]

Patten also linked giantism with longevity, suggesting these phenomena occurred together. He points to the incredible ages of some of the patriarchs in the Bible and how difficult it is for us to believe they could have lived so long, as we are confined to a much shorter lifespan. Vine Deloria Jr. was told many times by Indian elders that their ancestors lived in excess of 200 years.[94]

Patten concluded that in pre-flood times there was more carbon dioxide in the atmosphere and this would have stimulated growth increases in a majority of living things. Modern tests have confirmed that elevated carbon dioxide levels increase plant growth. An excess of it in the atmosphere has been known to trigger the hypothalamus gland and hormones that affect growth in humans.[95] It would also stimulate cerebral circulation and oxygenation. We never stop to think what life would have been like in deep prehistory, with something as simple as an extra ½ percent of carbon dioxide making us live longer, be bigger and stronger, and enhancing other powers within us.

THE YOUNGER DRYAS IMPACT

At the time known in Native tradition as the 'Dark Tent', all megafauna became extinct or decreased rapidly in size over a few generations. In one way, the surviving Indians saw this as a gift from the Great Spirit and it inspired them to keep it in their stories and pass it down through multiple generations to afford us today a version of what really happened in ancient America. The various descriptions of countrywide flooding, extreme cooling, wildfires and earthquakes are not mere fantasies. They were real stories describing the onslaught of the *Younger Dryas impact* that saw multiple comets hit the northern ice sheet and parts of North America that caused massive devastation across the entirety of the country, with the effect reaching the whole planet, as described in hundreds of worldwide myths, including Noah's flood.

The general *Younger Dryas impact hypothesis* states that about 12,900 years ago, air bursts or impacts from a comet set areas of the North American continent on fire, melted the ice sheets, and disrupted climate. It is also said to have caused a Quarternary extinction event in North America that resulted in the extinction of most of the megafauna, and the rapid demise of the Clovis culture who were present in America at the time. The Younger Dryas ice age lasted for about 1,200 years before the weather got back to normal and temperatures increased. These events are also seen as part of the Holocene extinction phenomenon.

The Antedeluvian world (before the flood) may have also been a golden age where all life was enhanced by this slight increase in CO_2. Large, healthy humans who lived to a great age, robust animal life with plants, vegetable and fruits, that grew abundantly in a temperate climate were the norm.[96] After 1,200 years of cold weather, dark skies and food shortages that all followed the flood, the improvement in the climate triggered an ancient worldwide civilizing effort. Within 200 years of the end of the Younger Dryas, a stable way of life emerged, focusing on megalithic and mound construction, agriculture, and a reverence for the Earth and fertility. The golden age had returned, but this time, they knew it may not last.

As humans and animals decreased in size after the great cataclysm, the few remaining giants may have become revered as gods or sages. This may have triggered the elite to protect signs of royalty and to selectively breed. Since the Younger Dryas had caused so much death and destruction, these giants who lived longer, and who were more physically powerful, became the natural rulers, shamans and leaders of isolated surviving tribes. Over time, their genetic traits became stronger due to selective breeding, and stories of the Tall Ones before the great cataclysm became the stuff of legend.

Whoever these exceptionally tall people were, they very likely invented an energy science to increase fertility in crops, maintain and enhance their royal traits, as well as develop other techniques for health and longevity that were essential for survival after the cataclysm.

The warriors and chieftans were always the tallest tribal members, and the prolonged wars and skirmishes may have been part of the reason the Tall Ones died off and the gene pool became weak in more recent times. This may have slowly decreased the height of the general populace, but did not affect everyone, and with the later migrations from other parts of the world, the giant genes lived on.

One of the last giant warriors in historical times was *Kots-a-to-ah* or Smoked Shield, who is shown in this painting by George Catlin on the Red River of Texas c.1830:

> *"Another of the extraordinary men of this tribe, nearly seven feet in stature, and distinguished, not only as one of the greatest warriors, but swiftest on foot, in the (Kiowa) nation. This man, it is said, runs down a buffalo on foot, and slays it with his*

knife or his lance, as he runs by his side!" [97]

"Kots-a-to-ah" or Smoked Shield stood at
nearly 7 ft. By George Catlin, c.1830.

Using anthropometric data originally collected by Franz Boas in the mid-1800s, it was found that the plains nomads were the tallest people in the world during the mid-nineteenth century,[98] suggesting it took some tribes much longer to lose these traits. There are very few instances of acromegaly, or pituitary induced gigantism throughout the known history of America. They were simply gigantic, healthy humans:

> *"Indians, generally, are about the size of white people. The Osages, and some other tribes, who are of remarkable height, and fine figure, are exceptions to this remark. In these respects they exceed any equally large body of white [sic] known among us. In the shape of their limbs, and their erect form, Indians have evidently the advantage over the whites. Some, whom I have seen, would be perfect models for the sculptor. Instances of deformity are rare."* [99]

The fact that the giants existed from as far back as 9,000 years ago, with legends placing them deep into pre-flood times, puts the whole story into a timeline that is starting to be pieced together. Although these very early inhabitants were probably not building mounds, there is one example dated to a staggering 22,000 years ago in California's Imperial Valley, where "Yuha Man" was excavated.[100] It was 9 feet by 12 feet wide and, if dated correctly, may be a clue to the true origins of the later Mound Builders.

Who the giants were and where they came from, as well as how they got so big is still not fully agreed upon, but the evidence for extremely early humans in the Americas poses an intriguing possibility that the giants may well have originated in this land mass and survived (in some tribes) up until the early 1900s.

As we have hypothesized in this chapter, the effects of the Bergmann Rule, along with heightened CO_2 levels may have been partly responsible for the genesis of the North American giants. Moreover, there is genetic evidence that the Denisovan genes made their way over to North America as early as 20,000 BC. Around 15,000 years ago the Solutreans arrived from Western Europe. The influence of the California Channel Islanders probably came inland at various times between 11,000 and 1,000 BC. The cave dwellers of Humbolt Lake in Nevada were terrorising the local Indians from as early as 8,000 BC, the same time the similarly red-haired bog mummies were alive and kicking in Florida. From the south around 6,000 BC, the Pericúes migrated north into the Southwestern states of America. Canadian giants, who couldn't stop growing, moved slowly south from the Great Lakes into the Ohio Valley around 5,000 BC, may have been the original Allegheni. Further waves of settlers from Northern Europe may well have arrived from the east, and the biblical Nephilim would have arrived around 1300 - 1500 BC.

It seems North America was inundated with immigrants, who all just happened to be of the tall persuasion, some no doubt had unusual teeth, as well as incredibly powerful jaws and bone structure—bringing their own unique genetic markers into North America. For some reason, giants from all over the world were magnestised to ancient America. In 1150 AD, Geoffrey of Monmouth tantalisingly wrote what might be a very early mention of *Turtle Island*, the ancient indigenous name of North America:

"Beyond the realms of Gaul, beneath the sunset Lieth an island,

girt about by ocean, Guarded by ocean—erst the haunt of giants." [101]

We have included evidence that America may have been the origin point of the Tall Ones, based on archaeological data and tribal folklore and it may be that these other exotic interlopers were simply latecomers to an already established culture of giants, some of whom may have simply been returning to their homeland after earlier migrations out of America.

This final chapter took us on a journey through some interesting (and quite bizarre) theories. We hope we have given some ideas for further research, as the mystery of the ancient giants of America is still in its infancy. With increasing carbon dioxide emissions, human hybridization, and a new understanding of earth energies in our current society, perhaps gigantism might be coming back, whether we like it or not. The time of the Tall Ones may be upon us once more.

Reconstruction of a (non-Adena) generalized 8 ft giant by forensic artist Gil Zamora.

Appendix

Gazetteer of Giants

Overall we have investigated some 1500 giant accounts, but that number is simply too many to include in this volume. This *Gazetteer of Giants* includes only those that are featured in this book, some of which are eyewitness accounts and some that are unverified. We shall continue to collate accounts and include them in future volumes. We hope the maps and tables detailing the discoveries in the next few pages becomes a useful tool to get started in the study of giantology.

The *date* is the year that the discoveries were made, rather than the date of the newspaper account—although some are simply the newspaper headline date, as there is no clarity on the original discovery dates. In the *features* box, this just gives a little information on the report and you can refer to the pages where these accounts are in the book.

The maps were put together by Cecelia Hall using Google Earth. We encourage researchers to compile further data, so we can create a comprehensive survey of giant skeletons that at some point will be too large for academia to ignore. We also urge Native Americans to get involved, as we feel this is an important study in understanding our true origins, from legends, elders and oral histories of the past.

We also encourage readers to check these accounts out for themselves and look for more examples that are yet to be discovered, because they can trigger ancestral memories of a reality that these giants were once inhabiting areas that became the cities and landscapes we currently live in.

367

E	LOCATION	SIZE	No.	FEATURES	PAGE
	ALABAMA (SEE GEORGIA MAP)				
1930	Moundville	6'5"-7'6"	Many	Once on display	122
	ALASKA				
1936	Aleutian Islands	?	1	Huge skull	238
1944	Aleutian Islands	7'	1	Buried in wheel form	241
1901	Prince William Sound	7' - 8'	Many	Mummified	304
1908	Fairbanks	Giant	1	Giant bone	305

DATE	LOCATION	SIZE	No.	FEATURES	PAGE
	ARIZONA				
1896	Prescott	Tall	1	Mummified	176
1900	Apache County	7'6"+8'6"	2	Cranial deformation	178
1911	Walnut Creek	Giant	1	Huge skull	229

368

DATE	LOCATION	SIZE	No.	FEATURES	PAGE

ARKANSAS

DATE	LOCATION	SIZE	No.	FEATURES	PAGE
1877	Chickasawba Mound	7'6" - 8'	Many	Flattened skulls	175
1913	Beaver Lake, Ozarks	10'	?	Now underwater	272

CALIFORNIA

DATE	LOCATION	SIZE	No.	FEATURES	PAGE
1540	Sonora Desert	?	1	Eyewitness	33
1540	South California	?	Many	Eyewitness	33
1540	Colorado River	?	Many	Eyewitness	34
1579	San Francisco	?	Many	Eyewitness	39
1775	Southern California	7' - 8'	Many	Eyewitness	46
1871	Kern County	7' 5"	1	Huge skull	162
1936	San Bernardino	?	1	Giant skull	168
1819	Lompock Rancho	12'	1	DRT	195
1862	Channel Islands	?	Many	DRT	197
1895	San Diego	8' 4"	1	Possible hoax	223
1897	Ukiah	Giant	1	Sent to Smithsonian	226
1934	Cascade Mountains	6'5" - 10'	Many	Caves	285
1947	Death Valley	8'- 9'	Many	Devil's Hole caves	286
1913	Catalina Island	8'	1	-	314
1920s	Catalina Island	7'8"-9'2"	Many	-	315
1938	Catalina Island	7'	1	-	316
1897	San Nicolas Island	Giant	Many	Taken to Long Beach	321
1875	San Buenaventura	?	?	DRT	321
1959	Santa Rosa Island	7'	Many	7,000 years old	322

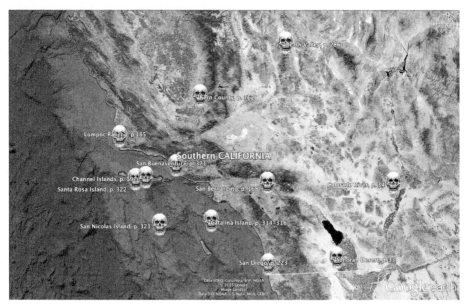

DATE	LOCATION	SIZE	No.	FEATURES	PAGE

CONNECTICUT (SEE MASSACHUSETTS MAP)

DATE	LOCATION	SIZE	No.	FEATURES	PAGE
1838	New Haven	8'	1	Covered in charcoal	140
1860	Hartford	7'+	1	With artifacts	140
1866	Norwich	Gigantic	1	With artifacts	141
1769	Norwalk	Giantess	1	Not Native American	141
1897	New Haven	8'	1	Petrified	141
1901	Shideler, nr. Hartford	Giant	1	Copper artifacts	142
1904	Shelton	6'8"	1	Unrecognisable metal	143

FLORIDA

DATE	LOCATION	SIZE	No.	FEATURES	PAGE
1528	Tampa Bay	?	2	7' & 8' later found	30
1540	Alachua County	8'	2	Eyewitness	35
1886	Wakulla	Giant	1	Jaw twice the size	154
1936	Cape Sable	8'	1	Thick skull	180
1875	Amelia Island	7'	1	3 sets of teeth	243
1914	St. Petersburg	9'	1	Massive skull	230
1925	Boca Grande	7'	1	Massive skull	231

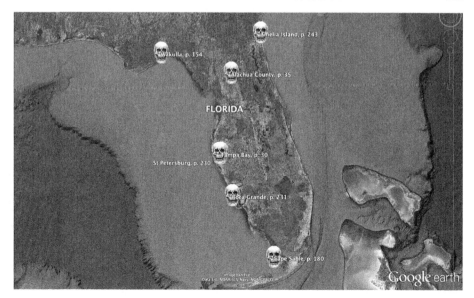

DATE	LOCATION	SIZE	No.	FEATURES	PAGE

GEORGIA

DATE	LOCATION	SIZE	No.	FEATURES	PAGE
1886	Etowah, Cartersville	14' & 7'	Many	Brass artifacts	220
1884	Etowah, Cartersville	9' 2"	8	Carved inscriptions	220
1936	Sea Island	7'	Many	Aleš Hrdlička involved	236

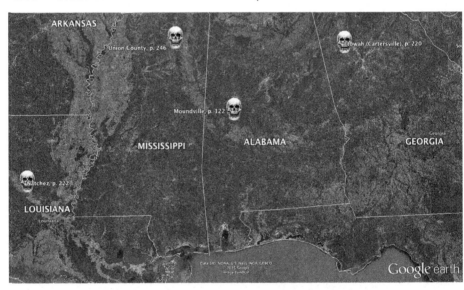

HAWAII

DATE	LOCATION	SIZE	No.	FEATURES	PAGE
1913	Waimea	7'+	3	Ancient warriors	309
1944	Big Island	7'	1	Beneath lava	310
1819	Hawi, Big Island	7'+	1	King Kamehameha	312
1881	Big Island	8'3"	1	-	313
1910s	Mauna Loa	7'+	1	-	311

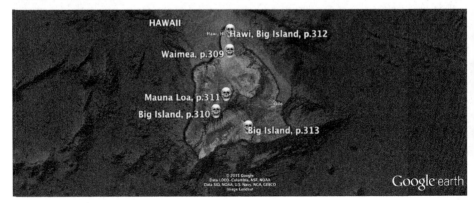

DATE	LOCATION	SIZE	No.	FEATURES	PAGE
			INDIANA		
1897	Connersville	9'	1	Femur - one yard long	155
1905	Sulphur Springs	7'+	1	Horned skull	173
1902	Noblesville	Giant	1	Claws on hands, DRT	195
1912	Lake Cicott	?	1	DRT	195
1915	Alcinda	Giant	1	Hieroglyphs reported	257
1925	South Bend	Giant	1	Copper armor	261
1915	Franklin County	7' 6"	1	Curious artifacts	269
1915	Kennard	8'	1	Ivory beads	270

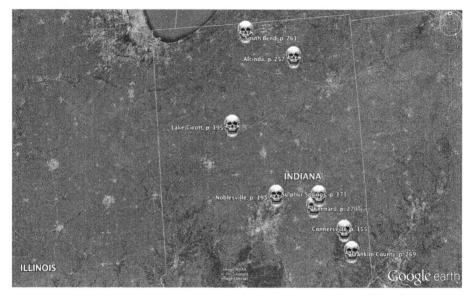

ILLINOIS (SEE MICHIGAN MAP)

DATE	LOCATION	SIZE	No.	FEATURES	PAGE
1891	Cahokia	Large	Many	DRTs	129+203
1886	Liverpool	Very large	Many	Found with steel anvil	154
1882	Red River Valley	Giant	1	Giant skull	165
1873	Anna, Union County	?	1	36 inch circ. skull	242
1877	Kishwaukee Mounds	Giant	3	Hunters tools	243
1880s	East Dubuque	7' - 8'	1	Crumbled to dust	245

IOWA (SEE MICHIGAN MAP)

DATE	LOCATION	SIZE	No.	FEATURES	PAGE
1897	Southeast Iowa	7' 6"	1	Large jaw	155+227

DATE	LOCATION	SIZE	No.	FEATURES	PAGE

KENTUCKY

DATE	LOCATION	SIZE	No.	FEATURES	PAGE
1959	Dover Mound	7'	1	-	119
1877	Morgantown	Giant	1	Large chin & teeth	152
1877	S/W of Richmond	7' or 8'	Many	Large jaw	152
1872	Rockport	10'	1	Complete skeleton	152
1841	Franklin	Giant	Many	Copper & silver beads	152
1852	Shippingsport	7'	1	Huge skull	160
1871	Jeffersonville	12'	1	3 ft thigh bone	162
1896	Elkwell Creek	8'+	1	Mummified	263
1903	Clay County	8' 6"	1	60 ft deep with corn in jar	356

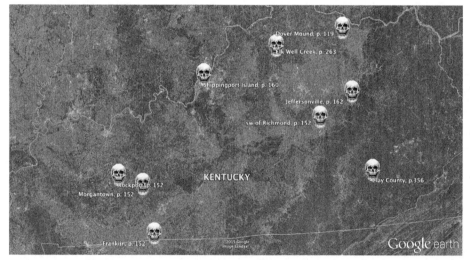

LOUISIANA (SEE GEORGIA MAP)

DATE	LOCATION	SIZE	No.	FEATURES	PAGE
1933	Natchez	7'+	Many	Smithsonian	222

MAINE

DATE	LOCATION	SIZE	No.	FEATURES	PAGE
1894	East Monmouth	7' 5"	1	-	145
1898	Swan Island	Large	Many	-	145
1907	Bath	6' - 7'	2	-	146
1912	Kennebunkport	7'	1	War or massacre	147

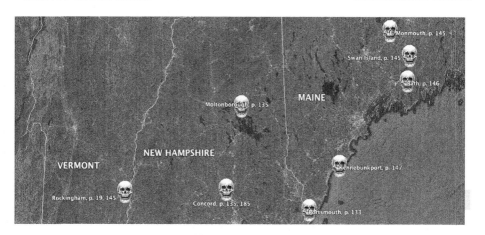

MASSACHUSETTS

1895	Deerfield	8'	1	DRT	18+193
1908	Marthas Vineyard	7'	1	DRT	18
1906	Middleboro	7' 8"	1	DRT	19+138
1600s	Lowell	7"	1	Chief Passaconeway	60
1855	Gill	Gigantic	1	Copper Tomahawk	136
1864	Hadley	7'	1	Reached age of 100 years	136
1891	Saugus	Enormous	1	Near megalithic Dolmen	137
1897	Edgartown	Large	1	Large jaw	138
1890s	Martha's Vineyard	7'	1	DRT	139+198
1873	Montague	7'	7	Sitting posture	140
1880	Newton	?	1	DRT	192

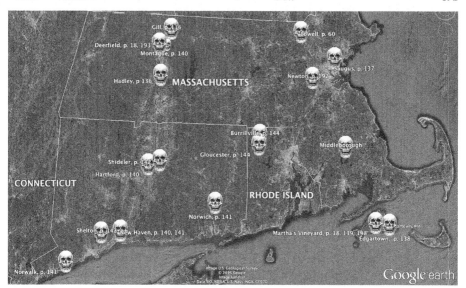

DATE	LOCATION	SIZE	No.	FEATURES	PAGE

MICHIGAN (SEE MINNESOTA MAP)

DATE	LOCATION	SIZE	No.	FEATURES	PAGE
1894	Cass County	11'	1	Large jawbone	156
1902	Lake County	7' & 8'	Many	-	157
1890	Detroit	?	5	Drilled skulls, DRT	199
1875	Bay County	?	1	Joe Fournier, DRT	208
1874	Battle Creek	7' - 8'	Many	Silver breastplate	262

MISSISSIPPI (SEE GEORGIA MAP)

DATE	LOCATION	SIZE	No.	FEATURES	PAGE
1880s	Union County	Large	1	Smithsonian Annual Rep	246

MISSOURI

DATE	LOCATION	SIZE	No.	FEATURES	PAGE
1800s	Osage River	7'+	Many	Eyewitnesses	47
1876	Wellsville	?	1	Large jaw	50+151
1883	Barnard	14' & 12'	2	40-inch skull	165
1925	St. Joseph	7' 2"	2	Flattened skulls	180
1933	Steelville	8'	1	Featured in TV show	231
1880s	Pike County	7'1"	1	Smithsonian Annual Rep	245

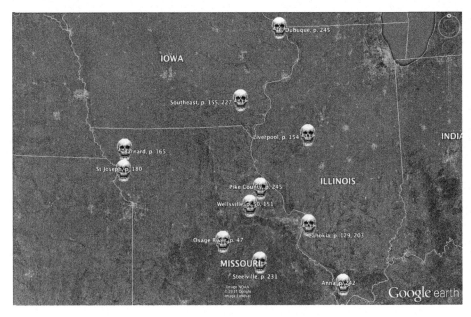

DATE	LOCATION	SIZE	No.	FEATURES	PAGE

Minnesota

DATE	LOCATION	SIZE	No.	FEATURES	PAGE
1873	Arcadia	7' & 11'	2	Large jaw	150
1893	Vasa	Giant	Many	DRTs	186
1878	Delano	?	3	Thigh bone 20 inches	187
1887	Crawford	8'2"& 9'	1	2' 2" inch wide pelvis	221

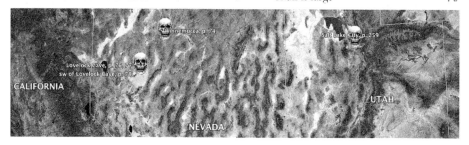

Nevada

DATE	LOCATION	SIZE	No.	FEATURES	PAGE
1904	Winnemucca	11'	1	Inspected by Dr. Samuels	74
1911	Lovelock Cave	6' 6"	1	Red hair	76
1914	Lovelock Cave	?	1	Robust skull	77
1967	S/W Lovelock Cave	?	1	Skull is large	78

New Hampshire (see Maine map)

DATE	LOCATION	SIZE	No.	FEATURES	PAGE
1821	Portsmouth	7'	1	DRT	133
1820s	Moltonborough	7'+	1	Large jaw	135
1856	Concord	Giant	9	DRT	135+185

New Jersey (see N.Y. map)

DATE	LOCATION	SIZE	No.	FEATURES	PAGE
1897	Cape May	?	1	Huge jaw	177

DATE	LOCATION	SIZE	No.	FEATURES	PAGE
NEW MEXICO (SEE ARIZONA MAP)					
1915	Silver City	8'	1	Elongated skull	179
NEW YORK					
1671	near New York	?	1	Eyewitness	45
1876	Cattaraugus County	9' & 7'	2	Male & female	162
1854	Rodman	?	1	DRT	193
1854	Watertown	Colossal	1	DRT	193
1819	Syracuse	?	1	DRT	194
1800s	Niagara	Giant	1	Copper artifacts	259

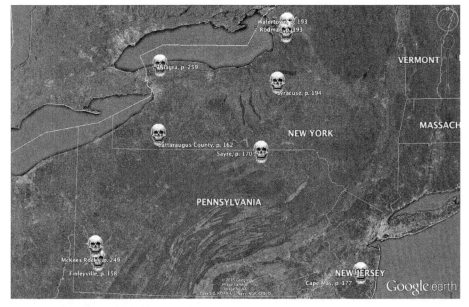

NORTH CAROLINA (SEE SOUTH CAROLINA MAP)

DATE	LOCATION	SIZE	No.	FEATURES	PAGE
1701	Unknown	?	1	Eyewitness	46
1890s	Patterson	7'	1	Beehive stone mound	121
1880s	Nelson Mound	7'	2	Smithsonian Annual Rep	246
1880s	Jones Mound	V. Large	1	Smithsonian Annual Rep	244

OHIO

DATE	LOCATION	SIZE	No.	FEATURES	PAGE
1882	Monroe County	8' 5"	1	Eyewitness	49
1858	Vermillion	?	?	Bearded men legend	60
1900?	Serpent Mound	7'	1	Postcard photo	97

DATE	LOCATION	SIZE	No.	FEATURES	PAGE
1894	Highland County	6'+	2	Near Serpent Mound	98
1891	Chillicothe	Massive	1	Encased in copper armor	101
1839	Miamisburg	Jaw	1	Large jaw only	105
1839	Miamisburg	9'+	1	10 ft stone grave	106
1898	Near Miamisburg	8' 1.5"	1	Strong teeth	108
1901	Marietta	7'	1	-	120
1882	Manchester	Giant	1	Large jaw	153
1800	Conneaut	Giant	Many	Large jaw	153
1898	Londonderry	8'	1	Skull one-third larger	156
1899	Akron	10'	1	Large jaw	157
1902	Cuyahoga County	8'	1	1,500 stone implements	158
1885	Whitewater	10' - 15'	1	Good teeth	167
1898	Toledo	7'	Many	Horned skulls	172
1904	Dayton	9'	1	Skull 6 x larger	178
1881	Medina County	?	9	Huge skull	188
1892	Proctorville	V. Large	1	Large jaw	189
1900	Eagle City	Giant	1	DRT	190
1872	Noble County	8'	1	DRT	190
1911	Morrow County	Large	1	DRT	191
1880s	Ripley	Large	?	Bones and skulls	249
1880s	Coshocton County	7'	1	Smithsonian Annual Rep	249
1880	Brush Creek	9'6"+ 8'9"	11	Brush Creek Tablet	254

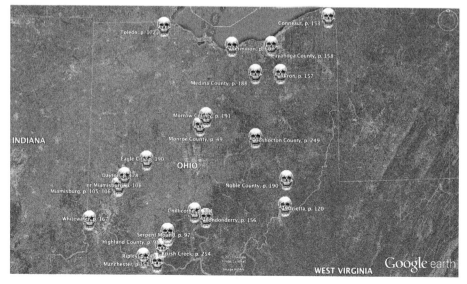

DATE	LOCATION	SIZE	No.	FEATURES	PAGE

OKLAHOMA (SEE ARKANSAS MAP)

DATE	LOCATION	SIZE	No.	FEATURES	PAGE
1934	Spiro Mound	7' - 9'	Many	-	126

PENNSYLVANIA (SEE NEW YORK MAP)

DATE	LOCATION	SIZE	No.	FEATURES	PAGE
1932	Finleyville	7'5" & 8'	Many	Huge teeth	158
1916	Sayre	7'	Many	Alleged horned skull	170
1870	West Hickory	18'	1	With 9 ft sword, DRT	186
1880s	McKees Rock	Large	1	Smithsonian Annual Rep	249
1932	Elrama/ Finleyville	7'5" - 8'	49	Smithsonian took bones	231+275

RHODE ISLAND (SEE MASS. MAP)

DATE	LOCATION	SIZE	No.	FEATURES	PAGE
1836	Burrillville	8'	1	Burial	144
1886	Gloucester	8'	1	-	144
1676	Cumberland	?	1	Colonial soldier, DRT	204

SOUTH CAROLINA (SEE TENNESSEE MAP)

DATE	LOCATION	SIZE	No.	FEATURES	PAGE
1523	Chicora	?	70	Eyewitness	29

TENNESSEE

DATE	LOCATION	SIZE	No.	FEATURES	PAGE
1883	Bristol	Giant	1	Given to Smithsonian	219
1880s	Roane County	7'	1	Smithsonian Annual Rep	246
1872	Bone Cave	?	1	Bones discovered	276

DATE	LOCATION	SIZE	No.	FEATURES	PAGE

TEXAS

DATE	LOCATION	SIZE	No.	FEATURES	PAGE
1939	Victoria County	?	3	Massive skull	169
1519	South of Galveston	Giant	Many	White skin	24
1830	Red River	7'	1	Kots-a-to-ah Warrior	363

UTAH (SEE NEVADA MAP)

DATE	LOCATION	SIZE	No.	FEATURES	PAGE
1891	Salt Lake City	8' 6"	1	Hieroglyphs	259

VERMONT (SEE MAINE MAP)

DATE	LOCATION	SIZE	No.	FEATURES	PAGE
1907	Rockingham	?	1	DRT	19+199

VIRGINIA (SEE W. VIRGINIA MAP)

DATE	LOCATION	SIZE	No.	FEATURES	PAGE
1606	Chesapeake Bay	7' - 8'	1	Eyewitness	43
1755	Winchester	7'	1	George Washington	54
1937	Stafford County	?		2100cc capacity	240
1880s	Barboursville	V. large	1	Smithsonian Annual Rep	249

WASHINGTON D.C. (SEE W. VIRGINIA MAP)

DATE	LOCATION	SIZE	No.	FEATURES	PAGE
1804	The White House	7'	1	With Thomas Jefferson	56
1932	?	8'	49	Sent to Smithsonian	231

WEST VIRGINIA

DATE	LOCATION	SIZE	No.	FEATURES	PAGE
1878	Charleston	8'	1	Ancient battlefield	90
1838	Grave Creek Mound	8' + 7' 4"	2	Male + female	112
1908	Friendly	6' 7"-7' 6"	Many	Flattened skulls	115

DATE	LOCATION	SIZE	No.	FEATURES	PAGE
1959	Cresap Mound	7' 2"	1	Heavy bones	117
1833	Shannondale Springs	7' & 11'	2	-	150
1883	Kingwood	14'	1	40-inch skull	166
1822	Mason County	Large	4	DRT	203
1883	Staunton Park	7'+	14	-	219
1889	Romney	Giant	11	Warren K. Moorehead	222
1884	Kanawha Valley	7'6" & 7'	4	Smithsonian Annual Rep	244
1880s	Spring Hill	7'	1	Smithsonian Annual Rep	246
1880s	Great Smith Mound	7' 8"	Many	Smithsonian Annual Rep	246
1880s	Poor House Mound	Large	Many	Smithsonian Annual Rep	249
1908	Huntington	7'	1	Copper bracelets	256

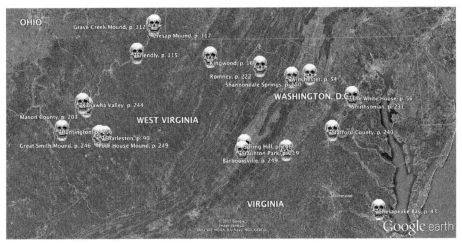

WASHINGTON

1913	Ellensburg	8'	1	Massive skull	167
1912	Craigshill	7'	11	DRT	192
1901	Tacoma	7' & 7'10"	2	Female & male	284

DATE	LOCATION	SIZE	No.	FEATURES	PAGE

WISCONSIN (SEE MINNESOTA MAP)

1891	Aztalan	Giant	1	Curious carved pipe	130
1870	Janesville	13'	1	32.5 inch skull	161
1870	Potosi	7'5 - 8'	2	DRT	198
1910	Fenyville	8' - 9'	1	-	211
1884	Sheboygan County	Large	1	Smithsonian Annual Rep	244

WYOMING

| 1879 | Niobrara County | 14'+ | 1 | Large bones witnessed | 91 |

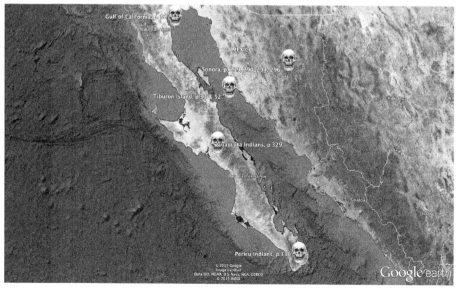

MEXICO

1900	Gulf of California	?	?	Eyewitness	52
1937	Sonora	Giants	Many	Smithsonian Annual Rep	239
1930	Sonora	6'8" - 8'3"	Many	Dr. Cummings	290
1934	Sonora	7'	34	Mummified	294
1935	Sonora	7'5"	Many	Mummified	296
1909	San Jose del Cabo	?	Many	Pericu Indians	330
1767	Baja California	?	Many	Guaycura Indians	329

DATE	LOCATION	SIZE	No.	FEATURES	PAGE
		CANADA			
1874	Labrador	?	1	Giant skull	259
1934	Simcoe, Ontario	8'	Many	Found with artifacts	306
1871	Cayuga	7'+	200	Curious artifacts	307
1910	Vancouver Island, B.C.	Giant	1	Stolen chief's skull	228

		PATAGONIA (SOUTH AMERICA)			
1520	Patagonia	10'	1	Eyewitness	26
1578	Patagonia	7' 7"	Many	Eyewitness	26
1592	Tierra del Fuego	12' & 9'	2	Eyewitness	27
1615	Patagonia	10' & 11'	2	Witnessed bones	27
1899	Antartica Islands	7' 2"	Many	Onas Indians, Eyewitness	51

Notes & References

FOREWORD BY ROSS HAMILTON

1. Edward Webb William. *Buffalo Land: an authentic account of the discoveries, adventures, and mishaps of a scientific and sporting party in the wild West*; p.384.
2. Vernon Kinietz and Erminie W. Voegelin, Editors. *Shawnese Traditions* (C. C. Trowbridge's Account), Occasional Contributions from the Museum of Anthropology of the University of Michigan, No. 9 University of Michigan Press, Ann Arbor, 1939.
3. Don Dragoo. *Mounds for the Dead*. McDonald and Woodward / Carnegie Museum.1963, p.72.

PREFACE

1. http://worldnewsdailyreport.com/smithsonian-admits-to-destruction-of-thousands-of-giant-human-skeletons-in-early-1900s/
2. http://www.worth1000.com/entries/105220/giant-skeleton
3. http://news.nationalgeographic.com/news/2007/12/photogalleries/giantskeleton-pictures/

INTRODUCTION BY HUGH NEWMAN

1. Anthony Roberts. *Sowers of Thunder*. Rider, 1978. p.xii.
2. II. C. Lofts. *Notes and Queries*, December 26th, 1874.
3. *Cherry Hinton Chronicle*, 27th May 1854. p.59.
4. Michelle Bullivant. *War Ditches 2010 Report*. Cambridge, 1854-2008, p.6.
5. Christopher Marlowe. *Legends of the Fenland People*. Cecil Palmer, London, 1926.
6. Eneas Mackenzie. *Historical, Topographical, and Descriptive view of the County of Northumberland*. 1825.
7. Wace. *Le Roman de Brut*. Dated to around 1150 AD. British Library: Egerton 3028.
8. Geoffry of Monmouth. *Histories of the Kings of Britain*, tr. by Sebastian Evans, 1904. and, Grinsell, L.V. *The Legendary History and Folklore of Stonehenge*, 1976.
9. Roy Norvill. *Giants: The Vanished Race of Mighty Men*, Aquarian Press, 1979. pp. 109-111.
10. www.damninteresting.com/king-arthurs-grave/
11. *Encyclopaedia Britannica*, 1967 ed., s.v. "Glastonbury."

CHAPTER 1 - EARLY EXPLORERS

1. Woodbury Lowery. *The Spanish Settlements*, New York: Russell & Russell. 1959, p.149.
2. ibid
3. ibid, p.64
4. Frederick Webb Hodge. ed. *Handbook of American Indians North of Mexico, Part 1*, 1971 pp.

657-658.

5. Daniel Garrison Brinton, ed. *Library of Aboriginal American Literature*, 1884

6. Lowery. p.161

7. Antonio Pigafetta. *Magellan's Voyage: A Narrative Account of the First Circumnavigation*. 1534, Yale University, 1969. p.46.

8. This work is based on the notes of Francis Fletcher, who sailed with Drake, and was compiled by Drake's nephew. *"The World Encompassed by Sir Francis Drake, Being His Next Voyage to That to Nombre de Dios Formerly Imprinted: Carefully Collected out of the Notes of Master Francis Fletcher, Preacher in This Imployment."* circa. 1628.

9. http://www.asimovs.com/2011_12/ref.shtml

10. ibid.

11. Captain Cook: *Explorations and Reassessments*, edited by Glyndwr Williams.

12. http://libweb5.princeton.edu/visual_materials/maps/websites/pacific/magellan-strait/patgonian-giants.html

13. John Bulkeley, & John Cummins. *A voyage to the South-Seas, in the years 1740-1 : containing, a faithful narrative of the loss of His Majesty's ship the Wager*. Pub. J.Robinson, London. 1743.

14. Detail from *"A Representation of the Interview between Commodore Byron and the Patagonians."* From volume 1 of John Hawkesworth's An Account of the Voyages Undertaken by the Order of His Present Majesty for Making Discoveries in the Southern Hemisphere and Successively Performed by Commodore Byron, Captain Wallis, Captain Carteret, and Captain Cook. London, 1773. Rare Books Division.

15. Danial Garrison Brinton. *Notes on the Floridian Peninsula*, 1859.

16. Pietro Martire d' Anghiera. 1457-1526; MacNutt, Francis Augustus, 1863-1927. *De orbe novo, the eight Decades of Peter Martyr d'Anghera;* New York, London, G.P. Putnam's Sons. (Kindle Locations 3670-3673).

17. http://www.examiner.com/article/did-giants-once-live-north-america

18. ibid.

19. A.Núñez Cabeza de Vaca. *American Explorers: The journey of Núñez Cabeza de Vaca*, 1922.

20. Article by Xaviant Haze. http://xavianthaze.blogspot.com/2013/04/the-conquistadors-encounters-with-giants.html

21. Steve Quayle. *Genesis 6 Giants: Master Builders of Prehistoric and Ancient Civilizations*. 2002. p.268.

22. The Florida Historical Quarterly, Volume 41,1963 p.95.

23. Pedro de Castaneda. *The Journey of Coronado: 1540-1542*, p25.

24. ibid. p.28.

25. ibid. p.27.

26. Bolton, Coronado, Herbert Eugene. *Knight of Pueblos and Plains*, New York and Albuquerque: McGraw-Hill Co., and The University of New Mexico Press, 1949, p.157.

27. ibid.

28. Bernard De Voto. *Westward the Course of Empire*. 1953.

29. http://www.bibliotecapleyades.net/gigantes/GiantsNAm1.html

30. ibid.

31. http://xavianthaze.blogspot.co.uk/2013/04/the-conquistadors-encounters-with-giants.html

32. Garcilaso de la Vega, *The Florida of the Inca*, ed. John and Jeanette Varner, Austin: University of Texas Press, 1951, p. 349.

33. *The World Encompassed by Sir Francis Drake, Being His Next Voyage to That to Nombre de Dios Formerly Imprinted: Carefully Collected out of the Notes of Master Francis Fletcher, Preacher in This Imployment*. This work of 1628 is the first edition of the earliest detailed account of the voyage around the world by Sir Francis Drake in 1577-80. http://www.wdl.org/en/item/624/

34. J. R. Mead. *Archeology of Catalina Island*, in Transactions of the Annual Meetings of the Kansas Academy of Science, vol 17, 199-1900.
35. www.thecatalinaislander.com/article/catalina%E2%80%99s-stonehenge
36. J. R. Mead. *Archeology of Catalina Island*, in Transactions of the Annual Meetings of the Kansas Academy of Science, vol 17, 199-1900.
37. *The Nautilus*, Volume 19, 1906, p.7.
38. New York Tribune, November 21, 1897. p.11.
39. William Stith, A.M. Williamsburg. *The History of the Discovery and Settlement of Virginia*, printed by Wilaim Parks, 1747. (from the diaries of John Smith)
40. https://www.nasa.gov/vision/earth/everydaylife/jamestown-transport-fs.html
41. *The Stature of A Susquehannock Population of the Mid-16th Century Based on Skeletal Remains from 46HM73*, Pennsylvania Archeologist, Volume 61, No. 2 September 1991.
42. Greensburg Daily Tribune, April 23, 1932 p.5
43. Henry Howe. *The Historical Collections of Virginia*,1852, pg 469
44. Greg Little. *Mound Builders: Edgar Cayce's Forgotten Record of Ancient America*. Eagle Wing Books Inc, 2001. p.8.
45. John Lawson. *A New Voyage to Carolina*, pg.24. 1709.
46. ibid p.180.
47. Gass. *Journals of the Lewis and Clark Expedition*, Friday, 1st June, 1804.
48. *The Gale Encyclopedia of Native American Tribes, vol 3*, 1998.
49. Thomas Nuttall. *Travels into the Arkansa Territory during the year 1819*, F. L. S. Philadelphia, 1821.
50. George Catlin. *Letters and notes on the manners, customs, and condition of the North American Indians, Volume 1*. William Shippard, 1841.
51. Joshua V.H. Clark, A.M. *Onondaga or Reminiscences of Earlier and Later Times Stoddard and Babcock, Syracuse*, 1849
52. Henry A. Ford, A. M. and Mrs. Kate B. Ford. *History of Hamilton County Ohio, Cleveland, Ohio*. L. A. Williams & Co. publishers, 1881.
53. *Bulletin of the American Geographical Society of New York, Volume 23*, By American Geographical Society of New York, p.260.
54. *Popular Photography Magazine*. Ziff-Davis Publishing: Chicago.
55. John W. Troutman. *St. Louis Republic*, Sept 1903 & *Overlord of the Savage World*, 1997.

CHAPTER 2 - PRESIDENTS AND GIANTS
1. *Collected Works of Abraham Lincoln*. Volume 2. pp.10-11. 1809-1865.
2. Wallace 1999, p.139 and n.18.

CHAPTER 3 - LEGENDS OF THE TALL ONES
1. Wilkins, *Fate Magazine*, January, 1952
2. Wm. H. Crane. *The Firelands Pioneer Memoirs of Townships*, November, 1858. Vermillion S.E. Quarter
3. https://en.wikipedia.org/wiki/Passaconaway
4. ibid.
5. Anthony Roberts. *Sowers of Thunder*. Rider, 1978. p.35.
6. Figure and history of Passaconeway thanks to C.F. Potter's History of Mansfield, New Hampshire, 1851.
7. http://www.boudillion.com/druidhill/druidhill.htm
8. Henry Schoolcraft. *Notes on the Iroquois*, 1846. p.158-159.
9. Erminnie A. Smith. SMITHSONIAN INSTITUTION—BUREAU OF ETHNOLOGY. MYTHS

OF THE IROQUOIS. Extracted from ARBAE 2 (1883): 51-116.

10. http://www.sacred-texts.com/nam/ca/dow/dow71.htm#fr_28

11. http://www.native-languages.org/mikmaq_culture.htm

12. Jeremiah Clark, S,B.A. *Rand and the Micmacs*, 1809.

13. Richard L. Dieterle, *Giants or Man Eaters (Wâ´gerútcge)* (chapter heading from The Encyclopedia of Hotcâk. Winnebago Mythology.

14. http://www.hotcakencyclopedia.com/ho.Giants.html

15. Ella Elizabeth Clark. *Indian Legends from the Northern Rockies*, University of Oklahoma Press, 1966, p.140.

16. ibid. p.141.

17. ibid. p.64.

18. ibid. p.15.

19. www.firstpeople.us/FP-Html-Legends/TheWomanandtheGiants-Paiute.html

20. Newark Sunday Call. May 17, 1891 pg 3.

21. Other geologists dated them to 50,000 years old, but there is a debate as to whether they are human or not. See full analysis at http://paleo.cc/paluxy/carson.htm

22. Sarah Winnemucca Hopkins. *Life among the Piutes, their wrongs and claims.* 1844-1891; Mann, Mary Tyler Peabody, 1806-1887, ed. p.75.

23. ibid. p.75.

24. Nevada State Journal, October 3, 1936 P.12.

25. ibid.

26. nevadamagazine.com/home/archives/prehistoric-storage/

27. http://hearstmuseum.berkeley.edu/blm/lovelock.pdf p.6,

28. Llewellyn L.. Loud; M. R. Harrington 1929. *Lovelock Cave.* U of California Publications in American Archaeology and Ethnology, Berkeley, p.87.

29. ibid. p.5.

30. Kathleen C. Warner. *The Quasi-prehistorical Validity of Western Numic* (Paviotso) Oral Tradition, Indiana University., 1978 - pg 151.

31. ibid.

32. Desert Magazine of the Southwest. Vol 38, No. 1 January 1975 p.38.

33. ibid.

34. Washington Post. Nov. 29, 1914.

35. The Telegraph-Herald. Dec 24, 1914 p.7.

36. Reed, E., (1967). An Unusual Human Skull from near Lovelock, Nevada, University of Utah Press. Miscellaneous Collected Papers, No.18.

37. http://patagoniamonsters.blogspot.co.uk/2014/01/lovelock-skull-and-spirit-cave-man.html

38. Katerina Harvati, Terry Harrison, eds. *Neanderthals Revisited: New Approaches and Perspectives*, Springer, 2007.

39. Nevada State Journal, Reno, Nevada. Sunday, August 3, 1952 p.6.

40. Sam P. Davis. *The History of Nevada,* 1913. p.892.

41. Llewellyn L. Loud; M. R. Harrington 1929. *Lovelock Cave.* U of California Publications in American Archaeology and Ethnology, Berkeley. p.13.

42. Mrs. Mary Eastman. *Dahcotah or, Life and Legends of the Sioux Around Fort Snelling*; prefaced by Mrs. C.M. Kirkland. Illustrated with drawings by Captain Eastman. New York, 1849, pp. 208-211.

43. Bureau of Indian Affairs, Philadelphia, 1852.

44. https://en.wikipedia.org/wiki/Henry_Schoolcraft

45. ibid. p.39.

46. ibid. p.93.

47. Vine Deloria, Jr. *Red Earth, White Lies: Native Americans and the Myth of Scientific Fact* 2000.

Fulcrum. p.139.

48. Nelson Lee. *Three Years Among the Comanches*. Baker Taylor Company. Albany, New York. 1859.

49. Micah Hanks. *Gods of the Hunt: Legends of Mysterious Slant-Eyed Giants*. http://mysteriousuniverse.org/2013/02/gods-of-the-hunt-legends-of-mysterious-slant-eyed-giants/

50. James Mooney. *Myths of the Cherokee*. From Nineteenth Annual Report of the Bureau of American Ethnology 1897-98, Part I. 1900.

51. Ross Hamilton. *A Tradition of Giants: The Elite Social Hierarchy of American Prehistory*. 2007. pp.40-41.

52. http://bf-field-journal.blogspot.co.uk/2012/06/bigfoot-cherokee-connection.html

53. Benjamin Smith Barton. *New Views of the Origin of the Tribes and Nations of America*, 1797.

54. Mooney. pp.22-23.

55. *The Discovery of America by Welsh Prince Madoc* - History Magazine, History, UK. 4 April 2013.

56. William L. Stone. *Life of Joseph Brant -Thayendanega, Includes the Wars of the American Revolution,* 1838.

57. Hamilton. p. 76

58. James Athearn Jones. *Traditions of the North American Indians,* Volume 2, 1830.

59. Hamilton. p. 75.

60. J. H. McCulloh. *Researches, philosophical and antiquarian, concerning the aboriginal history of America*.1829.

61. Hamilton. p.77.

62. ibid. p.79.

63. McCulloh. 1829.

64. Stevens Point Daily Journal, Stevens Point, Wisconsin, Saturday, November 12, 1881. Montello, Marquette County, WI—originated from the Black Rive Falls Independent.

65. *The North American Review*, Volume 6, Issue 18, November 1817, University of Northern Iowa, Cedar Falls, Iowa, p.137.

66. Danial Garrison Brinton, *Notes on the Floridian Peninsula*, 1859.

67. http://peabody.yale.edu/collections/archives/yale-college-scientific-expedition-1870

CHAPTER 4 - GIANTS IN THE MOUNDS

1. *History of Morrow County, Ohio - A Narrative Account,* Volume 1, 1911 p.14.

2. Webb and Snow noted that Kentucky had slightly earlier dating that Ohio.

3. J. Burke & K. Halberg. *Seed of Knowledge, Stone of Plenty*. Council Oak Books.2005. p.83

4.http://indiancountrytodaymedianetwork.com/2014/08/07/rethinking-ohios-history-serpent-mound-older-some-its-dirt-156268.

5. Ross Hamilton. *Star Mounds: Legacy of a Native American Mystery*, From Chapter 8, *The Ecliptic Plane and a Native American Zodiac*.

6. F.W. Putnam. *The Serpent Mound of Ohio*, Century Magazine Vol. XXXIX, 1889-1890.

7. Ross Hamilton. *A Tradition of Giants: The Elite Social Hierarchy of American Prehistory*, 2007. p.61.

8. Putnam, 1889-1890.

9. See details of their discoveries at http://www.earthworksconservancy.org/astronomically-aligned/

10.http://www.ohioarchaeology.org/resources/39-resources/research/articles-and-abstracts-2008/260-lidar-imaging-of-the-great-hopewell-road

11. https://www.ohiohistory.org/visit/museum-and-site-locator/miamisburg-mound

12. https://en.wikipedia.org/wiki/Miamisburg,_Ohio

13.http://www.daytondailynews.com/news/lifestyles/philosophy/how-was-mound-laboratory-allowed-to-do-so-much-har/nNJLG/

14. http://www.atlasobscura.com/places/west-virginia-state-penitentiary

15. *History of the Pan-Handle, Marshall County, West Virginia,* 1879.

16. Don W. Dragoo. *Mounds for the dead.* Annals of Carnegie Museum, Vol. 37. McDonald and Woodward / Carnegie Museum.1963. p.72.

17. ibid.

18. Larry and Christopher Merriam. *The Spiro Mound, A photo essay- photographs from the collection of Dr. Robert E. Bell,* 2004. p.36.

CHAPTER 6 - ANATOMIC ANOMALIES

1. Dragoo. p. 37.

2. William Smith Bryan. *A History of the Pioneer Families of Missouri - With Numerous Sketches.* 1876, p.101.

3. Annual Report of the Smithsonian Institution 1873. pp. 418 - 419.

4. Ellis and Nash. *History of Cattaraugus County,* 1879.

5. See lower segment http://www.pcgenweb.com/pcgs/membership/echo_2009-2011.htm

6. The Colonist, Volume LIV, Issue 13569, 9 November 1912. p.3.

7. Texas Archaeological Research Labatory archives - http://www.texasbeyondhistory.net/morhiss/credits.html

8. https://en.wikipedia.org/wiki/Cutaneous_horn

9. L.W. Murray. *Aboriginal Sites in and Near "Teaoga",* 1921. p.205.

10. www.surnateum.org/English/surnateum/collection/demonologie/exorciste.htm

11. Private email between Hugh Newman and the museum curator.

12. Minneapolis Journal, August 8, 1903.

13. Seymour Daily Republican, September 17, 1910.

14. Harrison Telegraph, Pa., June 28, 1917.

15. Letter with accession #6268, dated Nov. 22, 1877, to Professor Joseph Henry, Smithsonian Institution.

16. H. Terry Childsl and Charles H. McNutt. *Chickasawba.* 'Arkansas Archeological Society', Professor Emeritus, University of Memphis, 2009. p.35.

17. ibid. p.36.

CHAPTER 7 - DOUBLE ROWS OF TEETH

1. Chris Grooms. *The Giants of Wales:* Cewri Cymru. p.326

2. www.ncbi.nlm.nih.gov/pubmed/21967947

3. *The Natural History of the Human Teeth.* Thomas Cox, London, 1803. p.70.

4. Harold T. Wilkins. *Secret Cities of Old South America.* Reprint by Adventures Unlimited Press. p.419.

5. Jewish Encyclopedia, 1906. Deut. R. i.

6. Jewish Encyclopedia, 1906. Buber, "Tanhuma," Debarim, addition 7.

7. Jewish Encyclopedia, 1906. Hul. 60a.

8. Babylonian Talmud. Job xli. 5.

9. Babylonian Talmud. Cant. iv. 2.

10. Holy Bible, containing the Old and New Testaments ... with Notes, Critical, Explanatory, and Practical, 2nd edition, 1811–18, 5 vols.

11. Also reported in the Daily Star July 24, 1912. p.2.

12. Hubert Howe. *The Native Races of the Pacific states of North America.* 1875.

13. *Human Fossils In California from the Otago Witness*, Issue 644, April 2, 1864. p.18.
14. www.pcas.org/Vol36N2/18TitusWalker.pdf
15. See http://www.ncbi.nlm.nih.gov/pubmed/3473097
16. Bartelink, E., Willits, N., & Chelotti, K. *Earliest Evidence of Gigantism-Like Disease Found in 3,800-Year-Old California Skeleton. A probable case of acromegaly,* from the Windmiller culture of prehistoric Central California International Journal of Paleopathology, 4. 2014. pp.37-46 http://westerndigs.org/earliest-evidence-of-gigantism-like-disease-found-in-3800-year-old-california-skeleton/
17. ibid.
18. ibid.

Chapter 8 - The Smithsonian Files

1. www.si.edu/about/history
2. ibid
3. http://www.si.edu/about/history
4. S. Edgar Smoot. *Lost American Antiquities: A Hidden History*. Legends Library New York. 2013. p.170.
5. Neil M. Judd. *The Bureau of American Ethnology,* University of Oklahoma Press. 1967.
6. David Hatcher Childress. World Explorer Magazine, vol. 1, no. 3. 1993.
7. Hamilton, p.63.
8. Childress, 1993.
9. ibid.
10. Hamilton. p.46.
11. Science News letter, v13 #353 1928. pg.21.
12. *The First American: A study of North American Archaeology.* 1971.
13. Bernard K. Means, Ed. Kevin Kiernan: Preston Holder's WPA Excavtions in Glynn and Chatham Counties, Georgia, 1936-1938: *Shovel Ready: Archaeology and Roosevelt's NewDeal for America*, p.202
14. ibid.
15. Prof. Kevin Kiernan is a member of the Board of Directors for the Society for Georgia Archaeology 2008-2012, as well as a member of the Society for American Archaeology (SAA); Southeastern Archaeological Conference (SEAC); Society for Historical Archaeology (SHA); Society for Georgia Archaeology (SGA, Board of Directors); South Georgia Archaeological Research Team (SOGART), and Golden Isles Archaeological Society (GIAS, Executive Committee).
16. Smithsonian's Annual Report 1938. p.91. The official catalogue card for the skull: "Graham, Judge W. J., Washington, D. C. : Human skeletal material from 3 ossuaries near Potomac Creek, Stafford County, Va. (144975)."
17. Twelfth Annual Report of the Bureau of American Ethnology of the Smithsonian Institution, 1894. pg.610.

Chapter 9 - Curious Artifacts

1. E. Thomas Hemmings. *Grave Creek Mound*. 1984. p.3.
2. Full details and discussion of the skeletal remains are discussed in detail in the *Giants in the Mounds* chapter.
3. J.P. Maclean. *The Mound Builders: Being an Account of a Remarkable People That Once Inhabited the Valleys*. 1893. Reprint. London: Forgotten Books, 2013. pp.90-1.
4. ibid.
5. ibid. pp.98-99.
6. See http://www.econ.ohio-state.edu/jhm/arch/grvcrk.html

7. Barry Fell. *America B.C.: Ancient Settlers in the New World*. Times Books, 1976. p.21.

8. ibid.

9. ibid. p.158.

10. Ross Hamilton. *A Tradition of Giants*.

11. www.nps.gov/kewe/learn/historyculture/copper-mining-timeline.htm

12. Henry Sheltrone. *The Mound Builders*.1930. p.149.

13. ibid.

CHAPTER 10 - MYSTICS AND SECRET SOCIETIES

1. Edgar Cayce Reading 1298-1. F 43 (Business Woman, Polish Christian Background, Metaphysical Student). Part 20 & 21. Full reading here: http://www.aawmagazine.com/1298/001.html

2. Reading 364-11. Reading given by Edgar Cayce at his home in Pinewood on Lake Drive, Virginia Beach, Va., this 29th day of April, 1932. Part 8. Full reading here: http://www.aawmagazine.com/0364/011.html

CHAPTER 11 - CURSE OF THE GIANT HUNTERS

1. Archaeology Magazine, Volume 63, number 3, May/June 2010.

2. ibid.

3. David H. Childress. *Lost Cities of Ancient Lemuria and the Pacific*, AUP, 1988. p.213.

4. Philip Rife. *The Goliath Conspiracy*. iUniverse, 2001. pg.62.

5. http://www.s8int.com/giants9.html

6. Bourke lee. *Death Valley Men*. MacMillan Co., N.Y. 1932.

7. Rife. p.67.

CHAPTER 12 - GIANTS OF SONORA, MEXICO

1. Bourke Lee. *Death Valley Men*. MacMillan Co., N.Y. 1932.

CHAPTER 13 - FURTHER AFIELD

1. These dates have not been re-tested so they are classed as "Unconfirmed." See Michael J. Moratto. *California Archaeology*. Academic Press, 2014. p.58.

2. Louis Sahagun. *Bones flesh out an island's history: Files of man who dug up Indian skeletons could change views of early Catalina life*. April 2, 2012. http://articles.latimes.com/2012/apr/02/local/la-me-catalina-bones-20120402

3. See Marzulli's article here: https://lamarzulli.wordpress.com/tag/nephilim-catalina-island/

4. The Scientific American, Volume 6. P.227, from 1862.

5. Braje, et. al. (December 2010). "Channel Islands National Park: Archaeological Overview and Assessment" (PDF). Department of the Interior, National Park Service.

6. University of Oregon: *California islands give up evidence of early seafaring: Numerous artifacts found at late Pleistocene sites on the Channel Islands*. March 2, 2011. http://www.sciencedaily.com/releases/2011/03/110303141540.htm

7. ibid.

CHAPTER 14 - ORIGINS OF THE TALL ONES

1. Ross Hamilton. *A Tradition of Giants: The Elite Social Hierarchy of American Prehistory*. 2007. p.14.

2. ibid pp.57-58.

3. Greg Little, *Mound Builders: Edgar Cayce's Forgotten Record of Ancient America*. Eagle Wing Books Inc, 2001. p.182.

4. Hamilton. p.11.

5. https://en.wikipedia.org/wiki/Turtle_Island_(North_America)

6. Harriet Maxwell Converse and Arthur Caswell Parker. *Myth and Legends of the New York State Iroquois.* Albany: New York State Museum, 1906.p.3.

7. Little. p.182.

8. Vine Deloria, Jr. *Red Earth, White Lies: Native Americans and the Myth of Scientific Fact* 2000. Fulcrum. p.81.

9. www.jstor.org/stable/29542674

10. G.F. Carter. *On the Antiquity of Man in America.* Anthopological Journal of Canada, 1977. p.19.

11. http://www.sciencedaily.com/releases/2011/03/110303141540.htm

12. Michael J. Moratto. *California Archaeology.* Academic Press, 2014. p.58.

13.   www.latimes.com/science/sciencenow/la-sci-sn-native-american-origins-dna-20150721-story.html

14. http://coastaltec.com/rancho/indians.htm and www.ghosthuntingtheories.com/2015/01/tall-coastal-tribes-prove-denisovan.html

15. www.mexican-folk-art-guide.com/the-pericues.html#.Vahe52RdWSd

16. González-José et al. 2003; Rivet 1909, and www.bluecorncomics.com/stype492.htm

17. https://en.wikipedia.org/wiki/Peric%C3%BAes

18. www.bluecorncomics.com/stype492.htm. Originally from Discovery News Study: *Native Americans Weren't the First* By Jennifer Viegas, Sept. 6, 2004 and http://news.bbc.co.uk/1/hi/sci/tech/3634544.stm

19. Andrew Collins. Afterword, in *Path of Souls: The Native American Death Journey: Cygnus, Orion, the Milky Way, Giant Skeletons in Mounds, & the Smithsonian.* Archetype Books 2014 and *Denisovans and the American Giant Mystery* - http://www.andrewcollins.com/page/articles/denisovan.htm

20. https://en.wikipedia.org/wiki/Denisovan

21. http://siberiantimes.com/science/casestudy/news/n0407-new-dna-tests-on-ancient-denisovan-people-shows-them-occupying-altai-cave-170000-years-ago/

22. Collins, 2014 & Jamie Shreeve, *The Case of the Missing Ancestor: DNA from a cave in Russia adds a mysterious new member to the human family,* National Geographic, July 2013, http://ngm.nationalgeographic.com/2013/07/125-missing-human-ancestor/shreeve-text.

23. Collins, 2014.

24. www.thenakedscientists.com/HTML/interviews/interview/833/

25. https://youtu.be/SnAgOagVO2c - video by Michael Tellinger.

26. www.dailymail.co.uk/sciencetech/article-2928549/Have-fishermen-discovered-new-species-ancient-man-Chunky-jawbone-fossil-dredged-coast-Taiwan.html#ixzz3kQEb1NUk

27. Collins, 2014.

28. http://news.nationalgeographic.com/news/2014/01/140129-neanderthal-genes-genetics-migration-africa-eurasian-science/

29. Collins, 2014; Sandra Jacob, et al, *Ancient genome reveals its secrets,* Max-Plank-Gesellschaft, August 30, 2012. http://www.mpg.de/6328259/denisovan_genome1; Katherine Harmon, *New DNA Analysis Shows Ancient Humans Interbred with Denisovans,* Scientific American, August 30, 2012. http://www.scientificamerican.com/article/denisovan-genome/

30. ibid.

31. Prüfer, Kay, et al, *The complete genome sequence of a Neanderthal from the Altai Mountains,* Nature 505, January 2nd, 2014, 43-49; Sanders, Robert, *Neanderthal genome shows evidence of early human interbreeding, inbreeding,* UC Berkeley News Center, December 18th, 2013.

32. http://humanorigins.si.edu/evidence/genetics/ancient-dna-and-neanderthals/neanderthal-genes-red-hair-and-more

33. Bernardo T. Arriaza. *Beyond Death: The Chinchorro Mummies of Ancient Chile.* Washington:

Smithsonian Institution, 1995.

34. http://www.nbbd.com/godo/history/windover/

35. Little, Greg. Mound Builders pg. 62.

36. American Journal of Human Genetics, July 2001.

37. *Archaeology*, by Robert Kelly & David Thomas. p.255.

38. ibid.

39. Greg Little, *Mound Builders: Edgar Cayce's Forgotten Record of Ancient America*. Eagle Wing Books Inc, 2001. p.63.

40. John U. Terrell. *American Indian Almanac*. New York. Barnes & Noble, 1971; Snow, Dean. *The Archaeology of North America: American Indians and their Origins*. London: Thames & Hudson, 1976.

41. Wright, J. V. *A History of the Native People of Canada: 10,000-1,000 BC*. Gatineau, Quebec: Canadian Museum of Civilization, 1995. p.257.

42. Hamilton. p.96.

43. Wright, 1995. p.257.

44. Hamilton. p.38.

45. Shirley Andrews. *Lemuria and Atlantis: Studying the Past to Survive the Future*, Llewellyn Publications, 2004. pp.92-94.

46. ibid

47. Greg Little, *Mound Builders: Edgar Cayce's Forgotten Record of Ancient America*. Eagle Wing Books Inc, 2001. p.63.

48. https://en.wikipedia.org/wiki/Nephilim

49. Compiled by Joe Taylor, Mt. Blanco Fossil Museum, Texas.

50. https://answersingenesis.org/bible-characters/giants-in-the-old-testament/

51. Amos 2:9–10.

52. Numbers 13:32.

53. https://answersingenesis.org/bible-characters/giants-in-the-old-testament/

54. Walter Donlan. *The Aristocratic Ideal and Selected Papers*. 1980. p.60-61.

55. Steve Quayle. *Genesis 6 Giants: Master Builders of Prehistoric and Ancient Civilizations*. 2002.

56. www.assyriatimes.com/engine/modules/news/article.php?storyid=34056.

57. http://www.ualberta.ca/~swg/index.htm

58. Hamilton. 2007. p.30.

59. Michael Cremo, Richard Thomson. *Forbidden Archaeology: The Hidden History of the Human Race*. Bhaktivedanta Book Publishing, 1998.p.367.

60. Michael Cremo, Richard Thomson.*The Hidden History of the Human Race: Condensed Edition of Forbidden Archaeology*. Bhaktivedanta Book Publishing, 1999. p.91.

61. ibid. p.47.

62. ibid. p.123.

63. ibid. p.132.

64. http://www.independent.co.uk/news/science/does-skull-prove-that-the-first-americans-came-from-europe-134429.html

65. Paul Rincon. *Tribe challenges American origins*. BBC News. 7 Sept 2004.

66. G. F. Carter. *On the Antiquity of Man in America*. Anthopological Journal of Canada, 1977. p.19

67. Jeffrey Goodman Ph.D. *American Genesis: The American Indian and the origins of modern man*. Summit Books. 1981.

68. https://en.wikipedia.org/wiki/Cro-Magnon

69.http://anthropogenesis.kinshipstudies.org/anthropology-of-human-origins/out-of-america-family-of-hypotheses/

70. ibid.

71. Deloria p.63.

72. Goodman p.5.

73. Goodman p.142.

74. *Encyclopedia Americana, Volume 6: Cathedrals to Civil War,* Grolier Incorporated, 2001. p.85. OCLC 615043106.

75. http://webcentral.uc.edu/eProf/media/attachment/eprofmediafile_1777.pdf

76. Letter from James Wright to John Bartram, August 22, 1762, quoted by George Gaylord Simpson, *The Discovery of Fossil Vertebrates in North America.* Journal of Paleontology 17 1943.

77. France Densmore. *Teton Sioux Music.* Washington D.C.; Bureau of American Ethnology. Smithsonian Institution, 1918. pp.137-138.

78. Jane C. Beck, *The Giant Beaver: A Prehistoric Memory?* Ethnohistory 19, 1972. p119.

79. Deloria. p.136.

80. ibid.

81. ibid. p.138.

82. J.F.H. Claiborne, *Mississippi: As a Province, Territory, and State.* Baton Rouge, Louisiana State University Press, 1964. p.484.

83. Deloria. p.159.

84. Graham Hancock. *Magicians of the Gods: The forgotten wisdom of earth's lost civilisation.* Coronet, 2015. p.129.

85. Vine Deloria jr.. *The World We Used to Live in: Remembering the Powers of the Medicine Men.* p.127.

86. ibid.

87. John Burke, Kaj Halberg. *Seed of Knowledge, Stone of Plenty.* Council Oak Books. 2005.

88. Alanna Moore. *Stone Age Farming: Eco Agriculture for the 21st Century.* Castlemaine. Australia, 2001.

89. www.origin-life.gr.jp/3701/3701007/3701007.html

90. ibid

91. ibid

92. Hamilton. p.10.

93. Donald Patten. *A Comprehensive Theory on Aging, Giantism and Longevity,* in Catastrphism and Ancient History 2/1. 1979.

94. Deloria. p.153.

95. ibid.

96. Hancock. p.129.

97. George Catlin. *Letters and Notes,* vol. 2. p.75, pl. 182. Painted at the Comanche village in 1834.

98. http://economics.emory.edu/home/documents/workingpapers/carlson_10_06_paper.pdf

99. Report to the Secretary of War of the United states on Indian Affairs, Rev. Jedidiah Morse, D.D. Davis & Force, Washington, D.C. 1822.

100. W.M. Childers. *Preliminary Report on the Yuha Burial, California.* Anthropological Journal of Canada. 1974, pp. 2-9.

101. Geoffry of Monmouth. *Histories of the Kings of Britain.* tr. by Sebastian Evans, 1904.

Printed in Great Britain
by Amazon

28160815R00236